AP®

U.S. GOVERNMENT & POLITICS

PREMIUM PREP

23rd Edition

The Staff of The Princeton Review

PrincetonReview.com

Penguin Random House

The Princeton Review
110 East 42nd Street, 7th Floor
New York, NY 10017

Published in the United States by Penguin Random House LLC, New York.

Terms of Service: The Princeton Review Online Companion Tools ("Student Tools") for retail books are available for only the two most recent editions of that book. Student Tools may be activated only once per eligible book purchased for a total of 24 months of access. Activation of Student Tools more than once per book is in direct violation of these Terms of Service and may result in discontinuation of access to Student Tools Services.

ISBN: 978-0-593-51774-1
eBook ISBN: 978-0-593-51775-8
ISSN: 2690-7135

AP is a trademark registered and owned by the College Board, which is not affiliated with, and does not endorse, this product.

The Princeton Review is not affiliated with Princeton University.

The material in this book is up-to-date at the time of publication. However, changes may have been instituted by the testing body in the test after this book was published.

If there are any important late-breaking developments, changes, or corrections to the materials in this book, we will post that information online in the Student Tools. Register your book and check your Student Tools to see if there are any updates posted there.

Editor: Selena Coppock
Production Editors: Heidi Torres, Ali Landreau
Production Artist: Jason Ullmeyer
Content Developer: Gina Donegan

Printed in the United States of America.

10 9 8 7 6 5 4 3 2 1

23rd Edition

The Princeton Review Publishing Team

Rob Franek, Editor-in-Chief
David Soto, Senior Director, Data Operations
Stephen Koch, Senior Manager, Data Operations
Deborah Weber, Director of Production
Jason Ullmeyer, Production Design Manager
Jennifer Chapman, Senior Production Artist
Selena Coppock, Director of Editorial
Orion McBean, Senior Editor
Aaron Riccio, Senior Editor
Meave Shelton, Senior Editor
Chris Chimera, Editor
Patricia Murphy, Editor
Laura Rose, Editor
Isabelle Appleton, Editorial Assistant

Random House Publishing Team

Tom Russell, VP, Publisher
Alison Stoltzfus, Senior Director, Publishing
Emily Hoffman, Associate Managing Editor
Patty Collins, Executive Director of Production
Mary Ellen Owens, Assistant Director of Production
Alice Rahaeuser, Associate Production Manager
Maggie Gibson, Associate Production Manager
Suzanne Lee, Senior Designer
Eugenia Lo, Publishing Assistant

For customer service, please contact **editorialsupport@review.com**, and be sure to include:

- full title of the book
- ISBN
- page number

Acknowledgments

The Princeton Review would like to thank Gina Donegan for her wonderful contributions to the 23rd edition edition of this book. We also thank Jason Ullmeyer, Heidi Torres, and Ali Landreau for their detailed eyes and their time and attention to each page.

Permissions

Contents

Get More (Free) Content viii

Part I: Using This Book to Improve Your AP Score 1

   Preview: Your Knowledge, Your Expectations 2

   Your Guide to Using This Book 2

   How to Begin 3

Part II: Practice Test 1 7

   Practice Test 1 9

   Practice Test 1: Diagnostic Answer Key and Explanations 29

   How to Score Practice Test 1 51

Part III: About the AP U.S. Government and Politics Exam 53

   The Structure of the AP U.S. Government and Politics Exam 54

   How the AP U.S. Government and Politics Exam Is Scored 55

   Overview of Content Topics 56

   Primary Sources 58

   How AP Exams Are Used 59

   Other Resources 59

   Designing Your Study Plan 60

Part IV: Test-Taking Strategies for the AP U.S. Government
and Politics Exam 61

   Preview 62

1   How to Approach Multiple-Choice Questions 63

2   How to Approach Free-Response Questions 75

3   Using Time Effectively to Maximize Points 89

   Reflect 93

Part V: Content Review for the AP U.S. Government
and Politics Exam 95

4   Foundations of American Democracy 97

   Enlightenment Philosophies 98

   The Weaknesses of the Articles of Confederation 100

   The Constitution as an Instrument of Government 105

   Amendment Process 112

   State and Local Governments 113

   Chapter 4 Key Terms 114

   Chapter 4 Drill 115

   Summary 116

   Reflect 117

5   Interactions Among Branches of Government 119

     Congress 120

     Notable Legislation 132

     The President 134

     The Judiciary and the Law 140

     The Bureaucracy 147

     Chapter 5 Key Terms 159

     Chapter 5 Drill 161

     Summary 162

     Reflect 165

6   Civil Liberties and Civil Rights 167

     The Bill of Rights (December 15, 1791) 168

     The Extension of Civil Liberties Through American History 168

     First Amendment Rights and Restrictions 169

     The Second Amendment 176

     The Third Amendment 177

     The Fourth Amendment 177

     The Fifth Amendment 178

     The Sixth Amendment 180

     The Seventh Amendment 180

     The Eighth Amendment 181

     The Ninth Amendment 182

     The Right of All Americans to Privacy 182

     Civil Rights 183

     Chapter 6 Key Terms 190

     Chapter 6 Drill 191

     Summary 193

     Reflect 194

7   American Political Ideologies and Beliefs 195

     Characteristics of Public Opinion 196

     Polls Measure Public Opinion 197

     Where Does Public Opinion Come From? 198

     Political Ideologies 199

     Public Opinion and the Mass Media 201

     Chapter 7 Key Terms 204

     Chapter 7 Drill 205

     Summary 207

     Reflect 208

8 Political Participation 209

 Citizen Participation 210

 Political Parties 211

 Interest Groups 218

 Political Action Committees (PACs) and Super PACs 221

 527 Groups 222

 Elections 223

 The Election Cycle 224

 Media Influence on Elections 232

 Election Day 232

 Policy Making: Objectives 234

 Policy Making: Process 235

 Economic Policy 237

 Trade Policy 241

 Domestic Policy 242

 Chapter 8 Key Terms 247

 Chapter 8 Drill 249

 Summary 251

 Reflect 254

9 Chapter Drills: Answers and Explanations 255

Glossary 263

The Constitution of the United States of America 281

Part VI: Additional Practice Tests 299

 Practice Test 2 301

 Practice Test 2: Answers and Explanations 321

 Practice Test 3 337

 Practice Test 3: Answers and Explanations 361

 Practice Test 4 381

 Practice Test 4: Answers and Explanations 403

 Practice Test A .... online

 Practice Test A: Answers and Explanations .... online

 Practice Test B .... online

 Practice Test B: Answers and Explanations .... online

 Bubble Sheet .... online

Get More (Free) Content
at PrincetonReview.com/prep

As easy as 1•2•3

1 Go to PrincetonReview.com/prep or scan the **QR code** and enter the following ISBN to register your book:
9780593517741

2 Answer a few simple questions to set up an exclusive Princeton Review account. *(If you already have one, you can just log in.)*

3 Enjoy access to your **FREE** content!

Once you've registered, you can...

- Access and print Practice Tests A and B, as well as their Answers and Explanations

- Take a full-length practice SAT and ACT

- Get valuable advice about the college application process, including tips for writing a great essay and where to apply for financial aid

- Use our searchable rankings of *The Best 390 Colleges* to find out more information about your dream school

- Access a study guide and a variety of printable resources, including bubble sheets for the practice tests in this book, and a glossary of key terms to aid in your review

- Check out online digital flashcards to review core content

- Check to see if there have been any corrections or updates to this edition

- Get our take on any recent or pending updates to the AP U.S. Government and Politics Exam

LET'S GO MOBILE! Access free, additional resources by downloading the new Princeton Review app at www.princetonreview.com/mobile/apps/highschool or scan the QR Code to the right.

Need to report a potential **content** issue?

Contact **EditorialSupport@review.com** and include:
- full title of the book
- ISBN
- page number

Need to report a **technical** issue?

Contact **TPRStudentTech@review.com** and provide:
- your full name
- email address used to register the book
- full book title and ISBN
- Operating system (Mac/PC) and browser (Chrome, Firefox, Safari, etc.)

Look For These Icons Throughout The Book

 PREMIUM PORTAL

 ONLINE ARTICLES

 STUDY BREAK

 PROVEN TECHNIQUES

 ANOTHER APPROACH

 MORE GREAT BOOKS

 APPLIED STRATEGIES

 GOING DEEPER

 WATCH OUT

CONSIDERING AN AP® PREP COURSE?

Pick the Option That's Right For You

AP 5 TUTORING

OUR MOST POPULAR!

- 24 hours of 1:1 LiveOnline instruction
- Elite AP instructors
- Practice questions, practice tests, interactive score reports

AP 4 COURSE

- 24 hours of LiveOnline classroom instruction
- Elite AP instructors
- Practice questions, practice tests, interactive score reports

AP CRAM COURSE

SHORT ON TIME?

- 6 hours of expert LiveOnline instruction
- Practice tests & top-rated prep book
- Recordings of all class sessions

Learn More Online!

www.PrincetonReview.com | 1-800-2-REVIEW

Part I
Using This Book to Improve Your AP Score

- Preview: Your Knowledge, Your Expectations
- Your Guide to Using This Book
- How to Begin

PREVIEW: YOUR KNOWLEDGE, YOUR EXPECTATIONS

Your route to a high score on the AP U.S. Government and Politics Exam depends largely on how you plan to use this book. Respond to the following:

1. Rate your level of confidence about your knowledge of the content tested by the AP U.S. Government and Politics Exam.

    A. Very confident—I know it all
    B. I'm pretty confident, but there are topics for which I could use help
    C. Not confident—I need quite a bit of support
    D. I'm not sure

2. Circle your goal score for the AP U.S. Government and Politics Exam:

    5   4   3   2   1   I'm not sure yet

3. What do you expect to learn from this book? Circle all that apply to you.

    A. A general overview of the test and what to expect
    B. Strategies for how to approach the test
    C. The content the exam tests
    D. I'm not sure yet

YOUR GUIDE TO USING THIS BOOK

This book is organized to provide as much—or as little—support as you need, so you can use this book in whatever way will be most helpful for improving your score on the AP U.S. Government and Politics Exam.

Room to Write
On the actual test, you will be given space along with the bubble sheet to record your answers for each free-response question. You should use scrap paper for the free responses on these practice tests (diagrams that need to be completed have been included in this book). After you've gotten a hang of the timing, be aware of how much space each response is taking up, in case you need to write in smaller print or use fewer words on the test.

-   The remainder of **Part I** provides guidance on how to use this book and help you determine your strengths and weaknesses.

-   **Part II** of this book contains your first practice test, a Diagnostic Answer Key, detailed answers and explanations for each question, and a scoring guide. (Bubble sheets can be printed from your online Student Tools.) This is where you should begin your test preparation in order to realistically determine
    o   your starting point right now
    o   which question types you're ready for and which you might need to practice
    o   which content topics you are familiar with and which you will want to carefully review
    Once you have nailed down your strengths and weaknesses with regard to this exam, you can focus your test preparation, build a study plan, and be efficient with your time. Our Diagnostic Answer Key will assist you with this process.

- **Part III** of this book
  - provides information about the structure, scoring, and content of the AP U.S. Government and Politics Exam
  - helps you to make a study plan
  - points you toward additional resources

- **Part IV** of this book explores various strategies, including
  - how to answer multiple-choice questions
  - how to write high-scoring free-response answers
  - how to manage your time to maximize the number of points you can attain

- **Part V** of this book covers the content you need to get an edge on the AP U.S. Government and Politics Exam.

- **Part VI** of this book contains three additional practice tests, along with their answers, explanations, and scoring guides. If you skipped Practice Test 1, we recommend that you do all four (waiting at least a day or two between them) so that you can compare your progress. Additionally, taking the practice tests will help to identify any external issues: if you consistently get a certain type of question wrong, you probably need to review it. If you got it wrong only once, you may have run out of time or been distracted by something. In either case, examining your test results will allow you to focus on the factors that caused the discrepancy in scores and to be as prepared as possible on test day.

- **Online Resources** contain two additional practice tests. Follow the study guide found there based on the amount of time you have to study for the exam.

You may choose to use some parts of this book over others, or you may work through the entire book. This will depend on your needs and how much time you have. Let's now look at how to make this determination.

Once you register your book online, you can print the bubble sheets and scoring worksheets for your practice tests!

HOW TO BEGIN

1. **Take a Test**

   Before you can decide how to use this book, we recommend that you take a practice test. Doing so will give you an insight into your strengths and weaknesses, and the test will also help you make an effective study plan. If you're feeling test-phobic, remind yourself that a practice test is a diagnostic tool—it's not how well you do that matters but how you use the information gleaned from your performance to guide your preparation.

   So, before you read further, take Practice Test 1 starting on page 9 of this book. Be sure to do so in one sitting, following the instructions that appear before the test.

Scoring Worksheets
We've included a scoring worksheet for each of the Practice Tests. Remember that these worksheets are meant to serve as a rough guideline only. AP exam scores are weighted according to a statistical process that varies slightly every year based on how students perform on the exam. But you can use the worksheets to approximate your score!

2. **Check Your Answers**

Using the Diagnostic Answer Key on page 30, follow our three-step process to identify your strengths and weaknesses with regard to the tested topics. This will help you determine which content review chapters to prioritize when studying this book. Don't worry about the explanations for now, and don't worry about missed questions. We'll get to that soon.

3. **Reflect on the Test**

After you take your first test, respond to the following questions:

- How much time did you spend on the multiple-choice questions?

- How much time did you spend on each essay?

- How many multiple-choice questions did you miss?

- Do you feel you had the knowledge to address the subject matter in the free-response questions?

- Do you feel that you wrote well-organized, thoughtful free responses?

- Circle the content areas that were most challenging for you, and draw a line through the ones in which you felt confident and/or did well.

4. **Read Part III of this Book and Complete the Self-Evaluation**

Part III will provide information on how the test is structured and scored. It will also explain the areas of content that are tested.

As you read Part III, reevaluate your answers to the questions above. At the end of Part III, you will revisit those questions and refine your answers to them. Use the answer key to identify where you missed the most questions, as that may present you with a good place to begin your review. Make a study plan, based on your needs and available time, that will help you to use this book most effectively.

5. **Engage with Parts IV and V as Needed**

Notice the word *engage*. You'll get more out of this book if you use it intentionally than if you read it passively, hoping for an improved score through osmosis. In other words, focus on what you need as a learner.

The strategy chapters in Part IV will help you think about your approach to the types of questions on this exam. This part opens with a reminder to think about how you approach questions now and then closes with a reflection section asking you to think about how/whether you will change your approach in the future.

The content chapters in Part V are designed to provide a review of the content tested on the AP U.S. Government and Politics Exam, including the level of detail you need to know and how your knowledge of the content is tested. You will have the opportunity to assess your understanding of each chapter through test-appropriate questions and a reflection section at the end.

6. Take Another Test and Assess Your Performance

Once you feel you have developed the strategies you need and gained the knowledge you lacked, you should take Practice Test 2, which starts on page 301 of this book. You should do so in one sitting, following the instructions at the beginning of the test.

When you complete the test, check your answers to the multiple-choice section with the correct responses on page 322. Then, see whether a teacher will read your essays and provide feedback for your improvement.

Once you have taken the test, reflect on which areas you still need to work on, and revisit the chapters in this book that address those deficiencies. You have additional practice tests that you can use to prepare, so space those out as you complete your content review. Part VI includes practice tests 2, 3, and 4, and two more practice tests can be found online in your Student Tools. Finally, don't forget to consult your class materials (e.g., textbook, handouts) as well.

7. Keep Working

As discussed in Part III, there are other resources available to you, including a wealth of information on the official AP Students website. Here, you can continue to explore areas to improve upon and engage with right up until the day of the test. If you've followed our recommended approach, you'll have a total of five practice tests left at this point (three in the book, two online), and you should use a mix of Web resources and book review to solidify your understanding of any questions or subjects that you keep getting wrong.

You can find a course description and overview on the AP Students website, located here: apstudents.collegeboard. org/courses/ap-united-states-government-and-politics

This site also includes course details straight from the horse's mouth, so to speak, as well as links to .gov resources that provide primary source information on the Constitution, the Declaration of Independence, and the various branches of government.

Go Online!

Check us out on YouTube for test-taking tips and techniques to help you ace your next exam at youtube.com/The PrincetonReview.

Part II
Practice Test 1

Practice Test 1

1. YOUR NAME:
(Print) Last   First   M.I.

SIGNATURE: _____   DATE: ___ / ___ / ___

HOME ADDRESS: _____
(Print)   Number and Street

_____
City   State   Zip Code

PHONE NO. : _____
(Print)

IMPORTANT: Please fill in these boxes exactly as shown on the back cover of your test book.

2. TEST FORM

3. TEST CODE

4. REGISTRATION NUMBER

5. YOUR NAME

First 4 letters of last name				FIRST INIT	MID INIT

6. DATE OF BIRTH

Month	Day	Year
JAN		
FEB		
MAR	0 0	0 0
APR	1 1	1 1
MAY	2 2	2 2
JUN	3 3	3 3
JUL	4	4 4
AUG	5	5 5
SEP	6	6 6
OCT	7	7 7
NOV	8	8 8
DEC	9	9 9

The Princeton Review®
© The Princeton Review, Inc.
FORM NO. 00001-PR

Section 1

Start with number 1 for each new section.
If a section has fewer questions than answer spaces, leave the extra answer spaces blank.

1. A B C D
2. A B C D
3. A B C D
4. A B C D
5. A B C D
6. A B C D
7. A B C D
8. A B C D
9. A B C D
10. A B C D
11. A B C D
12. A B C D
13. A B C D
14. A B C D
15. A B C D

16. A B C D
17. A B C D
18. A B C D
19. A B C D
20. A B C D
21. A B C D
22. A B C D
23. A B C D
24. A B C D
25. A B C D
26. A B C D
27. A B C D
28. A B C D
29. A B C D
30. A B C D

31. A B C D
32. A B C D
33. A B C D
34. A B C D
35. A B C D
36. A B C D
37. A B C D
38. A B C D
39. A B C D
40. A B C D
41. A B C D
42. A B C D
43. A B C D
44. A B C D
45. A B C D

46. A B C D
47. A B C D
48. A B C D
49. A B C D
50. A B C D
51. A B C D
52. A B C D
53. A B C D
54. A B C D
55. A B C D

The Exam

AP® U.S. Government and Politics Exam

SECTION I: Multiple-Choice Questions

DO NOT OPEN THIS BOOKLET UNTIL YOU ARE TOLD TO DO SO.

At a Glance

Total Time
80 minutes
Number of Questions
55
Percent of Total Grade
50%
Writing Instrument
Pencil required

Instructions

Section I of this examination contains 55 multiple-choice questions. Fill in only the ovals for numbers 1 through 55 on your answer sheet.

Indicate all of your answers to the multiple-choice questions on the answer sheet. No credit will be given for anything written in this exam booklet, but you may use the booklet for notes or scratch work. After you have decided which of the suggested answers is best, completely fill in the corresponding oval on the answer sheet. Give only one answer to each question. If you change an answer, be sure that the previous mark is erased completely. Here is a sample question and answer.

<u>Sample Question</u>

Chicago is a
(A) state
(B) city
(C) country
(D) continent

<u>Sample Answer</u>

Ⓐ ⬤ Ⓒ Ⓓ

Use your time effectively, working as quickly as you can without losing accuracy. Do not spend too much time on any one question. Go on to other questions and come back to the ones you have not answered if you have time. It is not expected that everyone will know the answers to all the multiple-choice questions.

About Guessing

Many candidates wonder whether or not to guess the answers to questions about which they are not certain. Multiple-choice scores are based on the number of questions answered correctly. Points are not deducted for incorrect answers, and no points are awarded for unanswered questions. Because points are not deducted for incorrect answers, you are encouraged to answer all multiple-choice questions. On any questions you do not know the answer to, you should eliminate as many choices as you can, and then select the best answer among the remaining choices.

GO ON TO THE NEXT PAGE.

UNITED STATES GOVERNMENT AND POLITICS

Section I

Time—80 minutes

55 Questions

<u>Directions</u>: Each of the questions or incomplete statements below is followed by four suggested answers or completions. Select the one that is best in each case and then fill in the corresponding oval on the answer sheet.

Questions 1 and 2 refer to the graph below.

Congressional Job Approval Ratings

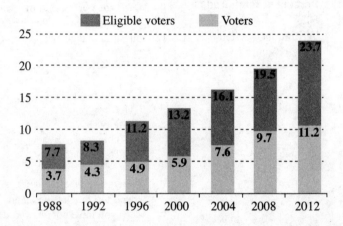

1. Which of the following best describes a trend in the line graph above?

   (A) The approval rating of Congress was higher in the early 1990s than in the late 1990s.
   (B) Congress was more popular in the mid-1990s than in the late 1980s.
   (C) Americans are usually displeased with Congress's performance.
   (D) A majority of Americans disapproved of the performance of Congress immediately after September 11, 2001.

2. Which of the following most likely caused congressional job approval ratings to change dramatically after 1993?

   (A) Since the 2000s, a greater number of congressional candidates have run as independents rather than as members of political parties.
   (B) Elected officials and candidates running for congressional office are increasingly using social media to reach out to voters and constituents.
   (C) Internet websites with political content have become less popular with younger people.
   (D) There has been an increased political polarization in the general public and in the members of Congress.

Questions 3 and 4 refer to the table below.

Latino Participation in Presidential Elections, 1988–2012
(in millions)

3. Which of the following statements is reflected in the data in the table?

   (A) No more than half of eligible Latino voters have ever participated in presidential elections.
   (B) The number of registered voters always increases between elections.
   (C) Latino voters were more dissatisfied with their electoral choices in the 1990s than they were during the 2000s.
   (D) Latino voters have become a larger voice in American politics.

GO ON TO THE NEXT PAGE.

4. Based on the table and your knowledge of typical voter behavior, which of the following statements explains Latino-American turnout between 1988 and 2012?

   (A) Latino voters, less financially well off than other racial groups, did not have the opportunity to learn about upcoming elections and candidates' positions.

   (B) Presidential candidates and their beliefs did not resonate with Latino voters or went against their beliefs entirely.

   (C) The large growth of Latino eligible voters between 1988 and 2012 meant that many were not politically socialized.

   (D) Most eligible Latino voters do not become active voters because of discriminatory voting policies at the state level.

Questions 5 and 6 refer to the infographic below.

Percentage of Voters for Democratic Candidates in Presidential Elections (1972–2012)

5. Which of the following accurately describes the information presented in the infographic?

   (A) If only men had voted in the 1980 election, Jimmy Carter would have won.

   (B) There is little difference in the level of support that the Republican Party receives from men and women.

   (C) The gender gap was more prominent in the 1980s and 1990s than it was in the 1970s.

   (D) In order for a Republican candidate to win, he or she must receive more votes from women than from men.

6. Which of the following could best explain the gender differences in the number of people who voted for Dole and Clinton in 1996?

   (A) Clinton had previously won the election of 1992 with a majority of male voters.

   (B) Dole's campaign received the majority of its funding from corporations, while Clinton's funding was largely from smaller donors and grassroots organizations.

   (C) Dole focused primarily on traditional Republican issues such as fiscal discipline, whereas Clinton attracted female voters of both parties by staking out moderate positions on a host of issues including crime, drugs, and education funding.

   (D) Since married women are more likely to vote for Democrat candidates, Clinton appealed to new voters in this demographic by focusing on domestic policy issues such as education, health care, and social welfare programs.

GO ON TO THE NEXT PAGE.

Questions 7 and 8 refer to the table below.

Dissemination of Medicare Benefits by Region
(Billions of $)

	2000	2004	2008	2012
North	12.4	13.2	14.0	16.4
Northeast	8.2	9.0	9.6	10.1
Midwest	12.0	13.2	14.2	15.0
West	14.8	16.2	15.8	17.0
East	9.8	10.4	10.4	11.0
South	11.8	13.6	16.2	18.4

7. Which of the following is an accurate statement about the information in the table?

   (A) The dissemination of Medicare funding has continually increased across all regions between 2000 and 2012.

   (B) The West received the most Medicare funding in 2012.

   (C) In 2008, the Northeast received approximately one and a half times the amount of Medicare funding as the North.

   (D) Of the regions listed, the South experienced the greatest increase in Medicare funding from 2000 to 2012.

8. Based on the information in the table and your knowledge of political ideology, which of the following statements best reflects how a Republican presidential candidate would address the trends in Medicare spending?

   (A) Medicare spending is becoming a burden on the national budget.

   (B) Medicare spending shows that the nation needs government-run health care.

   (C) Medicare spending shows that the program is working as intended.

   (D) Medicare spending is a crucial way to keep Americans healthy.

Questions 9 and 10 refer to the chart below.

Partisan Composition of State Legislatures

Years			
'78	31	8	11
'80	28	7	15
'82	34	6	10
'84	28	12	10
'86	27	14	9
'88	29	13	8
'90	29	15	6
'92	26	17	7
'94	22	13	15
'96	20	13	17
'98	20	13	17
'00	16	16	18
'02	16	13	21
'04	19	11	20
'06	23	11	16
'08	27	9	14
'10	27	9	14
'12	15	8	27
'14	19	4	27

Number of state legislatures
- ■ Democrats control both chambers
- □ Split D/R Control
- ▨ Republicans control both chambers

9. Which of the following statements is reflected in the data in the chart?

   (A) In most states, registered Democrats outnumber registered Republicans.

   (B) Democrats outnumbered Republicans in state legislatures throughout the early 1990s.

   (C) The number of Republican governors increased between 1990 and 1996.

   (D) The Democrats and Republicans controlled an equal number of state legislatures in 1996.

GO ON TO THE NEXT PAGE.

10. Which of the following was the most likely consequence of a trend illustrated in the bar chart?

    (A) After 1996, more candidates for state legislatures ran as independents rather than as members of political parties.

    (B) In the late 1990s, Democrats running for state office were more likely than Republicans to use social media to reach out to voters and constituents.

    (C) Compared to those in the late 1980s, Democrats in state legislatures in the 1990s were more likely to seek bipartisan support for their initiatives, especially on controversial policy issues.

    (D) The shift in party power in state legislatures in the 1990s led to increased political polarization in the general public.

Questions 11–14 refer to the passage below.

"It is in the context of the present world struggle between freedom and tyranny that the problem of racial discrimination must be viewed. The United States is trying to prove to the people of the world, of every nationality, race, and color, that a free democracy is the most civilized and most secure form of government yet devised by man. We must set an example for others by showing firm determination to remove existing flaws in our democracy.... The existence of discrimination against minority groups in the United States has an adverse effect upon our relations with other countries. Racial discrimination furnishes grist for the Communist propaganda mills."

– Attorney General James P. McGranery

11. Which of the following conclusions can be drawn based on McGranery's argument?

    (A) Since the civil rights of racial minorities are protected by the Bill of Rights, there is no need to enact additional legislation in these areas.

    (B) Civil rights legislation may have positive effects on foreign policy goals.

    (C) The protection of civil rights is essential for a functioning democracy.

    (D) Positive relationships with other countries are necessary to protect civil rights at home.

12. McGranery's statements were most likely made during the Supreme Court ruling on which of the following cases?

    (A) *Gideon v. Wainwright* (1963)

    (B) *Marbury v. Madison* (1803)

    (C) *Tinker v. Des Moines Independent Community School District* (1969)

    (D) *Brown v. Board of Education* (1954)

13. Which of the following constitutional provisions enables the power of the federal government in enacting legislation regarding the issues raised in McGranery's argument?

    (A) Equal protection clause of the Fourteenth Amendment

    (B) Faithful execution of the laws in Article II

    (C) Judicial review in Article III

    (D) Establishment clause in the First Amendment

14. Based on the text, with which of the following statements would McGranery most likely agree?

    (A) The United States Constitution explicitly prohibits racial segregation.

    (B) Without civil rights legislation, many people in foreign countries would be confused about the meaning of the United States Constitution.

    (C) Domestic policy can impact foreign policy.

    (D) Institutions that perpetuate racial discrimination ought to be held accountable for the spread of Communism in foreign lands.

GO ON TO THE NEXT PAGE.

Questions 15–17 refer to the passage below.

"The [Tenth] Amendment states but a truism that all is retained which has not been surrendered. There is nothing in the history of its adoption to suggest that it was more than declaratory of the relationship between the national and state governments as it had been established by the Constitution before the amendment or that its purpose was other than to allay fears that the new national government might seek to exercise powers not granted, and that the states might not be able to exercise fully their reserved powers."

—*United States v. Darby Lumber Co* (1941)

15. The Tenth Amendment most often comes into conflict with which section of the Constitution?

    (A) The "full faith and credit" clause
    (B) The "necessary and proper" clause
    (C) The provisions for the impeachment of a president
    (D) The clause prohibiting states from coining money and entering into treaties

16. The Supreme Court justice who wrote this opinion can be referred to as a

    (A) federalist
    (B) isolationist
    (C) loose constructionist
    (D) strict constructionist

17. Which of the following actions would be justified by the Tenth Amendment?

    (A) A city government asserts exemption from a federal environmental regulation.
    (B) A state asserts its right to waive federal minimum wage laws for part-time workers in a struggling industry.
    (C) The federal government provides financial incentives for state governments to expand Medicaid spending.
    (D) State police refuse to allow federal agents to enforce drug laws within state boundaries.

Questions 18 and 19 refer to the map below.

The Evolution of North Carolina's Congressional District 12

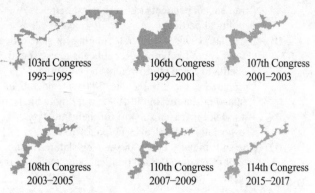

| 103rd Congress 1993–1995 | 106th Congress 1999–2001 | 107th Congress 2001–2003 |

| 108th Congress 2003–2005 | 110th Congress 2007–2009 | 114th Congress 2015–2017 |

Credit: Professor Alasdair Rae and the USGS.gov website

18. The map shows how the borders of a congressional district changed between 1993 and 2015. Which of the following statements, if true, could best explain the odd shapes of the district?

    (A) Due to an economic recession in 1999, moderate voters in North Carolina migrated to areas with greater opportunity in the inland portions of the state. After 2001, the migration ended and the district was restored to its prior boundaries.
    (B) Democrats and Republicans have negotiated cooperatively since 1993 to create a district with fair representation for all.
    (C) The boundaries of the district have been gerrymandered to create highly competitive elections.
    (D) The boundaries of the district have been drawn and redrawn over time to maintain a district with a majority of voters who are registered with the same party.

19. Which of the following has most likely been a consequence of the way the district is drawn on the map?

    (A) It has led to less competitive elections.
    (B) It has led to highly competitive elections.
    (C) It has been beneficial to independent and third-party candidates.
    (D) It has led to high voter turnout in most elections.

GO ON TO THE NEXT PAGE.

Questions 20 and 21 refer to the cartoon below.

Credit: Rick McKee, PoliticalCartoons.com

20. Which of the following best describes the message in the political cartoon?

   (A) Although voters may claim to want change in Congress, they often wind up reelecting their incumbents in primary elections.

   (B) Incumbents often win, despite the efforts of their local constituency to vote them out of office.

   (C) Incumbents often lose primary elections, though they tend to win in general elections.

   (D) Although voters wish to vote their local representatives out of office, they are apathetic about the overall makeup of the U.S. Congress.

21. Which of the following general trends in political elections most aligns with the message of the cartoon?

   (A) Senate incumbents are more likely to maintain their congressional seats than are incumbents in the House of Representatives.

   (B) Incumbents have a large advantage over their challengers, both in party support and campaign finance.

   (C) Since incumbents spend much of their time in Washington, D.C., voters are often unsuccessful in their attempts to communicate with their congressional leadership.

   (D) When voters become disgruntled with Congress, they often react by voting incumbents out of office.

Questions 22 and 23 refer to the graph below.

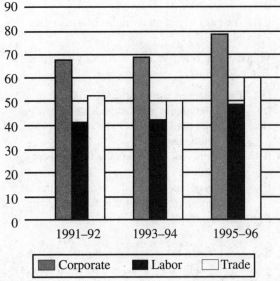

PAC Contributions to Candidates, in millions of dollars, by PAC Type

22. Which of the following conclusions is supported by the graph?

   (A) Corporations have more political influence than do labor unions.

   (B) Trade PACs are the fastest-growing sector of political activism in the United States.

   (C) Corporate PACs are more likely to donate to Republican candidates than to Democratic candidates.

   (D) For each two-year period provided, PACs consistently contributed more than $150 million to different candidates.

23. Based on the graph, which of the following claims would an opponent of PAC campaign contributions most likely make?

   (A) Corporations wield undue influence in politics by contributing a greater share of money to PACs.

   (B) Voter turnout will continue to be poor as long as PACs contribute more money to campaigns than individuals do.

   (C) The continued presence of PAC money in political campaigns will likely lead to election fraud.

   (D) PACs can more effectively influence politics by diverting their money into lobbying efforts rather than contributing to campaigns.

GO ON TO THE NEXT PAGE.

24. To which of the following concepts did the ratification of the Constitution in 1788 most clearly commit?

    (A) The idea of direct democracy
    (B) The principle of limited government
    (C) The abolition of slavery
    (D) The need to protect the rights of the accused

25. Which of the following most accurately describes *The Federalist Papers*?

    (A) The Federalist party platform during the presidency of John Adams, the first Federalist president
    (B) A popular anti-British booklet of the pre-Revolutionary era
    (C) A collection of essays arguing the merits of the Constitution
    (D) A series of congressional acts defining the relationship between the federal and state governments

26. A Supreme Court judge expresses the desire to change public policy and alter judicial precedent. Which of the following terms describes this action?

    (A) Judicial activism
    (B) Due process
    (C) Judicial restraint
    (D) *Ex post facto* lawmaking

27. Which of the following statements about Congress is true?

    (A) Congress cannot override a presidential veto.
    (B) A proposed constitutional amendment can be approved by two-thirds of the delegates in both houses of Congress.
    (C) Congress can establish an official church of the United States.
    (D) Congressional power over the bureaucracy is less than that of the president.

28. Which of the following demonstrates why the House Rules Committee is considered one of the most powerful groups in the House of Representatives?

    (A) It supervises the ethical conduct of House members.
    (B) It oversees the selection of federal judges.
    (C) It determines the number of subcommittees that a standing committee may establish at any given time.
    (D) It determines the scheduling of votes and the conditions under which bills are debated and amended.

29. Which of the following is the primary function of a political action committee (PAC)?

    (A) To contribute money to candidates for election
    (B) To coordinate local get-out-the-vote campaigns
    (C) To promote the defeat of incumbents in the federal and state legislatures
    (D) To organize protest demonstrations and other acts of civil disobedience

30. Voters who rely exclusively on television network news coverage of national elections are most likely to be aware of which of the following?

    (A) Which special interest groups have endorsed which candidates
    (B) Public opinion polls that show the relative strength of each candidate's support
    (C) Candidates' positions on international issues
    (D) Candidates' positions on domestic issues

31. Which of the following rights does the First Amendment protect?

    (A) Due process of the law in any criminal case
    (B) Retention of personal property unless justly compensated by the government
    (C) Not being subjected to excessive fines or unusual punishment
    (D) Petitioning the government for a redress of grievances

32. Which of the following cases focused on the right to privacy for all American citizens?

    (A) *United States v. Lopez*
    (B) *Tinker v. Des Moines Independent Community School District*
    (C) *Baker v. Carr*
    (D) *Griswold v. Connecticut*

33. Which principle of American government establishes concurrent state and national governments?

    (A) Federalism
    (B) Separation of powers
    (C) Checks and balances
    (D) Limited government

GO ON TO THE NEXT PAGE.

34. Which of the following is specifically mentioned in the U.S. Constitution?

    (A) Judicial review
    (B) The national census
    (C) Recall elections
    (D) The right to public education

35. The president wishes to influence the legislative process. Which of the following actions can he legally perform?

    (A) Call special sessions of Congress
    (B) Introduce bills to the floor of Congress
    (C) Address Congress during its debate on bills
    (D) Vote on acts of Congress

36. Which of the following presidential powers is shared with the Senate?

    (A) Deploying troops
    (B) Drafting appropriations bills
    (C) Negotiating treaties
    (D) Forcing Congress into session

37. Which of the following best describes why Republican presidential candidates who are successful in the primaries tend to be more conservative than rank-and-file Republicans?

    (A) Moderate Republicans are less likely than conservative Republicans to gain widespread support in the general election.
    (B) Most moderate Republicans have approved of the Democratic presidential candidate.
    (C) Most rank-and-file Republicans do not care whether their party's nominee shares their political views.
    (D) Party activists, whose political participation is disproportionate to their numbers, tend to be very conservative.

38. What is the primary reason that the committees in the House of Representatives are more influential than those found in the Senate?

    (A) The difference in size between the two chambers means that more work is done on the floor in the Senate and more work is done in committees in the House.
    (B) The Senate as a whole has confirmation powers that the House does not have.
    (C) Members are appointed to the committee in the House but are elected to committees in the Senate.
    (D) A member of any party can serve on a committee in the House, but only majority party members can serve on committees in the Senate.

39. Which of the following accounts for the fact that the power and prestige of the presidency have grown since 1932?

    (A) America's decreased role in international affairs
    (B) Increasing public confidence in the federal government
    (C) Decreased spending on entitlement programs
    (D) The president's increased visibility, due to the development of mass media

40. Which of the following generally results when the Senate and House of Representatives pass different versions of the same bill?

    (A) The president signs the version he prefers.
    (B) The bill goes back to each house's committee and restarts the legislative process.
    (C) All amendments to the bill are invalidated, and the original version of the bill is sent to the president to sign.
    (D) The two legislative bodies form a conference committee.

41. Which of the following statements concerning the likelihood that a person will vote is true?

    (A) When there is a strong front-runner in a state, people in that state are more likely to vote.
    (B) White-collar workers are more likely to vote than are blue-collar workers, with the exception of blue-collar workers who belong to unions.
    (C) Voters who are registered as independent are more likely to vote than those who are registered Democrats or Republicans.
    (D) There is no difference in the likelihood of voting among those with undergraduate degrees and those with postgraduate degrees.

42. A member of which of the following demographic groups is most likely to support a Republican presidential candidate?

    (A) Married white male
    (B) Unmarried white female
    (C) African American, male or female
    (D) People under the age of 25, male or female

GO ON TO THE NEXT PAGE.

43. Which of the following is an accurate comparison of the two court cases?

	United States v. Lopez (1995)	*McDonald v. Chicago* (2010)
(A)	Declared an act of Congress unconstitutional	Found that the personal right to own firearms is protected by the due process clause of the Fourteenth Amendment
(B)	Set limits to Congress's power under the commerce clause	Recognized the importance of state sovereignty and local control
(C)	Allowed for the possession of firearms on public school property	Ruled that state laws were supreme to national laws
(D)	Resolved uncertainty left in the wake of *District of Columbia v. Heller* as to the scope of gun rights in the states	Declared the Gun-Free School Zones Act unconstitutional

44. Which of the following is an accurate comparison of federal and state judiciaries?

	Federal Judiciaries	**State Judiciaries**
(A)	May overturn state decisions on any grounds	Are higher than federal courts
(B)	Do not hear cases which originated in state courts	Are entirely independent
(C)	May rule on the constitutionality of state court decisions	Are largely independent
(D)	Are appeals courts	Are trial courts

45. Which of the following is an accurate comparison of a pardon and a reprieve?

	Pardon	**Reprieve**
(A)	Lasts ten years	Lasts one year
(B)	Postpones legal punishment	Grants a release from legal punishment
(C)	Grants a release from legal punishment	Postpones legal punishment
(D)	Can be granted only by presidents	Can be granted only by governors

46. Which of the following is an accurate comparison of traditional Republican and Democrat views on government?

	Republicans	**Democrats**
(A)	Tend to be liberal	Tend to be conservative
(B)	Favor more governmental regulation of the marketplace	Favor personal privacy
(C)	Favor a national religion	Favor private education
(D)	Favor fewer regulations	Favor more governmental regulation of the marketplace

47. Which of the following is an accurate comparison of the First and Fourth Amendments to the Constitution?

	First Amendment	**Fourth Amendment**
(A)	Contains the establishment and free exercise clauses	Was clarified by the ruling in *Wisconsin v. Yoder*
(B)	Guarantees the right to an attorney, as stipulated by *Gideon v. Wainwright*	Protects citizens against unlawful searches and seizures
(C)	Protects freedom of religion	Requires that evidence illegally seized by law enforcement cannot be used in criminal prosecutions
(D)	Protects freedom of speech	Was used to justify the decision in *McDonald v. Chicago*

GO ON TO THE NEXT PAGE.

48. Congress used which of the following to justify the passage of the Civil Rights Act of 1964?

   (A) *Gideon v. Wainwright* (1963)
   (B) Southern States' Jim Crow laws
   (C) *Brown v. Board of Education* (1954)
   (D) The Fourteenth Amendment

49. According to Federalist No. 10, federalism has which of the following effects on political factions?

   (A) It provides a structured environment in which factions may flourish.
   (B) It limits the dangers of factionalism by diluting political power.
   (C) It allows factions to dominate on the national level while limiting their influence on state governments.
   (D) It eliminates any opportunity for factions to form.

50. The Constitution, as originally ratified, addressed which of the following weaknesses of the Articles of Confederation?

   (A) Inclusion of a chief executive office
   (B) National government's inability to levy taxes effectively
   (C) Imposition of a central authority to regulate interstate trade
   (D) Omission of a universal suffrage clause

51. Congress's power to determine national policy

   (A) usually increases as a president's popularity decreases, and vice versa
   (B) has declined steadily since the ratification of the Constitution
   (C) is severely limited by the "elastic clause" of the Constitution
   (D) increases during times of war

52. Which of the following statements about cabinet departments is true?

   (A) They are established by the judicial branch.
   (B) Their members sometimes do not share the president's goals.
   (C) They cannot all be run by leaders who belong to the same political party the president does.
   (D) Every federal agency is a cabinet department.

53. Which of the following statements about the Electoral College is correct?

   (A) Each state must split its electoral votes among all the candidates that receive votes.
   (B) Each state is equally represented in the Electoral College.
   (C) The Electoral College was created by an amendment to the Constitution.
   (D) The results of Electoral College voting tend to distort the winner's margin of victory when compared with the popular vote.

54. A newly elected member of the House of Representatives promised her constituents that she would fight to cut their taxes. Serving on which committee would help her keep this promise?

   (A) Appropriations
   (B) Financial Services
   (C) Oversight and Reform
   (D) Ways and Means

55. Which of the following would best represent a conservative view concerning social policy?

   (A) The federal government should have a strong role in regulating public education.
   (B) Gun-owners should be permitted to openly carry firearms in public.
   (C) Racial and gender considerations should be taken into account in state university admissions decisions.
   (D) Individuals should rely on government aid for their economic well-being.

STOP
END OF SECTION I

IF YOU FINISH BEFORE TIME IS CALLED, YOU MAY CHECK YOUR WORK ON THIS SECTION.
DO NOT GO ON TO SECTION II UNTIL YOU ARE TOLD TO DO SO.

UNITED STATES GOVERNMENT AND POLITICS

Section II

Time—1 hour and 40 minutes

<u>Directions:</u> You have 1 hour and 40 minutes to answer all four of the following questions. It is suggested that you spend approximately 20 minutes each on Questions 1, 2, and 3 and 40 minutes on Question 4. Unless directions indicate otherwise, respond to all parts of all four questions. In your response, use substantive examples where appropriate. It is recommended that you take a few minutes to plan each answer. You may plan your answers in this Questions booklet, but no credit will be given for notes written in this booklet. You will earn credit only for what you write in the Free Response booklet.

1. In March of 2010, Congress enacted a federal statute called the Affordable Care Act (ACA). The ACA greatly expanded federal regulation of the health care and health insurance industries, increased Medicaid benefits, and provided for subsidized health insurance for some eligible Americans. Perhaps the most controversial aspect of the ACA was its inclusion of an "individual mandate" that required uninsured individuals who did not qualify for Medicare or Medicaid benefits to purchase health insurance from private insurers or else pay fines and penalties.

   In *National Federation of Independent Business v. Sebelius* (2012), the Supreme Court ruled in a 5 to 4 decision that the individual mandate was not unconstitutional. Chief Justice John Roberts represented the majority opinion when he stated that "The individual mandate cannot be upheld as an exercise of Congress's power under the Commerce Clause… In this case, however, it is reasonable to construe what Congress has done as increasing taxes on those who have a certain amount of income but choose to go without health insurance. Such legislation is within Congress's power to tax." Justice Ruth Bader Ginsburg, in a minority opinion, wrote that "Congress had a rational basis for concluding that the uninsured, as a class, substantially affect interstate commerce."

   Although the ACA is still law, from 2010 to 2017, the Executive Branch did not enforce fines or penalties against Americans who lacked health insurance. In 2017, Congress finally repealed the individual mandate by passing the Tax Cuts and Jobs Act.

   After reading the scenario, respond to (A), (B), and (C) below:

   (A) Referencing the scenario, describe the enumerated power in Article I of the Constitution that the Supreme Court majority used to justify Congress's authority to require the "individual mandate" in the Affordable Care Act (ACA).

   (B) Explain ONE Constitutional reason why the majority on the Supreme Court may have rejected Justice Ginsburg's argument.

   (C) Explain ONE possible reason for the lack of enforcement and eventual repeal of the individual mandate.

GO ON TO THE NEXT PAGE.

Defense budgets, fiscal years 1948–2018

Source: Department of Defense

2. Use the information graphic to answer the questions.

(A) Which two presidents were responsible for the greatest increases of defense spending since 1953?

(B) Describe a trend in the data and draw a conclusion about the defense spending habits of Republican and Democratic presidents.

(C) Explain how the defense spending as shown in the graph relates to iron triangles within the federal government.

GO ON TO THE NEXT PAGE.

3. In March 1931, nine black men from Alabama were accused of sexually assaulting two young white women. Less than a week later, after a series of one-day trials, most of the defendants were sentenced to death. Prior to the trials, the defendants were not told they could hire lawyers or even contact their families. They had no access to a lawyer until shortly before trial. They appealed their convictions on the grounds that the group was not provided adequate legal counsel.

In the ensuing case, *Powell v. Alabama*, the Supreme Court reversed the convictions, reasoning that the right to retain and be represented by a lawyer was fundamental to a fair trial in death penalty cases, and that the trial judge must inform the defendant of this right. In death penalty cases in which the defendant cannot afford a lawyer, the court must appoint one sufficiently far in advance of the trial date.

    (A)   Identify a constitutional amendment or clause that was used to justify the decisions in both *Powell v. Alabama* (1932) and *Gideon v. Wainwright* (1963).

    (B)   Based on the constitutional amendment identified in Part A, explain how *Gideon v. Wainwright* expanded upon the decision in *Powell v. Alabama*.

    (C)   Describe historical changes that have been made to the prosecution of defendants since the *Gideon v. Wainwright* decision.

GO ON TO THE NEXT PAGE.

4. Develop an argument that explains whether increased power vested to the federal government or increased power vested to the states best achieves the founders' intent for American democracy in terms of ensuring a stable government run by the people.

In your essay, you must:

- Articulate a defensible claim or thesis that responds to the prompt and establishes a line of reasoning.

- Support your claim with at least TWO pieces of accurate and relevant information:
  - At least ONE piece of evidence must be from one of the following foundational documents:
    - Brutus 1
    - Articles of Confederation
    - Federalist No. 10
    - U.S. Constitution
  - Use a second piece of evidence from another foundational document from the list or your study of the electoral process.

- Use reasoning to explain why your evidence supports your claim/thesis.

- Respond to an opposing or alternative perspective using refutation, concession, or rebuttal.

END OF EXAMINATION

Practice Test 1: Diagnostic Answer Key and Explanations

PRACTICE TEST 1: DIAGNOSTIC ANSWER KEY

Let's take a look at how you did on Practice Test 1. Follow the three-step process in the diagnostic answer key below and go read the explanations for any questions you got wrong or you struggled with but got correct. Once you finish working through the answer key and the explanations, devise a study plan that helps you improve any areas that you may be struggling with.

STEP 1 》》 Check your answers and mark any correct answers with a ✔ in the appropriate column.

Q #	Ans.	✔	Chapter #, Section Title	Q #	Ans.	✔	Chapter #, Section Title
			Multiple-Choice				
1	C		**7,** Characteristics of Public Opinion	29	A		**8,** Changes to Campaign Financing
2	D		**7,** Characteristics of Public Opinion	30	B		**8,** Media Influence of Elections
3	D		**1,** Quantitative Analysis: Charts and Tables	31	D		**6,** First Amendment Rights and Restrictions
4	B		**8,** Election Day	32	D		**6,** *Griswold v. Connecticut*
5	C		**1,** Quantitative Analysis: Charts and Tables	33	A		**4,** Federalism
6	C		**7,** Determining Factors in Ideological and Political Behavior	34	B		**4,** The Constitution
7	D		**1,** Quantitative Analysis: Charts and Tables	35	A		**5,** The Formal Powers of the Presidency
8	A		**7,** Political Ideologies	36	C		**5,** The Formal Powers of the Presidency
9	B		**1,** Quantitative Analysis: Charts and Tables	37	D		**8,** The Election Cycle
10	C		**8,** Party Coalitions	38	A		**5,** Congressional Leadership
11	B		**6,** Civil Rights	39	D		**5,** Executive Office of the President
12	D		**6,** Civil Rights	40	D		**5,** Congressional Leadership
13	A		**6,** Civil Rights	41	B		**7,** Determining Factors in Ideological and Political Behavior
14	C		**6,** Civil Rights	42	A		**7,** Determining Factors in Ideological and Political Behavior
15	B		**4,** Federalism	43	A		**6,** The Second Amendment
16	D		**4,** Federalism	44	C		**5,** The Politics of the Judiciary
17	C		**4,** Federalism	45	C		**5,** The Formal Powers of the Presidency
18	D		**5,** Congressional Districts and Representation	46	D		**7,** Political Ideologies
19	A		**5,** Congressional Districts and Representation	47	C		**6,** The Fourth Amendment
20	A		**8,** The Election Cycle	48	D		**6,** Civil Rights Act of 1964
21	B		**8,** The Election Cycle	49	B		**4,** Federalist No. 10
22	D		**8,** Changes to Campaign Financing	50	B		**4,** Articles of Confederation
23	A		**8,** Changes to Campaign Financing	51	A		**5,** Congressional Leadership
24	B		**4,** The Constitutional Convention	52	B		**5,** The Executive Branch
25	C		**4,** The Federalist Papers	53	D		**8,** The Election Cycle
26	A		**5,** The Politics of the Judiciary	54	D		**8,** Legislation by Committee
27	B		**5,** The System of Checks and Balances	55	B		**7,** Political Ideologies
28	D		**5,** The Legislative Process				

	Free Response		
Q #	**Ans.**	**✔**	**Chapter #, Section Title**
1A	See Explanation		**4,** The Constitution
1B	See Explanation		**4,** The Constitution
1C	See Explanation		**4,** The Constitution
2A	See Explanation		**1,** Quantitative Analysis: Charts and Tables
2B	See Explanation		**8,** Fiscal Policy Making
2C	See Explanation		**5,** Iron Triangles
3A	See Explanation		**6,** Civil Liberties
3B	See Explanation		**6,** Civil Liberties
3C	See Explanation		**6,** Civil Liberties
4	See Explanation		**4,** Federalism

Tally your correct answers from Step 1 by chapter. For each chapter, write the number of correct answers in the appropriate box. Then, divide your number of correct answers by the number of total questions (which we've provided) to get your percent correct.

CHAPTER 1 TEST SELF-EVALUATION

CORRECT ANSWERS

$$\frac{\boxed{}}{\boxed{5}} = \boxed{} \%$$

PERCENT CORRECT

TOTAL QUESTIONS

CHAPTER 4 TEST SELF-EVALUATION

CORRECT ANSWERS

$$\frac{\boxed{}}{\boxed{13}} = \boxed{} \%$$

PERCENT CORRECT

TOTAL QUESTIONS

CHAPTER 5 TEST SELF-EVALUATION

CORRECT ANSWERS

$$\frac{\boxed{}}{\boxed{15}} = \boxed{} \%$$

PERCENT CORRECT

TOTAL QUESTIONS

CHAPTER 6 TEST SELF-EVALUATION

CORRECT ANSWERS

$$\frac{\boxed{}}{\boxed{12}} = \boxed{} \%$$

PERCENT CORRECT

TOTAL QUESTIONS

CHAPTER 7 TEST SELF-EVALUATION

CORRECT ANSWERS

$$\frac{\boxed{}}{\boxed{8}} = \boxed{} \%$$

PERCENT CORRECT

TOTAL QUESTIONS

CHAPTER 8 TEST SELF-EVALUATION

CORRECT ANSWERS

$$\frac{\boxed{}}{\boxed{12}} = \boxed{} \%$$

PERCENT CORRECT

TOTAL QUESTIONS

 Use the results above to customize your study plan. You may want to start with, or give more attention to, the chapters with the lowest percents correct.

PRACTICE TEST 1: ANSWERS AND EXPLANATIONS

Section I: Multiple Choice

1. **C** Upon a quick scan of the graph, a simple deduction is that Congress is usually "flunking" in the eyes of the American people. Choice (A) is incorrect because the approval rating of Congress was in the 20–40% range in the early 1990s and in the 30–50% range in the late 1990s. Choice (B) is incorrect because the approval rating of Congress was in the 20–40% range in the mid-1990s and between 35% and approximately 43% in the late 1980s. Choice (D) is incorrect because approximately 85% of Americans approved of Congress's performance immediately following September 11, 2001, and (D) says that Americans "disapproved" of Congress during that era. The correct answer is (C), since a majority of Americans (that is, more than 50%) approved of Congress's performance only from the late 1990s until about 2004: that's less than 10 years, and the graph shows data for more than 30.

2. **D** Use Process of Elimination. Choice (A) is incorrect, since it has always been extremely rare for congressional candidates to run as independents. Choice (B) is incorrect because social media as we know it did not come about until the early 2000s. Choice (C) is probably untrue, and has no obvious connection to congressional job approval ratings. This leaves (D), which is correct because since the early 1990s, both the Congress and the general public have become more politically polarized. This trend can explain the frequent swings in congressional approval.

3. **D** Use Process of Elimination. More than half of all eligible Latino voters participated in the elections of 1992, so (A) is contradicted right off the bat. (Additionally, this chart doesn't show any results prior to 1988 or after 2012, so avoid answers that draw conclusions about years not covered by the chart.) Choice (B) is unsupported by the data, since we aren't given the number of *registered* voters; in addition, it makes the same mistake as (A) by using the word always, which refers to years not covered as well as those in the chart. Choice (C) is incorrect, since the chart provides no information about "satisfaction," and may well be untrue, since the number of voters increased every year. Choice (D) is correct: the chart shows an increasing number of Latino voters.

4. **B** The question asks you to make connections between the data in the graph and typical voter behavior. Choice (A) is incorrect because the graph says nothing about Latino Americans' economic status compared to that of other racial groups. Choice (C) is incorrect because although the graph supports the statement that the Latino population grew, political socialization touches every American's life through media, parents, school, etc. There is no way that millions of Americans would not be politically socialized. Choice (D) is incorrect because the graph does not address that issue. Also, the Voting Rights Act of 1965 barred states from denying Americans the right to vote based on race. As a result, (B) is the correct answer. Between 1988 and 2012, Democratic and Republican presidential candidates were either Caucasian or African American. Also, the Republican Party advocates for restrictions on immigration, a significant issue with Latino Americans. These factors likely led to many eligible Latino voters deciding not to register.

5. **C** The chart shows little difference between the presidential votes of men and women in both the 1972 and the 1976 elections. Starting with the 1980 election, however, a clear gender gap can be seen, with women consistently giving greater support to the Democratic candidate than the men do. Choice (A) is incorrect, since the chart shows that, had only men voted, Ronald Reagan would have won the 1980 election by a greater margin than he actually did. Choice (B) is unsupported, since the chart is measuring Democrat voters, not Republicans, and actually suggests that from 1980 forward, a smaller percentage of women than men voted for the Republican presidential candidate. Because the chart illustrates only the percentage of votes from each gender, it is impossible to draw a conclusion about the number of votes that the candidates received from men and women, so (D) must be incorrect. Choice (C) is correct, because the black portions on the infographic are at roughly the same height for men as for women in 1972 and 1976 but noticeably higher for women than for men from 1980 through 1996.

6. **C** Some knowledge of the Dole/Clinton election may help here but is not necessary. Use Process of Elimination. Choice (A) is incorrect based on the data supplied in the graph, and it is not clear that the election of 1992 would have bearing on the results of the election of 1996. Choice (B) is incorrect, since both of the major parties tend to receive funding from corporations and trade unions. Also, it is unclear how funding would affect the gender voting gap. That leaves us with (C) and (D), the only answers that directly address the issue of gender. Choice (C) is better, since Clinton would have successfully captured votes from both Democrat women and moderate Republican women by appealing to domestic issues of concern to them. Dole was unsuccessful by appealing solely to his party's base. Choice (D) is incorrect, since married women do not swing Democrat in most elections.

7. **D** To eliminate (A), you'd have to find at least one instance in which Medicare funding does not increase; that's either the West or the East between 2004 and 2008. To eliminate (B), see whether there are any regions that got more than the West's $17,000,000,000 in funding; that would be the South, with $18,400,000,000. In 2008, the North (14.0) received approximately one and a half times the amount of Medicare funding as the Northeast (9.6), so eliminate (C). Accordingly, the correct answer is (D) because the South experienced the greatest increase in Medicare funding from 2000–2012, having increased by $6.6 billion over the 12-year period.

8. **A** Politicians often use the federal government's spending levels when making a point to potential voters. Choice (B) is a liberal position that Republicans have fought against for years. Choice (C) does not make sense because spending levels do not show either way whether a program is working. Choice (D) is incorrect because a Republican candidate would advocate for private insurance as a way to keep Americans healthy. As a result, (A) is correct as a Republican candidate would use rising Medicare costs in all regions as a way to argue that the program is becoming a burden on the national budget.

9. **B** Compare each of the four "Democratic" bars (on the left) with the corresponding "Republican" bars on the right and then run through the choices, eliminating those that don't match. Choice (A) is incorrect because the chart does not include information about registered voters. Choice (C)

is similarly incorrect because the chart does not include information about governors. (Remember that graph questions on the AP U.S. Government and Politics Exam ask that you identify indisputable conclusions. Do not try to "read between the lines" and interpret the data—you will only get into trouble that way.) Choice (D) is wrong because Democrats controlled 20 chambers in 1996, while Republicans controlled only 17. Only (B) is correct: Democrats controlled more seats through the early '90s before that trend began to reverse itself in 2000.

10. **C** According to the bar graph, throughout the 1990s and early 2000s, Republicans generally gained more seats in state legislatures, while Democrats generally lost seats. Therefore, the trend is toward a more equal balance of power. Choice (A) is incorrect, since there is no reason to conclude that more Republican victories would encourage third-party activity. Choice (B) is incorrect, since social media was virtually nonexistent in the 1990s and would not have been favored by either party in particular. Choice (D) is tempting, but we do not know whether the shift in party dominance was a cause or effect of political polarization; either is equally plausible. Only (C) matches the data, which is that despite having a majority in many legislatures, Democrats would have needed the support of at least a few Republicans for controversial pieces of legislation, so as to offset any Democrat legislators who might not vote in harmony with the majority of the party.

11. **B** Choice (A) would contradict McGranery's belief that resolving civil rights questions would be in the best interests of the United States overall. Choice (C) may look tempting, but is worded much more broadly than the thesis McGranery puts forward. Choice (D) is close, but actually reverses McGranery's argument: he thinks that "removing flaws in our democracy" promotes better relationships with other countries, not vice versa. The correct answer must be (B), which aptly summarizes the message in McGranery's remarks.

12. **D** Use Process of Elimination. Choices (A), (B), and (C) have no connection to racial civil rights, which is the topic of McGranery's quote. *Brown v. Board of Education* effectively reversed the "separate but equal" doctrine that had stood under *Plessy v. Ferguson*, so (D) is the best choice.

13. **A** McGranery dealt with the legal issues of providing African Americans around the country with "equal protection" from undue discrimination and with the unlawfulness of school segregation. Choices (B) and (C) are largely procedural in nature, and don't encompass the scope of this legislation. The establishment clause, (D), is bigger, but largely pertains to religious freedom cases, which are another category altogether. Choice (A) is correct because the Supreme Court has used the equal protection clause of the Fourteenth Amendment to provide justification for federal laws over state laws.

14. **C** This question is asking you to summarize McGranery's argument. Choice (A) is untrue, since the Civil Rights Act of 1964 was necessary to bring an end to discrimination laws in the South. Choice (B) may seem close, but there is no mention of "confusion" in McGranery's quote, nor would foreign nations necessarily concern themselves with our Constitution. Choice (D) is too strong and is not supported by McGranery's statements. Since McGranery believes that U.S. domestic policy regarding civil rights can affect our relationships with other countries around the world (foreign policy), (C) is the best choice.

15. **B** Recall that the Tenth Amendment clarifies whether the federal or state government has authority in any given situation. The "full faith and credit" clause requires states to honor one another's laws, licenses, and so on. It does not, however, deal with infringements on state governments by the national government, and so you can eliminate (A). The provisions for the impeachment of a president pertain only to the national government, so (C) can also be eliminated. The clause prohibiting states from coining money and entering into treaties appears in the body of the Constitution, which means that there is no conflict with the amendment, and (D) can be eliminated as well. Only the "necessary and proper" clause, often referred to as the elastic clause, creates an issue with the Tenth Amendment, as it allows Congress to pass new laws that would expand its authority over states' rights; this means that (B) is the correct answer.

16. **D** The term federalist, (A), refers either to those who support the federal system or to members of the Federalist Party, which existed from the late 1700s until the late 1810s. Either way, it describes a person who supports a strong central government, so eliminate it. The term isolationist, (B), refers to a person who believes that the government should avoid involvement with foreign governments and nations. Choice (B) can be eliminated. The term loose constructionist, (C), refers to a person who believes the national government should use the elastic clause to expand its powers. Loose constructionists argue that the national government may do anything not expressly forbidden by the Constitution. They do not see the Tenth Amendment as a significant limitation of federal power, and for this reason, (C) can be eliminated. Strict constructionists, (D), believe that the Constitution limits the national government to its specifically enumerated powers. They also believe that the vast majority of governance should be left entirely to the states. This makes (D) the correct answer.

17. **C** Although the Tenth Amendment grants that states often have discretion in how they govern their own affairs, they do not have the legal right to circumvent federal law. Attempts by state and local governments to assert actions such as those described in (A), (B), and (D) have consistently failed in federal courts. Choice (C) is an attempt by the federal government to influence the states, while not unduly coercing them, and so would be harmonious with the Tenth Amendment.

18. **D** Since the boundaries of the district are oddly shaped, this is a classic example of gerrymandering. Gerrymandering is a practice of designing districts with non-geographical considerations in mind, which rules out (A). Although racial gerrymandering is illegal, in some parts of the country parties routinely create districts with irregular boundaries in order to deliberately include (or exclude) certain cities or counties that have historically voted for one party or another. This is the opposite of what (B) and (C) suggest, so you can also eliminate those. Choice (D) is the best description of gerrymandering.

19. **A** Gerrymandered congressional districts such as the one in this map are designed to group together voters of a single party, with the hope that the results of an election in that district will be easily predicted. This leads to less competitive elections (A), not more competitive ones (B). There is no benefit to third-party candidates (C), nor is gerrymandering linked to high voter turnout (D). If anything, voters in the minority party may become less likely to participate, believing that their votes have less influence. The correct answer is (A).

20.　**A**　The first frame of the cartoon humorously depicts an angry voter holding up a newspaper indicating that it is congressional primary season. The voter says, "Throw the bums out!," a common refrain among citizens who have a low opinion of members of Congress generally. In the second frame, we see the headline "Entrenched Incumbents Win" and a smiling voter. We can infer that voters, no matter how upset they may be with Congress in general, tend to be loyal to their local senators and representatives. Thus, the makeup of Congress does not change dramatically from one election to another, despite its generally low approval ratings. Choice (B) is not supported by the second frame, which depicts the voter expressing happiness that his "entrenched incumbent" has won. Choice (C) is incorrect, since the cartoon is about primary elections. (Also, it would be virtually impossible to win general elections without winning primaries first.) Choice (D) is backward: according to the cartoon, voters are angry about Congress in general, but tend to reelect their local representatives. Choice (A) is the best match.

21.　**B**　Since the cartoon depicts incumbents winning elections, we are looking for a choice which is close to that. Choice (A) is not always true, and the cartoon does not distinguish between the two houses of Congress. Choice (C) is incorrect, since the cartoon is about voting, not communication. Choice (D) is going in the opposite direction. Choice (B) is true; incumbents do generally enjoy a tremendous advantage over their challengers.

22.　**D**　Compare each choice to what's shown in the graph and use Process of Elimination. Choice (A) can be ruled out immediately, as the graph measures money, not political influence. Choice (B) can be likewise dismissed, since we have no evidence that it is the "fastest-growing." Be careful with (C). Though it may be true, this graph does not break down contributions by political party. For (D), add the totals of all PAC contributions in each of the listed election. In each period shown, the sum is greater than $150 million, which means that (D) is the correct answer. (Remember that this is only the tip of the iceberg: candidates raise money from private donors and many other sources as well.)

23.　**A**　This question asks what an opponent of PAC contributions might claim, which means you're looking for a valid concern about PAC money. Voter turnout and election fraud are not clearly linked to PAC contributions, so rule out (B) and (C). Choice (D) is incorrect because opponents of PACs fear their influence in all aspects of politics, including lobbying. This leaves (A), which is a valid concern about how a politician might end up beholden to a few corporate sources, as opposed to representing many individual sources.

24.　**B**　A constitution specifies what a government is allowed to do, and also what it may not do. Eliminate any choice that does not match with the framers' intentions for the Constitution. Choice (A) describes a form of democratic government in which all citizens vote on all issues, but the Constitution established a representative democracy, in which citizens vote for representatives who, in turn, act on their behalf and assume the nation's legislative and executive duties. Eliminate (A). Choice (C) is also incorrect, as the abolition of slavery was not accomplished until the ratification of the Thirteenth Amendment in 1865. You can eliminate (D) for a similar reason; the Bill of Rights, which would protect the rights of the accused, was not ratified until 1791. This leaves (B) as the correct answer, and it is true that by setting limits on the government with the constitution, the framers hoped to prevent the government from seizing power, as the British monarchy had done.

25.   **C**   If you don't recall what *The Federalist Papers* were, use Process of Elimination to find wrong answers. You can eliminate (A) because the Federalist Party did not have a platform; platforms are the product of political conventions, which were not a part of American politics until after the Federalist Party. You may be able to eliminate (B) if you can recall that *The Federalist Papers* were neither anti-British nor, as they were written in 1787, pre-Revolutionary. Choice (D) can also be ruled out, as this is describing a portion of the U.S. Constitution. This leaves (C), which correctly identifies the collective essays of Alexander Hamilton, James Madison, and John Jay published in support of ratification of the Constitution.

26.   **A**   Consider whether each choice fits with the notion of changing public policy or altering precedent. The due process clause of the Fourteenth Amendment prohibits the states from depriving citizens of life, liberty, or property without a fair and impartial hearing; this has nothing to do with changing policy, so eliminate (B). Judicial restraint suggests an unwillingness to break with precedent or to overturn legislative and executive acts, which is the opposite of what the question is looking for, so you can also eliminate (C). An *ex post facto* law allows a government to prosecute citizens for acts that were legal at the time they occurred, but were later deemed illegal. Not only doesn't this match the question, but this form of lawmaking is explicitly prohibited by the Constitution, so throw out (D) as well. Judicial activism refers to the actions of a court that frequently strikes down or alters the acts of the executive and/or legislative branches, which perfectly describes the given scenario. Choice (A) is the correct answer.

27.   **B**   Use Process of Elimination. Congress can override a presidential veto, so eliminate (A). The First Amendment prohibits the establishment of a national religion, which rules out (C). And when it comes to control of the bureaucracy, Congress often has more power than the president, given that it can affirm or reject presidential appointments, abolish agencies, determine the funding an agency receives, and change agency jurisdiction if unsatisfied with policy implementation. Eliminate (D). Choice (B) is the correct answer, as Congress can approve a Constitutional amendment. After approval, the amendment goes to the states for ratification. Three-fourths of the states must ratify the proposed amendment before that amendment becomes part of the Constitution.

28.   **D**   The House Rules Committee is in charge, as you might expect from the name, of setting certain rules. The House Ethics Committee is in charge of investigating ethics charges against House members, so eliminate (A). The Senate, not the House, provides "advice and consent" to the president on judicial nominees, so rule out (B). The number of subcommittees is limited by budget and staffing considerations, not by a separate committee, so eliminate (C) as well. This leaves (D) as the correct answer: the Rules Committee controls the terms of debate and the scheduling of floor votes, which makes them quite powerful.

29.   **A**   Political action committees (PACs) want to see that those who represent their points of view are elected. Choice (B) wouldn't necessarily have this effect, as a get-out-the-vote campaign might lead voters to choose a different candidate. Choice (C) is also not specific enough; a PAC might try to defeat an incumbent, but would do so only if that incumbent failed to represent their point of view or actively worked against them. Choice (D) can be outright eliminated; a PAC's primary

function is not to organize protests or civil disobedience, which would be very indirect ways of influencing an election. Choice (A) is correct because a PAC largely exists to raise political funds for electoral campaigns and distribute them to candidates.

30. **B** Network news programs—which are separate from debates and long-form interviews—tend to favor information that changes regularly and can be communicated quickly. The endorsement of a special interest group is generally stable, and is likely to be reported on only once; eliminate (A). The same goes for candidates' positions on issues, which are not only complex and difficult to capture in sound bites or TV-friendly phrases and clips, but unlikely to change. As a result, you can eliminate (C) and (D) as well. The correct answer is (B), because public opinion is constantly shifting and is most likely to be repeated on a regular basis.

31. **D** This question is testing one of the less-discussed facets of the First Amendment. Be careful on questions like these, as the wrong answers—which appear in other amendments—will sound familiar. Choices (A) and (B) can be eliminated because they have to do with the Fifth Amendment, whereas (C) is from the Eighth Amendment. Choice (D) is the correct answer, as the First Amendment, which deals with different types of freedom of speech, states that "Congress shall make no law… abridging…the right of the people…to petition the Government for a redress of grievances."

32. **D** Use Process of Elimination. You can eliminate (A) because this case dealt with gun rights. You can cross off (B) because this case dealt with freedom of speech. Throw out (C) because this case involved redistricting of congressional districts. While the right to privacy is not explicitly mentioned in the Constitution, in *Griswold v. Connecticut* the Warren Court ruled that the Bill of Rights contained an implied right to privacy. Therefore, (D) is correct.

33. **A** Choices (B) and (C) can be eliminated as these terms refer to powers shared within the federal government. Choice (D) can be eliminated as *limited government* refers only to the federal government. As a result, (A) is correct, as *federalism* refers to the concurrent, or shared, powers between the state and national governments.

34. **B** If you don't remember, use POE to rule out answers that couldn't have been mentioned in the Constitution. Judicial review allows the Supreme Court to overturn laws on the basis of their constitutionality, but wasn't established until 1803, with Chief Justice John Marshall's decision in the 1803 *Marbury v. Madison* case; eliminate (A). Recall elections and public education would be covered at the state level, and so are not mentioned in the U.S. Constitution; eliminate (C) and (D). This leaves (B), the census, which must be taken every 10 years, according to Article I, Section 2 of the Constitution.

35. **A** Use Process of Elimination to rule out choices that you know aren't right. For instance, while the president may recommend bills to Congress and can strongly influence public sentiment on legislation, the president cannot directly introduce anything; eliminate (B). Likewise, the only point at which the president can address Congress is during the State of the Union (even then, Congress must invite them to do so), so eliminate (C). Don't overthink this question; the president may be able to influence congressional votes as the leader of their party, but the president cannot vote,

so eliminate (D) as well. Only (A) is a right granted by Article II, Section 3 of the Constitution, which states that the president may, "on extraordinary occasions, convene both Houses, or either of them."

36. **C** This question is looking for powers that are *shared* with the Senate, which means that you can eliminate any answers that are exclusive to the executive or legislative branches. Choices (A) and (D) are powers that can be exercised only by the president, and (B) is under the sole discretion of Congress; all three of these choices can be eliminated. This means that (C) is the correct answer, which fits with Article II, Section 2 of the Constitution, which requires that two-thirds of the Senate concur with a treaty.

37. **D** Consider the choices. If (B) were true, no Republican could ever win the presidency, because most Democrats and moderate Republicans would vote Democratic. Such a sizable coalition would win every election, so eliminate (B). If (C) were true, then how conservative a candidate was during the primaries wouldn't matter, so eliminate (C). The two remaining choices are opposites of one another, so consider the scenario. Those most active in both the Republican and Democratic parties tend to be further from the political center than average rank-and-file party members. Because party activists control much of the nomination process and are more likely than others to vote in primary elections, successful presidential nominees tend to reflect the political agendas of these activists. This has been particularly true of the Republican Party in recent years; most candidates for the Republican presidential nomination focus great effort on winning support from the party's small but powerful ultraconservative wing. Choice (A) does not reflect this reality, which means that (D) is the correct answer.

38. **A** Confirmation powers are not relevant to committees, so eliminate (B). In both the Senate and the House, members of committees are assigned by the majority party, so eliminate (C). Choice (D) is wrong, since committees in both the Senate and the House consist of members from both parties, although the majority party generally has more members. The correct answer is (A), as the large size of the House of Representatives means that more work can be done in committees than when all representatives are assembled on the floor.

39. **D** As chief of state, the president receives and negotiates with foreign leaders. This means that as America's role in world affairs increases, so too does the president's power. Since 1932, America has in fact enjoyed increased prominence in foreign affairs, so you can rule out (A). Choices (B) and (C) are false statements; public confidence in the federal government has generally decreased since the 1950s, while entitlement spending has increased. This means that (D) is the correct answer. Constant media exposure has given the American public greater awareness of each president since Franklin Roosevelt. The president is now better known and more widely heard than at any time in the past. This allows the president to influence voters in a way that no president before 1932 possibly could.

40. **D** The House and the Senate must pass the same version of a bill before the president may consider it, which means that (A) can be eliminated. Be careful regarding (B) and (C)—while a bill may ultimately end up going back to the House and Senate or might get sent to the president in its original form, neither of these is the first thing that would happen. Choice (D) is the correct answer: the legislative bodies would meet and first try to draft a compromise bill.

41. **B**   Use Process of Elimination. Choice (A) is incorrect because people are actually less likely to vote if they believe one candidate is too far ahead of the others. Choice (C) is wrong, because a strong party affiliation makes one more likely to vote. Choice (D) can also be eliminated, given that there is actually a strong correlation between higher education and a tendency to vote. Only (B) is true, given that—setting aside unions—white-collar workers vote more often than blue-collar workers.

42. **A**   While the overall voting habits of white females can vary, unmarried white females have historically favored the Democratic candidate; eliminate (B). Since Franklin Roosevelt's presidency, African Americans (C) have overwhelmingly identified as Democrats in a trend that continues to the present. Barack Obama won a whopping 96% and 93% of the African American vote in 2008 and 2012, respectively. Likewise, in the 2016 presidential election, Hillary Clinton received 88% of the African American vote. The majority of youths (D) voted for candidates Jimmy Carter (1976), Bill Clinton (1996), Barack Obama (2008 and 2012), and Hillary Clinton (2016). Married, white males have preferred the Republican candidate for president in every election since 1972, which makes the answer (A).

43. **A**   For a comparison question, remember that if one part of the choice is inaccurate, you can eliminate the entire choice. With that in mind, look to eliminate (B) and (C), because *McDonald v. Chicago* actually curtailed local control in favor of the Second Amendment. You can also eliminate (D), because the two choices have been swapped—it was *United States v. Lopez* that declared the Gun-Free School Zones Act unconstitutional. Choice (A) is the correct answer. *United States v. Lopez* held that Congress does not have the power to regulate guns near state-operated schools by invoking the commerce clause, and *McDonald v. Chicago* found that the right of an individual to "keep and bear arms" as protected under the Second Amendment was incorporated by the due process clause of the Fourteenth Amendment.

44. **C**   Use POE. The two parts of (A) contradict each other; if a state judiciary is higher than a federal one, then how is a federal one able to overturn state decisions? Federal courts are higher than state courts, and while they *may* overturn state court decisions, they can do so only on the grounds that a defendant's constitutional rights were violated. Eliminate (A). Additionally, you can eliminate (D), because federal courts are not solely appeals courts. Between the remaining choices, (B) is more extreme than (C), suggesting that state judiciaries are *entirely* independent, when in fact there are some exceptions, such as when state cases are appealed to federal courts on constitutional grounds, or when there is a jurisdictional concern. Choice (C) is the correct answer; eliminate (B).

45. **C**   Use POE to rule out unlikely choices. A reprieve is a postponement of legal punishment, whereas a pardon is an immediate forgiving of a crime. Neither one has a specific number of years associated with it, so (A) can be eliminated. Pay close attention to how extreme the choices in (D) are; would it make sense for a president to be able to pardon someone but not grant that person a reprieve? Eliminate (D). The final two choices are opposites of each other. Here, knowing the definitions of the words will help you to eliminate (B), which reverses the meanings, and to choose (C), the correct answer.

46. **D** Democratic Party platforms generally align more closely to liberal ideological positions, whereas the Republican Party generally favors conservative ideological positions, so rule out (A). Democrats, not Republicans, tend to favor more governmental regulation of the marketplace, so cross out (B). Neither party tends to favor a national religion, and Democrats are typically champions of public education, which means you can also eliminate (C). This leaves (D) as the correct answer.

47. **C** Start by eliminating anything that does not match with the First Amendment. Choice (B) mentions the right to an attorney, which was a judicial interpretation of the Sixth Amendment, not the First. Now turn to the Fourth Amendment; the ruling in *Wisconsin v. Yoder* pertains to the free exercise of religion, which is the First, not the Fourth, so eliminate (A). For the final two choices, you can eliminate (D) because *McDonald v. Chicago* pertained to the Second Amendment. Choice (C) is the correct answer, and accurately describes aspects of both amendments.

48. **D** The Civil Rights Act of 1964 was a landmark piece of legislation that struck down many discriminatory laws and policies throughout the United States. Choice (A) is incorrect; although *Gideon* helped people of all races receive legal counsel, Congress did not reference it to justify the Civil Rights Act. Choice (B) is incorrect; although Jim Crow laws were struck down because of the Civil Rights Act of 1964, Congress needed a constitutional justification to strike down these laws. Choice (C) is incorrect; although *Brown* did much to spur civil rights in the United States, the case solely dealt with schools, and could not have been used to justify the Civil Rights Act's provisions about voting and free access to public places. As a result, (D) is correct; Congress used the Fourteenth Amendment's guarantee of equal protection under the law as justification for the Civil Rights Act of 1964.

49. **B** Federalist No. 10 took a negative view of political factions and would not have approved of any political system that encouraged their growth, so eliminate (A). Likewise, Republican federalism was designed to limit the influence of political factions on all levels, so (C) can be cut as well. That said, James Madison acknowledged in Federalist No. 10 that political factions would form whenever people disagreed or put their personal welfare above the best interests of the state, so the extreme answer (D), "any opportunity," can also be eliminated. Choice (B) is the correct answer, as federalism diluted a faction's power by separating the powers and making it hard for any one faction to control the entire governing process.

50. **B** Under the Articles of Confederation, the national government was entirely dependent on the states to enforce national law, as it had no executive powers of its own, so eliminate (A). The Constitution rectified this problem by establishing the executive branch of government. Under the Articles of Confederation, the national government had no authority to regulate interstate trade. The Constitution grants this power to Congress, so eliminate (C). Neither the Articles nor the original Constitution had a universal suffrage clause, so (D) is also incorrect. Choice (B) is correct, since the Articles did not allow for any federal taxation, while the Constitution enabled the federal government to levy taxes in order to fund such efforts as the military.

51. **A** National policy can be set either by Congress or the president, so use POE on those choices that would have no effect on Congress's power. Choice (B) can be immediately eliminated, as Congress still retains the powers it gained in the Constitution: taxation, approving treaties, etc. The "elastic clause" actually *expands* congressional power, so eliminate (C) as well. As for (D), Congress is often reluctant to challenge the president during wartime, as many believe that it is most important for the country to remain unified, so Congress would actually *lose* power in this situation; eliminate (D). Ultimately, what most impacts the dynamic relationship between Congress and the presidency deals with the relative popularity of the two institutions, so the correct answer is (A).

52. **B** Cabinet leaders are appointed by the president, and the departments are established by Congress, so eliminate (A). There are no restrictions regarding whom the president can appoint, so (C) is incorrect. There are numerous federal sub-agencies and independent agencies within the bureaucracy, so (D) can also be eliminated. This leaves (B) as the correct answer: despite being appointed by the president, cabinet department leaders sometimes have goals that differ from those of the president.

53. **D** When using Process of Elimination here, remember to keep an eye out for any overly extreme examples. For instance, (A) says that *each* state needs to split its electoral votes, so if there's even one that allocates them by the winner-take-all method—there are, in fact, forty-eight that do just this—then you can eliminate (A). Each state is represented by a delegation equal in number to that state's total representation in Congress (senators and members of the House). However, the number of House members for a given state is determined by proportional representation based on population, so a large state like California winds up with 54 votes, whereas some states have only the minimum of 3. This is not equal representation, so eliminate (B). Finally, of the remaining choices, (C) can be eliminated on the grounds that the Electoral College was part of the Constitution as originally ratified, not as a later amendment. Choice (D) is therefore correct, which you may recall given that it is possible for a candidate to win the Electoral College (and the presidency) while still losing the popular vote.

54. **D** Congressional committees are where much of Congress's work happens. Choice (A) is incorrect because the Appropriations Committee deals with spending federal funds, not taxation. Choice (B) is incorrect because the Financial Services Committee oversees the banking, housing, and insurance industries. Choice (C) is incorrect because the Oversight and Reform Committee keeps federal agencies accountable through evaluating their efficiency and effectiveness. As a result, (D) is correct because the Ways and Means Committee writes and debates proposed tax laws.

55. **B** By and large, most conservatives believe in small government and individual responsibility, so rule out (A) and (D). Choice (C) describes a racial affirmative action program, which would be opposed—or simply not promoted—by most conservatives, so rule that out. Choice (B) is the correct answer, as most conservatives are staunch defenders of the Second Amendment right to bear arms.

Section II: Free Response

Remember that you need to answer all four free-response questions in 1 hour and 40 minutes, so you do not have time to waste, nor can you skip any questions. Nevertheless, you should take time to brainstorm some ideas and to organize what you come up with before you start to write each response. Otherwise, your responses will probably be incomplete, disorganized, or both.

You should take about 20 minutes each for Questions 1, 2, and 3 and about 40 minutes for Question 4. Make sure you read each question carefully and respond directly to each of its components in your response. The questions are about broad issues, but they ask for specific information. A general free response that fails to address specific concerns raised by the question will not earn a high score. Your replies to Questions 1–3 should be brief and to the point. The information below represents what you should consider before writing a concise answer.

Question 1

(A)   Referencing the scenario, describe the enumerated power in Article I of the Constitution that the Supreme Court majority used to justify Congress's authority to require the "individual mandate" in the Affordable Care Act (ACA).

As it may pertain to the ACA, try to incorporate as much of your knowledge about the Commerce Clause and taxation as you can. For Part A, you need to recognize that Justice Roberts, whose quote represents the majority view, did *not* think that the Commerce Clause would justify the individual mandate in the ACA. Rather, he thought that a penalty for not purchasing private health insurance could be considered a "tax" like any other and enforced as such. Article I, Section 8 of the Constitution states that "The Congress shall have Power To lay and collect Taxes, Duties, Imposts and Excises, to pay the Debts and provide for the common Defense and general Welfare of the United States; but all Duties, Imposts and Excises shall be uniform throughout the United States."

(B)   Explain ONE Constitutional reason why the majority on the Supreme Court may have rejected Justice Ginsburg's argument.

You need to recognize that Justice Ginsburg's invocation of the Commerce Clause was *not* agreed upon by the majority. The knowledge required for Part B includes an understanding of the Commerce Clause in Article I and why it may not justify an individual mandate to purchase health insurance. The clause states that the United States Congress shall have power "to regulate Commerce with foreign Nations, and among the several States, and with the Indian Tribes." Over the years, the Commerce Clause has increasingly been invoked by the Supreme Court to allow for more and more federal regulation of interstate commerce, though this power was partially curtailed by the decision in *United States v. Lopez*, which ruled that Congress may not use the Commerce Clause to make possession of a gun in a school zone a federal crime. In other words, the Congress can regulate "commerce," not other sorts of activities. In the case of the Affordable Care Act (ACA), if an individual chooses *not* to purchase health insurance, that individual is not engaged in commerce; and thus the justices most likely did not think that the Commerce Clause could be used to require commerce among citizens that did not exist. This would have represented an unprecedented application of the Constitution and could have had adverse consequences in the future, empowering Congress to mandate other unwanted financial transactions among citizens.

(C)   Explain ONE possible reason for the lack of enforcement and eventual repeal of the individual mandate.

Think about the political ramifications of the ACA's individual mandate and the reasons why it was never enforced. Although the ACA has enjoyed political support from many Americans, it is fair to conclude that the individual mandate was unpopular with most and ultimately failed. Since the Internal Revenue Service enforces other federal "taxes," a good answer to this question will not merely focus on the possible difficulties or costs of national enforcement. Other possible explanations include:

- **Voter Backlash.** Perhaps Presidents did not want to risk low approval ratings or losing a second-term election over the widespread imposition of fines on the uninsured, many of whom may be low-income taxpayers.
- **Risk of future repeal by Congress.** If the individual mandate were widely enforced, its unpopularity could lead to pressure on members of Congress to repeal the entire ACA, thus "throwing the baby out with the bathwater."
- **A regressive form of taxation.** Since many uninsured people have lower incomes, penalties from the individual mandate could have disproportionately affected the poor or working middle class.
- **Perception of collusion.** By requiring certain Americans to purchase private health insurance, politicians may have been perceived as colluding with private banks and corporations.

Question 2

(A)   Which two presidents were responsible for the greatest increases of defense spending since 1953?

First, identify the type of data that you're looking for. In this case, you're looking for increases, so you want to find steep rises on the graph. You can ignore the first, and steepest, increase, because it occurred before 1953. After that point, the two greatest increases occurred under the watch of President Reagan and President George W. Bush.

(B)   Describe a trend in the data and draw a conclusion about the defense spending habits of Republican and Democratic presidents.

- Defense spending spiked at the beginning of the Korean and Vietnam Wars, and again during the War on Terror (fought in Iraq and Afghanistan). As both Democratic and Republican presidents led the nation during these times, it appears as if presidents' political affiliation has little effect on defense spending during a time of war.
- You might also have written about the peacetime trend, in which the nation's defense budget falls to approximately four hundred billion dollars. As both Republican and Democratic presidents led during these eras, one can again conclude that factors besides politics influence defense spending decisions.

(C)   Explain how the defense spending as shown in the graph relates to iron triangles within the federal government.

Iron triangles represent the symbiotic relationship between Congress, the bureaucracy, and interest groups. In the case of defense spending, congressional committees related to defense, interest groups promoting military spending, and bureaucratic agencies overseeing defense spending, such as the DOD, make up an iron triangle. At the beginning of an armed conflict, Congress would increase funding to the DOD and accept ideas from interest groups, such as weapons manufacturers. In return, interest groups would raise money for congressional elections and lobby for the DOD. The DOD would execute Congress's wishes while granting special favors to lobbyists. This unique relationship also helps explain why defense spending returns to the $400 billion mark during peacetime. Although the nation may not need to spend this much on defense, the nature of iron triangles ensures a level of spending, political support, and granting of favors wherein all parties are satisfied.

Question 3

(A)   Identify a constitutional amendment or clause that was used to justify the decisions in both *Powell v. Alabama* (1932) and *Gideon v. Wainwright* (1963).

- *Powell* and *Gideon* were both in violation of the due process clause of the Fourteenth Amendment. For *Powell*, convictions had been made under unfair conditions—only one-day trials—and were thus invalid.
- Both were also in violation of the Sixth Amendment. There can be no fair trial if a defense attorney is not provided.

(B)   Based on the constitutional amendment identified in Part A, explain how *Gideon v. Wainwright* expanded upon the decision in *Powell v. Alabama*.

- *Powell* provided the right to representation to only those accused of capital crimes.
- *Gideon* provided the right to representation for all defendants. Between *Powell* and *Gideon*, cases like *Betts v. Brady* (1942) asserted that publicly appointed counsel was not required.
- Before *Gideon*, judges used their own discretion to determine whether defendants might receive court-appointed counsel, thus leading to unfair and uneven outcomes in criminal trials.

(C)   Describe historical changes that have been made to the prosecution of defendants since the *Gideon v. Wainwright* decision.

- Thousands of individuals around the country who had not received adequate representation in court were freed as a result of the *Gideon* decision.
- State and municipal courts adopted universal rules and established the offer of appointed counsel as a matter of right, without a defendant's need to petition the judge for a special appointment of counsel.
- States established Public Defender offices throughout their jurisdictions to accommodate the needs of defendants who do not have the desire or resources to acquire their own private attorneys.
- Defendants can waive their right to counsel by pleading guilty or by choosing to represent themselves in court. In lieu of these choices, however, a Public Defender will be assigned to such a case automatically.

Question 4

Develop an argument that explains whether increased power vested to the federal government or increased power vested to the states best achieves the founders' intent for American democracy in terms of ensuring a stable government run by the people.

- This essay is focusing on the principle of federalism, the power that the federal government has in relation to state governments. Over time, more and more power has tended to gravitate away from the states and toward Washington, D.C.

Articulate a defensible claim or thesis that responds to the prompt and establishes a line of reasoning.

- The two possible theses here are that more power entrusted to the federal government is beneficial for the smooth operation of society, or, alternatively, that the states are the rightful guardians of power and should not be usurped by Washington, D.C.

Support your claim with at least TWO pieces of accurate and relevant information.

- **Articles of Confederation.** Under these articles, which deprived the federal government of things like the power to levy taxes, the country ran into many social issues. Being unable to pay off the debts from the Revolutionary War, for example, weakened the economic progress of the new Republic. On the other hand, had states kept this autonomy, the federal government may not have later been able to abuse its power, as it did when enforcing new taxes (in the 1791 Whiskey Rebellion) or when suppressing voters in 1798's Alien and Sedition Acts.

- **Brutus No. 1** was one in a series of anonymous essays designed to raise skepticism regarding the early Constitution. The Anti-Federalist who wrote this paper objected to the overreach of federal power mainly on the grounds that it would detract from personal freedom. He demanded a Bill of Rights, warned of the power of Congress, and believed that a national standing army would be a threat to the liberty of both other nations and Americans themselves. Brutus favored a confederation of independent states with maximum autonomy. Most notably, Brutus warned that the **U.S. Supreme Court** would garner too much unchecked power.

- **Shays' Rebellion (1786)**, a Massachusetts farmers' rebellion, pointed out the weakness of the Articles and bolstered the **Federalist** cause to create a stronger federal government.

- **Bill of Rights (1787).** The first 10 Amendments to the Constitution were demanded by Anti-Federalists to serve as a bulwark against excessive federal power. The **Tenth Amendment** specifically grants all powers not delegated to the federal government to revert back to the sovereignty of individual states.

- **Sixteenth Amendment (1913).** This amendment arguably expanded federal power more than any other law had done up to this point, since it allowed Congress to levy a broad-based tax on personal and business income. For the first time, all Americans with income could be required to participate in the financial maintenance of government bureaucracy. The federal budget has expanded rapidly since the passage of a national income tax.

- **Seventeenth Amendment (1913).** This amendment ended the practice of the election of senators by state legislatures and provided for the direct election of senators by citizens at the ballot box. Although the amendment certainly gave more power to the populace, it took power away from state legislatures, thus radically altering the balance of federalism up to that point. Those who favored the amendment argued that it diminished the influence of corruption and cronyism at the state level. Opponents argued that direct election of senators would allow senators to disregard the concerns of their home states.

- **Loose Constructionism**. Putting more power in the hands of the federal government requires a flexible interpretation of the Constitution, since the Constitution does not explicitly grant many powers to Washington, D.C., (though it does not forbid them, either). The creation of the **First National Bank** by **Alexander Hamilton**, for instance, was opposed by Anti-Federalists who tended toward **strict constructionism** (limitation of federal power to only powers enumerated in Article I).

- **James Madison.** Fourth president and "Father of the Constitution," he co-authored *The Federalist Papers* (along with **Alexander Hamilton** and **John Jay**). Interestingly, Madison started out as a Federalist, favoring a strong central government, and then converted to Anti-Federalism in 1791, joining **Thomas Jefferson** in the newly formed (**Anti-Federalist) Democratic-Republican Party**. **Federalist No. 10** is particularly relevant to this topic, since Madison talks extensively about the dangers of factionalism and how a representative democracy is the proper antidote to imbalance of power. Madison specifically touts the virtues of a large republic over a small one, since it flattens out group differences. Thus, this document is a good choice if you are arguing in favor of federal power.

In addition to the documents above, you also have the freedom to reference the following issues. Many of them can be used to bolster either a pro-federal or pro-states argument:

- **Louisiana Purchase (1803)** and other historical **acquisitions of territory**. No doubt a positive manifestation of federal power, the Louisiana Purchase doubled the size of the United States. Such a vast tract of land could not have been acquired without federal money and influence. Napoleon ceded the Louisiana Territory in exchange for cash and debt forgiveness. Likewise, most of the modern land on which the United States stands was acquired through actions of the U.S. government, not the states. This is a powerful argument in favor of federal power.

- **Taxation/Debt**. Increased federal power inevitably leads to national taxation and debt. Republicans might argue that it is oppressive to tax working people to pay for expensive federal programs. Democrats might argue that a strong central government benefits everyone, including the working poor.

- *McCulloch v. Maryland* **(1819)**. Under Supreme Court Chief Justice John Marshall, this case allowed the federal government to pass laws not explicitly mentioned in the Constitution. It grants Congress **implied powers** in order to create a functioning national government. The case stopped the state of Maryland's tax on the Second Bank of the United States. The court ruled that this was a form of nullification that impeded the functioning of the federal government.

- **National Banking Acts of 1863–1866 and the Federal Reserve Act of 1913**. After the expiration of the Second Bank of the United States, this series of acts permanently established a nationally regulated banking system and a national currency.

- **New Deal (1933–1938)**. A tremendous assertion of federal power, the New Deal enacted various federally funded programs to help rebuild the American economy after the Great Depression. President Franklin D. Roosevelt's national government needed state and local government cooperation in order to implement its policies. The New Deal was highly controversial both because it required a significant outlay of federal dollars in order to succeed and because it bypassed state legislatures. President Lyndon Johnson's **Great Society** welfare programs of the 1960s were controversial for the same reasons.

- **Block grants (1980s)**. President Ronald Reagan attempted to turn some power back to the states by distributing federal money in the form of block grants. Unlike previous grants that greatly restricted the way federal money could be spent, block grants allowed states to spend money as they saw fit.

- **Decriminalization/Legalization of marijuana (1990s to present)**. Various states' attempts to legalize marijuana for either medicinal or recreational use have tested the boundaries of federalism in a power struggle that is not yet resolved. Several states currently have laws that allow for the medicinal cultivation, possession, and use of marijuana. As of November 2023, a total of 24 states have passed measures legalizing marijuana for recreational use: Alaska, Arizona, California, Colorado, Connecticut, Delaware, Illinois, Maine, Maryland, Massachusetts, Michigan, Minnesota, Missouri, Montana, Nevada, New Jersey, New Mexico, New York, Ohio, Oregon, Rhode Island, Vermont, Virginia, and Washington (plus Guam, Northern Mariana Islands, U.S. Virgin Islands, and District of Columbia). It's also decriminalized in 7: Hawaii, Louisiana, Mississippi, Nebraska, New Hampshire, North Carolina, and North Dakota. As more states continue to follow their lead, this issue will no doubt continue to be an important test of the balance of state and federal power.

- **Gun control.** Gun control is an interesting example of the see-saw of federalism. The Second Amendment of the Constitution guarantees the individual right to keep and bear arms, while states and cities have broad latitude to limit ownership in certain locales, set requirements for ownership of guns, and need not recognize the gun laws of other states. The federal government, on the other hand, asserts its authority upon states by requiring background checks, forbidding the ownership of guns by felons, and banning the possession of guns on school property.

Use reasoning to explain why your evidence supports your claim/thesis.

No matter what evidence you use to support your thesis, you need to do more than list facts. Spend 2–3 sentences describing why the evidence in question supports your thesis. For example, let's say you believe that more power to the federal government ensures a stable government run by the people. To support this claim, you can bring up the New Deal (see above). After describing the laws FDR passed, you could reason that these initiatives, although they increased the federal government's power over the states tremendously, preserved the U.S.'s representative democracy by making more extreme political ideologies (e.g., Communism and Fascism) less appealing to the American people.

Respond to an opposing or alternative perspective using refutation, concession, or rebuttal.

A good rebuttal to an opposing point of view requires knowing the pros and cons of each side of the debate.

Federal Power

Pros:
- Abundant financial resources
- National reach and scope
- Uniform laws and standards nationwide
- Extensive national infrastructure for implementation of laws and enforcement of policies

Cons:
- More potential for waste and inefficiency at a large scale of implementation
- A "one size fits all" approach that may not meet the needs of all states
- Takes power and decision making away from the people
- Allows one political party to gather power (factionalism)

State Power

Pros:
- State power allows for a diversity of approaches to tough problems.
- Solutions are targeted to the regional and demographic needs of each locale.
- Smaller programs tend to run more efficiently.
- Funding can come in a variety of ways, not always tied to an income tax.
- Through the election of state representatives and governors, the people have more direct participation in the process.

Cons:
- Too much variation from state to state can create confusion and irregular enforcement across state lines.
- States may struggle to fund initiatives that the federal government could fund more easily.
- Enforcement is limited by the resources in each state, county, and municipality.
- Some states may neglect to address issues altogether.
- Federalist No. 51 argues that the system of checks and balances set up in the then-proposed Constitution makes it impossible for any one faction to take control of the federal government. However, nothing is stopping a single faction from doing so if they retain the electorate's support. Also, the presidency, Congress, and Supreme Court's powers since the nation's founding have evolved, meaning that even if a faction gains control over just one branch, that faction may have greater power than the founders intended and can oppress a minority group.

Supreme Court Rulings

- Throughout U.S. history, various Supreme Court rulings have bowed to fringe or undemocratic ideas and beliefs promoted by minority factions within larger political parties. These decisions did not check the factions' beliefs and impinged on citizens' rights. At no point did the other two branches of government attempt to right these injustices.

    - *Buck v. Bell* (1927): The Court ruled in favor of states that required that citizens who were deemed mentally unfit undergo forced sterilization. This ruling was influenced by the progressive movement of the early 20th century.
    - *Korematsu v. United States* (1944): The Court ruled in favor of Japanese internment during the Second World War. Decades-long racial prejudice against Japanese and other Asian Americans—prejudice that a faction of nativist politicians on the West Coast had used since the late 19th century to win elections—influenced the U.S. government's policy tremendously.

Use reasoning.

- Political factions can gain tremendous influence during a political or national crisis (e.g., the Tea Party movement during the Great Recession, Anticommunists during the First and Second Red Scares). As a result, they can promote radical policies that have the chance to undermine citizens' rights.

- With the speed of modern communication, a faction can spread its message much faster than what the founders considered possible. As a result, a faction can influence public opinion and policy before the system of checks and balances can react.

Respond to an opposing perspective.

Opposing Perspective: The system of checks and balances has been successful in stemming the influence of political factions, such as McCarthyism in the 1950s.

Response (Concession): The Warren Court handed down a series of decisions in the 1950s that stopped the rise of McCarthyism. In this case, the Court acted as a check against a political faction that threatened citizens' civil liberties.

Opposing Perspective: The large number of factions within the modern Republican and Democratic Parties makes it impossible for a single one to dominate the party's policy and affect citizens negatively.

Response (Refutation): In the late 20th century, interest groups began to donate heavily to congressional and presidential campaigns. These groups, over time, became de facto political factions that held sway among multiple branches of government. For example, the NRA prevents gun control legislation (which has broad support among the electorate) from passing because of the organization's contributions to Republican congresspersons' and presidents' reelection campaigns. If the NRA (or similar groups) can retain influence long enough, policymakers install Supreme Court justices that align with that faction's beliefs. As a result, the system of checks and balances is no longer effective.

HOW TO SCORE PRACTICE TEST 1

Section I: Multiple Choice

_____ × 1.0000 = _____

Number of Correct   Weighted
(out of 55)   Section I Score
         (Do not round)

Section II: Free Response

Question 1   _____ × 4.5833 = _____
         (out of 3)   (Do not round)

Question 2   _____ × 3.4375 = _____
         (out of 4)   (Do not round)

Question 3   _____ × 3.4375 = _____
         (out of 4)   (Do not round)

Question 4   _____ × 2.2917 = _____
         (out of 6)   (Do not round)

Sum   = _____

Weighted Section II
Score (Do not round)

The following conversion chart provides only a rough estimate, as scoring ranges may vary from administration to administration. Check your online Student Tools for possible updates.

AP Score Conversion Chart U.S. Government and Politics

Composite Score Range	AP Score
83–110	5
72–82	4
56–71	3
38–55	2
0–37	1

Composite Score

_____ + _____ = _____

Weighted   Weighted   Composite Score
Section I Score   Section II Score   (Round to nearest
                                          whole number)

Part III
About the AP U.S. Government and Politics Exam

- The Structure of the AP U.S. Government and Politics Exam
- How the AP U.S. Government and Politics Exam Is Scored
- Overview of Content Topics
- Primary Sources
- How AP Exams Are Used
- Other Resources
- Designing Your Study Plan

THE STRUCTURE OF THE AP U.S. GOVERNMENT AND POLITICS EXAM

The AP U.S. Government and Politics Exam is a two-part test. The chart below illustrates the test's structure.

Section	Question Type	Number of Questions	Time Allowed	Percent of Final Grade
I	Multiple Choice	55	80 minutes	50%
II	Free Response	4	100 minutes	50%

There are several types of multiple-choice questions, which we'll discuss in Chapter 1, but they all pull from the five major topics of the AP U.S. Government and Politics course. **Not all subjects are tested equally;** the following list is a breakdown of how they are likely to appear on your test:

Subject	Percent of Questions	Covered in Chapter #
Foundations of American Democracy	15–22%	Chapter 4
Interaction Among Branches of Government	25–36%	Chapter 5
Civil Liberties and Civil Rights	13–18%	Chapter 6
American Political Ideologies and Beliefs	10–15%	Chapter 7
Political Participation	20–27%	Chapter 8

Questions on the exam expect you to be able to analyze data, get to the heart of short reading passages and quotes, and compare two distinct thoughts. Don't be thrown; these questions tend to boil down to the dynamics of how government operates within a political environment. For example, you may be asked how interest groups attempt to influence policy making in Congress and the bureaucracy or how the president attempts to influence Congress through public opinion. The test-writers want to know whether you understand the general principles that guide the U.S. government and the making of public policy.

In addition to the multiple-choice questions, there are four mandatory free-response questions. Be aware that you must manage your own time. Additional time spent on one question will reduce the time that you have left to answer the others. (Question 4 is more complex than Questions 1–3, so be sure to budget your time accordingly.) Writing more than is necessary to answer the questions will not earn you extra points, either.

The breakdown in the charts on this page represents the latest information to come from the College Board about its new test. Please check your online Student Tools for any late-breaking news!

We also strongly recommend checking the College Board's official AP Students website for any other free resources it may have released as the test approaches.

apstudents.collegeboard.org/courses/ap-united-states-government-and-politics

FREE-RESPONSE QUESTIONS

Question Type	Suggested Time	Percent of Final Grade
Question 1: Concept Application (3 points)	20 minutes	12.5%
Question 2: Quantitative Analysis (4 points)	20 minutes	12.5%
Question 3: SCOTUS Comparison (4 points)	20 minutes	12.5%
Question 4: Argument Essay (6 points)	40 minutes	12.5%

HOW THE AP U.S. GOVERNMENT AND POLITICS EXAM IS SCORED

The graders assign each of your free-response answers a numerical score. Weighting the average on the free responses and the score on the multiple-choice questions each as 50%, the graders create a final score from a low of 1 to a high of 5. The chart below tells you what that final score means.

Score	Percentage 2023	Credit Recommendation	College Grade Equivalent
5	12.8%	Extremely Well Qualified	A
4	11.3%	Well Qualified	A−, B+, B
3	25.1%	Qualified	B−, C+, C
2	24%	Possibly Qualified	–
1	26.8%	No Recommendation	–

*Percentages are based on the May 2023 administration of the exam.

To score your multiple-choice questions, award yourself one point for every correct answer, regardless of whether you guessed the answer or not. (You shouldn't have left any blanks, but if you did, they are worth nothing.)

Of course, if you follow our advice for how to write a good free-response essay, you could score higher on the free-response section than on the multiple-choice section and thus potentially increase your final score by one point. That's why it's important to have a teacher grade one of your practice free-response sections.

How Will I Know?
Your dream college's website may list information about how it treats AP scores, or you can contact the school's admissions department to verify AP exam score acceptance information.

Check your online tools for any possible updates on scoring info.

Go Online!
Check us out on YouTube for test-taking tips and techniques to help you ace your next exam at youtube.com/ThePrincetonReview.

Nine AP Exams Go Digital in 2025
College Board announced that in May 2025, nine AP exams will go fully digital! For the latest information regarding the specific AP subjects going digital and testing accommodations, visit the College Board website at apcentral. collegeboard.org/exam-administration-ordering-scores/digital-ap-exams.

OVERVIEW OF CONTENT TOPICS

As mentioned earlier, questions on the exam fall into five main units:

- Foundations of American Democracy
- Interaction Among Branches of Government
- Civil Liberties and Civil Rights
- American Political Ideologies and Beliefs
- Political Participation

Here are some key topics that fall into each of these categories:

Foundations of American Democracy	• Ideals of Democracy • Types of Democracy • Government Power and Individual Rights • Challenges of the Articles of Confederation • Ratification of the United States Constitution • Principles of American Government • Relationship Between States and the Federal Government • Constitutional Interpretations of Federalism • Federalism in Action
Interaction Among Branches of Government	• Congress: The Senate and the House of Representatives • Structures, Powers, and Functions of Congress • Congressional Behavior • Roles and Powers of the President • Checks on the Presidency • Expansion of Presidential Power • Presidential Communication • The Judicial Branch • Legitimacy of the Judicial Branch • The Court in Action • The Bureaucracy • Discretionary and Rule-Making Authority • Holding the Bureaucracy Accountable • Policy and the Branches of Government

Civil Liberties and Civil Rights	• The Bill of Rights • First Amendment: Freedom of Religion • First Amendment: Freedom of Speech • First Amendment: Freedom of the Press • Second Amendment: Right to Bear Arms • Amendments: Balancing Individual Freedom with Public Order and Safety • Selective Incorporation • Amendments: Due Process and the Rights of the Accused • Amendments: Due Process and the Right to Privacy • Social Movements and Equal Protection • Government Responses to Social Movements • Balancing Minority and Majority Rights • Affirmative Action
American Political Ideologies and Beliefs	• American Attitudes About Government and Politics • Political Socialization • Changes in Ideology • Influences of Political Events on Ideology • Measuring Public Opinion • Evaluating Public Opinion Data • Ideologies of Political Parties • Ideology and Policy Making • Ideology and Economic Policy • Ideology and Social Policy
Political Participation	• Voting Rights and Models of Voting Behavior • Voter Turnout • Political Parties • How and Why Political Parties Change and Adapt • Third-Party Politics • Interest Groups Influencing Policy Making • Groups Influencing Policy Outcomes • Electing a President • Congressional Elections • Modern Campaigns • Campaign Finance • The Media • Changing Media

Are You a Visual Learner?
If you're getting overwhelmed by all of the concepts for an AP course, consider looking at our *Fast Track* or *ASAP* books, available for some AP subjects. These handy guides focus on the most-tested content or present it in a friendly, illustrated fashion.

As you can see, the primary focus of the test is the nuts and bolts of the federal government. The test also emphasizes political activity—the factors that influence individual political beliefs, the conditions that determine how and why people vote, and the process by which groups form and attempt to influence the government. Be aware that the test is always changing, so keep an eye on every area, such as constitutional issues and civil rights, which are very important for providing context to the new scenario-based questions that appeared for the first time in the exam's 2019 version.

PRIMARY SOURCES

One thing the course now expects from students is that they've learned the major details of 14 different Supreme Court cases and that they are familiar with the ideas behind nine foundational documents. We touch on and reference these in the Part V content review, but you should definitely go above-and-beyond in familiarizing yourself with the following:

- *Marbury v. Madison*
- *McCulloch v. Maryland*
- *Schenck v. United States*
- *Brown v. Board of Education*
- *Baker v. Carr*
- *Engel v. Vitale*
- *Gideon v. Wainwright*
- *Tinker v. Des Moines Independent Community School District*
- *New York Times Co. v. United States*
- *Wisconsin v. Yoder*
- *Shaw v. Reno*
- *United States v. Lopez*
- *McDonald v. Chicago*
- *Citizens United v. Federal Election Commission*

- THE ARTICLES OF CONFEDERATION
- BRUTUS NO.1
  To the Citizens of the State of New-York
- THE CONSTITUTION OF THE UNITED STATES (INCLUDING THE BILL OF RIGHTS AND SUBSEQUENT AMENDMENTS)
- THE DECLARATION OF INDEPENDENCE
- FEDERALIST NO. 10
  The Same Subject Continued: The Union as a Safeguard Against Domestic Faction and Insurrection
- FEDERALIST NO. 51
  The Structure of the Government Must Furnish the Proper Checks and Balances Between the Different Departments
- FEDERALIST NO. 70
  The Executive Department Further Considered
- FEDERALIST NO. 78
  The Judiciary Department
- "LETTER FROM A BIRMINGHAM JAIL" (By Rev. Dr. Martin Luther King, Jr.)

Other Sources

While the primary sources listed above are the only ones that you'll be required to know for the exam, you should take the opportunity to widen your familiarity with other documents.

Reading political articles in newspapers and magazines, particularly those that present accompanying information in visual formats, can be helpful when preparing for the Quantitative Analysis questions. The Argument Essay in Section II allows you to cite from other sources, and the SCOTUS Comparison question will refer to lesser-known cases (although it will provide you with all the necessary facts).

If you do your own reading—and we highly recommend it!—make sure that you take into account the credibility of your sources. If you intend to reference anything on the test, make sure these other texts are both credible and reliable. That is, make sure they've been fact-checked and that they are both well-sourced and up-to-date.

HOW AP EXAMS ARE USED

Different colleges use AP exams in different ways, so it is important that you visit a particular college's website in order to determine how it accepts AP exam scores. The three items below represent the main ways in which colleges use AP exam scores.

- **College Credit.** Some colleges will give you college credit if you receive a high score on an AP exam. These credits count toward your graduation requirements, meaning that you can take fewer courses while in college. Given the cost of college, this could be quite a benefit, indeed.

- **Satisfy Requirements.** Some colleges will allow you to "place out" of certain requirements if you do well on an AP exam, even if they do not give you actual college credits. For example, you might not need to take an introductory-level course, or perhaps you might not need to take a class in a certain discipline at all.

- **Admissions Boost.** Even if your AP exam will not result in college credit or even allow you to place out of certain courses, most colleges will respect your decision to push yourself by taking an AP course, or even an AP exam outside of a course. A high score on an AP exam shows understanding of more difficult content than is typically taught in many high school courses, and colleges may take that into account during the admissions process.

OTHER RESOURCES

There are many resources available to help you improve your score on the AP U.S. Government and Politics Exam, not the least of which are your **teachers**. If you are taking an AP course, you may be able to get extra attention from your teacher, such as feedback on your essays. If you are not in an AP course, you can reach out to a teacher who teaches AP U.S. Government and Politics to ask whether they will review your essays or otherwise help you gain command of the content.

Nine AP Exams Go Digital in 2025
College Board announced that in May 2025, nine AP exams will go fully digital! For the latest information regarding the specific AP subjects going digital and testing accommodations, visit the College Board website at apcentral. collegeboard.org/exam-administration-ordering-scores/digital-ap-exams.

More AP Info Online!
We have put together even more goodies for a handful of AP Exam subjects. For short quizzes, high-level AP course and test information, and expert advice, head over to princetonreview. com/college-advice/ ap-exams.

Another wonderful resource is **AP Students**, the official website of the AP exams. The scope of the information available on this site is quite broad and includes the following:

- a course description, which includes further details on what content is covered by the exam

- sample questions from the AP U.S. Government and Politics Exam

- free-response question prompts and multiple-choice questions from previous years

The AP Students home page address is apstudent.collegeboard.org/home.

Finally, **The Princeton Review** offers tutoring, small group instruction, and admissions counseling. Our expert instructors can help you refine your strategic approach and enhance your content knowledge. For more information, call 1-800-2REVIEW.

DESIGNING YOUR STUDY PLAN

In Part I, you identified some areas of potential improvement. Let's now delve further into your performance on Practice Test 1, with the goal of developing a study plan appropriate to your needs and time commitment.

Read the answers and explanations associated with the multiple-choice questions (starting on page 33). After you have done so, respond to the following questions:

- What are your overall goals for using this book?

- Review the topic chart on pages 56–57. Next to each topic, indicate your rank of the topic as follows: 1 means "I need a lot of work on this," 2 means "I need to beef up my knowledge," and 3 means "I know this topic well."

- How many days/weeks/months away is your exam?

- What time of day is your best, most focused study time?

- How much time per day/week/month will you devote to preparing for your exam?

- When will you do this preparation? (Be as specific as possible: Mondays and Wednesdays from 3:00 P.M. to 4:00 P.M., for example.)

- Based on the answers above, will you focus on strategy (Part IV) or content (Part V) or both?

Looking to Guarantee a 5?
We now offer one-on-one tutoring for a guaranteed 5 on the AP U.S. Government and Politics Exam. For information on rates and availability, visit PrincetonReview.com/college/ap-test-prep.

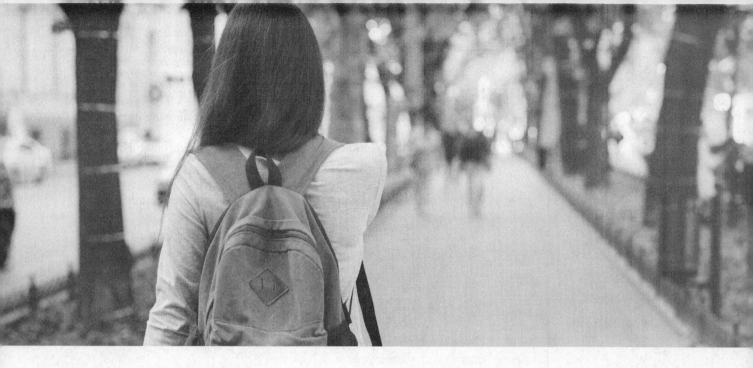

Part IV
Test-Taking Strategies for the AP U.S. Government and Politics Exam

- Preview
1 How to Approach Multiple-Choice Questions
2 How to Approach Free-Response Questions
3 Using Time Effectively to Maximize Points
- Reflect

PREVIEW

Review your Practice Test 1 results and then respond to the following questions:

- How many multiple-choice questions did you miss even though you knew the answer?

- On how many multiple-choice questions did you guess randomly?

- How many multiple-choice questions did you miss after eliminating some answers and guessing based on the remaining answers?

- Did you find any of the free-response questions easier or harder than the others—and, if so, why?

- Did you run out of time in Section II—and, if so, how did the questions challenge you?

HOW TO USE THE CHAPTERS IN THIS PART

Before reading the following strategy chapters, think about what you are doing now. As you read and engage in the directed practice, be sure to think critically about the ways you can change your approach.

Chapter 1
How to
Approach
Multiple-Choice
Questions

Bonus Tips and Tricks...
Check us out on YouTube for additional test-taking tips and must-know strategies at youtube.com/ThePrincetonReview.

HOW TO CRACK THE MULTIPLE-CHOICE SECTION

The AP U.S. Government and Politics Exam is, by the College Board standards, a straightforward test. Unlike the SAT, for example, the questions and answer choices on the AP U.S. Government and Politics Exam are not designed to trick you. These questions are not subjective, but are based on the content you've learned in your AP course, and which you can review in this book. You should, however, not be lulled into believing the test is easy because it covers material that can be readily obtained from reading the newspaper and watching television. This secondhand information is not enough to ensure a passing grade on the exam. While being able to recall specific examples may help to flesh out your free-response questions, the majority of the knowledge you'll need is academic, so be sure that you review your textbook, especially for the topics that you feel least comfortable with.

In short, if you've paid attention in class, you should do well on this test. That said, if you haven't paid close attention, it's not too late, especially since you have this book! You may still be able to truly comprehend the material if you review intensively, which means using both this book and course materials. You can use the content review in this book as your guide, helping you to remember what you may have forgotten. Ultimately, you will do better if you know what to expect from the test. In the next few pages, we'll discuss some things that all AP U.S. Government and Politics Exam multiple-choice sections have in common.

The Question Types Are Varied

As you will see from the breakdown of question types on page 66, the new AP U.S. Government and Politics Exam has a lot of complicated ways in which to ask what might otherwise be familiar questions. You may find some questions easier than others, or you may prefer to work with the context provided by Quantitative Analysis and Qualitative Analysis questions more than with the more formal knowledge questions. You are allowed to answer questions in any order that you wish, so don't feel as if you have to start with the material that slows you down.

There Are No Trivial Pursuit Questions on This Exam

Here's some more good news. The AP U.S. Government and Politics Exam doesn't ask about trivial matters. You will probably never see a question such as this one on the exam.

1. The American equivalent of the British Exchequer is the

    (A) House Finance Committee
    (B) Internal Revenue Service
    (C) United States Mint
    (D) Office of Management and Budget

To answer this question correctly, you would have to be fairly familiar with the British government. The AP U.S. Government and Politics Exam does not require such knowledge. This question is atypical in another way as well: it does not have a varied selection of possible answers. Even if you had known that the British Exchequer has something to do with money and government, you could not have eliminated any of the incorrect answers on this question. On an actual AP test, at least one of these answers would have been completely unrelated to finance, and you could have eliminated that choice to guess from among the remaining answers.

Process of Elimination

For questions that you do not confidently know the correct answer to, it is important to utilize the Process of Elimination (POE). This highly effective method for solving a multiple-choice question relies on the fact that incorrect answers are much easier to identify than correct ones. Try it! Chances are that when you look for the correct answer, you'll try to justify why an answer might be correct. That's nice and forgiving, but what you need is brutal honesty. Look for the wrong answers, and then eliminate them with extreme prejudice. If you've done your job well, only the correct answer will be left standing at the end; at the very least, if you have to guess from only two or three choices as opposed to four, you'll be increasing your odds of answering difficult questions correctly.

Common Sense Can Help

Sometimes, answers on the multiple-choice section contradict common sense. Eliminate those answers, because common sense works on the AP U.S. Government and Politics Exam.

Think about which of the answer choices to the question below go against common sense.

Be a Shark
Good test-takers take multiple-choice tests aggressively. They sift through the answer choices, discard incorrect answers without remorse, guess with impunity, and prowl the test searching for questions they can answer, all with the tenacity and ruthlessness of a shark. All right, maybe that's a bit overdramatic, but you get the point.

2.   Which of the following best explains the way in which federal legislation is implemented?

(A)   Most laws outline general goals and restrictions, which the federal bureaucracy interprets and translates into specific guidelines.

(B)   The manner of implementing federal legislation is negotiated between a joint congressional committee and a presidential advisory committee.

(C)   After a bill is signed, all disputes pertaining to its implementation are decided by the congressional committee responsible for the bill.

(D)   The details of implementing congressional legislation are worked out in the courts on a case-by-case basis.

Here's How to Crack It

2. **A** You should have been able to apply common sense to eliminate (C) and (D) pretty quickly. Congressional committees work on bills *before* they reach the floor for a vote, and this work takes up all their time. They would hardly have time to hear all disputes concerning bills that have already passed. Furthermore, such a system would violate the system of checks and balances, because the responsibility for interpreting laws belongs to the judiciary. All the same, the details of congressional legislation could never be worked out in the courts. There would simply be too many cases for the courts to be able to process them all. Similarly, (B) contradicts the principle of separation of powers. It is the executive branch's responsibility to enforce the law; it is not required to confer with Congress on the manner in which it performs this task. The correct answer, by POE, is (A).

THE BASICS

Section I of the AP U.S. Government and Politics Exam consists of 55 multiple-choice questions, and you will be given 80 minutes to complete it. The types of questions are as follows:

Knowledge Questions: Nearly half of the AP Exam is made up of multiple-choice questions that test your recall of terms, principles, processes, institutions, policies, and behaviors, and how well you can apply those to a variety of political scenarios.

Quantitative Analysis: Roughly 30% of the test is given over to the analysis of charts, tables, infographics, maps, diagrams, and political cartoons.

Text-Based Analysis: About 13% of the test is passage-based. You'll be presented with two short excerpts of 100–150 words, each of which will then be followed by 3–4 questions.

Comparison Questions: About 9% of the questions ask you to select the choice that best identifies a similarity or difference between two political concepts.

Each of these questions has four choices: (A), (B), (C), and (D). Only one of these is correct for each question.

There is no penalty for getting a question wrong; your total score is assessed entirely by the number of questions you get correct, so make sure you don't leave any questions blank!

Knowledge Questions

The majority of questions in the multiple-choice section of the test are testing the various AP Government topics that you would have learned in class. Here's an example.

3. In which of the following situations can a president use a pocket veto?

    (A) Congress amends a bill.
    (B) The president is out of the country.
    (C) A bill passes Congress with a greater than two-thirds majority in each house.
    (D) A bill reaches the president's desk within 10 days of the end of a congressional session.

Stuck on a knowledge question? Break down the different parts of the question and use Process of Elimination to guide your thinking!

Here's How to Crack It

3. **D** Quickly brainstorm the key term, "pocket veto." The answer choices mostly deal with *when* a veto can be applied, so focus your recall on that aspect. In general, a veto is applied to something that has already been passed, so (A) can be eliminated. Choice (B) can also be eliminated, as a veto is an action—it has nothing to do with a president's physical location. Choice (C) is tricky, because it refers to the fact that a veto can be overridden by a two-thirds majority vote in each house, but has nothing to do with when the veto can be used. The remaining choice correctly identifies the "pocket" part of the veto, indicating that it is a special kind of veto in which the president simply runs out the clock on Congress, an act the president can do only when there are fewer than 10 days left in a congressional session (as the bill would otherwise become law after 10 days). Choice (D) is correct.

When approaching the charts, maps, and cartoons in quantitative analysis questions, always read the questions first.

Quantitative Analysis

There will be several questions at the beginning of the section asking you to interpret a graph or chart. These questions come in paired sets: first you'll see the image, and then answer two separate questions pertaining to it.

Charts and Tables

For statistics-based questions, the first question is often very direct, simply asking you to interpret the data, while the second may ask about causes and effects, or it may require you to make knowledge-based judgments. You will *not* have to answer one of the two questions correctly in order to answer the other, so even if you can't figure out the first, you should still read the second.

Be sure that you don't overinterpret the data. The correct answers will be indisputably supported by the information in the chart.

Here's an example.

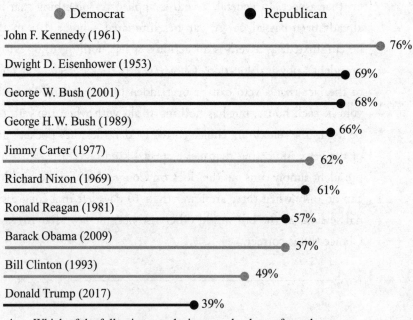

U.S. Presidential Approval Ratings After First Year in Office, 1953 to 2017

4. Which of the following conclusions can be drawn from the information presented in the chart above?

(A) Eisenhower was the most consistently popular president in the nation's history.

(B) Kennedy received greater congressional support for his programs than did any other president from 1953 to 2017.

(C) Nixon's approval rating was largely a result of the Watergate scandal.

(D) Kennedy's first-year approval ratings were the greatest for any president from 1953 to 2017.

5. Which of the following explains why, despite shifts in public approval, incumbent presidents usually win reelection?

    (A) The approval ratings of incumbent presidents typically rise in the months immediately before an election.
    (B) Incumbents generally have better name recognition and campaign finance advantages than their opponents.
    (C) Incumbent presidents since 1974 have experienced generally higher approval ratings than their predecessors.
    (D) National polls do not accurately capture the true sentiments of voters in presidential elections.

Don't get overwhelmed by the data presented to you on the Quantitative Analysis questions: first identify the key words in the question stems, and then find the matching term in the chart, table, or graph!

Here's How to Crack It

4. **D** Charts and tables require you to find a needle in a haystack. As with all questions paired with charts/tables/passages, read the question first to find out what the question wants you to discover. The first question after the chart/table/passage will always be a simple knowledge question. For the second question, you need to draw a conclusion about the data as a whole. Now take a look at the answer choices. Immediately notice that (A), (B), and (C) all refer to information not present in the table. Even before looking at (D), we know it is the correct answer.

5. **B** The second question after a chart/table/passage will typically ask you to make an inference about the information or make a connection between the information and what you learned throughout the AP U.S. Government and Politics course. Quickly skim the question to see whether you'll need to refer to any data and, if you don't, save time by ignoring the image entirely. Choice (C) seems odd, as some of America's most beloved presidents served before 1974. So does (D), as most polls, if done correctly, are accurate. Left with (A) and (B), choose the one that makes the most sense. During an election, the incumbent president's opponent is likely to put out attack ads, which means that the president's approval ratings are likelier to drop than to rise; eliminate (A). However, the incumbent president, having likely served for a full term at this point, will have the advantage of being already established as a presidential candidate, and will generally be more recognized and better funded, which makes (B) the correct answer.

You don't need to be an art historian to ace political cartoon questions! Political cartoons will often portray caricatures of key figures to emphasize the character of those individuals, provide labels to convey key information, and use symbolism to emphasize a particular message. Once you identify the key players or general theme of the political cartoon, use Process of Elimination to get rid of answers that are not aligned with your findings!

Maps, Diagrams, and Cartoons

A few questions will ask you to interpret an illustration, often a map or a political cartoon. The key is not reading too much between the lines. Here's an example.

Source: Adam Zyglis, PoliticalCartoons.com

6. Which of the following principles of government is most relevant to the cartoon?

(A) Judicial restraint
(B) Checks and balances
(C) Federalism
(D) Executive privilege

Here's How to Crack It

6. **B** When analyzing a political cartoon, you need to first understand what the cartoon portrays. On the left, a man (President George W. Bush) stands in front of GITMO, the prison camp in Guantanamo Bay, Cuba. On the right of a line marked "Constitution," a judge holds up a document imprinted with the words "Habeas Corpus –S.C." *Habeas corpus* refers to an American's right to appear in front of a judge and not be held indefinitely without trial. Now that we know the basics, we can determine which principle of government is relevant to the cartoon. Choice (A) can be eliminated as judicial restraint refers to the actions of the Supreme Court; the cartoon appears to be criticizing the president's actions. The president is standing outside the "U.S. Constitution" line. Choice (C) can be eliminated as the cartoon does not depict the relationship between

the federal government and the states. Choice (D) can be eliminated as the president's actions and words do not suggest executive privilege, the president withholding information from the public in the name of national security. As a result, (B) is correct; the conflict between the president and Supreme Court as depicted in the cartoon is an example of checks and balances. At GITMO, President Bush attempted to keep prisoners indefinitely, but the Supreme Court invoked habeas corpus.

―――――――――――○―――――――――――

Text-Based Analysis

As with the Quantitative Analysis format, Text-Based Analysis questions come in sets. The difference is that instead of being about images or data, these are based on short text passages. One or two of these questions will simply test your comprehension of the meaning of the passage, which means you can solve these based entirely on the provided context, while the remaining questions will require you to apply outside knowledge. Here is an example:

―――――――――――○―――――――――――

THERE is an idea, which is not without its advocates, that a vigorous Executive is inconsistent with the genius of republican government…Energy in the Executive is a leading character in the definition of good government. It is essential to the protection of the community against foreign attacks; it is not less essential to the steady administration of the laws; to the protection of property against those irregular and high-handed combinations which sometimes interrupt the ordinary course of justice; to the security of liberty against the enterprises and assaults of ambition, of faction, and of anarchy. Every man the least conversant in Roman story, knows how often that republic was obliged to take refuge in the absolute power of a single man, under the formidable title of Dictator, as well against the intrigues of ambitious individuals who aspired to the tyranny, and the seditions of whole classes of the community whose conduct threatened the existence of all government, as against the invasions of external enemies who menaced the conquest and destruction of Rome.

—Alexander Hamilton,
The Federalist paper number 70 (1788)

While you aren't required to do the test questions in a specific order, it's best to do paired questions at the same time. However, don't get bogged down when reading dense text on Qualitative Analysis questions.

First, read the questions related to the text to guide your reading. Knowing what you're looking for will ensure that you don't waste time analyzing portions of the text that aren't related to the exam questions.

When relating information in the text to other events, identify common themes, ideologies, or policies. If there's no commonality, eliminate that answer choice!

7. Which of the following statements best summarizes Hamilton's reasoning for why the new nation requires an executive?

   (A) The United States must model itself on the Roman Republic.
   (B) The Executive can act decisively to protect the United States.
   (C) Giving the legislative branch all the power would lead to ruin.
   (D) The legislative branch lacks energy.

8. Which of the following events from the 20th century would support Hamilton's argument?

   (A) President Wilson creating the League of Nations
   (B) President Nixon breaking the law during the Watergate Scandal
   (C) President Roosevelt's leadership during World War II
   (D) President Reagan signing tax cuts

Here's How to Crack It

7. **B** With a passage-based Qualitative Analysis question, you should start by skimming the questions so that when you go back and read the text, you know what you're looking for. Begin by seeking out "Executive." You can also cross out any choices that aren't directly claimed in the passage, since you're being asked to summarize it: this means (C) and (D) can be eliminated. Choice (A) is tricky, as Hamilton does talk about the Roman Republic; but as you dig deeper, the text reveals that Hamilton mentions this model as a warning, which means you can eliminate (A). The correct answer is (B): like the leaders of the Roman Republic, the Executive defends the United States from external and internal threats.

8. **C** While you may choose to skip around through the test, it's a good idea to do paired questions like this one in order, because you can take some of the work you've already done—summarizing the passage—in order to now find a historical event to link it with. Choices (A) and (D) deal with topics that Hamilton does not address in his defense of the Executive, so both can be eliminated. Choice (B) can also be ruled out, as President Nixon's crimes would be an argument against Hamilton's opinions of the Executive. Only the correct answer, (C), calls back to Hamilton: "It is essential to the protection of the community against foreign attacks."

Comparison Questions

These questions will present you with two columns containing two similar or opposing ideas or Supreme Court cases. Your job is to choose the answer which matches the correct characteristics to both columns. Here is an example:

When tackling Comparison Questions, tackle one term at a time. As soon as you eliminate an answer from one column, the entire answer choice can be eliminated: remember, half right is all wrong!

9.   Which of the following is an accurate comparison of the themes and views expressed in Federalist No. 10 and Brutus No. 1?

	Federalist No. 10	Brutus No. 1
(A)	Was written by James Madison	Warned against the "mischiefs of faction"
(B)	Advocated for the delegation of authority to elected representatives	Advocated for a strong federal government
(C)	Warned of the dangers of a large, centralized government	Warned of the inefficiency of power diffused to individual states
(D)	Supported the notion of a large republic in order to control factionalism	Was written by an Anti-Federalist

Here's How to Crack It

9.   **D**   In comparison questions, if one part of the comparison is wrong, that whole answer is wrong. Before diving into the options, remind yourself that Federalists were in favor of a powerful government and a large republic. The Anti-Federalists, which included Brutus, were for the opposite. Remembering these few bits of information helps you eliminate (B) and (C). If you're stuck between the remaining two choices, pick the one that you're most confident about; would an Anti-Federalist have warned against "the mischief of faction"? Would a Federalist have supported a large republic? The correct answer is (D).

Summary

o   Remember not to leave any questions blank. There is no "guessing penalty" on this exam!

o   Rest assured that the AP U.S. Government and Politics Exam tests a relatively small amount of information. Be confident: you can review this material fairly quickly and still get a good score on this exam.

o   Familiarize yourself with the different types of questions that will appear in the multiple-choice section.

o   Remember that most of the questions on this exam are of medium difficulty. The test does not bother with trivial matters or minute exceptions to general trends. The test-writers want to know that you understand the general principles underlying U.S. government.

o   Tailor your studying to suit the test's most common topics. Don't spend a lot of time studying civil rights and civil liberties until you have completely reviewed the workings of the federal government and the basics of political behavior.

o   Use POE on all but the easiest questions. Once you have worked on a question, eliminated some answers, and convinced yourself that you cannot eliminate any other incorrect answers, you should guess and move on to the next question.

o   Use common sense.

Chapter 2
How to
Approach
Free-Response
Questions

Forget the idea of crafting a fine piece of writing that convinces the reader of your opinion. Instead, think "just the facts, ma'am."

Need More Help on Essays?

We've got just the book for that! *How to Write Essays for Standardized Tests* contains advice and examples of best practices on an assortment of AP exams, plus ACT and others!

OVERVIEW OF THE FREE-RESPONSE SECTION

You may be surprised to see the words "free response" at the start of this chapter. What is a "free response," anyway? The first thing to be aware of is that this response is hardly free. The College Board wants a very specific type of writing, and it is one that you might not be used to. Your basic goal here is to read the questions and answer them to the best of your ability. Don't get too hung up on crafting a perfectly organized essay with transitional phrases—this section of the AP exam should almost stand for "Answer the Prompt"—just crank out a straightforward, clear answer, and show the graders that you know your stuff in the fewest number of words possible.

You will have 100 minutes to answer four questions, so be sure to budget your time well. Give as much detail as necessary to answer the question, but no more! Above all, don't worry. So long as you know the basics of American government, this section should be a breeze.

PLANNING AND WRITING YOUR FREE RESPONSE

There are two essential components to writing a successful timed free response. The first is to plan what you are going to write before you start writing. The second is to use a number of tried-and-true writing techniques that will make your response better organized, better thought out, and better written.

Step 1: Know the Question

Read the question carefully and figure out what you are being asked.

Step 2: Brainstorm the Topic

Brainstorm for a minute or two. In your test booklet, write down everything that comes to mind about the subject; there is room on the back pages of the booklet and in the blank space at the bottom of the question pages. Think of a question as a lock; this is the point at which you're shaking out your mental pockets to try to find the right key.

Step 3: **Match Your Knowledge to the Question**

Look at your notes and consider the results of your brainstorming session as you decide which points you will argue in your response. Tailor your argument to the information, but don't make an argument that you know is wrong or with which you disagree. It's always best to stick with what you know so as to maximize your chance of getting full credit on a response: graders only see whether you have a thorough understanding of the topic as written.

Step 4: **Answer the Question(s)**

Readers are looking for substantive examples, so don't generalize or beat around the bush. **Describe, explain,** and **identify** what's being asked for, and **provide** anything that you're prompted for. If there are multiple parts, clearly label each and address each in turn. In short, be short! (This approach will be a little more in-depth for the argument essay, but we'll get to that in the next section!)

WHAT ARE THE FREE-RESPONSE QUESTIONS LIKE?

The AP U.S. Government and Politics free-response section contains four free-response questions. Each contains multiple parts that are scored individually. The entire free-response section counts as 50% of your examination grade. At least one of the essay prompts will test your knowledge of public policy initiatives. This is most likely to occur in the Concept Application question.

The Concept Application Question

The Concept Application question features a short passage that outlines a scenario, followed by three related questions. The passage will typically be pertinent to a law or constitutional amendment that you have learned about in your AP Government class. The Concept Application question is worth 3 points and has a 12.5% exam weight. A point is awarded for sufficiently answering each of the three questions. It should take about 20 minutes to complete. Let's look at an example.

1. "There is recognition abroad that we are in many ways a sexist country. Sexism is judging people by their sex when sex doesn't matter. Sexism is intended to rhyme with racism. Both have been used to keep the powers that be in power… Women who get good jobs do it by outsexing the sexism. They persuade the boss that a woman's intuition is needed. Or that women pay more attention to detail. They know it isn't so, but they use the sexist arguments to get around prejudice."

Caroline Bird, "On Being Born Female," published on November 15, 1968

After reading the scenario, respond to A, B, and C below:

(A) Describe a law which was passed to legally address the problem described in the quote.
(B) For the law described in Part A, evaluate the extent of its effectiveness.
(C) In the context of the scenario, explain how the actions of the federal government can be helped or hindered by the states.

Step 1: Know the Question

In the case of a Concept Application question, in which text has been provided, the scenario itself is a part of the question. Read through the scenario, and then after reading Part A, go back through the scenario, underlining key words and determining the central message or theme. In this case, Caroline Bird is defining sexism and comparing it to racism, specifically mentioning the struggle to compete in the workplace.

Step 2: Brainstorm the Topic

Throw out a list of laws and/or constitutional policies that may pertain to sexism, either in general or specifically at the workplace. You might think of the Equal Pay Act of 1963, the Lily Ledbetter Fair Pay Act of 2009, or even Title IX of the Higher Education Act of 1973. If these are unfamiliar, you could even use the Civil Rights Act of 1964, which has undoubtedly promoted more fair treatment for women of color.

Step 3: Match Your Knowledge to the Question

Choose the law or amendment that you know the most about. Note that you're going to have to answer Part B and Part C based on your choice for Part A, so stick with the strongest core of your knowledge base. This also applies to either/or options like "helped or hindered"; choose the approach that is easiest to defend given your brainstormed knowledge.

Step 4: Answer the Question(s)

Describe the law you've chosen. **Evaluate** its effectiveness. For the final part, **explain** either how a state has hindered or helped the federal government.

The Quantitative Analysis Question

The Quantitative Analysis question will provide you with a chart, graph, or table with numerical data in it. Typically, one or two of the questions will simply ask you to accurately interpret the data as given, while the other remaining question(s) will require your outside knowledge. The Quantitative Analysis question is worth 4 points and has a 12.5% exam weight. A point is awarded for sufficiently answering each of the four questions. It should take about 20 minutes to complete. The following is an example of a quantitative analysis question.

To unlock a trove of Free-Response Questions from previous years, go to https://apcentral. collegeboard.org/courses/ ap-united-states-government-and-politics/ exam/ap-us-government-and-politics-past-exam-questions

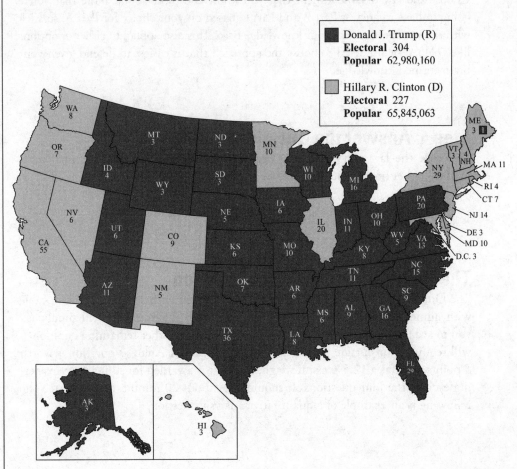

2016 PRESIDENTIAL ELECTION RESULTS

Donald J. Trump (R)
Electoral 304
Popular 62,980,160

Hillary R. Clinton (D)
Electoral 227
Popular 65,845,063

2. Use the information graphic to answer the questions.

   (A) Identify a regional trend in presidential elections
       as illustrated by the graphic.

   (B) Explain the discrepancy in each candidate's accrual
       of electoral votes and popular votes in the 2016
       presidential election and how that discrepancy
       affected the outcome of the election.

   (C) Identify one campaign strategy presidential
       candidates might use to influence the outcome of
       electoral votes in various states or regions.

Step 1: Know the Question

For any Quantitative Analysis question, the graphic is a part of the question. Pay close attention to the labels, units, and sidebars provided. In this case, one shade represents Republican votes, while the other represents Democrat votes. Note that electoral votes are shown on the map, while the key shows the popular votes and candidate names. Read through the questions, and circle any relevant information in the graphic that could be used to answer Part A or Part B.

Step 2: Brainstorm the Topic

You need to brainstorm only when outside knowledge is required, so just look at Part C. Think about campaign strategies you've learned about in class. Perhaps you have heard of presidential candidates campaigning heavily in swing states while neglecting reliably Republican or Democratic states.

Step 3: Match Your Knowledge to the Question

Michigan, Pennsylvania, and New Hampshire are all swing states. You could point out that Trump campaigned heavily in Michigan and Pennsylvania to capture the swing electoral votes in those states. You could suggest that Clinton did not put enough resources into those states, thus losing the electoral race.

Step 4: Answer the Question(s)

Identify a trend, referring specifically to regions shown in the graphic. **Explain** the difference between electoral votes and popular votes by calling out the electoral worth of each state on the graphic. Using everything you've brainstormed, **identify** an electoral strategy that may have been used.

The SCOTUS Comparison Question

The SCOTUS Comparison question will require you to read a description of a historical Supreme Court case and then compare or contrast it with another case. Chances are, the case provided in the description will be an obscure case you have not seen before, while the second case will be more familiar, having been covered in your AP Government class. The two cases will be related in topic, but will contain important differences. Your job is to identify the similarities and differences and use them as the primary evidence with which to answer the questions. The SCOTUS Comparison question is worth 4 points and has a 12.5% exam weight. A point is awarded for sufficiently answering each of the four questions. It should take about 20 minutes to complete.

Here is an example:

The SCOTUS Comparison free-response question is worth 12.5% of the exam and can be intimidating because of the qualitative analysis required.

Don't panic! Break the process down into bite-sized pieces, and attack the passage and questions systematically using the four steps for success!

3. The Jehovah's Witnesses are a small Christian denomination which has existed in the United States since the mid-19th century. Since they believe that the law of God supersedes that of worldly governments, they take literally Exodus 20:4, which says: "Thou shalt not make unto thee any graven images... thou shalt not bow down thyself to them nor serve them." They consider that the American flag is an "image" within this command and thus their children refuse to recite the Pledge of Allegiance or participate in the morning flag salute at public schools. In the 1930s and 1940s, children of Jehovah's Witnesses throughout the country had been disciplined or even expelled from school for taking this stand. Parents of such children were prosecuted for upholding their children's actions.

In 1943, the Supreme Court decision in *West Virginia State Board of Education v. Barnette* held that the Constitution protects students from being forced by public schools to salute the American flag or say the Pledge of Allegiance in public school. The majority opinion in *Barnette* is considered one of the Court's most decisive statements regarding the Bill of Rights.

(A) Identify the constitutional clause that is common to both *West Virginia State Board of Education v. Barnette* (1943) and *Tinker v. Des Moines Independent Community School District* (1969).

(B) Based on the constitutional clause identified in Part A, describe how *Tinker v. Des Moines Independent Community School District* further expanded and clarified the rights at stake in *West Virginia State Board of Education v. Barnette*.

(C) Describe one circumstance, real or hypothetical, in which the rights established by *West Virginia State Board of Education v. Barnette* and *Tinker v. Des Moines Independent Community School District* may still be limited.

Step 1: Know the Question

For a SCOTUS Comparison question, you need to *identify* the known (required) SCOTUS case and the obscure one described in the prompt, as well as the main issue covered by the case—in this case, freedom of speech in schools *(Tinker)*. This is the longest of the essay prompts, so you may want to underline or circle key terms as you go through, and consult with Part A to assess whether you should be looking for a similarity or a difference between the two cases—in this case, you want one that is "common," or similar.

Step 2: **Brainstorm the Topic**

On a SCOTUS Comparison question, you're given everything you need to know about one case, so you really need to brainstorm only on the second case, the one that was a required Supreme Court case from your class. You also don't need to brainstorm *everything* about that case—only the portions that are similar (or different) from the one that you've been given. Here, the main similarity is freedom of expression by underage school children.

Step 3: **Match Your Knowledge**

For Part A, you should think about constitutional clauses that apply to both, such as the First Amendment—the freedom of speech. (There might not always be more than one amendment.) You should also think about differences between the two, such as the way in which *Tinker* allowed for discretionary freedom of expression (wearing black armbands to protest the Vietnam War), while *Barnette* was simply concerned with the unconstitutionality of compelling school children to engage in enforced speech (saluting the flag). Finally, for Part C, you should consider various exceptions to the law, such as how schools still restrict speech in certain situations. If nothing comes to mind, remember that you can use hypothetical situations; try to imagine a context in which they could be challenged.

Step 4: **Answer the Question(s)**

Identify the common constitutional clause, being specific. Describe the differences between how *Tinker* and *Barnette* distinguished those rights. Using either a real-world or hypothetical example, describe how the rights granted by *Tinker* might still be limited.

The Argument Essay

Although the Argument Essay is worth no more than the other three free-response questions, the College Board suggests that you spend up to 40 minutes writing this essay. That's because the directions are more detailed, and because you'll need to rely heavily on primary source material, both of which may require more time and effort. The Argument Essay is worth 6 points and has a 12.5% exam weight. Points are awarded based on a scoring rubric (see page 85). It should take about 40 minutes to complete. The following is an example of an argument essay question.

The Argument Essay is the only part of the AP U.S. Government and Politics Exam where you get to express your views—and you don't need to be an expert on every historical document to ace this free-response question.

Brainstorm to identify the evidence that you feel most knowledgeable about, choose an argument you can confidently support, and then develop your thesis. Remember to play to your strengths—you can achieve full points, regardless of perspective, as long as you provide a complete answer!

4. Develop an argument that explains how effectively the United States government has used its legal authority to ensure civil rights for various social groups throughout its history.

In your essay, you must:

- Articulate a defensible claim or thesis that responds to the prompt and establishes a line of reasoning.

- Support your claim with at least two pieces of accurate and relevant information:
  o At least ONE piece of evidence must be from one of the following foundational documents:
    - Federalist No. 10
    - The Declaration of Independence
    - "Letter from a Birmingham Jail" (MLK)
  o Use a second piece of evidence from another foundational document from the list or your study of civil rights:
    - U.S. Constitution
    - Federalist No. 51
    - Federalist No. 78
- Use reasoning to explain why your evidence supports your claim/thesis.

- Respond to an opposing or alternative perspective using refutation, concession, or rebuttal.

Step 1: Know the Question

As opposed to the other free-response questions, which have targeted, specific questions, the Argument Essay largely leaves you to craft an argument on your own. There are still specific tasks, represented by each bullet, but there's no question. That's fine! It just means *you* get to ask it. In this case, rephrase the prompt and ask, "When has the United States "effectively (or ineffectively)" used its legal authority to ensure civil rights?"

Step 2: Brainstorm the Topic

This step is also a bit different from those of the other free-response questions, because this time, there are restrictions on what you can use. Begin, then, by choosing which documents you'll use as evidence, allowing the one that's provided to help influence the direction of your brainstorming for the second piece of evidence. Perhaps you know "Letter from a Birmingham Jail" like the back of your hand, and perhaps you are well-versed in the Civil Rights Act of 1964. If you use the documents you know best, any argument you choose will be easier to support. Another reason to choose a topic that you're very familiar with is that you'll need to include an opposing perspective, which you should mull over in this step.

Step 3: Match Your Knowledge to the Question

The heart of your essay is a clear and complete thesis statement, so be sure you have this nailed down before you start writing. Typically, you will have the freedom to argue a "pro" stance, such as "The Federal Government has done an excellent job of defending civil rights throughout our recent history" or a "con" stance, such as "The Federal Government has generally neglected the civil rights of its citizens" or a moderated stance, such as "Despite some setbacks, the defense of the civil rights of all Americans is making greater strides over time." Choose the argument that you feel most comfortable with; you won't get any extra points for attempting a more nuanced, trickier essay. Because there's less structure here than there was on the other free responses, you may also want to briefly outline how you'll connect each piece of evidence to your thesis statement.

Step 4: Answer the Question(s)

The prompt for the essay changes for each test, as do the foundational documents that you can choose between, but the directions themselves are largely the same. That means that you should always expect to have to **articulate** a thesis, **support** that thesis with evidence (**explaining** each connection in detail), and use **refutation, concession,** or **rebuttal** to respond to the opposing point of view.

Scoring Rubric for Question 4: Argument Essay			6 points
Reporting Category	**Scoring Criteria**		
Row A Claim/Thesis (0–1 points)	0 points		1 point Responds to the prompt with a defensible claim or thesis that responds to the prompt rather than restating the prompt and establishes a line of reasoning
Row B Evidence (0–3 points)	0 points	1 point Provides one piece of evidence that is relevant to the topic of the prompt	2 points Uses one piece of specific and relevant evidence to support the claim or thesis 3 points Uses two pieces of specific and relevant evidence to support the claim or thesis
Row C Reasoning (0–1 points)	0 points		1 point Explains how or why the evidence supports the claim or thesis
Row D Responds to Alternative Perspectives (0–1 points)	0 points		1 point Responds to an opposing or alternative perspective using refutation, concession, or rebuttal

**Don't Rush . . .
But Don't Gush**

The scoring rubric does not award any extra points for having a fancy introduction or an in-depth conclusion. Even though you're writing an essay, you should still approach this as if you're answering individual parts of a question, and don't waste time on things you won't be graded on.

**Some More
Useful
Transitions:**
- Additionally
- Contrastingly
- Furthermore
- However
- Likewise
- Therefore
- Thus

AS YOU ARE WRITING

Here are some general tips to keep in mind as you write.

- **Keep sentences as simple as possible.** Long sentences get convoluted very quickly and may give both you and your graders a headache.

- **Use appropriate political science terminology.** Just as a picture is worth a thousand words, so too is the right word. That said, don't overdo it. Good writing doesn't have to be complicated, and you should use political terms only if they help you more succinctly state your point. *Never* use a word if you are unsure of its meaning or proper usage. A malapropism may give your graders a good laugh, but it won't earn you any points and may cost you points, especially if it changes the intended meaning of your response.

- **Write clearly and neatly.** Here's an easy way to put graders in a good mood. Graders look at a lot of chicken scratches; it strains their eyes and makes them grumpy. Also keep in mind that they have as little as two minutes to read each response. Neatly written essays make them happy. When you cross out, do it neatly. Write in blue or black ink. If you're making any major changes—for example, if you want to insert a paragraph in the middle of your response—make sure you indicate them clearly.

- **Define your terms.** Most questions require you to use terms that mean different things to different people. One person's "liberal" is another person's "conservative" and yet another person's "radical." The folks who grade the test want to know what you think these terms mean. When you use them, define them. Take particular care to define any such terms that appear in the question. Almost all official College Board materials stress this point, so don't forget: define any term that you suspect can be defined in more than one way.

- **Use structural indicators to organize your paragraphs.** Another way to clarify your intentions is to organize your response around structural indicators. For example, if you are making a number of related points, number them ("First, . . . Second, . . . Finally, . . ."). If you are attempting to compare and contrast two viewpoints, use the indicators "on the one hand" and "on the other hand" or "whereas."

- **Stick to your outline.** Unless you get an absolutely brilliant idea after you've brainstormed and while you're in the middle of writing, don't deviate from your outline. If you do, you risk muddying your response, or forgetting to answer the actual question. (That's why planning is so important!)

- **Back up your ideas with examples.** When a part of a question calls for evidence or reasoning, be prepared to provide it, and remember to always be specific, especially when indicating data points on the Quantitative Analysis question. Don't just throw half-baked ideas out there and hope that the reader will connect the dots for you. You will score big points if you substantiate your claims with facts, and remember that at least in the SCOTUS Comparison, you may be able to use hypothetical situations to illustrate your point, if no real-world ones spring to mind. However, real-world examples are preferable.

- **Answer each part of the question directly.** You can label each part of a question that you're responding to, but to make sure you stay on track and help the reader follow, it helps to restate that question in your response. For instance, if asked how Jefferson's concern about term limits is relevant today, begin by restating the question: "Jefferson's concern is relevant (or irrelevant) today."

- **Watch your time.** You need to average about 20 minutes per question for the first three prompts, with about 40 minutes devoted to the Argument Essay. The biggest mistake you can make, with the exception of skipping a question entirely, is failing to leave yourself enough time to answer all four questions. It's okay to spend as much as 25 minutes on a given question, but you'd better make it worthwhile. (You also probably don't want to spend that much time on the first essay—preferably 15 minutes max—or you'll feel rushed while writing the remaining three.)

- **If you draw a total blank on a question, take a deep breath and ask yourself what you do know about the topic.** You may realize that you know more than you think. Try to figure out what the question is asking and/or how you can approach it. Remember that you can get partial credit if you're able to answer only some parts correctly.

Don't Panic
As you scan the four questions, you may well come to rest on one that deals with a subject your teacher didn't cover or you didn't get around to studying. Don't worry: everyone finds some questions harder than others. To build your confidence, answer the question you find easiest before turning to the intimidating one.

Summary

o   Use the four-step approach so that you stay on target for each free-response question.

o   Read all parts carefully and be sure that you address each of them.

o   Mark up the question. You may bracket the core of the question, underline the operative words such as *identify*, *discuss*, *describe*, and *analyze*, or circle limiters like, "since 2016," "give one example," and "list three."

o   Look out for questions that require a definition of a term. If a question asks for a definition, write one; even if a question doesn't ask for a definition, make sure that you understand the terms used.

o   Always back up your statements with evidence.

o   Don't start writing until you have brainstormed and chosen a thesis, if required. Consider writing a brief outline at least for the Argument Essay.

o   Write clearly and neatly. Don't use sentences that are too long. Toss in a couple of political science terms that you know you won't misuse. When in doubt, stick to simple syntax and vocabulary.

o   Take a watch to the exam and check it several times throughout the section so that you internalize how much time is left for each question.

o   Every piece of data that supports your argument should be linked to it. Do not just list information without relating it to the point you are trying to make.

Chapter 3
Using Time Effectively to Maximize Points

Very few students stop to think about how to improve their test-taking skills. Most assume that if they study hard, they will test well, and if they do not study, they will do poorly. Most students continue to believe this even after experience teaches them otherwise. Have you ever studied really hard for an exam, and then blown it on test day? Have you ever aced an exam for which you thought you weren't well prepared? Most students have had one, if not both, of these experiences. The lesson should be clear: factors other than your level of preparation influence your final test score. This chapter will provide you with some insights that will help you perform better on the AP U.S. Government and Politics Exam, as well as on other exams.

PACING AND TIMING

A big part of scoring well on an exam is working at a consistent pace. The worst mistake that inexperienced or unsavvy test-takers make is to come to a question that stumps them, and rather than just skip it, panic and stall. Time stands still when you're working on a question you cannot answer, and it is not unusual for students to waste five minutes on a single question (especially a question involving a graph or the word EXCEPT) because they are too stubborn to cut their losses. It is important to be aware of how much time you have spent on any given question and on the section on which you are working. There are several ways to improve your pacing and timing for the test.

When calculating your average pace, make sure that your practice questions include all question types. It also makes sense to take your practice tests at the same time you will take the AP Exam in order to mirror testing conditions and build up your endurance.

- **Know your average pace.** While you prepare for your test, try to gauge how long you take on 5, 10, or 20 questions. Knowing how long you spend on average per question will help you identify how many questions you can answer effectively and how best to pace yourself for the test.

- **Have a watch or clock nearby.** You are permitted to have a watch or clock nearby to help you keep track of time. It is important to remember, however, that constantly checking the clock is in itself a waste of time and can be distracting. Devise a plan. Try checking the clock after every 15 or 20 questions to see whether you are keeping the correct pace or whether you need to speed up; this will ensure that you're cognizant of the time while not permitting you to fall into the trap of dwelling on it.

- **Know when to move on.** Since all questions are scored equally, investing appreciable amounts of time on a single question is inefficient and can potentially deprive you of the chance to answer easier questions later on. If you are able to eliminate answer choices, do so, but don't worry about picking a random answer and moving on if you cannot find the correct answer. Remember, tests are like marathons; you do best when you work through them at a steady pace. You can always come back to a question you don't know. When you do, very often you will find that your previous mental block is gone, and you will wonder why the question perplexed you the first time around (as you gleefully move on to the next question). Even if you still don't know the answer, you will not have wasted valuable time that you could have spent on easier questions.

- **Be selective.** You don't have to do any of the questions in a given section in order. If you are stumped by an essay or multiple-choice question, skip it or choose a different one. In the section below, you will see that you may not have to answer every question correctly to achieve your desired score. Select the questions or essays that you can answer, and work on them first. This approach will make you more efficient and give you the greatest chance of answering the most questions correctly.

- **Use Process of Elimination on multiple-choice questions.** Many times, one or more answer choices can be eliminated. Every choice that you eliminate using Process of Elimination raises your odds of selecting the right answer significantly.

Remember, when all the questions on a test are of equal value, no one question is that important. Your overall goal for pacing is to get the most questions correct. Finally, you should set a realistic goal for your final score. In the next section, we will break down how to achieve your desired score and ways of pacing yourself to do so.

GETTING THE SCORE YOU WANT

AP exams in all subjects do not include any guessing penalty for incorrect answers. Instead, students are assessed solely on the total number of correct answers. A lot of AP materials, even those you receive in your AP class, may not include this information. It is really important to remember that if you are running out of time, you should fill in all the bubbles before the time for the multiple-choice section is up. Even if you don't plan to spend a lot of time on every question and even if you have no idea what the correct answer is, you need to fill something in.

There are multiple ways to achieve your desired score. It is important to remember that guessing is not penalized and that you must put in energy and effort on the essays to perform well.

TEST ANXIETY

Everybody experiences anxiety before and during an exam. To a certain extent, test anxiety can be helpful. Some people find that they perform more quickly and efficiently under stress. If you have ever pulled an all-nighter to write a paper and ended up doing good work, you know the feeling.

Nine AP Exams Go Digital in 2025
College Board announced that in May 2025, nine AP exams will go fully digital! For the latest information regarding the specific AP subjects going digital and testing accommodations, visit the College Board website at apcentral.collegeboard. org/exam-administration-ordering-scores/digital-ap-exams.

Here are some more test anxiety tips you can use to make sure you have a successful test day:
- Go to bed early the night before the test.
- Eat breakfast (or lunch if you have an afternoon test), but watch out for overly fatty or sugary foods.
- Go to the bathroom right before the test.
- Make sure to walk around a little during the break.
- Plan to do something nice for yourself after the test. This plan should put you in a positive frame of mind.

However, too much stress is definitely a bad thing. Some students experience physical symptoms: upset stomach, sweating, and hyperventilating. If you find that you stress out during exams, here are a few preemptive actions you can take. Following these steps will not only put you at ease, but also very likely raise your score!

- **Take a reality check.** Evaluate your situation before the test begins. If you have studied hard, remind yourself that you are well prepared. Remember that many others taking the test are not as well prepared, and (in your classes, at least) you are being graded against them, so you have an advantage. If you didn't study, accept the fact that you will probably not ace the test. Make sure you get to every question that you know something about. Don't stress out or fixate on how much you don't know. Your job is to score as high as you can by maximizing the benefits of what you do know. In either scenario, it is best to think of a test as if it were a game. How can you get the most points in the time allotted to you? Always answer questions you can answer easily and quickly before you answer those that will take more time.

- **Try to relax.** Slow, deep breathing works for almost everyone. Close your eyes, take a few slow, deep breaths, and concentrate on nothing but your inhalation and exhalation for a few seconds. This is a basic form of meditation, and it should help you to clear your mind of stress and, as a result, concentrate better on the test. If you have ever taken yoga classes, you probably know some other good relaxation techniques. Use them when you can (obviously, anything that requires leaving your seat and, say, assuming a handstand position won't be allowed by any but the most free-spirited proctors).

- **Eliminate as many surprises as you can.** Make sure you know where the test will be given, when it starts, what type of questions are going to be asked, and how long the test will take. You don't want to be worrying about any of these things on test day or, even worse, after the test has already begun.

The best way to avoid stress is to study both the test material and the test itself. Congratulations! By buying or reading this book, you are taking a major step toward a stress-free AP U.S. Government and Politics Exam.

REFLECT
Think about what you learned in Part IV, and respond to the following questions:

- How much time will you spend on multiple-choice questions?

- How will you change your approach to multiple-choice questions?

- What is your multiple-choice guessing strategy?

- How much time will you spend on the free-response questions?

- How will you change your approach to the free-response questions?

- Will you seek further help, outside of this book (such as from a teacher, tutor, or AP Students), on how to approach multiple-choice questions, free-response questions, or a pacing strategy?

Part V
Content Review for the AP U.S. Government and Politics Exam

4   Foundations of American Democracy
5   Interactions Among Branches of Government
6   Civil Liberties and Civil Rights
7   American Political Ideologies and Beliefs
8   Political Participation
9   Chapter Drills: Answers and Explanations

Chapter 4
Foundations
of American
Democracy

"Revolt is the right of the people."

— John Locke

CONCEPTS

- Why did the Articles of Confederation fail?
- What was the immediate impact of Shays' Rebellion?
- What motivated the framers of the Constitution? Were they elitists or pragmatists?
- Why did the framers create a republican form of government?
- Why did the framers create a federal system of government?
- What is the purpose of checks and balances and the separation of powers?
- Why are plurality systems democratic but unstable?

Although the Enlightenment philosophers are important for their influence on the framers of the Constitution, they are not directly tested on the AP U.S. Government and Politics Exam.

ENLIGHTENMENT PHILOSOPHIES

The framers of the Constitution lived in a unique time, when new ideas about government challenged conventional wisdom regarding the roles of people and their governments. The Enlightenment was an 18th-century philosophical movement that began in Western Europe with roots in the Scientific Revolution. The focus was on the use of reason, rather than tradition, to solve social dilemmas.

Major Enlightenment Philosophers

Thomas Hobbes: Hobbes's famous work *Leviathan* (1660) argued that if humans were left to their own devices, chaos and violence would ensue. In a state of nature, life would be "solitary, poor, nasty, brutish, and short." He argued that the best way to protect life was to give total power to an absolute monarch because man cannot be trusted to rule himself. Hobbes also advocated for the rule of law and believed that for the government to protect the natural rights of its citizens, individuals would need to view the government as an authority to be respected. In essence, citizens enter a **social contract** with the government, sacrificing some freedoms to be protected by the federal government.

John Locke: While Hobbes was concerned primarily with the protection of life, Locke went further and argued in his ***Second Treatise on Civil Government*** (1690) that liberty and property also needed to be respected. Locke believed that all individuals are born on neutral footing with a blank slate, or *tabula rasa*, and everything that an individual knows or does is shaped by experience, a concept known as *empiricism*. According to Locke, life, liberty, and property were natural rights granted by God; it was the duty of all governments to respect and protect these rights. If the government did not, Locke contended, the citizens had the right to revolution.

Charles de Montesquieu: A critic of the monarchy and advocate for democracy, Montesquieu was a French philosopher who greatly influenced the founders. His *De l'Esprit des Lois* (*The Spirit of the Laws*, 1748) advocated for the separation of power into three branches of government, believing that such separation promoted a system of checks and balances to limit the power of each branch.

Jean-Jacques Rousseau: Rousseau believed that humans are naturally born good, but are corrupted by society; those who remain uncorrupted are noble savages. Stating, "man is born free and everywhere he is in chains," Rousseau believed that individuals should act in the best interests of the greater good, rather than out of self-interest. Rousseau argued in *The Social Contract* (1762) that the only good government was one that was freely formed with the consent of the people. This consent was shown by a powerful agreement among people.

Voltaire: Famous for *Candide*, a satirical novel that reflected his aversion to Christian power regimes and the nobility, Voltaire was a proponent of rationality. Voltaire was also a fierce advocate of freedom of thought, speech, religion, and politics.

Denis Diderot: The producer and editor of the first encyclopedia, Diderot intended to change the way individuals thought by including his own philosophies and those of other Enlightenment thinkers in his work. Diderot advocated for freedom of expression and educational access for all, while criticizing the theory of divine right and traditional values and religion.

Enlightenment philosophers favored democracy over absolute monarchy. Here are some of the forms a representative democracy can take:

- **Participatory democracy** emphasizes broad participation in politics and civil society by citizens at various levels of socioeconomic status.
- **Pluralist democracy** implies organized group-based activism by citizens with common interests all striving for the same political goals.
- An **elite democracy,** on the other hand, would discourage participation by the majority of citizens and cede power to the educated and/or wealthy.

The American Founding Fathers were most politically influenced by Enlightenment thought in their promotion of Republicanism. Republicanism espouses individual liberty and God-given rights, asserts that all governmental power is derived from the people, rejects aristocracy, and encourages broad-based civic participation in political affairs. American Republicanism is characterized by **representative democracy,** the principle of elected officials representing a group of people, as in the U.S. Congress and state legislatures. Direct democracy is not the primary mode of governance in the United States, although many states do allow for referenda (direct voting by the people). Also, most towns in New England still require a direct vote by the people on budgetary and legislative matters. Perhaps the stability of the American system of democracy is its use of diverse systems at different levels of government.

Many Enlightenment philosophers promoted the idea of **popular sovereignty,** the notion that the authority of a government is created and sustained by the consent of its people, through their elected representatives. Benjamin Franklin once said, "In free governments, the rulers are the servants and the people their superiors and sovereigns."

You can read the Declaration of Independence in full at https://www.archives.gov/founding-docs/declaration.

The Declaration of Independence

Although the American colonies and Great Britain had already been involved in armed conflict for more than one year, the Declaration of Independence was a formal declaration of war between the two groups. The majority of the document outlines the various injustices perpetrated by King George III against the colonies, which author Thomas Jefferson uses to explain why the colonies are declaring their independence. Not only was the Declaration a foundational document for the United States, but in the following centuries other nations would also use it as a template when declaring their independence from colonial powers.

THE WEAKNESSES OF THE ARTICLES OF CONFEDERATION

The first government of the newly born United States of America was formed under the **Articles of Confederation**, the predecessor to the Constitution. These Articles were informally followed from 1776 to 1781 when they were ratified and so named. The government under the Articles achieved some notable accomplishments, including the following:

ARTICLES OF CONFEDERATION

- Set the precedent of **federalism**, whereby the states and central government shared governing responsibilities

- Negotiated the treaty that ended the Revolutionary War (on favorable terms for the United States' victorious army)

- Established the **Northwest Ordinance**, creating methods by which new states would enter the Union

However, the Articles of Confederation suffered from insurmountable weaknesses that placed the newly independent states at risk. The year 1783 was the official end of the American Revolution, and the post-revolution transitional period was marked by states being wholly unprepared to manage their own affairs. By 1787, trade between the states was in decline, the value of money was dropping, potential threats from foreign enemies were growing, and there was the real threat of social disorder from groups within the country. The inability of the state of Massachusetts to effectively deal with **Shays' Rebellion**, a six-month rebellion in which more than 1,000 armed farmers attacked a federal arsenal to protest the foreclosure of farms in the western part of the state, was a major concern at the Constitutional Convention. The nation's leaders began to see the necessity of a stronger central government, as Shays' Rebellion frightened the politicians and exposed the weakness of the Articles of Confederation.

Compounding the problems exposed by Shays' Rebellion was the fact that the central government did not have the power to impose taxes. In order to avoid the perception of "taxation without representation," the Articles of Confederation only allowed state governments to levy taxes. Indeed, the national government had no way to pay for its own expenses, and could only acquire funds by requesting money from the states, borrowing from foreign governments, or selling western lands. In turn, the central government could neither maintain an effective military nor back its own paper currency. Quite simply, the Articles of Confederation hindered the ability of a strong central government to exist.

The federal government under the Articles:

- could not draft soldiers
- was completely dependent on the state legislatures for revenue—the federal government was not permitted to tax citizens
- could not pay off the Revolutionary War debt
- could not control interstate trade
- had no Supreme Court to interpret law
- had no executive branch to enforce national law
- had no national currency
- had no control over import and export taxes imposed between states
- needed unanimity to amend the Articles
- needed approval from 9 out of 13 states to pass legislation (69% majority)
- could not raise a national army to quash uprisings
- had no ability to ensure states complied with national laws
- lacked enforcement mechanisms for requests from within the federal government

These deficiencies of the Articles of Confederation were the direct causes for calling a convention. But amending the articles became so difficult that James Madison easily persuaded the other delegates that a complete rewrite was necessary. The result was the **Constitution,** and the convention came to be known as the **Constitutional Convention**.

Review Source Documents
Many students mix up the Constitution with the Declaration of Independence. Be sure to read through the Constitution (found on page 281) and the Declaration of Independence a few times before your exam.

The Constitutional Convention

When the framers of the Constitution met in Philadelphia in 1787, they were divided over their views of the appropriate power, structure, and responsibilities of government. Some saw the current government, formed under the Articles of Confederation, as weak and ineffective, while others believed that changes to the Articles would be infringements on the responsibilities of state governments and intrusions into the lives of citizens. Some historians see the convention as an elitist conspiracy to protect the wealth of the rich, while others see the convention as a meeting of political pragmatists who knew that by protecting everyone's property and rights, they could best protect their own. Today, the generally accepted view is that the framers were pragmatists.

The delegates agreed that a stronger central government was necessary, but they were fearful of the corrupting influences of power. How to control the federal legislature was a central theme at the convention. The two main plans presented at the convention resulted in a compromise.

One of the most heated debates at the Constitutional Convention related to the composition of the legislative branch of the federal government. Specifically, the framers debated whether the legislative branch should be **unicameral**, consisting of a single house, or **bicameral**, consisting of two houses.

Madison's Virginia Plan called for a bicameral legislature based on population size, which was supported by the larger states as they would be afforded greater representation. Smaller states, however, supported the New Jersey Plan, wherein the legislature would be unicameral and each state would have a single vote; this was similar to what was proposed in the Articles of Confederation.

The Virginia Plan

The large states seized the agenda at the beginning of the convention and proposed the **Virginia Plan**, a recipe for a strong government with each state represented proportionately to its population.

The New Jersey Plan

The small states worried that a government dominated by the large states would be overly strong, so they proposed the **New Jersey Plan**, under which each state would be represented equally.

The Great Compromise

The Great (or "Connecticut") Compromise created the solution: a bicameral (two-house) legislature with a House of Representatives, based on population, and a Senate, with equal representation for all states.

Another major conflict arose over the representation of enslaved people. (Remember that enslaved people could not vote then.) Northerners felt that enslaved people should not be counted when determining each state's number of electoral votes, while Southerners disagreed. The "solution" was the infamous **Three-Fifths Compromise:** the decision was that enslaved people would each count as three-fifths of a person when apportioning seats in the House of Representatives.

Under the Articles of Confederation, there was no executive authority to enforce laws. The framers of the Constitution corrected that problem by addressing the issue of a chief executive, or president. Under the Constitution, the executive is the enforcer of law and a second check on the power of the legislature. Before bills become law, they require presidential approval, and the president has the power to veto acts of the legislature. However, presidential power is not absolute. Congress can override a presidential veto if two-thirds of both houses of the legislature vote to do so.

In order to arbitrate disputes between the Congress and the president, between states, and between the states and the central government, the framers created the Supreme Court.

Despite all of the compromises that were reached at the convention, acceptance of the Constitution was by no means assured. It had to be submitted to the states for ratification. Supporters and opponents of the Constitution broke into two camps, **Federalists** and **Anti-Federalists**. Alexander Hamilton, James Madison, and John Jay wrote a series of newspaper articles supporting the Constitution, collectively known as *The Federalist Papers*. These essays are the primary source for understanding the original intent of the framers. They were designed to persuade the states of the wisdom of a strong central government coupled with autonomous political power retained by the states.

The Anti-Federalists opposed the creation of a stronger national government, arguing that a Constitution would threaten citizens' personal liberties and effectively make the president a king. Keep in mind that only 12 years prior, these people had declared independence from Britain, and many were fearful that a large government would recreate that same state of tyrannical control from which they had just escaped.

The opposition to the Constitution centered on the lack of a **Bill of Rights** that would protect the rights of individuals from government infringement. Once the Federalists guaranteed that a Bill of Rights would be added to the Constitution immediately after ratification, opposition diminished, and the Constitution became the foundation of American government.

The Constitutional Convention also led to the creation of the **Electoral College**, which was originally created because the Founding Fathers did not believe that citizens were educated enough to choose a president of a high caliber. Furthermore, the Founding Fathers believed that the Electoral College would safeguard against the influence of small groups and ensure that states with larger populations did not completely overshadow states with smaller populations.

Compromises, Compromises
Each state had its own interests to pursue and protect, which led to some key issues being temporarily tabled so as to ratify the Constitution. For instance, despite moral objections, delegates at the Constitutional Convention agreed that the international slave trade could not be ended until at least 1808. And while Southern states—which heavily relied on foreign trade—opposed tariffs being placed by Congress on exported goods, they did concede a tax on imports, something that would be a major issue of contention down the road when determining states' rights.

Did You Know?
Only five times in history have presidential candidates won the popular vote, but lost the Electoral College. The last time this occurred was in 2016, when Hillary Clinton won the popular vote by over two million votes, but Donald Trump won the Electoral College by 77 votes.

Still used today, although hotly debated, the electoral college is composed of elected officials from each state, based on the given state's population, for a total of 538 electors. Each state is given two votes for the two U.S. senators and one vote for every member the state has in the House of Representatives. For example, Texas has 38 votes in the Electoral College, while Maine has four electoral votes. Each state's political parties choose their own slate of potential electors. In modern elections, the presidential candidate who receives 270 electoral votes first wins the election—regardless of the popular vote.

The Federalist Papers and Anti-Federalist Dissent

Brutus No. 1

Basic Philosophy—Brutus No. 1 was the first publication that began the series of essays known as the *Federalist* and *Anti-Federalist Papers*. In Brutus No. 1, the anonymous author posed a series of questions about and critiques of the then-proposed Constitution. The main critiques included that the proposed national government had too much power, a standing army could diminish liberty, and representatives would not truly represent the people.

Major Dissent—*The Federalist Papers* were an attempt to answer the questions and assuage the concerns posed by Brutus and other Anti-Federalist writers.

Federalist No. 10

Basic Philosophy—James Madison addressed the dangers of factionalism and how to protect minority factions in a nation founded on majority rule. Madison argued that a large republic ensures multiple factions so as to avoid any one faction taking control, which could lead to a suppression of minority opinion.

Major Dissent—Anti-Federalists argued that Madison's claims were naïve, as a nation with multiple factions would never form the "perfect union" proclaimed in the Constitution. Anti-Federalists believed that no nation larger than one of the states could survive for long. They believed that states' separate interests would tear them apart, as happened during the American Civil War.

Federalist No. 51

Basic Philosophy—James Madison argued that separation of powers and checks and balances would guarantee that no one faction would take total control of the national government. Also, separation of powers would make the national government more efficient, as each branch had specific responsibilities.

Major Dissent—Anti-Federalists claimed that there was no perfect way to separate powers and that, eventually, one branch of government would hold more power.

You can read Brutus No. 1 in full at teachingamericanhistory. org/document/brutus-i.

You can read Federalist No. 10 in full at teachingamericanhistory. org/document/ federalist-no-10/.

You can read Federalist No. 51 in full at teachingamericanhistory. org/document/ federalist-no-51/.

Federalist No. 70

Basic Philosophy—Alexander Hamilton argued that the executive branch should consist of a single person, a president. Hamilton looked to the British monarchy as an example; the king had significant power but was checked by the House of Commons. Hamilton went a step further by proposing term limits as another check on the executive's power. (Term limits were not set until the ratification of the Twenty-Second Amendment in 1951.)

Major Dissent—Anti-Federalist critics claimed that with executive power vested in one person, only the president's "minions" would influence him. Other Anti-Federalists were alarmed at the prospect of giving control of the military to a single person.

You can read Federalist No. 70 in full at teachingamericanhistory. org/document/ federalist-no-70/.

Federalist No. 78

Basic Philosophy—Alexander Hamilton addressed Anti-Federalist critiques on the power of the federal judiciary by arguing that under the Constitution, the judicial branch would have the least amount of power. Even so, Hamilton reaffirmed that the Judicial Branch would have the power of judicial review, acting as a check on Congress.

Major Dissent—Anti-Federalists argued that a federal judiciary would overshadow the states' judicial systems, making state courts all but powerless. Also, Anti-Federalists claimed that federal judges' lifetime appointments could lead to corruption.

You can read Federalist No. 78 in full at teachingamericanhistory. org/document/ federalist-no-78/.

THE CONSTITUTION AS AN INSTRUMENT OF GOVERNMENT

The Constitution is vague and skeletal in form, containing only about 5,000 words. It was intended to be a blueprint for the structure of government and a guide for guaranteeing the rights of citizens. It was written to allow change, anticipating unknown needs of future generations, through amendments that require widespread support. The branches of government have all grown and evolved since the ratification of the Constitution.

You can find the full text of the Constitution in this book (page 281).

- The first three articles of the Constitution set up the threefold separation of powers that are the **legislative**, **executive**, and **judicial branches**. More on that in a few pages.

- The **necessary and proper clause** of the Constitution (Article I, Section 8) allows Congress to "make all laws" that appear "necessary and proper" to implement its delegated powers. This is also called the **elastic clause.** For example, there is nothing in the Constitution that creates the Federal Reserve System, which is the central bank for the United States. Neither is there any mention of a cabinet in the executive branch. The Federal District Courts and the Courts of Appeals were both created by congressional elaboration.

- The Constitution states, "The executive power shall be vested in a President of the United States of America." This statement has given presidents the power to issue **executive orders,** which have the same effect as law and bypass Congress in policy making. Executive orders are not mentioned in the Constitution. Presidents use this power as part of the enforcement duties of the executive branch. **Executive agreements** between heads of countries have many of the same elements as treaties. These agreements bypass the ratification power of the Senate but are not mentioned in the Constitution. An extreme example of an executive order is Executive Order 9066, in which Franklin D. Roosevelt ordered people removed from a military zone. It was no coincidence that these people were Japanese American and German American. This order paved the way for all Japanese Americans on the West Coast to be sent to internment camps for the duration of World War II. A much smaller number of German Americans and Italian Americans were also sent to internment camps under executive order.

- When the Supreme Court decided the case of *Marbury v. Madison* in 1803, it drastically increased its own power by granting itself the ability to overturn laws passed by the legislature. This new power came to be known as **judicial review.**

- Finally, custom and usage have changed the system to meet differing needs. The political party system, with its organization, technology, and fundraising capabilities, was created from custom and usage. The rules used in Congress were also created from custom and usage.

Federalism

Central to the Constitution is the idea that the United States government is a federal government. The term federalism describes a system of government under which the national government and local governments (state governments, in the case of the United States) share powers. Other federal governments include those of Germany, Switzerland, and Australia. Contrast this with a **confederation**, a system in which many decisions are made by an external member-state legislation; decisions on day-to-day matters are not taken by simple majority but by special majorities, consensus, or unanimity—and changes to the Constitution require unanimity. But let's get back to federalism for now.

The Supreme Court (which we'll discuss in depth later) handed down a few important decisions concerning the relationship between the national government and local governments. Know these two, in particular, for your exam:

- **Essential Case:** *McCulloch v. Maryland* **(1819)**   The court ruled that the states did not have the power to tax the national bank (and, by extension, the federal government). This decision reinforced the supremacy clause of the Constitution, which states that the Constitution "and the laws of the United States which shall be made in pursuance thereof . . . shall be the supreme law of the land; and the judges in every state shall be bound thereby, anything in the Constitution or laws of any State to the contrary notwithstanding." In short, the court both ruled that Congress has implied powers necessary to implement its enumerated powers and established the supremacy of the Constitution and federal laws over state laws.

- **Essential Case:** *United States v. Lopez* **(1995)**   The case arose after a challenge to the Gun-Free School Zones Act of 1990, which banned the possession of handguns on school property. The Court held that the commerce clause did not extend to the regulation of the carrying of handguns. This ruling marked a new phase of federalism, in which the importance of state sovereignty and local control was emphasized.

Powers Under Federalism

Delegated, or Enumerated, Powers

Delegated, or **enumerated**, **powers** are those that belong to the national government only. These powers include

- printing money
- regulating interstate and international trade
- making treaties and conducting foreign policy
- declaring war
- establishing post offices
- establishing lower courts
- establishing rules of naturalization
- establishing copyright and patent laws
- raising and supporting armed forces
- making all laws "necessary and proper" to carry out responsibilities

The Tenth Amendment

The Tenth Amendment defines the relationship between the states and the national government under the concept of federalism. It states that when powers are not de-fined or delegated by the Constitution, the states have reserved power to make their own individual judgments—so long as they do not infringe on the explicit rules of the Constitution and the federal government. State issues such as the death penalty, speed limit, and drinking age are within the jurisdiction of the states to decide so long as they do not contradict the Constitution.

Reserved Powers

Powers that belong exclusively to the states are called **reserved powers**. According to the **Tenth Amendment**, these powers include any that the Constitution neither specifically grants to the national government nor denies to the state governments. These powers are not listed in the Constitution; in fact, they are made up of all powers not mentioned in the Constitution. These powers include

- o   issuing licenses
- o   regulating intrastate business (business within a state)
- o   conducting elections
- o   establishing local governments
- o   maintaining a justice system
- o   educating residents
- o   maintaining a militia (National Guard)
- o   providing public health, safety, and welfare programs

Concurrent Powers

Concurrent powers are those that are shared by federal and state governments. These powers include

- o   levying and collecting taxes
- o   building roads
- o   operating courts of law
- o   establishing courts
- o   chartering banks and corporations
- o   eminent domain
- o   paying debts and borrowing money

The Constitution specifies which powers are denied to the national government and which powers are denied to the states. Those powers are listed on the next page.

The Constitution also obliges the federal government to guarantee the states a republican form of government and protection against foreign invasion and domestic rebellion. The federal government must also prevent the states from subdividing or combining to form new states without congressional consent. The states, in turn, are required by the Constitution to accept the court judgments, licenses, contracts, and other civil acts of all the other states.

The precedent set by *McCulloch v. Maryland* requires conflicts between federal law and state law to be resolved in favor of federal law. State laws that violate the Constitution, federal laws, or international treaties can be invalidated through the supremacy clause.

The nature of federalism has changed over time. For the first part of the nation's history, the federal and state governments remained separate and independent. What little contact most Americans had with the government occurred on the state level, as the national government concerned itself primarily with international trade; the construction of roads, harbors, and railways; and the distribution of public land in the West.

The Federal Government Does Not Have the Power to	**The State Governments Do Not Have the Power to**
• suspend the writ of *habeas corpus* (which protects against illegal imprisonment), except in times of national crisis • pass *ex post facto* (retroactive) laws or issuance of bills of attainder (which declare an individual guilty of a capital offense without a trial) • impose export taxes • use money from the treasury without the passage and approval of an appropriations bill • grant titles of nobility	• enter into treaties with foreign countries • declare war • maintain a standing army • print money • pass *ex post facto* (retroactive) laws or issuance of bills of attainder (which declare an individual guilty of a capital offense without a trial) • grant titles of nobility • impose import or export duties

Most federal government programs—such as those to aid the poor, clean the environment, improve education, and protect those with disabilities—are administered through the states. The federal government pays for these programs through grants-in-aid, which are outright gifts of money to the states. Some politicians prefer to tie strings to the grants, ensuring that the federal government maintains control over the money. Others want no strings attached, leaving decisions about how the grant money is to be used to state and local governments, who they believe know how best to spend it.

Those who favor federal power like **categorical grants**, which are a form of aid with strict provisions from the federal government on how it may be spent. Those committed to states' rights like **block grants**, which permit the states to experiment and use the money as they see fit. In the final analysis, however, the federal government can use a number of techniques, including direct orders and preemption, to force the states to abide by federal law. The federal government can also use a crossover sanction, which requires a state to do something before a grant will be awarded. An example would be to raise the drinking age to 21 before federal highway money to build state roads is released.

Types of Grants
Examples of categorical grants include Head Start, Medicaid, and SNAP. Examples of block grants include Temporary Assistance for Needy Families (TANF), often referred to as welfare, the Community Development Block Grant, and the Social Services Block Grant. Remember that block grants have a broad range of eligible activities typically addressing a general problem area.

Advantages of Federalism

- Mass participation: Constituents of all ages, backgrounds, races, and religions can participate by voting on both local and national issues.
- Regional autonomy: States retain some rights and have choices about public policy issues such as gun control, property rights, abortion, and euthanasia.
- Government at many levels: Politicians are in touch with the concerns of their constituents.
- Innovative methods: States can be laboratories for government experimentation, to see whether policies are feasible.
- Diffusion of Power: Due to the separation of powers, it is difficult for a single political party or interest group to dominate all branches of government.
- Diversity: The electoral process allows for diverse populations to participate in the democratic process and hold positions of power in government.

Disadvantages of Federalism

- Lack of consistency: Differing policies on issues like gun control, capital punishment, and local taxes can clog the court system and create inequality in states.
- Inefficiency: Federalism can lead to duplication of government and inefficient, overlapping, or contradictory policies in different parts of the country.
- Bureaucracy: Power can be spread out among so many groups that it can result in corruption and a stalemate.
- Resistance: National unity is hard to both achieve and maintain, and state governments may be resistant to national policies.
- Inequity: Federalism can lead to legislation and judicial outcomes that lead to both economic and racial inequity.

Separation of Powers

The framers of the Constitution decided that no one faction of the government should be able to acquire too much power. To prevent this, they borrowed the concept of the **separation of powers** from the French political philosopher Charles de Montesquieu. The framers delegated different but equally important tasks to the three branches of government. The legislative branch (Congress) makes the laws; the executive branch, led by the president, enforces the laws; and the judicial branch interprets the laws.

Separation of powers also prevents a person from serving in more than one branch of the government at the same time. For example, a congressperson (legislative branch) may not simultaneously be either a judge (judicial branch) or a cabinet member (executive branch). If a congressperson were appointed to one of these positions, they would first have to resign their seat in Congress.

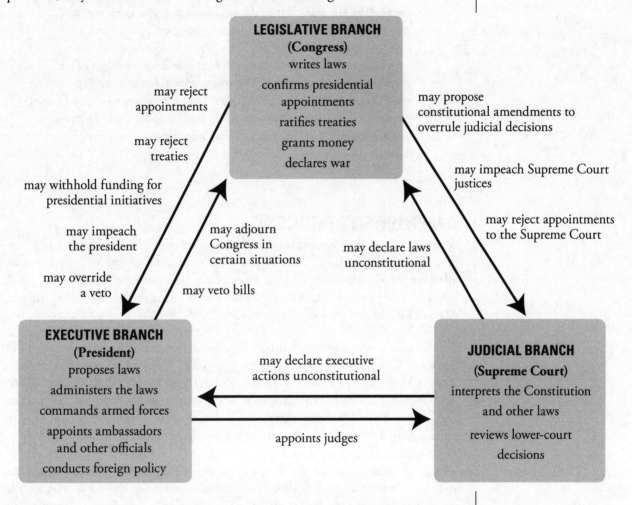

The System of Checks and Balances

The system of **checks and balances** is another constitutional safeguard designed to prevent any one branch of government from becoming dominant. The system of checks and balances requires the different branches of government to share power and cooperate with one another to accomplish anything of importance.

- **Nomination of federal judges, cabinet officials, and ambassadors.** The president chooses nominees for these positions. However, the president's nominees must be approved by the Senate.

- **Negotiation of treaties.** The president is empowered to negotiate treaties. No treaty can go into effect, however, until it is approved by two-thirds of the Senate.

Under "Enactment of legislation," to the right, note the use of the word *encourages*. As can be seen with regards to President Obama's support of the Affordable Care Act, the legislative bodies still have the freedom to choose their own approach to a law.

- **Enactment of legislation.** Only Congress may pass laws. However, the president has the power to **veto**, or reject, legislation. The president's veto power encourages the legislature to consider the president's position on a law, and to negotiate with the president to prevent a veto. Congress can also check the president's veto by **overriding** the veto, but to do so it must pass the same law with a two-thirds majority in both houses (a congressional override is difficult, but not impossible). If Congress succeeds in overriding the president's veto, the legislation becomes law regardless of the president's position. Finally, the courts may determine the constitutionality of the law. Thus, the courts have the power to overturn laws passed by Congress and approved by the president (only on constitutional grounds, however; judges may not overturn laws simply because they don't like them).

AMENDMENT PROCESS

One reason that the Constitution has lasted more than 200 years is that it is flexible. (Think of the elastic clause!) Many of its provisions require interpretation, allowing the document to become more conservative or progressive as the times warrant. Furthermore, the Constitution can be changed through **amendments** (the addition of provisions to the document).

To amend the Constitution, a proposed amendment must be introduced to both houses of Congress and approved by a two-thirds majority in each. The amendment is then passed on to each of the 50 state legislatures. Three-fourths of the state legislatures must **ratify** (approve) the amendment for it to become part of the Constitution. The states themselves are allowed to determine the number of votes required to ratify an amendment. Most states require a simple majority of their legislatures, but seven states require either three-fifths or two-thirds majorities. Also, rather than use the state legislatures, Congress can mandate that each state use a **ratifying convention**, with delegates expressly elected to vote on the proposed amendment. This method was once used to ratify the Twenty-First Amendment, which ended Prohibition in 1933.

The Constitution allows for a second means of amendment. Two-thirds of the state legislatures can petition Congress to call a constitutional convention. Because no constitutional convention has ever taken place, nobody knows for certain how extensively conventioneers would be allowed to alter the Constitution. Could they rewrite it entirely, or would they be restricted to amendments mentioned specifically in their petitions for a convention? Fear that a constitutional convention could attempt drastic alterations has persuaded many state legislators to oppose any call for a convention. There are ongoing movements in many states to call a constitutional convention to add a balanced budget amendment to the Constitution. While 29 state legislatures have approved a convention, the movement has not yet met the bar of 34 states required to call the convention.

Ways to Change the Constitution	Ways to Ratify the Change
• **Proposed amendment** wins $\frac{2}{3}$ majority in the House and Senate. • Used for all 27 amendments.	• $\frac{3}{4}$ of all state legislatures approve of the amendment. • Used 26 times (not for Twenty-First Amendment).
• A **constitutional convention** is called by $\frac{2}{3}$ of state legislatures. Any amendment can now be proposed at the convention. • This method has never been used.	• $\frac{3}{4}$ of special state-ratifying conventions approve the amendment. • Used only once, for the Twenty-First Amendment (repeal of prohibition).

STATE AND LOCAL GOVERNMENTS

The Constitution does not stipulate the form state governments must take. The states are instead free to form whatever governments they choose, provided that the government is defined by a state constitution and that the constitution is approved by Congress. However, most state governments are structured after the federal government.

All states have an executive branch led by a **governor**, whose duties to the state are similar to the president's duties to the nation. Governors direct state executive agencies, which oversee areas such as education, roads, and policing. They command the state National Guard and may grant **pardons** and **reprieves.** Most have the power to appoint state judges, with the "advice and consent" of one of the state's legislative bodies. Governors have veto power over acts of the state legislature.

All states but one have bicameral legislatures modeled after the House of Representatives and the Senate. In the same way that Congress enacts federal law, the state legislatures enact state law. The legislatures have the power to override the **gubernatorial veto** (the word *gubernatorial* means *relating to the governor*). Governors have many of the same executive powers as presidents. However, many governors may use a **line-item veto** to reject only parts of bills. Presidents were denied this power by the Supreme Court under the ruling that a federal line-item veto would take too much power away from the legislative branch.

All states also have state judiciaries to interpret state law. These judicial systems consist of trial courts and appeals courts, as does the federal judiciary. They hear both criminal cases (in which an individual is accused of a crime) and civil cases (in which disputing parties can sue to receive compensation).

An Exception
Nebraska has a unicameral legislature, meaning that the state has one legislative chamber or house.

CHAPTER 4 KEY TERMS

Thomas Hobbes
Leviathan
Social Contract
John Locke
Second Treatise on Civil Government
Charles de Montesquieu
De l'Esprit des Lois
Jean-Jacques Rousseau
The Social Contract
Voltaire
Candide
Denis Diderot
Participatory democracy
Pluralist democracy
Elite democracy
Representative democracy
Popular sovereignty
Articles of Confederation
Federalism
Northwest Ordinance
Shays' Rebellion
Constitution
Constitutional Convention
Unicameral
Bicameral
Virginia Plan
New Jersey Plan
The Great (Connecticut)
   Compromise
Three-Fifths Compromise
Federalists

Anti-Federalists
The Federalist Papers
Bill of Rights
Electoral College
Legislative branch
Executive branch
Judicial branch
Necessary and proper clause
   (elastic clause)
Executive orders
Executive agreements
Judicial review
Confederation
Delegated (enumerated) powers
Reserved powers
Tenth Amendment
Categorical grants
Block grants
Separation of powers
Checks and balances
Veto
Overriding
Amendments
Ratify
Ratifying convention
Governor
Pardons
Reprieves
Gubernatorial veto
Line-item veto

Chapter 4 Drill

See Chapter 9 for answers and explanations.

Questions 1 and 2 refer to the passage below.

The United States in Congress assembled shall never engage in a war, nor grant letters of marque or reprisal in time of peace, nor enter into any treaties or alliances, nor coin money, nor regulate the value thereof, nor ascertain the sums and expenses necessary for the defense and welfare of the United States, or any of them, nor emit bills, nor borrow money on the credit of the United States, nor appropriate money, nor agree upon the number of vessels of war, to be built or purchased, or the number of land or sea forces to be raised, nor appoint a commander in chief of the army or navy, unless nine States assent to the same.

—The Articles of Confederation, 1781

1. Which of the following statements best illustrates the central idea of this excerpt from the Articles of Confederation?

    (A) States kept their sovereignty under the Articles of Confederation.
    (B) States had the authority to declare war without the approval of the national government.
    (C) Congress was the only branch of government.
    (D) A majority of states had to agree on major decisions affecting the new nation.

2. The excerpt best supports which of the following arguments?

    (A) The Articles of Confederation created a strong national government.
    (B) The Articles of Confederation gave more power to Congress than to the states.
    (C) The Articles of Confederation created an inefficient national government.
    (D) The Articles of Confederation gave Congress a different set of powers than those in the Constitution.

3. Which of the following decided the issue of the representation of enslaved people?

    (A) Three-Fifths Compromise
    (B) Connecticut Compromise
    (C) Commerce and Slave-Trade Compromise
    (D) Bill of Rights

4. Which of the following is an accurate comparison between the New Jersey Plan and the Virginia Plan?

	Virginia Plan	New Jersey Plan
(A)	Equal representation in Congress	Representation in Congress based on population
(B)	Bicameral legislature	Unicameral legislature
(C)	Supported by smaller states	Supported by larger states
(D)	President elected by the people	President elected by the Electoral College

5. Which of the following is American federalism most clearly exemplified by?

    (A) A system of checks and balances among the three branches of the national government
    (B) A process by which international treaties are completed
    (C) The special constitutional status of Washington, D.C.
    (D) The Tenth Amendment to the Constitution

6. Which of the following statements best illustrates the significance of Shays' Rebellion in American history?

    (A) It led to the overthrow of British rule.
    (B) It terrified American elites, leading to the adoption of the Constitution.
    (C) It led to the enactment of slavery in the South.
    (D) It narrowly avoided overthrowing the government of Vermont.

7. Which of the following is NOT an enumerated power of the Constitution?

    (A) To declare war
    (B) To print money
    (C) To regulate interstate commerce
    (D) To levy and collect taxes

Summary

- Remember that the Articles of Confederation were ultimately too weak to serve as a viable governing constitution for the new nation.

- Know the important philosophers that influenced the framers: Hobbes, Locke, Montesquieu, and Rousseau.

- The Constitutional Convention in Philadelphia resulted in a new governing document that sought to balance the autonomy of the states with a stronger federal government.

- The vagueness of some sections of the Constitution, along with elements like the elastic clause, makes the document adaptable to changing times.

- The United States, through the Constitution, was the first nation to practice federalism: a balance of power between the states and the federal government.

- In keeping with the principles of Montesquieu, the Founders created a government split into three branches and gave each branch the power to check the other two.

- Many powers that are not formally declared in the Constitution have been taken on by the president and Congress—you should be aware of this "unwritten Constitution."

- Know a bit about how state and local governments function and how they interact with the federal government.

REFLECT

Respond to the following questions:

- Of which content topics discussed in this chapter do you feel you have achieved sufficient comprehension to answer multiple-choice questions correctly?

- Of which content topics discussed in this chapter do you feel you have achieved sufficient comprehension to discuss them effectively in an essay?

- On which content topics discussed in this chapter do you feel you need more work before you can answer multiple-choice questions correctly?

- On which content topics discussed in this chapter do you feel you need more work before you can discuss them effectively in an essay?

- Which parts of this chapter are you going to re-review?

- Will you seek further help, outside of this book (such as from a teacher, tutor, or AP Students), on any of the content in this chapter—and, if so, on what content?

Chapter 5
Interactions Among Branches of Government

"The accumulation of all powers, legislative, executive and judiciary, in the same hands, whether of one, a few, or many, and whether hereditary, self-appointed, or elected, may justly be pronounced the very definition of tyranny."

— James Madison

CONGRESS

Concepts

- Why do congressional incumbents have an advantage over challengers?
- Why did the Supreme Court strike down majority-minority voting districts?
- Why does Congress continue to maintain the seniority system?
- What is it about the way Congress operates that promotes factionalism?
- Why has it been argued that Congress contributes to the fragmentation of policy making?
- Why do we hate Congress but love our congressperson?
- Why would members of Congress vote against campaign finance reform?
- Why would members of the Senate engage in a filibuster?
- Why is the House Rules Committee so important?
- How does politics enter into the nomination process for independent agencies and the judiciary?
- What impact has the high cost of campaigning had on the legislative process?
- What are the powers of the leaders in the House and Senate?

Congressional Structure

Congress is the bicameral (two-house) legislature responsible for writing the laws of the nation. Congress also serves other functions, such as overseeing the bureaucracy, building consensus, clarifying and legitimizing policy, and representing diversity. It is made up of a **House of Representatives** of 435 members and a **Senate** of 100 members. The Senate is designed to represent states equally, with two senators elected from each state, while the House is designed to represent the state population, with the number of state representatives based on the population of the state.

Every 10 years, a **census** is taken by the federal government to count the population and determine the number of each state's **congressional districts**. Each state must then redraw its congressional boundaries to ensure that each district is equal in population. Congressional **redistricting** is done by each state legislature. Therefore, the political party in control of the state legislature controls how the districts are drawn. As much as is legally possible, the legislature will **gerrymander** the district boundaries to give the majority party an advantage in future elections. This is true in every state except Iowa and California, who use independent commissions to form districts. In some states, such as Alaska and Wyoming, the populations are so small that the entire state becomes a congressional district; all states are guaranteed at least one seat in the House.

Did You Know?

Gerrymandering leads to fewer competitive U.S. House districts and provides safety for incumbents following redistricting. Due to the lack of an independent redistricting committee, partisan distortions exist in both politically drawn and commissioned plans. Such aggressive gerrymandering makes elections far less competitive and leads to congressional chambers failing to represent the population.

Congressional Elections

Elections for all the 435 seats of the House of Representatives occur every two years. House members must reside in the district they represent, be a citizen of the state, and be at least 25 years old. Election to the House takes place within each congressional district. The constituencies of representatives are relatively small compared with those of senators, and the House incumbent election rates are very high, averaging more than 90%. Many House members have safe seats and are not seriously challenged for reelection.

Elections for one-third of the Senate occur every two years, with a senator's term lasting six years. Prospective senators must be at least 30 years old, must be U.S. citizens (at least 9 years), and must reside in their district. Every state is guaranteed two senators, elected on a staggered basis in statewide elections. Senate elections are generally more competitive, expensive, and high-profile. In addition, they often draw candidates from other elected offices.

Essential Case: *Baker v. Carr* (1962)

Facts: In 1960, Tennessee had not redrawn its state legislative districts since the turn of the century. Charles Baker sued the state as his county's population had grown considerably in that time without benefiting from increased representation in the state legislature. The defendant in the case was Tennessee's secretary of state.

Issue: Did Tennessee's refusal to redistrict violate the Fourteenth Amendment's guarantee of "equal protection of the law"? Lawyers representing Tennessee argued that redistricting was a state issue.

Holding: After nearly a year of deliberations, the Supreme Court ruled in a 6-2 decision that the federal government can force states to redistrict every 10 years after the national census. The ruling in this case facilitated the development of the "one person, one vote" doctrine and afforded federal courts the right to weigh in on legislative redistricting. Dissenting justices claimed that the ruling imperiled the separation of powers between the legislative and judicial branches.

Essential Case: *Shaw v. Reno* (1993)

Facts: After the 1990 national census, the federal government reapportioned seats in the House of Representatives to reflect changes in the population. The North Carolina legislature began to redraw its congressional map.

Issue: The proposal the North Carolina legislature submitted to the Department of Justice suggested that the state legislature was attempting to use gerrymandering to isolate African American voters into the 12th Congressional District. White voters living in the 12th sued. When a federal District Court dismissed their lawsuit, the case went to the Supreme Court.

Holding: In a 5-4 decision, the Supreme Court ruled that North Carolina's 12th Congressional District was a clear case of the state using racial bias in its congressional map. The court ruling held that claims of racial redistricting must be "held to a strict standard of scrutiny under the equal protection clause." Dissenting justices noted that it was not the court's place to make this determination, as the plaintiffs were not African American. North Carolina was forced to redraw its congressional map.

Congressional Districts and Representation

Descriptive representation means that the elected legislature should reflect the demographic characteristics of the constituency. Minorities and women have always been underrepresented in Congress and state legislatures, which is why the **Voting Rights Act of 1965** encouraged states to take measures to increase minority representation in Congress. Into the early 1980s, little progress had been made. Women and minority groups continued to be underrepresented. In 1982, Congress amended the Voting Rights Act to encourage states to create majority-minority districts, concentrating Black and Hispanic populations into distinct congressional districts. These districts were created to make it more feasible for minority candidates to get elected.

Following the 1990 census, many states redrew their congressional districts, which resulted in an increase of Black representation by 50% and Hispanic membership by 70%. Various districts were drawn to conform to the Voting Rights Act. However, the shape of these districts was sometimes quite bizarre. North Carolina District 12, for example, stretched in a narrow band 160 miles down Interstate Highway 85. A Duke University professor joined with four other white plaintiffs to challenge the constitutionality of District 12. In *Shaw v. Reno* (1993), the Supreme Court surprised many with a split decision. The court invalidated the district in question because its boundaries were neither contiguous nor compact and were drawn with the intent to discriminate through the use of racial gerrymandering. The court ruled that any racial gerrymandering by the state required a compelling state interest, and it did not see such a compelling interest in this district. On the other hand, the Supreme Court has heard other redistricting cases like this one, and has upheld the redistricting or simply declined to take the challenge. The following maps show how the individual counties voted for the 2012 and 2016 elections.

2012 Presidential Election Map by County

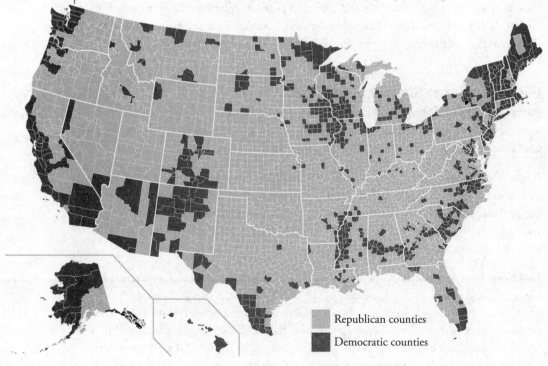

Republican counties

Democratic counties

2016 Presidential Election Map by County

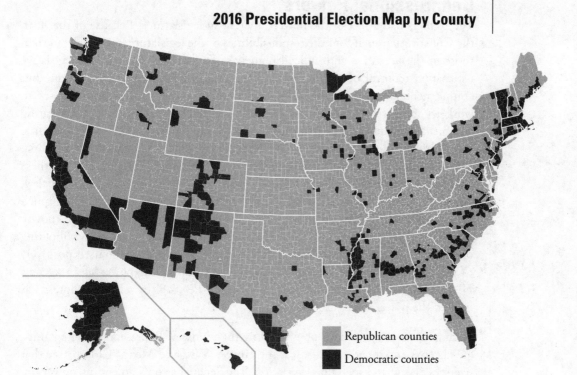

Republican counties

Democratic counties

Legislators in North Carolina, Georgia, Texas, and many other states have been accused of playing dirty politics with redistricting. Black and (to a lesser degree) Hispanic voters are overwhelmingly Democrat. (Cuban Americans in Florida tend to vote Republican.) Critics claim that Republican-controlled state legislatures were not motivated by any sense of duty. Instead, they stand accused of trying to remove racial-minority Democrats from other districts to ensure that more Republicans get elected. The political trade-off was to create a guaranteed Democratic district and at the same time gain more Republican seats from the surrounding districts.

Packing and Cracking
Isolating minorities in the district is known as "packing." Dividing them across many districts is "cracking."

To add to the representation controversy, population shifts in the last 20 years have given additional seats in the House to Southern states while reducing the number from other regions. In addition, suburban representation has increased, at the expense of both rural and urban areas.

Hijacking and Kidnapping
"Hijacking" redraws two districts in a way that forces two incumbents to oppose each other in a single district when redistricting. "Kidnapping" moves an incumbent's home address into another district when redistricting.

Finally, Congress draws its members primarily from the legal and business worlds. Almost half of the members in the House and more than half of the members in the Senate have a legal background. The reason seems to be that lawyers have many of the prerequisites needed for a successful run for Congress: interest and experience in the law, prominence within the community, and the personal wealth to at least partially fund an election campaign.

Congressional Powers

The framers had a fear of the power inherent in legislatures. Because of that fear, the Constitution spells out the responsibilities of the legislature in more detail than those of the executive and judicial branches. To further guard against legislative usurpation (control of one house over the other), both houses have unique but complementary powers. The delegated powers, which require both houses to work in concert with each other, include taxing, borrowing money, regulating commerce, raising an army, creating and making rules for the federal courts, establishing naturalization laws, establishing post offices, providing for a militia, and making any law that is deemed necessary and proper for carrying out these powers. In Article I, Section 9, Clause 7 (the appropriations clause) and Article I, Section 8, Clause 1 (the taxing and spending clause), the Congress is given much control over **budgetary** spending. The **power of the purse**, as this is known, gives Congress power to influence the president or bureaucrats by withholding or putting conditions on funding. The power of the purse can be used positively to promote certain programs or negatively to diminish the power of an agency. Historically, the power of the purse has been a key tool by which Congress has limited the power of the executive branch.

Each house also has unique powers. Only the House of Representatives may initiate tax laws and spending bills. It is the **House Ways and Means Committee** that oversees taxing and spending legislation. The Senate has only amending powers on revenue bills.

The Senate's unique powers include confirmation of presidential nominations to the federal courts and ambassadorships to foreign countries. The Senate must also ratify all treaties signed by the president.

The Nonlegislative Tasks of Congress

Congress's primary responsibility is to fulfill the legal needs of the nation by writing laws. However, Congress also performs other equally important functions. These include the following:

- **Oversight.** Through its committees and subcommittees, Congress reviews the work of the federal agencies. This helps check the executive branch. It investigates charges of corruption and waste, and it holds **hearings** in which experts and citizens discuss the government's problems and suggest solutions. All committee chairs have the power to subpoena (legally compel) witnesses to appear and testify. It is also the role of the Senate to confirm the members of the president's cabinet as well as to approve nominees for all positions in the federal court system.

- **Public education.** Committee hearings and floor debates increase public awareness of government and societal problems. Floor debates over issues such as gun control, tax cuts, Social Security reform, health care reform, and sending armed troops abroad all help to focus national attention.

- **Representing constituents within the government.** As representatives of their electorates, also known as **politicos,** members of Congress not only vote on laws but also help constituents in their dealings with the government. They receive and can act on complaints about federal services, sponsor voters who seek scholarships or federal contracts, and solicit constituents' suggestions on how to improve the government. In performing this last task, some members of Congress consider themselves **delegates** whose job it is to mirror the views of their home districts. This is known as the **Delegate Model** or representational view. Others see themselves as trustees who should consider their constituents' views but should ultimately use their best judgment as experts when deciding how to vote. This is known as the **Trustee Model** or attitudinal view.

- **Constitutional Amendments.** Congress has the power to propose Constitutional Amendments by a two-thirds vote in both the House and the Senate. Alternatively, amendments can be proposed by a convention called by the legislatures of two-thirds of the states; however, such a convention has never been called.

- **Electoral Duties.** If neither candidate receives the required 270 Electoral College votes, the House may be called upon to elect the next president. Similarly, the Senate may be called upon to elect the Vice President in the same scenario.

- **Impeachment.** The House has exclusive power over impeachment, a formal accusation of misconduct in office. If the majority of the House votes to impeach a public official, the Senate conducts the impeachment trial of that official. If two-thirds of the Senate votes against the official, the official is convicted and removed from office.

- **Confirmation Duties.** The Senate holds the power to approve both presidential appointments and federal officials.

- **Ratification.** The Senate has exclusive power to ratify treaties between the U.S. and other nations. If two-thirds of the Senate votes affirmatively, a treaty is ratified. This power allows the Senate to influence foreign policy and international relations.

- **Investigation.** Investigations can be conducted by either a standing or select committee and may last for months as committee members gather evidence and schedule witnesses. The majority of investigations lead to new legislation to address the issue at hand, changes in government programs, or the removal of officials from office.

The insurrection that took place on January 6, 2021, was an attempt to halt the standard process and install a candidate who had not received 270 Electoral College votes (former President Donald Trump).

Did You Know?
Only three U.S. presidents have been formally impeached: Andrew Johnson, Bill Clinton, and Donald Trump. Only Donald Trump was impeached twice during his single term in office.

No U.S. president, however, has ever been removed from office through impeachment.

The Legislative Process

The legislative process is, by design, slow and complicated. This is to prevent Congress from acting hastily. The framers intended for the process to foster compromise. The result has been that the final versions of bills are often radically different from the initial versions. Without compromise, there would be no legislative process.

As many as 10,000 bills are introduced on the floor of Congress each year. Some are written by members of Congress and their staffs; others are drafted by the executive branch and are introduced by a sympathetic member of Congress. Many are suggested or written by interest groups and their lawyers. Regardless of who authors a bill, a bill can be proposed only by a member of Congress. Whoever introduces a bill is called the **sponsor** of the bill.

The legislative process requires the two houses to work cooperatively with each other. All bills must pass both houses in exactly the same form. While the bills must be the same, the debate and voting processes in the two houses differ. Because there are 435 members of the House of Representatives, the process by which bills are debated is limited. The Senate, which is smaller, has fewer rules governing the legislative process.

Unlike the Senate, the House has a **Rules Committee,** which is responsible for determining how long a bill will be debated and whether to allow an open or closed rule for amending the bill. Open rules allow amendments; closed rules prohibit amendments. When Republicans gained control of the House of Representatives in 1994, they promised most bills would be debated under open rules. Allowing 435 members an opportunity to add amendments to bills became so cumbersome, however, that the House leadership returned to the closed rule process. Because the House Rules Committee controls crucial aspects of the legislative process, it is considered the most powerful committee in the House. The Rules Committee can kill a bill by delaying a vote or by making it easy for opponents to add **poison-pill** (or "**killer**") **amendments**. The House Rules Committee can also bring bills up for an immediate floor vote.

While the House strictly controls debate, the Senate does not. There are no time restraints placed on senators. A **filibuster** is a tactic used to delay a vote on a bill and tie up the work of the Senate, usually by a senator making a speech that continues for hours on the Senate floor. A filibuster can also happen without continuous speeches (the mere threat of filibuster now carries almost the same weight as an actual filibuster). The only way to end a filibuster is to vote for **cloture**, but this requires the votes of 60 members, which is difficult to achieve when the two parties are evenly represented.

Meat Lovers

"Bringing home the bacon" is one of the reasons incumbent reelection rates are so high. The members of both houses love pork-barrel legislation.

The Senate has no closed rules for amending legislation. Amendments, called riders, do not have to be relevant to a bill. This allows individual senators an opportunity to add amendments, such as "pet" issues or projects for their home state, or to prohibit the actions of executive agencies. "Pet project" riders designed to bring federal money to a home state are called **pork barrels. Earmarks**—provisions within legislation that appropriate money to a specific project—appear in appropriation bills and authorization bills. There are a few groups that monitor earmarking in the U.S. Congress, but earmarks are no longer allowed by the House.

After debates, bills usually end up passing the House and Senate in different forms, so both versions are sent to a **conference committee**. The members of these conference committees come from the respective committees of the two houses that wrote the bill. The conference committee tries to negotiate a compromise bill, acceptable to both houses of Congress. Once a compromise version has been written, the bill is returned to the two houses for a vote. Failure to pass a bill from a conference committee will kill a bill. If the bill is passed in both houses, it is sent to the White House for the president's signature.

The president has options. If the president does nothing for 10 days, the bill becomes law without their signature. However, there is an exception. If a congressional session ends during those 10 days, the president must sign every bill into law. If the president doesn't, the bill will be **pocket vetoed**, requiring that the bill go through the entire legislative process again. If there are more than 10 days left in a congressional session, and a president wants to prevent a bill from becoming law, they may veto the entire bill. The president returns the legislation to the house in which it originated, usually with a message explaining why (though an explanation isn't required).

At that point, Congress has choices. The two houses may make the required changes, or they may attempt to override the president's veto by a two-thirds vote. If the bill passes both houses by the required two-thirds vote, the bill becomes law without the president's signature. If the house of origination (where the bill was originally introduced) does nothing with the presidential veto, the bill is dead.

In 1996, Congress gave President Clinton the **line-item veto,** empowering the president to veto individual parts of a bill. The constitutionality of the line-item veto was immediately challenged in the Supreme Court (*Clinton v. City of New York*). The court struck down the line-item veto as an unconstitutional delegation of legislative authority to the president.

Congress has also attempted to give itself veto power over the actions of the president. In specific instances, Congress would write legislation giving the president broad powers to act but reserve the right to void presidential actions by a vote of one or both houses. This legislative veto was declared unconstitutional by the Supreme Court in *INS v. Chadha* (1983). The only form of veto mentioned in the Constitution is that used by the president.

More Than Just a Bill
A **signing statement** is a written message issued by the president when they sign a bill into law. The statements typically begin with "This bill, which I have signed today" and continue with several paragraphs of commentary. Signing statements have recently become controversial, having been used extensively by Presidents George W. Bush and Barack Obama. Critics fear that signing statements may function as attempts to modify the law or undermine the principle of separation of powers.

Clinton v. The City of New York and *INS v. Chadha* are not on the list of required court cases for the test.

The following chart summarizes the legislative process.

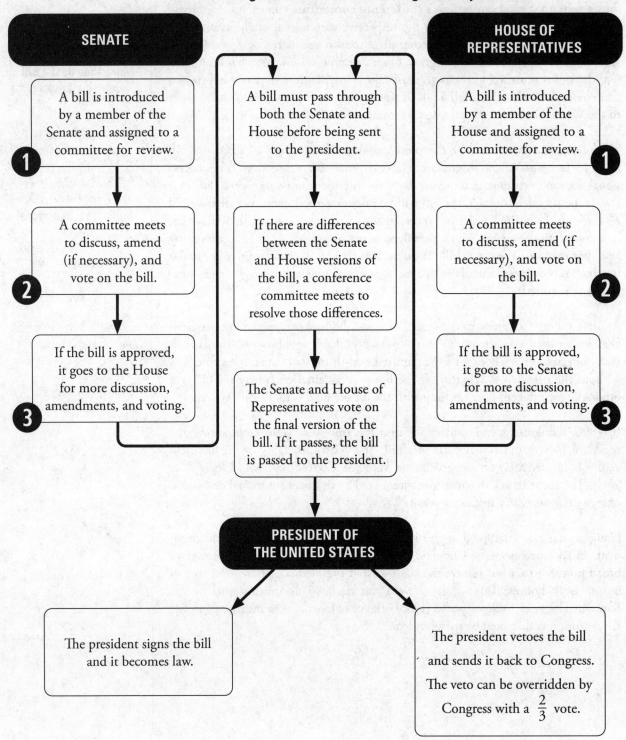

Legislation by Committee

Most of the legislative business of Congress occurs in committees. Who serves on which committee and what position they hold is determined by a number of factors. The majority party of each house holds all the committee chairs. The majority party will also hold a majority of the seats on each committee, effectively controlling all the business of the committee. On the important committees, the majority usually holds two-thirds of the committee seats.

Generally, the committee member of the majority party with the most seniority becomes the chair, and the senior member from the minority party becomes the ranking member. The ranking member becomes chair if the minority party becomes the majority party. This happened in 2001 when a member of the Republican-controlled Senate left the Republican Party to become an Independent. All Democrat ranking members of Senate committees became the chairs, while the Republican chairs became the ranking members. The same principle applies in the House of Representatives.

Committee assignments in the House and Senate are determined by the House and Senate leadership and a caucus of the two political parties. Members of Congress attempt to get on the committees that will allow them to do the most constituent service and help them get reelected. For example, representatives and senators from farm states try to get assigned to agriculture committees.

Committees serve as mini-legislatures, performing the tasks of investigating and debating bills that, due to time constraints, could never otherwise receive the consideration of Congress. Often, the congressional committee assigns the bill to an even smaller group, called a **subcommittee,** for initial consideration. Recently, there has been a proliferation of subcommittees. Subcommittees, which often determine how money is spent, have therefore become very powerful.

The fate of a new bill depends on much more than its content. The membership of the committee and subcommittee that first considers the bill is crucial. Bill sponsors attempt to draft bills in such a way as to steer them toward sympathetic committees. Supporters of a bill must also decide which house of Congress should consider their bill first, because with the exception of revenue bills, federal bills may originate in either house. To build political momentum, supporters attempt to have the bill introduced in the house most sympathetic to their cause.

The House has more committees than the Senate. House members, however, tend to become more specialized because they serve on fewer committees. As a result, they are considered to have more expertise than senators.

There are four types of committees in Congress.

1. **Standing committees** are permanent, specialized committees. Examples include the House Ways and Means Committee, the Senate Judiciary Committee, and the Senate Armed Services Committee. There are 20 standing committees in the House and 17 in the Senate.

2. **Joint committees** are made up of members of both the House and the Senate. These committees are normally used for communicating to the public or for investigations but generally do not send bills to the floor for votes.

3. **Select committees** are temporary committees organized in each house for some special purpose. These committees usually carry out investigations for the purpose of writing special legislation. The House Watergate Committee and the Senate Select Committee on Unfair Campaign Practices are examples from the Nixon era. The work of these committees eventually led to campaign reform.

4. **Conference committees** are temporary and include members from the committees of the two houses who were responsible for writing a bill. These committees try to negotiate compromise bills, which are then submitted to the two houses for an up or down vote without amendments. Once a compromise bill has been negotiated, the conference committee disbands.

Most bills die almost immediately in a subcommittee because of a lack of interest from committee members; unless a committee member takes a special interest in a bill, the bill will either be quickly rejected or ignored until it dies a natural death at the end of the congressional session. That is, a bill that is not enacted at any point in a two-year Congress dies when that Congress adjourns. It may be reintroduced in the next Congress with a new bill number.

Committees and subcommittees function by calling interested parties and expert witnesses who have some information to give. Lobbyists often testify as expert witnesses. Congress can subpoena reluctant witnesses, forcing them to appear in hearings, and can grant immunity to compel them to testify. Once their investigations have concluded, committees begin amending and rewriting sections of bills in meetings called markup sessions.

Committees will sometimes refuse to vote a bill out, hoping to keep it from being considered by the House. A bill stuck in a House or Senate committee is said to be **pigeonholed.** The parliamentary mechanism to force a bill out of committee for a floor vote is called a **discharge petition.**

Committees have responsibilities in addition to writing laws. For example, they are responsible for the oversight of many bureaucratic agencies and departments. Heads of regulatory agencies, which are responsible for enforcing the laws, often appear to give testimony before congressional committees with oversight jurisdiction. If the agency has not followed the intent of the law, the agency head will be in for a rough time. A recent example comes from a congressional investigation of the Secret Service and subsequent resignation by Director Julia Pierson after multiple security lapses involving President Obama and the White House. Congressional committees also have the power to subpoena witnesses, which legally orders individuals to appear or produce requested documents. Furthermore, these committees can require witnesses to testify under oath, and those who fail to tell the truth can be prosecuted for perjury, or lying under oath. If an individual fails to cooperate or submit to a subpoena request, the committee can either hold them in contempt or willful obstruction of Congress.

Committees also hear testimony from agency heads pleading for money and personnel. Congressional budget cutting and agency reorganization can have a profound impact on an agency's ability to carry out its responsibilities. This is one way that Congress can use the budget to shape policy.

Congressional Leadership

The House

The leader of the House of Representatives is the **Speaker**, who is chosen by the majority party in a special election. The Speaker is powerful because they can direct floor debate and have influence over committee assignments and over the Rules Committee. The Speaker can also control which bills go to which committees. The **majority leader** of the House keeps party members in line and helps determine party policy and the party's legislative agenda. The **minority leader** keeps the minority party members in line and helps determine the minority party's legislative agenda. The House majority and minority **whips** also help their respective party leaders keep the members loyal to the party's legislative agenda. They coordinate members of each party and help garner support for proposed legislation.

The Senate

The vice president is the president of the Senate, and this is their only constitutionally delegated responsibility. However, the vice president is rarely on the floor of the Senate and votes only to break a tie. When the vice president is absent during Senate sessions, the **president *pro tempore*** is the presiding officer. The president *pro tempore* is largely an honorary position and is usually given to the most senior member of the majority party of the Senate. The majority leader has the real power in the Senate because they control the legislative agenda and act as a power broker and policy initiator. The minority leader can act as a power broker but usually cannot initiate policy or control the agenda.

The Speaker of the House and Majority Leader of the Senate serve as spokespeople for their parties' positions on issues. Both are elected at the beginning of each Congress by members of their respective party.

To date, Nancy Pelosi has been the only woman elected to the Speaker of the House position, and there has not yet been an elected female Senate majority leader.

Why Do They Vote That Way?

Congresspersons are always cross-pressured to influence their vote. These pressures come from their own party and from the opposition. They also come from the president through jawboning (trying to influence) and from their colleagues by **logrolling** ("you help me on this bill, and I'll help you on yours"). Political Action Committees (also known as PACs) try to influence votes through contributions, as do constituents and interest groups. Personal ideology and religious beliefs can also impact a congressperson's judgment. The most important factor in determining the vote of a congressperson is party affiliation. Members of Congress usually—but not always—vote with their parties.

NOTABLE LEGISLATION

National Growth, Expansion, and Institution Building

- **Northwest Ordinance (1787, 1789).** One of the few successes of the Articles of Confederation, providing clear guidelines for the settlement of new territories and a path to statehood. Reaffirmed by Congress under the Constitution in 1789.

Regulation of Government and Industry

- **Pendleton Act (1883).** Eliminated the spoils system of patronage in selection for government jobs and set up an exam-based merit system for qualified candidates.

- **Sherman Anti-Trust Act (1890).** Provided Congress with authority to regulate and break up monopolies—or trusts—in the United States. Abused, however, to break up labor unions.

- **Hatch Act (1939).** Permitted government employees to vote in government elections but forbade them from participating in partisan politics.

- **Freedom of Information Act (1966).** Declassified government documents for public use.

- **Air Quality Act (1967) and various Clean Air Acts (1960s–1990s).** The beginning of a series of acts to regulate impacts on the environment by establishing emission standards for cars and factories.

- **Federal Election Campaign Acts (1971, 1974).** Established the Federal Election Commission and required disclosures of contributions and expenditures, as well as limitations on contributions and presidential election expenditures. Also provided subsidies for presidential candidates.

- **War Powers Act (1973).** Limited the president's power to use troops overseas in hostilities, put a time limit on use, and gave Congress final power to withdraw troops. Since 1973, every president, Democrat and

Republican, has claimed that the War Powers Act was not constitutional and has ignored it.

- **Budget and Impoundment Control Act (1974).** Established congressional budget committees and the Congressional Budget Office, as well as gave Congress the power to prevent the president from refusing to fund congressional initiatives (known as "impoundment").

- **Gramm-Rudman-Hollings Bill (1985).** Set budget reduction targets to balance the budget. Failed to eliminate loopholes.

- **Unfunded Mandates Reform Act (1995).** Requires the Congressional Budget Office to analyze the impact of unfunded mandates on the states, and it requires a separate congressional vote on bills that impose such unfunded mandates.

- **No Child Left Behind Act (2001).** Requires states to adopt education accountability standards, mandates annual progress testing of students, and sanctions schools that fail to meet adequate yearly progress goals.

Rights and Freedoms

- **Espionage Act (1917), Sedition Act (1918).** Severely curtailed the civil liberties of Americans during wartime and greatly increased the power of the federal government in controlling public activity. The Sedition Act was repealed by Congress in 1921.

- **Immigration Act (1924).** This law stringently limited the number of immigrants admitted into the United States and set strict quotas for entry.

- **Voting Rights Act (1965).** Suspended literacy tests, empowered federal officials to register voters, and prohibited states from changing voting procedures without federal permission. Also empowered federal officials to count ballots and to ensure that citizens could vote.

- **Age Discrimination in Employment Act (1967).** Banned age discrimination in jobs unless age is related to job performance.

- **Civil Rights Act** or **Fair Housing Act (1968).** Title II banned discrimination in public places on the basis of race, color, national origin, or religion. Title VII prohibited employment discrimination based on gender.

- **Title IX Education Act (1972).** Prohibited gender discrimination in federally funded education programs.

- **Americans with Disabilities Act (1990).** Protected civil liberties of disabled Americans and mandated "reasonable accommodations" to public facility use. Bans job discrimination if reasonable accommodation can be made, requires access to facilities for disabled persons, and permits non-paid leave of absence, in certain situations, without fear of employer termination.

- **National Voter Registration Act (1993).** Also known as **The Motor Voter Act**, this law allowed people to register to vote when applying for driver's licenses.

- **Patriot Act (2001).** In response to the terrorist attacks of September 11, 2001, Congress granted broad police authority to the federal, state, and local government to interdict, prosecute, and convict suspected terrorists. This law is formally known as the USA-PATRIOT Act, an acronym for "Uniting and Strengthening America by Providing Appropriate Tools Required to Intercept and Obstruct Terrorism."

Government Aid to the People

- **New Deal Legislation (1933–1939).** Legislation that expanded the role of government in the economy and society. Created entities like Social Security, the Securities and Exchange Commission, and the Tennessee Valley Authority. These laws also dramatically expanded the role and size of the federal government.

- **Personal Responsibility and Work Opportunity Reconciliation Act (1996).** The Welfare Reform Act signaled a change in the role of the federal government in its relationship with the states. This law sought to increase the role of personal responsibility in welfare recipients and shifted many responsibilities for welfare provision to state governments. It ended the federal entitlement status of welfare, replacing it with block grants to states to administer welfare. Recipients of these grants must work within two years and cannot receive benefits for more than five years.

- **Bipartisan Campaign Reform Act (2002).** Often known as the **McCain-Feingold Bill**, this law banned soft money contributions to national political parties and raised hard money limits to $2,000. In a controversial decision in the case of *Citizens United v. Federal Election Commission* (2010), the Supreme Court struck down several provisions in this law, especially those related to contributions made by corporations to political campaigns.

THE PRESIDENT

Concepts

Want to read more? Article II, Section 2 of the Constitution discusses the power of the executive branch and the president. Turn to page 287 to read it in full.

- How do presidents use their formal and informal powers to get their legislative agenda passed?
- How can Congress curb the foreign policy-making powers of the president?
- How does the president use the appointment power to ensure that policies are carried out?
- What techniques can presidents use to promote their legislative agendas in the face of divided government?
- What impact does the White House staff have on policy making?
- Why would Congress give the president a line-item veto?
- Do executive agreements go against the intent of the framers of the Constitution?

The Formal Powers of the Presidency

The powers delegated by the Constitution to the executive branch are in Article II, Section 2, but they are less specific than the formal powers of Congress. The broadly defined powers were intended to give flexibility, but they have instead resulted in greatly expanded power.

> ### Chief of State
> While primarily a ceremonial role, the President serves as the embodiment of America and the head spokesperson for the United States. As a key actor in international events and a host to foreign emissaries, the President is the ultimate representative of the nation.

The president is responsible for enforcing the laws, handling **foreign policy**, and serving as the ceremonial head of state. They are also the administrative head of the government. They can force Congress into session, must brief Congress on the State of the Union, and can veto legislation, as well as grant reprieves and pardons. But regardless of these expansive powers, they must cooperate with Congress because the powers of the presidency are intermingled with the powers of the legislature. The president's appointments of federal judges, Supreme Court justices, ambassadors, and department secretaries all require Senate approval. The president negotiates treaties, but they must be ratified by two-thirds of the Senate. Because Senate ratification is sometimes difficult to achieve—a good example is the defeat of the Treaty of Versailles in 1919—the broad powers of the president to initiate foreign policy came to include **executive agreements** (which do not require Senate approval). These are agreements between heads of countries; under international and U.S. law, they are as binding as a treaty. However, executive agreements usually deal with more routine, administrative matters.

The President as Commander in Chief

The president also serves as **commander in chief** of the armed forces. But the framers created a complex institutional situation regarding armed conflict. Only Congress has the power to declare war, but only the president can make war. The President can mobilize the armed forces at their command, and first strike abilities are not subject to checks and balances by any other branch of government. The last official declaration of war by Congress was against Bulgaria, Hungary, and Romania during World War II. While the United States has involved itself in numerous armed conflicts since that time, no formal declarations of war were ever made.

> ### Presidential Powers in Wartime
> In the post-Vietnam War era, Congress has attempted to place controls on the war-making powers of the president. Congress passed the **War Powers Act** in 1973 in an attempt to force the president to seek congressional approval before making war. The act specifically limits the president to 10,000 troops for 60 days, with 30 additional days to withdraw the troops, unless Congress grants an extension or declares war. The Supreme Court has never ruled on the War Powers Act, and Congress has never invoked it, although whenever the president commits troops overseas, members of Congress have threatened the president with imposition of the War Powers Act.

While the president is the chief strategist and director of the military forces of the United States, they are at at the mercy of Congress for the money to wage war. However, once the president has committed troops in a conflict, it is unlikely that Congress would refuse to fund the weapons needed for the military. For members of Congress, such an action would be potentially career-ending and probably lead to a constitutional crisis within the U.S. government.

In a national crisis, the other branches of government and the American people look to the president for leadership. Initially, presidents will have strong support for their policies. This helps explain why Congress, in 1964, passed the **Gulf of Tonkin Resolution,** giving the president the broad powers to commit unlimited numbers of troops for an unlimited length of time in the Vietnam conflict. President Johnson was unable to bring that war to a conclusion. Strong criticism of his handling of the war led to a general lack of support for his policies, undermining his ability to govern. The same thing happened to President Carter when he was unable to successfully end the Iranian hostage crisis. As president during the Gulf War, George H. W. Bush's ability to quickly bring the war to a conclusion while suffering relatively few casualties resulted in the second-highest approval rating of any president, at 89%.

The Informal Powers

The presidential powers that are not enumerated in the Constitution are referred to as the informal powers, and they are sometimes more important than the formal ones. How well presidents use the informal powers can determine the success of their presidencies.

Chief of Party

While political parties are never mentioned in the Constitution, they play an undeniable and important role in the U.S. political system. The president, who holds the ultimate political position, has tremendous influence on their political party's issues, agenda, policy, electoral strategy, and overall direction. In this role, the president also acts as a key fundraiser, raising money for candidates across the country who align with their party's views.

When the president and the majorities in both the House and Senate are of the same political party, it is referred to as a **unified government**. When the president and the majorities in both the House and Senate are not of the same political party, it is referred to as a **divided government**.

Presidents are supposed to be morale builders. President Carter's failure to improve the morale of the country contributed to his reelection defeat. President Reagan was an expert at morale building, and this characteristic helps explain why he remained popular with the American people.

Presidents serve as legislative leaders and coalition builders. Failure to set and lead the legislative agenda and build coalitions in Congress can doom presidents, particularly when there is divided government (when one or both houses of the legislature are controlled by the opposition party). George H. W. Bush became the "foreign policy president" when he was unable to get his domestic policy agenda passed in a Democrat-controlled Congress. Ronald Reagan and his advisers were experts in building coalitions with Republicans and southern conservative Democrats. This coalition of Republicans and southern Democrats gave Reagan his legislative agenda.

Perhaps the president's most important informal powers are as a policy persuader and communicator to Congress and the American people. Clinton and Reagan were superior communicators. The ability of a president to communicate well with the American people by way of the **bully pulpit** is a very powerful tool for pressuring Congress. Communicating with Congress is also important. Having the congressional leadership down to the White House for lunch and a photo op is another way that presidents try to persuade members of Congress to pass their legislative agendas.

Executive Office of the President

The Executive Office of the President helps carry out the president's administrative responsibilities. It is made up of more than half a dozen agencies involved in the day-to-day operations of the White House and is basically divided into three areas: domestic, foreign, and military affairs. It is staffed by hundreds of personnel located in the White House and the Executive Office Building. All are directly responsible to the president or their designees.

- The **chief of staff** is the top aide to the president. They are a person in whom the president has complete trust and are probably a longtime associate and friend. Considered one of the most powerful persons in Washington, the chief of staff is responsible for managing the Executive Office and can control access to the president, thus potentially controlling the information that the president receives. Some presidents, such as Bill Clinton, permitted easy access; others, such as Richard Nixon, tended to insulate themselves. Whomever the president chooses as chief of staff can have a tremendous impact on presidential effectiveness. Clinton's first chief of staff, Thomas McClarty, a Washington outsider and Clinton friend, ran an undisciplined White House, prone to many errors. He was replaced by a Washington insider, former Congressperson Leon Panetta, who established order and discipline, emerging as a key policy player in the Clinton administration. In 2009, Panetta became Director of the Central Intelligence Agency. He later resigned from that post to become Secretary of Defense. In 2010, Barack Obama's first chief of staff, former Congressperson Rahm Emanuel, left the position to run for mayor of Chicago, an election he won.

There are a few theories that exist about how the president can choose to exercise their power.

According to the **literalist doctrine**, the president only has the powers that are specifically stated in Article II of the Constitution. This doctrine holds that the president should not exercise any power that is not granted by the Constitution, giving the president and executive branch only limited power. Since the 1920s, this doctrine has not been followed by any president.

The **stewardship doctrine** provides the president the ability to exercise power in multiple ways and multiple arenas. According to this doctrine, the president is free to exercise any power unless it is specifically prohibited by the Constitution. The stewardship doctrine increases the power of the presidency significantly and allows the president to influence vast portions of public policy.

A more controversial view is held in the **unitary executive theory**, which affords the president and executive branch virtually unlimited power. This theory provides the president with complete power within the executive branch to develop rules and policies as they deem necessary.

- **The National Security Council (NSC)** is headed by the national security advisor, who has direct access to the president in matters relating to military and foreign policy. The NSC has been involved since the late 1940s in the decision-making process during national emergencies. President Kennedy used the NSC during the Cuban missile crisis, President Reagan during the Iran-Contra affair, and President George H. W. Bush during the Gulf War. Unlike the State Department, the NSC is largely free from congressional oversight. For this reason, it has become one of the most favored institutions for many presidents.

- **The Domestic Policy Council** assists the president in formulating policies relating to energy, education, agriculture, natural resources, economic affairs, health and human resources, welfare reform, drug abuse, and crime.

- **The Office of Management and Budget (OMB)** is responsible for preparing the budget of the United States and can be used to control and manage the executive agencies for the president. The OMB has enormous power because of its ability to allocate money to the cabinet departments through the budget process of the executive branch. Increasing or decreasing a department's budget affects how it carries out its responsibilities.

- **The Council of Economic Advisors** is responsible for helping the president make national economic policy. The council is usually made up of economists who advise the president on policies that are designed to increase prosperity.

- **The U.S. Trade Representative** is responsible for negotiating complex trade and tariff agreements for the president. Trade agreements such as GATT (the General Agreement on Tariffs and Trade) and USMCA (United States-Mexico-Canada Agreement) are negotiated by the Trade Representative on behalf of the president, with the guidance of the White House.

The Cabinet

The **cabinet** is not mentioned in the Constitution but was created through custom and usage. Each cabinet department was instituted by an act of Congress to help administrate the responsibilities of the executive branch. A President's cabinet is their "squad," to put it in pop-culture parlance.

Each cabinet secretary is appointed by the president and confirmed by the Senate. **Secretaries** can be dismissed at the president's will. Cabinet secretaries are supposed to run their departments and carry out the president's policies. Those who disagree with presidential policy are expected to resign. Secretaries tend to be lightning rods to be used for deflecting criticism, and they are responsible for explaining and promoting presidential policies. Over time, secretaries have tended to represent their own departments more than the president's policies. They are expected to fight for their department's budget, jurisdiction, and personnel. This creates competition and friction between departments and accounts for the reason presidents usually do not hold full cabinet meetings. Presidents just don't have the time or inclination to listen to the bickering and arguing between department heads.

Still, despite these institutional shortcomings, cabinet secretaries do rule over vast departmental bureaucracies—each containing numerous powerful government agencies. With the recent addition of the **Department of Homeland Security,** there are now 15 cabinet departments. After the September 11 attacks, it was felt that a cabinet-level department was necessary to counter possible threats to the United States, and more than 22 agencies were consolidated into the new department, making it the third-largest executive branch department. Agencies as disparate as the Bureau of Citizenship and Immigration Services (formerly the INS), the Coast Guard, and the Secret Service were consolidated to shape a coherent agenda to protect the United States against potential attacks. The Department of Homeland Security has four functions: to protect the borders; to support local agencies like police and fire departments; to detect chemical, biological, and nuclear weapons; and to analyze intelligence.

A New Addition
Homeland Security is the first top-level government position created since the Energy Department was formed in 1977 and the first large-scale government reorganization since Harry Truman created the Department of Defense in 1947.

Impeachment

The Constitution gives Congress the power to remove the president from office for "treason, bribery, or other high crimes and misdemeanors." The Constitution does not define high crimes and misdemeanors, leaving those definitions to politicians. The only direction in the Constitution is that the House of Representatives impeaches the president (or brings the charges) by a simple majority vote. If the impeachment passes, the Senate holds a trial, with the Chief Justice of the Supreme Court presiding. Removal of the president requires a two-thirds vote of the Senate. The entire process in Congress has been developed as a result of guesswork, custom, and usage.

Because the definition of an impeachable offense is left to the House, **impeachment** is a highly charged political process. Most constitutional scholars place the standard for impeachment as an act against the government or the Constitution, but there seems to be political disagreement over what standard should be used. Conservatives seem to have one standard, while liberals seem to have another. Every impeachment, or near-impeachment, has divided the Congress along party lines, and some scholars have accused members of Congress of using the process to try to undo the result of an election.

No president of the United States has been removed from office. While the House successfully impeached Andrew Johnson for his violation of the Tenure in Office Act, the Senate fell just one vote short of removing him from office. This act was later invalidated by the Supreme Court. The **Watergate** scandal caused Richard Nixon to resign before imminent impeachment proceedings could begin. He knew that the Senate would convict if given the opportunity to vote. The impeachment of President Clinton for lying under oath was very political. All parties knew before the trial began that there was little chance of a Senate conviction. Clinton's defenders claimed that while Clinton's behavior had been improper and had brought dishonor to the Office of the President, his conduct had not risen to the level of an impeachable offense. The same result occurred for President Trump, whom the House impeached for abuse of power and obstruction of Congress. However, the Senate did not convict.

Federal judges are appointed for life and can be removed only by the impeachment process. Fifteen federal judges have been impeached. Of those fifteen, eight were convicted by the Senate, four were acquitted by the Senate, and three resigned before an outcome at trial.

THE JUDICIARY AND THE LAW

Concepts

- What circumstances are required for a case to be brought before the Supreme Court?
- How do politics enter into Supreme Court decisions?
- Why can it be said that all judicial decisions are activist?
- Why can it be said that a president's strongest legacy is found in the judiciary?
- What control does Congress have over the judiciary?

American Legal Principles

Although the United States plays host to the interlocking systems of state and federal law, a few underlying principles make up the foundation of our legal system. They are **equal justice under the law**, **due process of law**, the **adversarial system,** and **presumption of innocence**.

All who appear in court in the United States must be treated as equals. The founders were very concerned that the new nation avoid the hierarchical legal systems that plagued many other nations and, as a result, enshrined many amendments in the Constitution that establish equal justice under the law. For example, whenever jurors hear a criminal case, they are instructed not to privilege the testimony of a police officer over that of a defendant.

Due process can be divided into two types: **substantive due process** and **procedural due process**. Substantive due process law deals with the question of *whether laws are fair*. Fairness is determined by looking at the Constitution, specifically the Bill of Rights and the Fourteenth Amendment. A law that made it illegal for people with blue eyes to ride motorcycles would constitute a violation of substantive due process. Procedural due process law is concerned with the question of *whether laws are fairly applied*. This might seem less important than substantive due process, but procedural issues are actually at the heart of our legal system. If suspects in certain types of crimes were held for 10 years before they ever had a trial, this would be a violation of procedural due process, because the law guarantees everyone a speedy trial. Even if a nation has laws that are fair and just, if they are not applied fairly, they are meaningless.

TAKE A BREAK

Right now, you're about half way through this chapter. Give yourself a break—take a short walk, go get a snack, listen to a song you love and dance it out. It's important to let yourself take a beat before you continue on.

Strange as it may seem to those of us raised in the United States, many nations do not require both sides of legal cases to be represented by advocates. This inquisitorial system, as it is known, is not used in the United States—we use the adversarial system. As you can probably guess from the name, this principle is based on the premise that the best way to work out questions of fact is to have two sides—or adversaries—debate the burden of guilt or liability in a situation. Some critics say that this system creates too many conflicts—particularly in areas such as family law and divorce, and recommend an increased role for mediators who seek an establishment of harmonious relations and can make legally binding decisions.

In both England and America, the idea that accused individuals are innocent until proven guilty—the presumption of innocence—is one of the bedrock principles of the legal system. As a result, the burden of proof is on the prosecutor in criminal cases, and if there is any reasonable doubt as to a person's innocence, juries are instructed to acquit.

Types of Law

In the United States, most legal cases involve either **civil law** or **criminal law**. The distinction between these two types of law is very important, and knowing the differences and similarities can help a great deal when you are taking the AP exam. The chart on the following page highlights the different processes involved in criminal and civil cases.

In his *Commentaries on the Laws of England*, English jurist and professor William Blackstone said, "Better that ten guilty persons escape than that one innocent suffer," and this number became known as the Blackstone ratio. Benjamin Franklin expanded this, writing "that it is better [one hundred] guilty Persons should escape than that one innocent Person should suffer."

Criminal Law vs. Civil Law

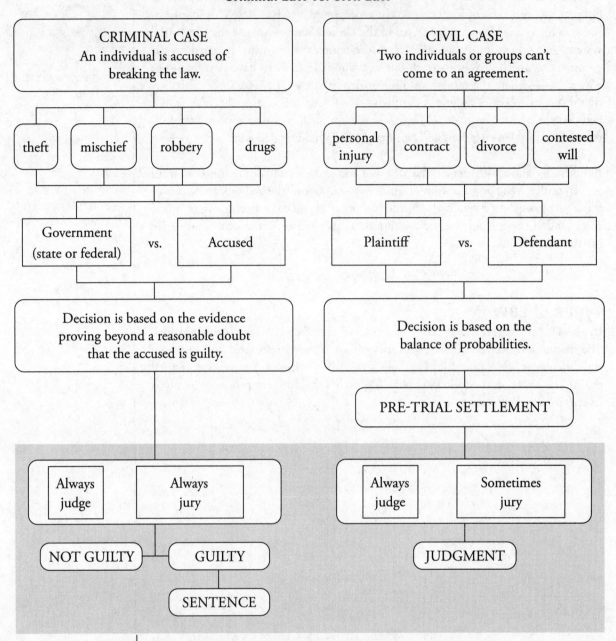

Anyone who watches television police or law dramas has at least some familiarity with the trappings of criminal law. This type of law deals with serious crimes that harm individuals or society. If physical violence is involved, the action will probably end up in the criminal justice system, but fraud and extortion are also crimes. In criminal law, a suspect is arrested and must be indicted. This is done (in most states and at the federal level) by a **grand jury**: a group of 24 to 48 jurors who decide only one thing—whether a trial should commence. Since the grand jury is not deciding guilt or innocence, an accused person does not have many protections at the grand jury level. The prosecution usually has to meet a certain standard of evidence. In fact, defense attorneys are not even allowed to address grand juries. Once the accused is indicted, that person then has the option of **plea bargaining** with the prosecution to agree to a less serious crime and sentence.

Still, many cases go to trial. Here it is important to note that in criminal trials, the state (at the state level) or the United States (at the federal level) is the party opposing the accused person. The attorney for the state or the United States represents "the people," and that's why it's often "The People vs. So-and-so." Even if your loved one has been killed, it is not you versus the accused killer, but the government against the accused killer—the government acts as the prosecution. This reflects the basic Lockean premise that when we enter into a society or community, we cede our fundamental right to vengeance and punishment to the state in exchange for protection. Since the presumption of innocence is so important to our legal system, the burden of proof is on the prosecution to prove guilt beyond a **reasonable doubt**. Criminal trials are held before **petit juries** (these are what most of us think of as simply "juries" that are composed of 12 people) as opposed to grand juries. The decision of the jury is known as the **verdict**, and a guilty verdict can be returned only if all 12 jurors vote to convict. A split jury is known as a "hung jury" and results in a mistrial.

Civil law may not seem as exciting as criminal law, but that shouldn't detract from its importance. The civil law system is what determines the results of disputes over things like contracts, property, custody of children, or an issue of liability. Unlike in criminal law cases, the government is involved in a civil case only if it happens to be the party being sued. There is no prosecution; instead, a plaintiff squares off against a defendant. If a person thinks that they have been wronged, they issue a complaint in **civil court**. If that complaint is answered—that is, if a judge or jury thinks the complaint has merit—then the case moves forward. As with plea bargaining in criminal law, civil law also has a mechanism to avoid trial—the **settlement**. In a settlement, the parties negotiate, and the issue becomes how much each party is willing to give up to end the lawsuit. If no settlement can be reached, the case goes to trial.

Since the stakes in civil law are not nearly as high as they are in criminal law—a defendant cannot be jailed or executed—the burden of proof is lighter. In order to win a case, a plaintiff need not prove that they are right beyond a reasonable doubt. Instead, they merely need to show that a **preponderance of evidence** favors their side of the case. This is the equivalent of proving that 51% of the evidence points their way. Juries are also used in civil cases, but many states do not require 12 members; some allow as few as 5 or 6. Winning can mean either the payment of monetary damages or **equity**, in which the loser may be forced to stop doing something that was annoying or harmful to the winner.

Structure and Jurisdiction

The federal courts are responsible for interpreting and settling disputes arising out of federal law; state courts are responsible for interpreting and settling disputes arising out of state law. It is possible for a citizen to commit a single act that violates both state and federal law—trading in drugs and tax evasion are two examples.

Yes, Pleas
Despite what law dramas show on TV, approximately 95% of all criminal cases end in plea bargains.

There are three levels of federal courts: the Federal District Courts, which have **original jurisdiction;** the Federal Circuit Courts of Appeals, which hear cases on appeal from the District Courts; and the **Supreme Court**, which hears appeals of cases dealing with constitutional questions from the Circuit Courts and, in rare instances, original suits between states. The Supreme Court also has original jurisdiction in cases involving foreign ministers, which is intended to prevent states from deciding such cases.

The Supreme Court does not have a jury. It is considered a collegial court because its decisions are made by the nine justices. When the court acts in **appellate jurisdiction,** it can decide only issues of law and never the facts of a case.

There are 94 **Federal District Courts**, created by Congress to fulfill its delegated responsibility of creating courts inferior to the Supreme Court. Federal District Courts decide both civil and criminal cases in original jurisdiction. The trial court that determines guilt or innocence is the court of original jurisdiction. These courts hear evidence and can use juries to decide the verdict. Federal District Courts can also decide liability in civil cases in which monetary losses have occurred. Civil cases can also have juries. It is always possible for a defendant to ask a judge to decide a case, but a judge can refuse the request and force the defendant to have a jury trial. (The Constitution guarantees a jury trial but not a trial decided by a judge.)

There are 13 **Circuit Courts of Appeals**, which hear cases on appeal from the Federal District Courts or from a state Supreme Court. In these cases, someone has to claim that a federal constitutional right has been violated. The Circuit Courts decide issues of law and never issues of fact. Circuit courts have no juries. The decisions of these courts are made by panels of appointed judges. In almost every case, the Circuit Court of Appeals is the court of last resort because the Supreme Court rarely agrees to hear cases appealed from the Circuit Courts. Additionally, most Supreme Court justices rise from the Circuit Courts.

The Politics of the Judiciary

All judges in the federal judiciary (only those on the Supreme Court are called justices) are appointed by the president for lifetime terms. Appointees must go through a **confirmation** process in the Senate. To maintain judicial neutrality and integrity, impeachment is the only method of removal.

The appointment process has become very political. Some presidents have required potential appointees to fill out a judicial questionnaire to determine their political and judicial ideology. Nominees are almost always of the same party as the president. In nomination hearings before the Senate Judiciary Committee, members of both parties try to determine how potential judges would rule in cases dealing with issues such as abortion rights, affirmative action, or school prayer. The American Bar Association is asked to evaluate a nominee's qualifications, and interest groups often present their opinions. Senators in a state where an appointee will sit

Did You Know?
Supreme Court Justice nominations have become extremely partisan over the past couple of decades—something Alexander Hamilton feared would happen when he said in Federalist No. 78 that the judiciary branch was the weakest of the proposed branches.

In 1993, the late Justice Ruth Bader Ginsburg was confirmed to the Supreme Court in a vote of 96-3. In 2020, Justice Amy Coney Barrett was confirmed along partisan lines in a vote of 52-48.

have traditionally exercised **senatorial courtesy**—they submit a list of acceptable names of nominees to the president. Presidents usually choose a nominee from the list submitted. Senatorial courtesy is expected only when the president and senators are of the same party.

While the Supreme Court can only judge a case on its merits, ideological changes in the makeup of the Court because of the partisan nature of the nomination process have resulted in the Court's establishment of new precedents and the rejection of existing precedents. Since the 1950s, the Court has overturned twice as many precedents as it had in over 150 years. Liberals and conservatives often argue over a nominee's judicial philosophy or level of judicial activism. The central point of the argument is whether the nominee is more or less inclined to second-guess a legislative enactment. As the conservatives see it, the courts are the least democratic branch of government (because judges are appointed, not elected), and when they overturn an act of a legislature, they are overruling the will of the people, as expressed in the most democratic branch of government (the legislature). Judges who are reluctant to overturn the acts of a legislature are said to practice **judicial restraint.** Liberals often see judges as constitutional interpreters who should reflect current values. A judge who has no qualms about overturning a legislative action is considered a **judicial activist.** Compromise over these two positions is sometimes very difficult to achieve. The nomination of Robert Bork to be a Justice of the Supreme Court was defeated by liberals because of his judicial philosophy on civil rights. Clarence Thomas and Amy Comey Barrett had remarkably close Senate votes (52 to 48), but Brett Kavanaugh holds the record for the closest Senate vote in U.S. history (50 votes in favor, 48 against, 2 did not vote) over concerns related to his intemperate manner during testimony and allegation of multiple instances of sexual assault.

Process by Which Cases Reach the Supreme Court

The process that the Supreme Court uses to hear cases is not part of the Constitution. The process is a result of custom and usage, time, and tradition.

The Supreme Court will not grant an appeal until all opportunities have been exhausted in the lower appellate courts. In the vast majority of cases, the court refuses to hear the appeal because it agrees with the lower court decision. However, the court may choose to review the decisions of lower courts. If four justices agree to this review, the court issues a **writ of *certiorari*,** a legal document used to request the lower court transcripts of a case.

The Supreme Court will rule only in cases that are real and adverse, which means that the case must involve an actual legal dispute. Such cases are said to be **justiciable.** Disputes over political issues cannot be decided by courts—that is, political disputes are not justiciable. The Supreme Court cannot give advisory opinions. It can rule only in an actual legal case involving litigants. In other words, the court will not rule on hypothetical cases.

The court also places limits on who may bring cases before it. Simply disliking or disagreeing with a law is not sufficient to bring a case. The petitioner (the person who brings the case) must have some vested interest in the outcome of the case. Such petitioners are said to have **standing.**

In *Lujan v. Defenders of Wildlife*, the Supreme Court made a major ruling on the issue of standing. The case involved a challenge to a rule related to the Endangered Species Act of 1973. The Court found that the plaintiffs did not have the standing necessary to bring suit, because any injury caused was to certain species of animals and not to the plaintiffs themselves.

Judicial Review

The Constitution does not specifically grant the Supreme Court the right to judge the constitutionality of laws. That power was established by the case of *Marbury v. Madison* (1803). This extremely important power is called **judicial review** and was established by John Marshall, the fourth Chief Justice of the Supreme Court (he served from 1800 to 1835). Marshall was a Federalist who worked to increase the powers of the federal government over the states.

Essential Case: *Marbury v. Madison* (1803)

Facts: In the closing hours of his presidency, John Adams commissioned William Marbury as a Justice of the Peace in the District of Columbia. (Article II, section 3, of the U.S. Constitution requires the President to formally **commission** federal judges by providing them with a signed and sealed document authorizing their power to act on the President's behalf.) Although the commission was approved by the Senate, President Thomas Jefferson, upon taking office, ordered Secretary of State James Madison not to deliver the commission.

Issue: What was the extent of the Supreme Court's power regarding judicial review as outlined in Article III, Section 2 of the Constitution? Although Marbury filed his suit with the Supreme Court, did it have original jurisdiction over the case?

Holding: In a unanimous decision, the Supreme Court ruled that although Marbury was entitled to his position as Justice of the Peace, the provision of the Judiciary Act allowing the Supreme Court to grant this position was unconstitutional. The ruling, therefore, set a precedent that future courts have followed: when a law comes into conflict with the Constitution, the Supreme Court considers that law unconstitutional. This practice is the foundation of judicial review, the power of the court to rule on the constitutionality of laws, acts, statutes, and executive orders.

How the Court Hears Cases

Once the Supreme Court decides to take a case, a complicated legal dance swings into motion. Both sides of the case submit summaries of their arguments and legal foundations for them. These summaries are known as **briefs**. At the same time, interest groups affiliated with both sides of the case submit their own briefs to the Supreme Court. These *amicus curiae* ("friend of the court") **briefs** constitute an effort to sway the justices to one side or the other, and they can be quite influential in determining the outcome of the case.

Every year from October to April, the court hears **oral arguments** for the cases it has chosen to take. Usually in oral arguments, lawyers for each party have a half hour each to stand before the nine justices and present their arguments. Often, the federal government will take one side or the other, and in these cases the **solicitor general** gets a portion of that half hour to argue on the government's behalf. The solicitor general is the second-ranking member of the justice department (after the attorney general) and typically makes many appearances before the high court— so much so that the solicitor general is sometimes called the "tenth justice." After the oral arguments, the justices meet for a highly secretive conference. At this point, all the justices cast votes, and opinion-writing duties are handed out.

There are four different types of **opinions**: unanimous, majority, concurring, and dissenting. A **unanimous opinion**, as was the case in *Brown v. Board of Education*, occurs when all of the justices agree—this opinion carries the most force in future legal cases and when legislatures draft new laws. When the justices split, the opinion with the most votes is the **majority opinion**, and it is the opinion that decides the result of the case. Sometimes, justices may vote with the majority but take issue with its legal reasoning; these are called **concurring opinions**. Those justices in the minority on an opinion can write a **dissenting opinion**, questioning the reasoning of the winning side. Though these dissents have no immediate significance, if the ideological composition of the court changes, they can sometimes become the legal foundation for future majority opinions.

The power of the Supreme Court can be limited through:

- Constitutional amendments
- Judicial confirmations and appointments
- Legislation that modifies the jurisdiction of a court
- Legislation intended to counteract the ramifications of Supreme Court decisions
- The president's and the states' refusal to comply with Supreme Court decisions

THE BUREAUCRACY

Concepts

- To what degree is the bureaucracy able to maintain political neutrality?
- How do iron triangles and issue networks foster democratic principles?
- How does Congress control the bureaucracy?
- How does the bureaucracy act to implement the intent of Congress?
- How do regulatory agencies work to protect society?
- How do presidents control their policy preferences through the bureaucracy?

The **bureaucracy** (system of government in which power is divided among departments and officials) is responsible for ensuring that the policies and programs enacted by Congress and the executive departments are carried out. Because the bureaucracy is responsible for executing the laws, providing for defense, and administering social programs, it is considered part of the executive branch of government. To ensure impartiality, bureaucratic agencies are supposed to function above partisan politics and also ensure that the laws are administered without prejudice.

Bureaucrats are not elected. Bureaucrats operate under the merit system that hires and promotes individuals based on their skills and experience rather than political patronage. The 15 cabinet secretaries and the heads of independent agencies are appointed by the president with the consent of the Senate. Most of the hundreds of thousands of civilian employees who work for the government work for one of the 15 executive departments or one of the other cabinet-level agencies considered by the White House to be part of the cabinet (such as the Director of Management and Budget or the Director of the Drug Control Office). These other cabinet-level offices are not actual cabinet departments. The civil service is comprised of the professional branches of government administration. Unlike the Legislative and Executive branches, and in some sense the Judicial branch, of government, the civil service is nonpartisan in nature.

The largest department, the Department of Defense, is administered by the **Secretary of Defense**. This person, who must be a civilian, reports directly to the president. Each of the five military services is headed by a uniformed chief of staff, and the five chiefs work together as the **Joint Chiefs of Staff**, headed by a chairperson. The Joint Chiefs and their chairperson are responsible for carrying out defense policy, and they directly report to both the Secretary of Defense and the president. The military is, therefore, subject to civilian control.

Take a look at the chart on the following page, which shows how the United States bureaucracy is organized.

Bigger than Walmart
With over 2.8 million employees that include all armed services personnel, the Department of Defense is the largest employer in the world.

> **Policy implementation** is the primary role of the federal bureaucracy. Laws and executive orders often lack specific details regarding how the policy should be enacted, but the federal bureaucracy has discretionary authority to determine the process for turning policy into reality once a law or executive order is passed.
>
> An agency must act within the bounds of the Constitution and the scope of their agency's jurisdiction, but agencies have tremendous power over the way in which a policy is interpreted and implemented. Agencies also have the power to develop rules to govern policies and procedures, which are often the subjects of cases heard before the courts. Unlike other branches of government, no system of checks and balances exists within the bureaucracy.

Bureaucratic Structure of the U.S. Government

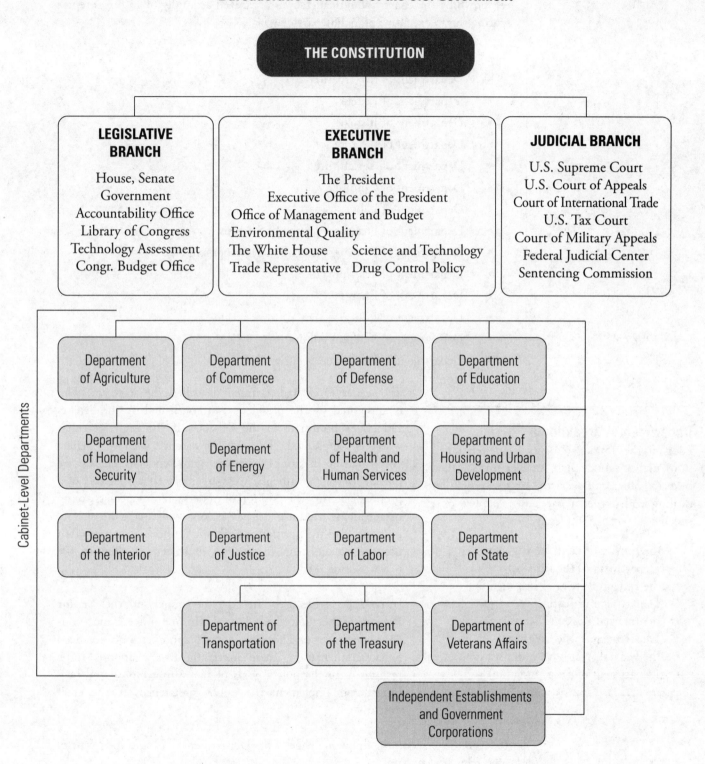

THE CONSTITUTION

LEGISLATIVE BRANCH

House, Senate
Government
Accountability Office
Library of Congress
Technology Assessment
Congr. Budget Office

EXECUTIVE BRANCH

The President
Executive Office of the President
Office of Management and Budget
Environmental Quality
The White House   Science and Technology
Trade Representative   Drug Control Policy

JUDICIAL BRANCH

U.S. Supreme Court
U.S. Court of Appeals
Court of International Trade
U.S. Tax Court
Court of Military Appeals
Federal Judicial Center
Sentencing Commission

Cabinet-Level Departments

Department of Agriculture

Department of Commerce

Department of Defense

Department of Education

Department of Homeland Security

Department of Energy

Department of Health and Human Services

Department of Housing and Urban Development

Department of the Interior

Department of Justice

Department of Labor

Department of State

Department of Transportation

Department of the Treasury

Department of Veterans Affairs

Independent Establishments and Government Corporations

As shown by the chart, the bureaucracy is organized as a tally of 15 boxes representing the 15 executive branch departments:

- Department of State
- Department of the Treasury
- Department of Defense
- Department of Justice
- Department of the Interior
- Department of Agriculture
- Department of Commerce
- Department of Labor
- Department of Health and Human Services
- Department of Housing and Urban Development
- Department of Transportation
- Department of Energy
- Department of Education
- Department of Veterans Affairs
- Department of Homeland Security

Departmental Breakdown

Each of the 15 departments is broken down into smaller units. These smaller units, called bureaus, offices, or services, are responsible for dealing with either a particular clientele or a specific subject. Examples are:

- The Bureau of Land Management (Department of the Interior)
- The Federal Bureau of Investigation (Department of Justice)
- The Internal Revenue Service (Department of the Treasury)
- The Federal Aviation Administration (Department of Transportation)

The leader of each department is called the secretary, who is appointed by the president and confirmed by the Senate. Directly subordinate to the secretary is the undersecretary, who is appointed by the president without Senate confirmation. Because secretaries and undersecretaries are presidential appointments, they are replaced at the end of a president's term. The position of undersecretary attracts young professionals. Because the pay is low compared with private industry, and the position is temporary, undersecretaries often use the appointment to step up to better positions in the private sector.

Below the secretaries are the personnel of the **Senior Executive Service**, including both appointees and non-appointees. Senior Executive Service appointees do not need Senate confirmation. These career officials are supposed to be responsive to the policy goals of the White House and help bureaucrats implement the policy preferences of the chief executive.

Refer to the chart on the following page of the Department of Homeland Security hierarchy as an example.

Bureaucratic Structure of the U.S. Department of Homeland Security

Did You Know?
Government corporations provide services that could be provided by the private sector.

Government Corporations

Government corporations are hybrid organizations. They are a cross between a private business corporation and a government agency. Corporations are supposed to have freedom of action and flexibility and produce at least enough revenue to support themselves. Amtrak, the government corporation created to provide railroad passenger service, is an example. Unfortunately, Amtrak has never made a profit and must ask Congress for subsidies to keep itself from declaring bankruptcy and ending intercity passenger rail service in the United States.

Originally created as a cabinet position, the United States Postal Service has become a government corporation. The intent of Congress was to create a mail delivery system that pays its own way without government assistance. Because of electronic messaging systems and competition from package delivery companies, the post office has had to increase its fees, but it is no longer solvent.

More successful, but at times controversial, is the Corporation for Public Broadcasting, which produces and airs both television and radio programs. Funding for the Public Broadcasting System (PBS) comes from both private and government subsidies. Most of its programming is related to public affairs, news, and culture. The controversy often occurs when groups object to the content of programs. Still others object to the government being involved in any service that could be provided by private sector corporations.

Regulatory Agencies and Commissions

Government entities that are not within the 15 cabinet departments fall into two categories: the **independent agencies** and the **regulatory agencies,** sometimes called **independent regulatory commissions.** While independent agencies are generally run-of-the-mill bureaucracies with broad presidential oversight, regulatory commissions are given an extraordinary degree of independence to act as watchdogs over the federal government. Congress and the president are not supposed to become enmeshed in the workings of regulatory commissions. The safety regulations for nuclear power plants or securities exchange should not be regulated by politics.

In contemporary societies, the difficulties and complexities of writing legislation are often beyond the abilities and expertise of lawmakers. The result is that legislation is often written in general terms with many gaps that need to be filled in by the agency with jurisdiction. Independent agencies that have the responsibility for filling in these gaps and writing rules are referred to as **quasi-legislative agencies.** Those responsible for rule enforcement and punishing violators are **quasi-judicial agencies.**

Members of Congress do not have the education to deal with the scientific details that are often required to implement legislation. For example, House and Senate members who sit on committees that deal with environmental issues do not generally have advanced degrees in chemistry. It is the experts who work in the enforcing agencies who have that knowledge. Compounding the problems for Congress are the many competing interests that surround every major issue. Environmentalists have their agenda, while the petroleum industry, electric utilities, and lumber interests have theirs. Even the regulating agency with jurisdiction has its own agenda. These competing interests often delay or prevent legislation. This is the clash of the special interests.

In an age of science and technology, it is the bureaucrat the public knows nothing about who often has the answers for Congress. These bureaucrats, on the one hand, are asked for advice and expertise, and on the other hand, are often ignored because of the pressures from interest groups. Working within the regulatory commissions, they are the people responsible for writing and enforcing rules that regulate the environment, the economy, or industry. If they fail to implement the intent of Congress, they are criticized by Congress and the parties regulated, usually for being too restrictive with their rules and too strict in their enforcement policies.

Examples of regulatory agencies include the following:

- **The Federal Trade Commission** is responsible for preventing fraud in the marketplace by preventing price fixing and deceptive advertising.

- **The Securities and Exchange Commission** protects investors by regulating stock markets and policing corporations to prevent false and misleading claims of profits in an effort to increase stock prices.

- **The Nuclear Regulatory Commission** controls how electric power companies design, build, and operate nuclear reactors.

- **The Federal Communications Commission** is responsible for assigning broadcast frequencies, for licensing radio and television stations, and for regulating the use of wireless communication devices.

- **The Food and Drug Administration** is responsible for ensuring the health of the American people by inspecting the food supply for contaminants and spoilage. The agency is also responsible for regulating the sale of over-the-counter drugs and patent medicines.

- **The Federal Energy Regulatory Commission** is responsible for preventing price fixing and price manipulation in electric utilities, interstate oil and gas pipelines, and natural gas suppliers.

- **The Occupational Safety and Health Administration** is responsible for ensuring workers are employed in a safe work environment. For example, OSHA can regulate the type of ventilation in a factory, as well as the type of clothing worn and tools used.

Did You Know?
Each regulatory commission is responsible for a certain sector of the economy.

Case Studies

Considered to be one of the most controversial government bureaucracies, the **Environmental Protection Agency (EPA)** was created in 1970 as an independent body. Its mission is the enforcement of the environmental laws passed by Congress. One of the agency's first responsibilities was to enforce the **1970 Clean Air Act.** The intent of the law was to reduce automobile pollution and increase automobile gasoline mileage. The automobile industry lobbied hard to defeat the bill and claimed that they could not meet the requirements of the law by the time specified. They were granted extensions and eventually complied, although trucks and SUVs are still exempt from the law.

The Clean Air Act was amended in 1990 as a result of scientific evidence indicating that the refrigerants used in air conditioners were instrumental in depleting the ozone layer. The EPA successfully pressured chemical companies and air-conditioning manufacturers to find alternatives to the ozone-destroying chemicals. The EPA has also been successful in reducing the pollutants that cause acid rain.

Clean air is not the EPA's only problem. It is responsible for the enforcement of the **Endangered Species Act.** This highly controversial law is intended to protect endangered wildlife habitats from human encroachment. To implement this goal, environmental impact statements are required whenever construction projects are planned. If there is any possibility that an endangered species could be adversely affected, the EPA has the power to prohibit construction. The EPA's ban on lumbering in areas of the Pacific Northwest—the habitat for the spotted owl—and its decision to block the construction of a dam in Tennessee because of the endangered snail darter fish are two examples. In the Tennessee dam case, Congress overruled the decision of the EPA, even though the Supreme Court had sided with the EPA to stop construction. In addition, Congress further weakened the EPA's enforcement powers by amending the Endangered Species Act to permit exemptions in the future.

Another agency that provokes political contention is the **Equal Employment Opportunities Commission (EEOC).** Created by the 1964 Civil Rights Act, the EEOC is responsible for enforcing the antidiscrimination laws of the United States. This commission has been susceptible to political pressure from both Congress and the White House. It is the EEOC's responsibility to implement affirmative action programs for minorities, to bring suits in cases of racial or sexual discrimination, and to enforce the **Americans with Disabilities Act.** The head of the EEOC is a presidential appointment and is supposed to carry out the policies of the president. If the law conflicts with presidential policy, the EEOC has a problem.

The critics of affirmative action claim the policy is a form of reverse discrimination. Feeling pressure from voters, Congress, and the president, the EEOC first promoted affirmative action and then discouraged the policy. The attempts by this agency to implement the will of Congress have been complicated because both Congress and the White House seem to change their mind at will.

Congress and the EPA

The EPA can sometimes become a foe of Congress, which originally gave the EPA its mandate to act.

The Americans with Disabilities Act requires the EEOC to enforce laws against employers who discriminate against disabled employees or job seekers. In addition, part of the Disabilities Act requires that public buildings and large businesses be accessible to those with disabilities. Critics claim that this attempt at helping disabled people live normal lives has cost taxpayers hundreds of millions of dollars, and the cost is too high in relation to the number of persons benefited.

Who Runs Regulatory Agencies?

Independent regulatory agencies are run by panels of administrators called Boards of Commissioners. These commissioners are appointed by the president with the consent of the Senate. The terms of these commissioners usually overlap the term of the appointing president. The staggered term is intended to minimize political pressure from the White House. Depending on the commission, terms can range from 3 to 14 years.

Perhaps the best-known regulatory board is the **Federal Reserve Board** (the Fed) because its policies directly affect the buying power of the public. The Fed accomplishes this by regulating banks, the value and supply of money, and interest rates. Its members serve 14-year terms. Its chairperson serves a four-year term.

Because the Fed is an independent agency, its policies can sometimes conflict with the policies of the president. In 1993, in the first weeks of the Clinton administration, Fed Chairperson Alan Greenspan told the president that the condition of the economy was worse than the previous Bush administration had told the American people. In addition, the national debt, as bad as it was perceived to be, was actually even greater than anyone realized. Clinton wanted an economic stimulus tax cut to get the economy out of recession. Greenspan told the president a tax cut should not be pursued, and if the White House went forward with the plan, the Fed would raise interest rates. Clinton was forced to break his campaign pledge to lower taxes. Even though the chairperson and the president disagreed over economic policy, the president was powerless to do anything about it. In time, the Greenspan policy helped to get the economy out of the recession and into the longest economic boom in American history. Things went so well that Clinton reappointed Greenspan as chairperson. Greenspan's legacy would later come into question as a result of the economic collapse of 2008–2009.

Who Controls the Bureaucracy?

Because most boards of commissions and regulatory agencies are appointed by the president with Senate consent, political considerations always play a part in the appointment process. However, presidents come and go with great regularity, as do the appointed governing boards and commissions. It is the rank-and-file bureaucrats who are permanent, and they do not like political meddling.

Fed-really!
Janet Yellen, appointed by Barack Obama in 2014, was the first woman to hold the position of Fed Chairperson.

Fast Fact!
Economist, sociologist, and jurist Max Weber coined the term bureaucracy, claiming that it was a rational way for modern society to conduct government business. Weber believed that a bureaucracy must operate on a merit system with a hierarchical authority structure, task specialization, and comprehensive rules regarding processes and procedures in order to be successful and efficient.

While in office, presidents do have the power to promote their supporters and to use the budget to increase or decrease the influence of an agency. Reducing an agency's budget reduces its staff, which reduces its effectiveness. Increasing the agency's budget can have the opposite effect. Presidents can also reorganize an agency.

Congressional power over the bureaucracy is greater than that of the president. The Senate can affirm or reject presidential appointments. Congress can also abolish an agency or change its jurisdiction if it is unhappy with policy implementation. Finally, it is the Congress, through the appropriations process, that has the final say over how much money agencies will receive.

Rule Setting, Alliance Building, and Iron Triangles

The regulatory agencies carry out their responsibilities by setting rules and regulations that industry must follow. Setting regulations is a participatory process, in which industry becomes actively involved in determining the rules. Agencies welcome public participation by holding public hearings for testimony and advice. In most instances, the law requires agencies to consult with industry before rules and regulations can go into effect.

Iron Triangles

The rule-making process has fostered the creation of **iron triangles.** Typically, iron triangles are informal alliances made up of three groups: (1) a particular industry and its lobbyists (for example, weapons manufacturers), (2) the congressional committee dealing with that industry (the Armed Services Committees of the Senate and House), and (3) the agency that actually is affected (in this case, the Pentagon).

The groups that make up an iron triangle work together to formulate and implement policy in their area of interest. Lobbyists representing industries promote their special-interest agendas by claiming each is in the best interest of the American people. For example, drug companies may lobby the Food and Drug Administration to speed up the certification process for a medication because it will benefit the sick faster. Patients and drug companies will pressure Congress, which then pressures the FDA. These are powerful arguments, but speeding up the process can cause the FDA to overlook something dangerous about the medication.

Special interests also contribute money to congressional campaigns. Large contributors are never shy about asking for help from congressional representatives, who are asked to help put pressure on regulators, or at a minimum, to listen to the arguments that the special interests put forward for their cause.

Political scientists have recently seen a more complex political process at work. When issues affect many groups, pro and con coalitions of interest groups, members of Congress, and bureaucrats form a close working relationship. This political process is called either an **alliance network** or an **issue network**, and it is far more complicated than a simple three-part iron triangle.

For example, if a large factory was a polluter but had marginal profits, it would probably fight expensive environmental regulations. Compliance might drive the company into bankruptcy. But more is at stake than just the company. There are jobs involved, as well as secondary industries that supply the raw materials for production at the company. A local government, which relies on the tax revenues from the company, also has something at stake. Environmental groups are also going to be involved. This complicated situation would certainly result in the creation of issue networks for the purpose of influencing the regulatory agency's decisions.

After all the opportunities for input and debate have been exhausted, the regulatory agency writes and publishes the rules (this is its quasi-legislative function). If the industry still objects to the regulation, it can seek remedies in the courts by suing the regulatory agency. In the above example, if the company is forced to comply with the environmental laws, it could appeal the decision to the courts.

Because regulatory agencies invite so much controversy, there has been a recent trend toward deregulating the marketplace (removing government restrictions and regulations). Those in favor of **deregulation** claim that the competition of the marketplace is all the regulation that is needed. The deregulators say that regulation is too expensive and time-consuming, and it involves too much unnecessary red tape. They note that over the past 25 years, the **Civil Aeronautics Board**, which was responsible for regulating the airline industry, and the **Interstate Commerce Commission**, which regulated railroads and the trucking industry, were successfully phased out with little negative impact on consumers.

The Civil Service and Maintaining Neutrality

Today, the majority of government jobs are filled through the competitive **civil service system**. This system was established in 1883 with the passage of the Pendleton Act, a law that ended the "**patronage system**," or the practice of handing out government jobs in exchange for political support. The Office of Personnel Management (OPM) acts as the bureaucracy's employment agency. OPM administers the civil service examination, publishes lists of job openings, and hires on the basis of merit. The intent is to create a competent, professional bureaucracy instead of one based on the "patronage system." A Merit Systems Protection Board investigates charges of agency corruption and incompetence, and it is supposed to protect "whistle blowers."

To ensure bureaucratic neutrality, Congress passed the Hatch Act in 1939. This law permitted bureaucrats the right to vote but not the right to actively campaign for political candidates, work for parties, or run for office. The act's revision of 1993 is less restrictive, allowing bureaucrats to join political parties, make campaign contributions, and display political advertising in the form of buttons and bumper stickers. Bureaucrats still cannot run for public office at any level, solicit campaign funds from subordinates, or make political speeches.

Did You Know?
While nonpartisan in nature, both congress and the president attempt to influence the bureaucracy through agency appointments, altering the budgets of agencies, agency reorganization, legislation, and executive orders.

CHECKS AND BALANCES

JUDICIAL BRANCH
(SUPREME COURT)

- *interprets the Constitution and other laws*

Judicial Review
The Supreme Court supervises Congress and the president. Using the Constitution as a guide, the Supreme Court determines whether or not laws and executive actions are legal or unconstitutional, and therefore subject to reversal.

EXECUTIVE BRANCH
(PRESIDENT)

- *administers the laws*
- *may suggest laws*
- *appoints ambassadors and other officials*
- *conducts foreign policy*
- *commands armed forces*

Veto Power
The president has the power to veto any legislation written by Congress, meaning the president can prevent any newly written bill from becoming a law. (This power is limited. Congress can override a veto with enough votes.)

LEGISLATIVE BRANCH
(CONGRESS)

- *declares war*
- *writes laws*
- *ratifies treaties*
- *grants money*
- *confirms presidential appointments*

Impeachment
Congress has the power to impeach the president or justices on the Supreme Court. Members can bring charges against federal judges or the president, hold a trial, and determine whether or not that individual should be removed from office.

CHAPTER 5 KEY TERMS

Congress

House of Representatives

Senate

Census

Congressional districts

Redistricting

Gerrymander

Voting Rights Act of 1965

Budgetary

Power of the purse

House Ways and Means Committee

Hearings

Politicos

Delegates

Delegate Model

Trustee Model

Sponsor

Rules Committee

Poison-pill (killer) amendments

Filibuster

Cloture

Pork barrels

Earmarks

Conference committee

Pocket veto

Line-item veto

Subcommittee

Pigeonhole

Discharge petition

Speaker

Majority leader

Minority leader

Whips

President *pro tempore*

Logrolling

McCain-Feingold Bill

Foreign policy

Executive agreements

Commander in chief

War Powers Act

Gulf of Tonkin Resolution

Unified government

Divided government

Bully pulpit

Chief of staff

Literalist doctrine

Stewardship doctrine

Unitary executive theory

Cabinet

Secretaries

Department of Homeland Security

Impeachment

Watergate

Equal justice under the law

Due process of law

Adversarial system

Presumption of innocence

Substantive due process

Procedural due process

Civil law

Criminal law

Grand jury

Plea bargaining

Reasonable doubt

Petit juries

Verdict

Civil court

Settlement

Preponderance of evidence

Equity

Original jurisdiction

Supreme Court

Appellate jurisdiction

Federal District Courts

Circuit Courts of Appeals

Confirmation

Senatorial courtesy

Judicial restraint

Judicial activist

Writ of *certiorari*

Justiciable

Standing

Marbury v. Madison (1803)

Judicial review

Stare decisis/legal precedent

Commission

Briefs

Amicus curiae briefs

Oral arguments

Solicitor general

Opinions

Unanimous opinion

Majority opinion

Concurring opinions

Dissenting opinion

Bureaucracy

Secretary of Defense

Joint Chiefs of Staff

Policy implementation

Senior Executive Service

Independent agencies

Regulatory agencies

Independent regulatory commissions

Quasi-legislative agencies

Quasi-judicial agencies

Environmental Protection Agency
(EPA)

1970 Clean Air Act

Endangered Species Act

Equal Employment Opportunities
Commission (EEOC)

Americans with Disabilities Act

Federal Reserve Board

Iron triangles

Alliance (issue) network

Deregulation

Civil Aeronautics Board

Interstate Commerce Commission

Civil service system

"Patronage System"

Chapter 5 Drill

See Chapter 9 for answers and explanations.

Questions 1 and 2 refer to the passage below.

Why does a judge swear to discharge his duties agreeably to the Constitution of the United States, if that Constitution forms no rule for his government? If it is closed upon him, and cannot be inspected by him?

If such be the real state of things, this is worse than solemn mockery. To prescribe, or take this oath, becomes equally a crime.

It is also not entirely unworthy of observation that, in declaring what shall be the *supreme* law of the land, the Constitution itself is first mentioned; and not the laws of the United States generally, but those only which shall be made in pursuance of the *Constitution*, have that rank.

Thus, the particular phraseology of the Constitution of the United States confirms and strengthens the principle, supposed to be essential to all written constitutions, that a law repugnant to the Constitution is void; and that *courts*, as well as other departments, are bound by that instrument.

—John Marshall, Chief Justice of the Supreme Court
(1801–1835)

1. Which of the following statements best summarizes the whole passage?

   (A) Justices must interpret the Constitution, although they do not explicitly have this power.
   (B) There are many questions about why justices have the power to interpret the Constitution.
   (C) Marshall is unsure about how to properly perform his job.
   (D) Justices are loyal to the Constitution because they swear an oath of allegiance.

2. It can be inferred from this passage that Marshall was arguing for which legal doctrine?

   (A) *Ex post facto* laws
   (B) Judicial restraint
   (C) Judicial review
   (D) *Amicus curiae* briefs

3. Who is the official head of the Senate?

   (A) President of the United States
   (B) Vice president of the United States
   (C) President *pro tempore*
   (D) Chief whip

4. Which of the following is an accurate comparison of the bureaucratic responsibilities of the Executive and Legislative Branches?

	Legislative Branch	Executive Branch
(A)	Library of Congress	Technology Assessment
(B)	Department of Energy	Government Publishing Office
(C)	Department of Justice	Department of State
(D)	Government Accountability Office	Drug Control Policy

5. Which of the following is one of the most important legislative powers of Congress?

   (A) The ability to tax and spend
   (B) The power to choose a president
   (C) The ability to propose amendments to the Constitution
   (D) The power to ratify treaties (in the Senate)

6. How do House congressional districts gain their shapes?

   (A) A vote held in the Senate by the majority party
   (B) An executive order of the president
   (C) A census and the various state legislatures
   (D) A nonpartisan commission

7. How are cabinet members chosen?

   (A) By the president and then confirmed by the Senate
   (B) By the president and then confirmed by both houses of Congress
   (C) By the Supreme Court
   (D) By the president alone, without confirmation

8. Which of the following are NOT part of the formal federal bureaucratic structure?

   (A) Independent regulatory commissions
   (B) Interest groups
   (C) Independent executive agencies
   (D) Government corporations

Summary

- Remember that Congress is a bicameral (two-house) legislature, split into the Senate (in which all states receive equal representation) and the House of Representatives (in which representation is proportionate to population).

- The number of House seats a state gets is based on its population as determined by a census. Once the number of seats is determined, the state legislature draws the districts—often using partisan gerrymandering to ensure a majority for one party or the other.

- Congress has numerous powers that range from creation of all law, to funding all executive agencies, to declaring war. It is the first institution defined in the Constitution, and most scholars think that the Founders intended it to be the most powerful of the branches.

- How does a bill become a law? It is introduced to the House or Senate, referred to a committee, amended and debated, reintroduced to the general House and Senate, debated and amended once more, harmonized with its counterpart that has traveled through the other legislative body, voted on again, and signed by the president.

- Given the large size of both houses of Congress, committees do most of the work of legislating. Committees can be standing, select, or joint, and are often further divided into subcommittees.

- The House is led by the speaker, while the Senate has two ceremonial leaders (the vice president and the president *pro tempore*) and one actual power broker—the majority leader.

- This chapter has a ton of laws. Try to remember them by using the four categories: (1) National Growth, Expansion, and Institution Building; (2) Regulation of Government and Industry; (3) Rights and Freedoms; and (4) Government Aid to the People.

- The president is the chief executive of the nation and is responsible for enforcing all laws. Over the years, the power of the presidency has grown dramatically—often at the expense of Congress.

- Even though the Constitution gives Congress the power to declare war, the nature of modern warfare has given the president control of this area. Though Congress does have tools to stop a wartime president, using them would be potentially career-ending.

o   Being a good president often means going beyond the powers explicitly listed in the Constitution. Grasp of these "informal powers"—like consensus-building or boosting the morale of the nation—often determines presidents' successes.

o   The president relies a great deal on the Executive Office of the President (EOP)—his personal staff, which is ensconced within the West Wing of the White House. The EOP is also home to a number of agencies that serve the president and are largely free from congressional oversight.

o   America has 15 cabinet departments, and each contains a huge array of agencies and bureaucracies designed to help enforce the law of the land. The cabinet secretaries are supposed to advise the president, but due to conflicting loyalties, most presidents have kept them out of the loop and relied on the EOP and other informal advisors when making policy decisions.

o   If a president has committed "treason, bribery, or other high crimes and misdemeanors," they can be impeached by a majority vote in the House and then removed from office with a two-thirds vote in the Senate.

o   Remember that America has two legal systems—state and federal—and all people are under the jurisdiction of both. The federal system was created by the Constitution—all federal judges are appointed by the president and approved by the Senate, and the nation is divided into 91 federal districts.

o   The Supreme Court rules on some very divisive social issues, and the battle to appoint new members has become more intense. Increasingly, presidents are looking to appoint younger and more ideological candidates who share their political philosophies.

o   The Supreme Court is America's court of last resort. Most of its cases come through appeals from lower courts or by granting writs of *certiorari*, which cause cases to jump straight to their chambers.

o   Though it is not mentioned in the Constitution, the Supreme Court's most important power is judicial review: the ability to strike down any state or federal law that is unconstitutional. This power was established in the case of *Marbury v. Madison* in 1803.

o   Often called "the fourth branch of government," bureaucrats staff the large executive agencies that run the federal government. To get these jobs, applicants must take competitive exams. Bureaucrats play a huge role in creating public policy by making rules that flesh out vague laws passed by Congress.

o   We see four different types of bureaucracy in Washington: cabinet departments, independent agencies, regulatory commissions, and government corporations. Regulatory commissions are largely free of political control and have broad oversight responsibilities, while government corporations like the Postal Service are expected to turn a profit in the free market.

o   Because the issues dealt with by bureaucrats are so technical and often pertain to a small interest group, we see the formation of iron triangles—cooperation between a bureaucracy (like the Department of Defense), a congressional committee (like the Senate Armed Services Committee), and a special interest group (like weapons and aircraft manufacturers).

o   Bureaucrats are supposed to be politically neutral and stable, while their political higher-ups shift due to election results. Still, many suspect that they may take sides, and laws like the Hatch Act were designed to prevent this from happening.

REFLECT

Respond to the following questions:

- Of which content topics discussed in this chapter do you feel you have achieved sufficient understanding to answer multiple-choice questions correctly?

- Of which content topics discussed in this chapter do you feel you have achieved sufficient understanding to discuss them effectively in an essay?

- On which content topics discussed in this chapter do you feel you need more work before you can answer multiple-choice questions correctly?

- On which content topics discussed in this chapter do you feel you need more work before you can discuss them effectively in an essay?

- Which parts of this chapter are you going to re-review?

- Will you seek further help, outside of this book (such as from a teacher, tutor, or AP Students), on any of the content in this chapter—and, if so, on what content?

Chapter 6
Civil Liberties and Civil Rights

"Power concedes nothing without a demand. It never did and it never will."
— Frederick Douglass

CONCEPTS

- Why would Justice Thurgood Marshall blame the Supreme Court for the racial policies practiced in the United States before the *Brown* decision?

- Why did the Supreme Court allow the use of affirmative action programs?

- Why is it said that the Warren Court took the handcuffs off the criminals and put them on the police?

- What mechanism did the Supreme Court use to ensure the rights of defendants in state criminal prosecutions?

- What impact has the interpretation of speech as a preferred right had on the government's power to censure?

- How does the Supreme Court interpret the right to privacy on matters dealing with human reproduction?

- How has the Supreme Court changed its reasoning in dealing with religious activities in schools financed by the public?

Did You Know?

Civil liberties are freedoms and guarantees established by the constitution that protect citizens, opinions, and property against arbitrary interference.

THE BILL OF RIGHTS (DECEMBER 15, 1791)

The first 10 amendments were added to the Constitution within three years of its ratification. These amendments are known collectively as the Bill of Rights. Originally written by James Madison, many provisions of the Bill of Rights have been expanded and clarified over the years.

The term **civil liberties** generally applies to those protections (enjoyed by all Americans) from the abuse of government power. The term **civil rights** is used specifically to describe protections from discrimination based on race, gender, or other minority status. Often, the term is used to refer specifically to the struggles of African Americans for equal status (for example, the Civil Rights Movement).

THE EXTENSION OF CIVIL LIBERTIES THROUGH AMERICAN HISTORY

In *Barron v. Baltimore* (1833), the Supreme Court determined that the Bill of Rights restricted the national government but not the state governments. It was not until 1925 that the court overturned this ruling, citing Fourteenth Amendment restrictions on the states ("no state shall…deprive any person of life, liberty, or property, without due process of law; nor deny to any person within its jurisdiction the equal protection of the laws"). That case, *Gitlow v. New York*, concerned freedom of speech and freedom of the press. The court ruled that state limits on speech and the press could not exceed the limits allowed by the national government.

Since then, the court has applied the Bill of Rights to state law on a case-by-case basis. This process is called **selective incorporation.** Currently, the following rights have NOT been incorporated and may thus be restricted by the states:

- the Third Amendment protection against forced quartering of troops in private homes
- the Fifth Amendment right to **indictment** by a grand jury
- the Seventh Amendment right to a jury trial in civil cases

All other provisions of the Bill of Rights, however, apply equally to the states and the national government. In defining individual rights, the court has consistently weighed the rights of individuals against the needs of society at large. Therefore, none of the rights guaranteed in the Bill of Rights is absolute.

FIRST AMENDMENT RIGHTS AND RESTRICTIONS

Supreme Court Justice Benjamin Cardozo said that the First Amendment of the Bill of Rights contains "the fundamental principles of liberty and justice which lie at the base of all of our civil and political institutions." The **First Amendment** guarantees **freedom of speech, freedom of the press, freedom of petitioning the government, freedom of assembly,** and **freedom of religion.** None of these important rights, however, is absolute. Throughout the nation's history, the Supreme Court has ruled that these rights may be limited in the interest of the greater public good. It has also ruled, however, that such restrictions must be well justified, well defined, and limited only to those few instances in which the public welfare is genuinely threatened.

Freedom of Speech

Congress may not pass a law that prevents citizens from expressing their opinions, either in speech or in writing. Nevertheless, the Supreme Court has placed some limits on these freedoms. The most famous limit on free speech is the **clear and present danger test.** In the case of *Schenck v. United States* (1919), Justice Oliver Wendell Holmes argued that a person may not falsely scream "fire!" in a crowded theater, because doing so would likely result in panic. The court has also ruled that there is no constitutional protection for false defamatory speech (called **slander** when it is spoken and **libel** when it is in a more permanent form, such as print), **obscenity**, or speech intended to incite violence.

Since the 1940s, the court has followed the **preferred position doctrine** in determining the limits of free speech. The doctrine reflects the court's belief that freedom of speech is fundamental to liberty; therefore, any limits on free speech must address severe, imminent threats to the nation. They must also be limited to constraining those threats; any restriction that fails to meet this test would probably be overturned by the Supreme Court. The court continues to protect offensive

Did You Know?
The way in which the Bill of Rights, which consists of the first ten amendments of the Constitution, is applied is based on the interpretations and rulings of the courts. While the Bill of Rights enumerates the liberties and rights of individuals, the way in which those rights and liberties are construed in current society is based on judicial interpretation; this is one reason that judicial appointments and nominations have become increasingly partisan.

but nonthreatening speech such as flag burning (usually undertaken by protesters, who burn the flag as a symbolic indication that the country has failed to protect American values such as democracy and freedom for all).

Essential Case: *Schenck v. United States* (1919)

Facts: During the First World War, the United States prosecuted thousands of dissenters. Near the end of the war, Charles Schenck, a Socialist, was arrested in Philadelphia for handing out leaflets calling on men not to enlist. Schneck was arrested and convicted of violating the Espionage Act of 1917. He appealed to the Supreme Court.

Issue: Schneck's attorney argued that the Espionage Act of 1917 violated the First Amendment.

Holding: In a unanimous decision, the Supreme Court ruled that Schneck's conviction was constitutional and that his speech posed "a clear and present danger" to the United States. Thus, the Court held that the First Amendment does not protect speech that creates a "clear and present danger," stating that free speech can be curtailed if the speech will "bring about the substantive evils that Congress has the right to prevent."

Although *Schenck* has never been formally overturned, the court loosened its stance on what defined a clear and present danger in *Brandenburg v. Ohio* (1969). It ruled that for speech to be "a clear and present danger," the speaker must be making a specific threat, and not just advocating violence in general.

Essential Case: *Tinker v. Des Moines* (1969)

Facts: The mid-1960s saw the beginnings of anti-Vietnam War protests throughout the United States. In 1965, teenagers John and Mary Beth Tinker wore black armbands to school as a form of silent anti-war protest. After multiple warnings, the Tinkers were suspended for their actions. The ACLU helped the Tinker family take their case to the Supreme Court.

Issue: In *West Virginia State Board of Education v. Barnette* (1943), the Supreme Court had ruled that the First Amendment protects minors at school under certain circumstances. However, the court needed to consider whether the First Amendment and *West Virginia State Board of Education* applied to the Tinkers' protest.

Holding: In a 7-2 decision, the Supreme Court ruled that children in public schools were protected fully by the First Amendment as long as their speech did not violate specific, constitutional regulations. In this case, the court held that students in public schools could wear black armbands to school as a means of protesting the Vietnam War. The Court held that students can exercise their First Amendment rights in public school if those actions do not cause a "substantial disruption." The dissenting justices argued that although the speech was constitutional, specific locations, such as schools, were not an appropriate venue for anti-war protests.

Important Cases

Gitlow v. New York (1925). This case created the "Bad Tendency Doctrine," which held that speech could be restricted even if it has only a tendency to lead to illegal action. Though this element of the decision was quite restrictive, Gitlow also selectively incorporated freedom of speech to state governments.

Bethel School District v. Fraser (1986). This case gave public school officials the authority to suspend students for speech considered to be lewd or indecent. The Court held that schools have the right to regulate the use of explicit speech, obscene language was not covered by the First Amendment, and schools can punish a student if such speech fails to have educational value.

Hustler Magazine v. Falwell (1988). In this much-publicized case, the court held that intentional infliction of emotional distress was permissible First Amendment speech—so long as such speech was about a public figure and could not reasonably be construed to state actual facts about its subject. In other words, parody is not an actionable offense.

Texas v. Johnson (1989). *Johnson* established that burning the American flag is an example of permissible free speech, and struck down numerous anti-flag-burning laws. The Court held that political or symbolic speech could not be regulated by the government, even if offensive to some populations.

Morse v. Frederick (2007). This case was known as the "Bong Hits 4 Jesus" case, in which the Supreme Court limited students' free speech rights. The justices ruled that Frederick's free speech rights were not violated by his suspension over what the majority's written opinion called a "sophomoric" banner.

Gitlow v. New York, Bethel School District v. Fraser, Hustler Magazine v. Falwell, Texas v. Johnson, and *Morse v. Frederick,* while important to understanding the limits to free speech, are not on the list of required cases.

Freedom of the Press

Criticism of the government and its politics is protected. When it comes to censoring the press, there are few instances in which the government can use **prior restraint**—crossing out sections of an article before publication. On occasion, the government has tried to control the press, usually claiming national security interests. This occurred during the 1990 Persian Gulf War, when the Pentagon limited media access to the war zone and censored outgoing news reports. The media objected to these limitations. Such conflicts usually end up in the courts, where judges are forced to weigh conflicting national interests: the need to be informed versus security concerns.

An even more contentious issue involves the media's responsibility to reveal the sources of their information. The Supreme Court has ruled that reporters are not exempt from testifying in court cases and that they can be asked to name their sources. Reporters who refuse to do so, as many have, can be jailed. A number of states have enacted **shield laws** to protect reporters in state cases, but in other states and in federal cases reporters have no such protection.

Did You Know?
Prior restraint is a method of censorship that allows the government to review, censor, and prevent the publication of printed materials.

As mentioned earlier, libel and obscenity are not protected by the First Amendment. In the case of *Miller v. California* (1973), the court established a **three-part obscenity test.**

- Would the average person, applying community standards, judge the work as appealing primarily to people's baser sexual instincts?
- Does the work lack other value, or is it also of literary, artistic, political, or scientific interest?
- Does the work depict sexual behavior in an offensive manner?

Essential Case: *New York Times v. United States* (1971)

Facts: In 1971, Daniel Ellsberg leaked the Pentagon Papers, a top-secret report on the country's role in Vietnam, to *The New York Times*. When the *Times* began summarizing the finding of the report in a series of articles, the government sued and sought a restraining order. When *The Washington Post* began publishing the Pentagon Papers, the government filed a lawsuit that went to the Supreme Court.

Issue: The government claimed that the release of the Pentagon Papers violated the Espionage Act of 1917 and that it had the right to use prior restraint—the suppression of harmful information.

Holding: In a 6-3 decision, the Supreme Court ruled that the newspapers could publish the Pentagon Papers, as the government had not met the burden of proof necessary to enact prior restraint. Dissenting justices noted that the court did not have enough time to adequately research information relevant to the case, as the Pentagon Papers spanned over 7,000 pages. With this holding, the Court established a "heavy presumption against prior restraint," including in situations that involve national security. Accordingly, the Court is unlikely to find cases regarding government censorship unconstitutional.

Near v. Minnesota, New York Times v. Sullivan, and *Hazelwood School v. Kuhlmeier,* while important to understanding limits of freedom of the press, are not on the list of required cases.

Important Cases

Near v. Minnesota (1931). *Near* established that state injunctions to prevent publication violate the free press provision of the First Amendment and are unconstitutional. This case is important in that it selectively incorporates freedom of the press and prevents prior restraint.

New York Times v. Sullivan (1964). If a newspaper prints an article that turns out to be false but that the newspaper thought was true at the time of publication, has the newspaper committed libel? This case said no.

Hazelwood School v. Kuhlmeier (1988). In *Hazelwood*, the court held that school officials have sweeping authority to regulate free speech in student-run newspapers.

Freedom of Assembly and Association

The First Amendment protects the right of people to assemble peacefully. That right does not extend to violent groups or to demonstrations that would incite violence. Furthermore, the government may place reasonable restrictions on crowd gatherings, provided such restrictions are applied equally to all groups. Demonstrators have no constitutional right, for example, to march on and thereby close down a highway. They may not block the doorways of buildings. In short, crowd gatherings must not unnecessarily disrupt day-to-day life. That is why groups must apply for licenses to hold a parade or street fair.

The court has also ruled that the combined rights of freedom of speech and freedom of assembly imply a **freedom of association**. This means that the government may not restrict the number or type of groups or organizations people belong to, provided those groups do not threaten national security.

When Assembly Was Persecuted: Martin Luther King Jr.'s "Letter from a Birmingham Jail"

In April 1963, Martin Luther King Jr. was arrested in Birmingham, Alabama, for his role in helping to organize a series of marches and sit-ins to protest racial segregation. From his jail cell, King wrote an open letter to the city's African American religious leaders. This letter outlined many of his key ideas regarding the importance of nonviolent resistance in the form of peaceful assembly. His letter convinced many, and African Americans and their supporters continued to use nonviolent resistance to dismantle legal segregation throughout the South.

Important Cases

Thornhill v. Alabama (1940). Labor unions have been controversial since the dawn of the Industrial Revolution—did their strikes constitute a form of unlawful assembly? In *Thornhill*, the court held that strikes by unions were not unlawful.

Cox v. New Hampshire (1941). When a group of Jehovah's Witnesses was arrested for marching in New Hampshire without a permit, they claimed that permits themselves were an unconstitutional abridgment of their First Amendment freedoms. In *Cox*, the court held that cities and towns could legitimately require parade permits in the interest of public order.

Lloyd Corporation v. Tanner (1972). This case allowed the owners of a shopping mall to throw out people protesting the Vietnam War. The key element here is that malls are private spaces, not public. As a result, protesters have substantially fewer assembly rights in malls and other private establishments.

Did You Know?
Reverend Dr. Martin Luther King Jr. is considered by many to be the most influential civil rights leader of the 20th century. Famous for delivering his "I Have A Dream" speech to over a quarter of a million people during the 1963 March on Washington, King was a fierce advocate for nonviolent protest as a way to eliminate social injustice.

You can read "Letter from a Birmingham Jail" in full at billofrightsinstitute.org/ primary-sources/letter-from-birmingham-jail.

Though *Thornhill v. Alabama*, *Cox v. New Hampshire*, *Lloyd Corporation v. Tanner*, and *Boy Scouts of America v. Dale* are important to understanding the limits of freedom of assembly, they are not on the list of required cases.

Update:
The Boy Scouts removed the ban for youth effective January 2014, and for adults in July 2015.

Boy Scouts of America v. Dale (2000). Private organizations' First Amendment right of expressive association allows them to choose their own membership and expel members based on their sexual orientation even if such discrimination would otherwise be prohibited by antidiscrimination legislation designed to protect minorities in public accommodations. As a result of this case, the Boy Scouts of America were allowed to expel any member who was discovered to be gay.

Freedom of Religion

The Constitution guarantees the right to the **free exercise** of religion, meaning that the government may not prevent individuals from practicing their faiths. This right is not absolute, however. Human sacrifice, to give an extreme example, is not allowed. The courts have ruled that polygamy is not protected by the Constitution, nor is the denial of medical treatment to a child, regardless of individual religious beliefs. However, the court has ruled that Jehovah's Witnesses cannot be required to salute the American flag and that Amish children may stop attending school after the eighth grade. In all cases, the court weighs individual rights to free religious exercise against society's needs.

The Constitution also prevents the government from establishing a state religion (**the establishment clause**). The establishment clause has been used to prevent school prayer, government-sponsored displays of the Christmas nativity, and state bans on the teaching of evolution (because such bans were religiously motivated). However, the wall between church and state is not rock solid. The court has allowed government subsidies to provide some aspects of parochial education (such as lunches, textbooks, and buses). It has also allowed for tax credits for non-public school costs. In deciding whether a law violates the establishment clause, the court uses a three-part test, called the **Lemon test** after the case *Lemon v. Kurtzman* (1971).

Lemon v. Kurtzman is not on the list of required cases.

- Does the law have a secular, rather than a religious, purpose?
- Does the law neither promote nor discourage religion?
- Does the law avoid "excessive entanglement" of the government and religious institutions?

Essential Case: *Engel v. Vitale* (1962)

Facts: In the early 1960s, a group of Jewish families in New York brought suit against their children's school district for imposing prayer in the classroom. The New York Court of Appeals upheld school prayer before the families took the case to the Supreme Court.

Issue: The families argued the school prayer violated the First Amendment's establishment clause.

Holding: In a 6-1 decision (one justice was ill, and another recused himself based on the fact he was not a member of the court during oral arguments), the court ruled that school prayer violated the First Amendment's establishment clause. The lone dissenting justice argued that forbidding prayer in school denied children the nation's "spiritual heritage."

Essential Case: *Wisconsin v. Yoder* (1972)

Facts: The Amish faith discouraged higher education so as to preserve the Amish way of life. In the early 1970s, Wisconsin fined three Amish families $5 for taking their children out of school after the eighth grade. The Amish families appealed the case, and after the state supreme court ruled in the families' favor, the state took the case to the Supreme Court.

Issue: In a conflict between the free expression of religious belief and state laws regarding compulsory education, who wins?

Holding: In an 8-1 decision, the Supreme Court ruled that Amish families taking their children out of school after the eighth grade was protected by the First Amendment's free exercise clause. The single dissenting justice argued that allowing parents to take their children out of school sets a dangerous precedent.

Important Cases

Abington School Dist. v. Schempp (1963). Given the court's ruling in *Engel*, it's not surprising that in *Abington* they decided that the establishment clause of the First Amendment forbids state-mandated reading of the Bible, or recitation of the Lord's Prayer in public schools.

Epperson v. Arkansas (1968). In line with the establishment clause, *Epperson* prohibited states from banning the teaching of evolution in public schools.

Employment Division v. Smith (1990). This case determined that the state could deny unemployment benefits to a person fired for violating a state prohibition on the use of peyote, even though the use of the drug was part of a religious ritual. In short, states may accommodate otherwise illegal acts done in pursuit of religious beliefs, but they are not required to do so.

Though *Abington School Dist. v. Schempp, Epperson v. Arkansas,* and *Employment Division v. Smith* are important for understanding limits on freedom of religion, they are not on the list of required cases.

THE SECOND AMENDMENT

The Second Amendment to the Constitution, which protects citizens' rights to keep and bear arms, has led to a debate over whether the Constitution protects citizens' rights to bear arms under all circumstances, or only when those citizens serve in "well-regulated militias." Thus far, the Supreme Court's rulings on the Second Amendment have upheld the individual right to keep and bear arms, while allowing for wide variations in gun laws from state to state and in large cities. Future court decisions are likely to revolve around concerns about public safety and the ways in which governmental regulation of firearms may promote or interfere with public safety and individual rights.

The Second Amendment Goes to Court

Essential Case: *McDonald v. Chicago* (2010)

Facts: In 2008, Otis McDonald, a Chicago resident, wanted to purchase a handgun for self-defense. However, he could not buy one due to the city's laws restricting new handgun registrations. McDonald and a group of other Chicago residents sued the city.

Issue: Lawyers representing McDonald argued that Chicago's laws violated the Fourteenth Amendment's due process clause. As McDonald had not committed a crime, the city had no right to deny him the right to own a handgun.

Holding: In a 5-4 decision, the Supreme Court used the Fourteenth Amendment to incorporate the Second Amendment to the states, striking down gun control laws in Chicago and other cities. The Court held that states do not have the power to impede their citizens' rights to keep and bear arms granted by the Second Amendment. Dissenting justices argued that the case was not the right vehicle for incorporation, as self-defense is not mentioned in the Second Amendment.

Essential Case: *United States v. Lopez* (1995)

Facts: In 1992, high school senior Alfonso Lopez was arrested for taking a gun to school. He was tried and convicted for violating the Gun-Free School Zones Act of 1990. He appealed the decision to the Supreme Court.

Issue: Lopez argued that the Gun-Free School Zones Act of 1990 violated the Constitution, as the federal government did not have the power to regulate public schools. The federal government argued that the law was constitutional based on the commerce clause—firearms were interstate commerce.

Holding: In a 5-4 decision, the Supreme Court struck down the Gun-Free School Zones Act of 1990. The majority argued that merely carrying a gun did not qualify as commerce. The Court's holding affirmed the broad lawmaking power of Congress under the commerce clause, but ruled that the commerce clause does not grant Congress the power of firearm regulation. The dissenting justices argued that school shootings violently disrupt children's education, education being a crucial component for financial success later in life. In this way, they believed that guns in schools interrupted interstate commerce.

THE THIRD AMENDMENT

The most antiquated of all the amendments—though important at the time of its creation—the Third Amendment forbids the government from forcing citizens to allow soldiers to live in their homes at all during peace and only when allowed by law during war. It was a direct reaction to the British practice of using civilian support to conduct military operations.

THE FOURTH AMENDMENT

The Fourth Amendment places restrictions on government agencies regarding criminal or civil procedural investigations and does much to protect an individual's "person, house, papers, and effects against unreasonable searches and seizures." When the police want to search private property, in most circumstances they must first go before a judge and justify the search. If the judge is convinced that the search is likely to uncover evidence of illegality—called **probable cause**—the judge issues a **search warrant**, which limits where the police may search and what they may take as evidence. Evidence found by police who disregard this procedure may not be admitted as evidence in trial. This is called the **exclusionary rule**. Questions regarding probable cause, traffic stops, stop-and-frisk searches, and search warrants have led to challenges regarding the interpretation of the exclusionary rule regarding evidence seized without proper procedures. In its original form, the exclusionary rule holds that all evidence unlawfully gathered must be excluded from judicial proceedings.

As with all constitutional rights, however, there are exceptions to this rule. In 1984, the Supreme Court established the **objective good faith** exception, which allows for convictions in cases in which a search was not technically legal (either because it violated the warrant or because the warrant itself was faulty) but was conducted under the assumption that it was legal. The court has also determined that illegally seized evidence that would eventually have been found legally is also admissible in court. This principle is known as the **inevitable discovery rule**. There are also circumstances under which the police may conduct a search without a warrant. Police may conduct an immediate search following a legal arrest, for example. Police may also conduct an immediate search of private property if the owner consents to that search. Evidence found in plain view may be seized immediately; if, for example, a person is growing marijuana on their front lawn, the police may seize that evidence without first acquiring a search warrant. Finally, police may conduct an immediate search if they have probable cause to believe they will find evidence of criminal activity, especially when there are

Did You Know?
In *Mapp v. Ohio*, the Court established the Exclusionary Rule, which prohibits the government from using evidence that is gathered in violation of the Constitution.

exigent circumstances—reason to believe that someone may be harmed or that evidence could disappear by the time they received a warrant and returned. The police later have to demonstrate in court that they had probable cause.

In recent times, the primacy of the Fourth Amendment has been challenged by the ease with which government agencies can gather data on citizens digitally through such methods as wiretapping, bulk collection of phone records, and computer hacking. Fears of internal and external terrorism have led some Americans to support the Patriot Act, USA Freedom Act, and warrantless searches at airports, while others fear that government intrusion into privacy may confer too much power to an anonymous elite. With regard to privacy concerns and self-incrimination, the Court has placed limitations on the bulk collection of telecommunications metadata collected under the Patriot and USA Freedoms Acts.

Did You Know?

The Fifth Amendment defines the processes and procedures for indictment by grand jury, prohibits self-incrimination, protects the right to due process, and eliminates the possibility of double jeopardy.

THE FIFTH AMENDMENT

The Fifth Amendment does the most to protect an individual from the broad powers of the federal government. It provides a guarantee of a **grand jury** when a suspect is held for a capital or other "infamous" crime. It eliminates the possibility of a person being maliciously prosecuted for the same crime again and again by prohibiting **double jeopardy**. It establishes the right of the government to seize property for public use under the auspices of **eminent domain**, but only if such seizure can be "justly compensated." The most significant attribute of the Fifth Amendment is its mandate that the federal government not deprive an individual of "life, liberty, or property by any level unless **due process of law** is applied." **Rights granted to the accused** are a fundamental protection against governmental abuse of power. Many of these rights are found in the Fifth Amendment. Without them, the government could imprison its political opponents without trial, or it could guarantee conviction through numerous unfair prosecutorial tactics. However, these rights are also controversial. Anticrime organizations and politicians frequently decry these protections when arguing that it is too difficult to capture, try, and imprison criminals. These accusations have grown louder and more frequent since the 1960s, when the Warren Court (the Supreme Court under Chief Justice Earl Warren) greatly expanded those protections that are granted to criminal defendants. *Miranda v. Arizona* (1966) is the most dramatic and well-known of the Warren Court decisions. The court found that all defendants must be informed of all their legal rights before they are arrested. (It is thanks to *Miranda* that we all know the phrase "You have the right to remain silent..." and that you can't get through an episode of *Law & Order* without hearing it at least once.)

Essential Case: *Gideon v. Wainwright* (1963)

Facts: In 1961, Earl Gideon was accused of breaking-and-entering, destruction of property, and theft. During the trial, the judge did not appoint him an attorney, as the crimes Florida charged him with were non-capital offenses. A jury convicted Gideon of the crime. From prison, Gideon studied constitutional law and drafted a handwritten appeal to the Supreme Court.

Issue: Gideon argued that Florida had violated his Sixth Amendment right to an attorney.

Holding: The Supreme Court unanimously ruled that Florida had violated Gideon's right to an attorney. This ruling had the effect of incorporating the Sixth Amendment to the states, expanding the rights of the accused. Since *Gideon*, all defendants in jury trials must have the option of having an attorney represent them.

Capital crimes are those for which, if the defendant is found guilty, a jury can sentence that person to death.

Important Cases

Weeks v. United States (1914). Though the Constitution is unequivocal when it forbids unlawful search and seizure, such ill-gotten evidence was still commonly used to prosecute defendants. *Weeks* established the exclusionary rule, which held that illegally obtained evidence could not be used in federal court.

Powell v. Alabama (1932). The Constitution is clear in the Sixth Amendment when it guarantees all those accused of a federal crime the right to have a lawyer. But what about those accused of state crimes? Should they get a lawyer if they can't afford one? In *Powell*, the court ruled that state governments must provide counsel in cases involving the death penalty to those who can't afford it.

Betts v. Brady (1942). The *Betts* case established that state governments did not have to provide lawyers to indigent defendants in capital cases.

Mapp v. Ohio (1961). By 1961, the exclusionary rule meant that any unlawfully gathered evidence could not be introduced in federal court, but such evidence was introduced all the time in state courts. The *Mapp* case extended the exclusionary rule to the states, increasing the protections for defendants.

Escobedo v. Illinois (1964). *Escobedo* is another important Warren Court decision. Here, the court held that any defendant who asked for a lawyer had to have one granted to him—or any confession garnered after that point would be inadmissible in court.

Although *Weeks v. United States*, *Powell v. Alabama*, *Betts v. Brady*, *Mapp v. Ohio*, *Escobedo v. Illinois*, and *Miranda v. Arizona* are important cases to understand the rights of the accused, they are not on the list of required cases.

Protection from Self-Incrimination

The Constitution protects individuals from **self-incrimination.** A defendant cannot be forced to testify at trial, and the jury is instructed not to infer guilt when a defendant chooses to not testify. Furthermore, a defendant must be notified of their right to remain silent, their right to a lawyer, and their protection against self-incrimination at the time of their arrest.

Did You Know?
The Fifth Amendment protects against self-incrimination, a situation in which an accused individual is compelled to be a witness against themselves in a court of law.

However, the Court has held that unwarned interrogation can stand as direct evidence in court when dealing with matters concerning "public safety."

For years, the courts rarely admitted into evidence confessions from arrestees who had not been properly "Mirandized." In recent years, however, the Supreme Court has defined some situations in which such confessions are admissible. In 1991, the court ruled that a coerced confession does not automatically invalidate a conviction. Rather, an appeals court may consider all evidence entered at trial. If the court decides that a conviction was probable even without the confession, it may let the guilty verdict stand.

THE SIXTH AMENDMENT

This amendment allows persons accused of a crime to be prosecuted by an impartial jury. Individuals have the right to be informed of their charges, to confront witnesses, to subpoena witnesses for their defense, and to have a lawyer for their defense. The Sixth Amendment forms the basis for **habeas corpus**, which protects against unlawful imprisonment and ensures that a person cannot be held indefinitely without being formally charged before a judge or in a court, or without a legal reason to extend their detention. In 1932, the Supreme Court used the Fourteenth Amendment to incorporate this right in capital cases ("the Scottsboro boys" case). In the 1963 case *Gideon v. Wainwright*, the court ruled that all criminal defendants in state courts were entitled to legal counsel. In both cases, the court ruled that the state must provide a lawyer to defendants who are too poor to hire a lawyer. The court has since extended this protection to misdemeanor cases, provided those cases could result in jail time for the defendant. However, the court has held that states are not required to provide a lawyer to litigants in civil cases.

The Sixth Amendment also guarantees defendants the **right to a speedy trial.** The courts have become so overburdened with cases that the Supreme Court recently imposed a 100-day limit between the time of arrest and the start of a trial. The limit has had little practical effect, however, because both prosecutors and defense attorneys can request an extension to prepare their cases. Courts have generally granted such extensions. As a result, it is not unusual for a defendant to wait a year or more between their arrest date and a trial.

THE SEVENTH AMENDMENT

Statutory, or written, law has come to replace or supersede common law, which is based on past court decisions. The Seventh Amendment allows for trial by jury in common-law cases.

THE EIGHTH AMENDMENT

The **Eighth Amendment** states that "excessive bail shall not be required, nor excessive fines imposed, nor cruel and unusual punishments inflicted." The government is not required, however, to offer bail to all defendants. In 1984, Congress passed the Bail Reform Act to allow federal judges to deny bail to defendants considered either dangerous or likely to flee the country. The protection from excessive bail has *not* been incorporated, and states are therefore free to set bail as high as state law permits.

The **cruel and unusual punishment** clause of the Constitution lies at the heart of the debate over the death penalty. The court has placed limits on when the death penalty can be applied; however, it has upheld the constitutionality of the death penalty when properly applied. Critics point out that, statistically, those convicted of killing Black people are far less likely to receive the death penalty than those convicted of killing white people. The court has rejected this argument. In recent years, the court has moved to make it easier for states to carry out the death penalty by limiting the number and nature of appeals allowed by convicted murderers on death row. Recently too, however, some states have enacted moratoriums on the death penalty for reasons including methodology problems, flawed trial processes, and ethical objections.

Important Cases

Furman v. Georgia (1972). Here, the court looked at the patchwork quilt of nationwide capital punishment decisions and found that its imposition was often racist and arbitrary. In *Furman*, the court ordered a halt to all death penalty punishments in the nation until a less arbitrary method of sentencing was found.

Woodson v. North Carolina (1976). North Carolina tried to satisfy the court's requirement that the imposition of the death penalty not be arbitrary—so they made it a mandatory punishment for certain crimes. The court rejected this approach and ruled mandatory death penalty sentences as unconstitutional.

Gregg v. Georgia (1976). Georgia was finally able to convince the court that it had come up with a careful and fair system for trying capital offenses. As a result, the court ruled that under adequate guidelines the death penalty did not, in fact, constitute cruel and unusual punishment. Thus *Gregg* allowed the resumption of the death penalty in the United States.

Atkins v. Virginia (2002). Here, the United States lined up with most other nations in the world by forbidding the execution of defendants who have intellectual disabilities.

Roper v. Simmons (2005). Building on *Atkins*, the court declared the death penalty unconstitutional for defendants whose crimes were committed as minors, even if they were charged as adults.

Did You Know?
The Eighth Amendment protects criminal defendants from egregiously harsh penalties from the federal government, either as the price for receiving pretrial release or as punishment post-conviction.

Although *Furman v. Georgia, Woodson v. North Carolina, Gregg v. Georgia, Atkins v. Virginia,* and *Roper v. Simmons* are important to understanding limits on protections from cruel and unusual punishment, they are not on the list of required cases.

THE NINTH AMENDMENT

The Ninth Amendment reaffirms the principles of a limited federal government. "The enumeration in the Constitution, of certain rights, shall not be construed to deny or disparage others retained by the people" means that rights not specifically mentioned in the Constitution are still protected—everyone has the right to brush their hair, for example—even though that right is mentioned nowhere in the Bill of Rights. Although somewhat vague in its premise, the Ninth Amendment has led to the implied right to privacy and other questions regarding individual rights not identified or even understood at the time of the creation of the Constitution.

THE RIGHT OF ALL AMERICANS TO PRIVACY

The right to privacy is not specifically mentioned in the Constitution. However, in the 1965 Supreme Court case of *Griswold v. Connecticut*, the court ruled that the Bill of Rights contained an **implied right to privacy.** The court ruled that the combination of the First, Third, Fourth, Fifth, Ninth, and Fourteenth Amendments added up to a guarantee of privacy. The *Griswold* case concerned a state law banning the use of contraception; the Supreme Court decision overturned that law. *Griswold* also laid the foundation for the landmark *Roe v. Wade* case of 1973, which legalized abortion.

Important Cases

Roe v. Wade (1973). In a 7-2 decision, the court ruled that abortion was protected by the right to privacy established in *Griswold*, supported by the Ninth and Fourteenth Amendments. The Court held that state bans on abortion are unconstitutional. Their ruling held that states had no control over abortion decisions during the first trimester of pregnancy, though states could limit abortions in the second and third trimesters. *Roe v. Wade* was a controversial decision, both in the legal and political spheres. It was ultimately overturned in 2022 by *Dobbs v. Jackson Women's Health Organization*, which once again granted to the states absolute decision-making power in all abortion-related matters.

Webster v. Reproductive Health Services (1989). This case did not overturn *Roe v. Wade*, but it did give states more power to regulate abortion.

Planned Parenthood v. Casey (1992). A Pennsylvania law that would have required a woman to notify her husband before getting an abortion was thrown out, but laws calling for parental consent and the imposition of a 24-hour waiting period were upheld. All in all, the message was that states *can* regulate abortion but not with regulations that impose an "undue burden" upon women.

Lawrence v. Texas (2003). With this ruling, the Supreme Court struck down a sodomy law that had criminalized gay sex in Texas. The court had previously addressed the same issue in *Bowers v. Hardwick* (1986), in which it did not find constitutional protection of sexual privacy. *Lawrence* explicitly overruled *Bowers*, saying that consensual sexual conduct was part of the liberty protected under the Fourteenth Amendment.

Although *Griswold v. Connecticut*, *Roe v. Wade*, *Webster v. Reproductive Health Services*, *Planned Parenthood v. Casey*, and *Lawrence v. Texas* are important to understand the right to privacy, they are not on the list of required cases.

CIVIL RIGHTS

The AP U.S. Government and Politics Exam occasionally tests your knowledge of key civil rights legislation. Here is what you need to know about civil rights for the test.

Civil Rights and African Americans

Prior to the Civil War, most of the African American population in the United States consisted of enslaved people who were denied virtually any legal rights whatsoever. Free Black people were also denied basic civil rights such as the right to vote and the right to equal protection under the law. Because the Supreme Court had ruled in 1833 that the Bill of Rights applied to the federal government only, states were free to enact discriminatory and segregationist laws. Many did so to ensure the oppression of African Americans.

The Civil War began the long, slow development toward equality of the races before the law. Here is a list of key events in that process.

- **The Civil War (1861–1865).** The Civil War began, at least in part, over the issue of slavery (the debate over the relative powers of the federal and state governments was also a major cause of the war). The war was more clearly defined as a war about slavery in 1863, when President Lincoln issued the **Emancipation Proclamation,** which declared the liberation of enslaved people in the rebel states. The Civil War also influenced the civil rights process in a less direct and less immediate way, as it resulted in an increase in the power of the federal government. One hundred years later, the increased power vested in the federal government would be the means of imposing and enforcing equal rights laws in the states.

- **Thirteenth Amendment (1865).** The Thirteenth Amendment, ratified after the Civil War, made slavery illegal. With the exception of having committed a crime (that is, people in prison), this amendment also prohibited indentured servitude.

- **Fourteenth Amendment (1868).** The Fourteenth Amendment, ratified during Reconstruction, declared that all persons born in the U.S. were citizens and that all citizens were entitled to equal rights, which are protected by due process. The amendment was designed to prevent states in the South from depriving formerly enslaved persons of their rights. Its clauses guaranteeing **due process** and **equal protection** were later used by the Supreme Court to apply most of the Bill of Rights to state law. However, in the 1880s, the Supreme Court interpreted the amendment narrowly, allowing the states to enact segregationist laws. The Fourteenth Amendment also made African Americans citizens of the nation and of their home states, overruling the *Dred Scott v. Sandford case* (1857), which had ruled that enslaved people and their descendants were not citizens.

Although the *Dred Scott* case is important to understanding the background for the Fourteenth Amendment, it is not on the list of required cases.

Did You Know?
The Civil Rights Act of 1964 and the Voting Rights Act of 1965 granted Black Americans more federally protected power in an attempt to make the goal of social equity easier to obtain.

- **Fifteenth Amendment (1870).** The Fifteenth Amendment banned laws that would prevent African Americans from voting on the basis of their race or the fact that they previously were enslaved people.

- **Civil Rights Act of 1875.** The Civil Rights Act of 1875 banned discrimination in public places such as hotels, restaurants, and railroad cars, as well as in selection for jury duty. The Supreme Court overturned portions of the Act in 1883.

- **Jim Crow laws and voting restrictions.** As the federal government exerted less influence over the South, states, towns, and cities passed numerous discriminatory and segregationist laws. The Supreme Court supported the states by ruling that the Fourteenth Amendment did not protect Black Americans from discriminatory state laws, and that Black Americans would have to seek equal protection from the states, not from the federal government. In 1883, the court also reversed the Civil Rights Act of 1875, thus opening the door to legal segregation. These segregationist laws are known collectively as **Jim Crow laws.** The states also moved to deprive Black Americans of their voting rights by imposing **poll taxes** (a tax that must be paid in order to vote) and literacy tests. To allow poor, illiterate white people to vote, some states passed **grandfather clauses** that exempted from these restrictions anyone whose grandfather had voted. Grandfather clauses effectively excluded Black Americans whose grandparents had been enslaved people and therefore could not have voted.

- **Equal Pay Act of 1963.** This federal law made it illegal to base an employee's pay on race, gender, religion, or national origin. The Equal Pay Act was also important to the women's movement and to the civil rights struggles of other minorities.

- **Twenty-Fourth Amendment (1964).** This outlawed poll taxes, which had been used to prevent Black people and poor white people from voting.

- **Civil Rights Act of 1964.** The Civil Rights Act of 1964 was a landmark piece of legislation. It not only established new rights for Black Americans and other minorities, but also gave the federal government greater means of enforcing the law. The law banned discrimination in public accommodations (public transportation, offices, and so on) and in all federally funded programs. It also prohibited discrimination in hiring based on race and gender. Finally, it required the government to cut off funding from any program that did not comply with the law, and it gave the federal government the power to initiate lawsuits in cases of school segregation. States that had previously ignored federal civil rights mandates now faced serious consequences for doing so.

- **Voting Rights Act of 1965.** The Voting Rights Act was designed to counteract voting discrimination in the South. It allowed the federal government to step into any state or county in which less than 50% of the population was registered to vote, or in areas that used literacy tests to prevent voting. In those areas, the federal government could register voters (which is normally a function of the states).

- **Civil Rights Act, Title VIII (1968).** This banned racial discrimination in housing.

- **Civil Rights Act of 1991.** This law was designed to address a number of problems that had arisen in civil rights law during the previous decade. Several Supreme Court decisions had limited the abilities of job applicants and employees to bring suit against employers with discriminatory hiring practices; the 1991 act eased those restrictions.

Essential Case: *Brown v. Board of Education* (1954)

Facts: In 1951, a group of 20 families from Topeka, Kansas, filed suit against the city's board of education for enforcing school segregation. A District Court upheld school segregation as it did not violate *Plessy v. Ferguson* (1896). The families appealed the case to the Supreme Court, where the case was heard alongside four other school segregation cases.

Issue: Did the Fourteenth Amendment's equal protection clause apply to school segregation?

Holding: In a unanimous decision, the Supreme Court struck down school segregation nationwide. The Court held that "separate educational facilities are inherently unequal" due to the detrimental impact that racial segregation has on minorities. In fact, many justices had made up their minds long before hearing the case, as racial segregation was tarnishing America's image abroad. The ruling overturned the precedent set by *Plessy*, arguing that separation is harmful even when the "tangible qualities" of a situation are identical.

Important Cases

Plessy v. Ferguson (1896). This case famously allowed Southern states to twist the equal protection clause of the Fourteenth Amendment by allowing "separate but equal" facilities based on race.

Brown v. Board II (1955). One year after *Brown v. Board of Education*, the Warren Court saw that segregation was still ubiquitous. So in *Brown II*, they ordered schools to desegregate "with all due and deliberate speed."

Heart of Atlanta Motel, Inc. v. United States (1964). Did the Federal Civil Rights Act of 1964 mandate that places of public accommodation are prohibited from discriminating against Black Americans? Yes, said the court.

Although *Plessy v. Ferguson*, *Brown v. Board II*, *Heart of Atlanta Motel, Inc. v. United States*, *Katzenbach v. McClung*, *Regents of the University of California v. Bakke*, *Grutter v. Bollinger*, *Gratz v. Bollinger*, and *Shelby County v. Holder* are important to understanding the history of civil rights, they are not on the list of required cases.

Did You Know?
While *Brown* was hailed as a victory of the Civil Rights Movement, the Court's holding was met with resistance from southern governments. In the Deep South, politicians developed and implemented "Massive Resistance," a program intended to stop school integration at all costs. In order to combat such resistance, the federal government sent the National Guard to aid in the integration of schools in both Alabama and Louisiana. Memorable photos show Ruby Bridges, the first African American student to integrate in the South, being escorted to school by U.S. Marshals following the Court's ruling.

Katzenbach v. McClung (1964). The Civil Rights Act of 1964 prohibited discrimination in public places, but what about in private businesses? The *Katzenbach* case established that the power of Congress to regulate interstate commerce extends to state discrimination statutes. This ruling made the Civil Rights Act of 1964 apply to virtually all businesses.

Regents of the University of California v. Bakke (1978). Alan Bakke was a white applicant who was rejected from medical school because of an affirmative action plan to boost the number of Black students. The court ruled that Bakke had been unfairly excluded and that quotas requiring a certain percentage of minorities violated the Fourteenth Amendment. But the court also held that race-based affirmative action *was* permissible so long as it was in the service of creating greater diversity.

Grutter v. Bollinger (2003) and *Gratz v. Bollinger* (2003). These cases involved the University of Michigan Law School and the University of Michigan undergraduate school. Both used affirmative action, but the undergraduate school did so by giving minority applicants a large boost in the score used by officers deciding on admission. The court threw out the undergraduate system of selection, but generally upheld *Bakke*.

Shelby v. Holder (2013). The Supreme Court struck down Section 4 of the Voting Rights Act, which required federal pre-clearance of voting law changes for states with a history of voter discrimination. The ruling spurred fear among minorities, as concern about voter suppression rose.

Although the number of major new civil rights laws has decreased in the past decades, the fight for civil rights for Black Americans and other minority groups is far from over. Although legally enforced segregation of public facilities no longer exists, racial segregation remains a national concern. Most public school systems remain essentially segregated because the neighborhoods that feed into them are segregated. The impact of this ***de facto* segregation** (as opposed to ***de jure* segregation,** which is segregation by law) is increased by the disparity in average incomes between white people and Black people. Because many local school systems are supported by property taxes, lower-income neighborhoods end up with poorly funded, overcrowded schools.

Attempts at Integration

In the 1970s, the Supreme Court ruled that the government could bus children to different school districts to achieve the goal of integration, provided the affected districts had been intentionally segregated. Busing plans failed, however, due to public protest and the abandonment of cities by white residents.

Furthermore, discrimination continues in employment, housing, and higher education. Because such discrimination is subtler—few employers tell job applicants, "I won't hire you because you're Black"—it is more difficult to enforce antidiscrimination laws and punish offenders in these areas. **Affirmative action** programs—which seek to create special employment opportunities for minorities, women, and others who suffer from discrimination—address these questions but have become increasingly controversial and politically unpopular in recent years. In *Regents of the University of California v. Bakke* (1978), the Supreme Court ruled that affirmative action programs could not use quotas to meet civil rights goals; however, it did say that gender and race could be considered among other factors by schools and businesses practicing affirmative action. Opponents of affirmative action programs argue that such programs penalize white people and thus constitute **reverse discrimination,** which is illegal under the Civil Rights Act of 1964.

Civil Rights and Women

The granting of equal rights for women in the United States is a relatively recent phenomenon. Women were not given the right to vote in all 50 states until 1920. Employment discrimination based on gender was not outlawed until 1964. As recently as the early 1990s, women were not guaranteed leave from work after giving birth (this finally changed with the **Family and Medical Leave Act of 1993,** which gives 12 weeks of unpaid leave to parents of newborns). Those who fought for the failed **Equal Rights Amendment** to the Constitution (1972–1982) continue to argue that women do not yet have a full guarantee of equality under the law from the federal government.

Here is a list of events of the women's rights movement that the AP U.S. Government and Politics Exam sometimes tests.

- **Nineteenth Amendment (1920).** Granted women the right to vote.
- **Equal Pay Act of 1963.** This federal law made it illegal to base an employee's pay on race, gender, religion, or national origin. Prior to this bill, many businesses and organizations maintained different pay and raise schedules for their male and female employees. In fact, many continued to do so after the bill passed. Federal enforcement of the law, however, has helped narrow the gap between the salaries and wages of the genders.
- **Civil Rights Act of 1964.** The provision pertaining to gender discrimination was included in the Civil Rights Act of 1964 by an opponent of the bill. Representative Howard Smith of Virginia believed his proposal was ridiculous and would therefore weaken support for the bill. Much to his surprise, the bill passed with the gender provision—prohibiting employment discrimination based on gender—included. The Ledbetter Fair Pay Act of 2009 enhanced those protections.

Did You Know?
Founded in 1966, the National Organization for Women (NOW) mission has been to promote feminist ideals, lead social change, eliminate discrimination, and achieve and protect the equal rights of all women and girls in all aspects of social, political, and economic life. NOW's message is simple: equality for women.

NOW's 1966 statement of purpose stated: "The purpose of NOW is to take action to bring women in to full participation in the mainstream of American society now, exercising all the privileges and responsibilities thereof in truly equal partnership with men. We organize... to break through the silken curtain of prejudice and discrimination against women in government, industry, the professions, the churches, the political parties, the judiciary, the labor unions, in education, science, medicine, law, religion, and every other field of importance in American society."

- **Title IX, Higher Education Act (1972).** This law prohibits gender discrimination by institutions of higher education that receive federal funds. Title IX has been used to force increased funding of women-only programs, such as women's sports. The **Civil Rights Restoration Act of 1988** increased its potency by allowing the government to cut off all funding to schools that violate the law (and not just to the specific program or office found in violation). As a result of these laws mandating equity in college athletics spending, colleges have eliminated many less popular men's sports, resulting in a backlash against Title IX and the Civil Rights Restoration Act.

- **Lilly Ledbetter Fair Pay Act of 2009.** This law closed a loophole that limited suits on discriminatory pay based on the timing of the issuance of the first discriminatory paycheck. The Ledbetter Act expanded those limits to allow suits based on any discriminatory paycheck, an important adjustment for employees who learn of inequities in wages or salary only after they have persisted for some time.

As women have entered the workplace in greater numbers, the issue of sexual harassment at work has gained prominence. **Sexual harassment** is defined as any sexist or sexual behavior—physical or verbal—that creates a hostile work environment. It can range from suggestive remarks to attempts to coerce sex from a subordinate. Like other forms of discrimination, it is difficult to prove legally. Efforts to combat it range from public-awareness programs to sensitivity training to increased legal penalties for harassers.

Other Major Civil Rights Advances

- **Age Discrimination Act of 1967.** As its name states, this law prohibits employment discrimination on the basis of age. The law makes an exception for jobs in which age is essential to job performance. An amendment to this law banned some mandatory retirement ages and increased others to 70.

- **Twenty-Sixth Amendment (1971).** Extended the right to vote to 18-year-olds.

- **Individuals with Disabilities Education Act (1975).** Ensured that children with disabilities can receive a free, appropriate public education, just like other children.

- **Voting Rights Act of 1982.** This law requires states to create congressional districts with minority majorities in order to increase minority representation in the House of Representatives. The law has resulted in the creation of numerous strangely shaped districts, such as one in North Carolina that was 160 miles long and, at points, only several hundred yards wide. The Supreme Court nullified the district just described, leaving it unclear how the government may both achieve the goals of the Voting Rights Act and maintain the regional integrity of congressional districts.

- **Americans with Disabilities Act of 1990.** This law requires businesses with more than 24 employees to make their offices accessible to people with disabilities. It also requires public transportation, new offices, hotels, and restaurants to be wheelchair-accessible whenever feasible. Finally, it mandated the development of wider telephone services for the hearing-impaired.

Other Important Cases

Federalism

Marbury v. Madison (1803). This most important of all decisions established **judicial review**—the Supreme Court's power to strike down acts of United States Congress that conflict with the Constitution.

McCulloch v. Maryland (1819). This case is important because it established that states could not interfere with implied powers of the federal government.

Gitlow v. New York (1925). *Gitlow* began the process of selective incorporation—the practice of transferring protections that Americans had from the federal government and applying them to state governments.

South Dakota v. Dole (1987). The federal government mandated the 21-year-old drinking age by threatening to withhold federal highway funds from all states that did not comply. In this case, such withholding was held to be constitutional.

Although *Gitlow v. New York* and *South Dakota v. Dole* are important cases for understanding federalism, they are not on the list of required cases. *Marbury v. Madison* and *McCulloch v. Maryland*, however, ARE required cases.

Executive Power

Korematsu v. United States (1944). This case was not the Supreme Court's finest hour, as it ruled that American citizens of Japanese descent could be interned and deprived of basic constitutional rights due to executive order.

United States v. Nixon (1974). In this case, Congress claimed that there was no such thing as executive privilege as it went after tapes that President Nixon had made of all his conversations in the Oval Office. The court disagreed and allowed for executive privilege, but it forbade its usage in criminal cases, which meant that Nixon ultimately did have to turn over the tapes.

Clinton v. City of New York (1998). This case banned the presidential use of a line-item veto as a violation of legislative powers.

Although *Korematsu v. United States, United States v. Nixon,* and *Clinton v. City of New York* are important to understanding executive power, they are not on the list of required cases.

CHAPTER 6 KEY TERMS

Civil liberties

Civil rights

Selective incorporation

Indictment

First Amendment

Freedom of speech

Freedom of the press

Freedom of petitioning the government

Freedom of assembly

Freedom of religion

Clear and present danger test

Slander

Libel

Obscenity

Preferred position doctrine

Prior restraint

Shield laws

Three-part obscenity test

Freedom of association

Free exercise

The establishment clause

Lemon test

Probable cause

Search warrant

Exclusionary rule

Objective good faith

Inevitable discovery rule

Exigent circumstances

Grand jury

Double jeopardy

Eminent domain

Due process of law

Rights granted to the accused

Self-incrimination

Habeas corpus

Right to a speedy trial

Eighth Amendment

Cruel and unusual punishment

Implied right to privacy

Emancipation Proclamation

Due process

Equal protection

Dred Scott v. Sandford (1857)

Jim Crow laws

Poll taxes

Grandfather clauses

De facto segregation

De jure segregation

Affirmative action

Reverse discrimination

Family and Medical Leave Act of 1993

Equal Rights Amendment

Civil Rights Restoration Act of 1988

Sexual harassment

Judicial review

Chapter 6 Drill

See Chapter 9 for answers and explanations.

Questions 1 and 2 refer to the passage below.

We should never forget that everything Adolf Hitler did in Germany was "legal" and everything the Hungarian freedom fighters did in Hungary was "illegal." It was "illegal" to aid and comfort a Jew in Hitler's Germany. Even so, I am sure that, had I lived in Germany at the time, I would have aided and comforted my Jewish brothers. If today I lived in a Communist country where certain principles dear to the Christian faith are suppressed, I would openly advocate disobeying that country's antireligious laws.

—Martin Luther King Jr., "Letter from a Birmingham Jail"

1. Which of the following statements best reflects King's message in this passage?

    (A) Nazi Germany and the suppression of Hungarian freedom fighters were both cruel events.
    (B) All laws are corrupt.
    (C) A law does not automatically mean that something is right or wrong.
    (D) The law can be a dangerous tool when used by dictators.

2. Which of the following statements best explains why King included this passage in "Letter from a Birmingham Jail"?

    (A) To claim that the United States was as bad as Nazi Germany and Communist Hungary
    (B) To show how segregationist laws were comparable to unjust laws in oppressive states
    (C) To promote himself as an activist who would work under the harshest conditions
    (D) To educate readers on the horrors of Nazi Germany and Communist Hungary

3. Which Supreme Court case established the right to always have counsel present in criminal court cases?

    (A) *Powell v. Alabama*
    (B) *Betts v. Brady*
    (C) *Gideon v. Wainwright*
    (D) *Miranda v. Arizona*

4. Which of the following is an accurate comparison between civil liberties and civil rights?

	Civil Liberties	Civil Rights
(A)	Enshrined in the Bill of Rights	The equal application of the law to all Americans
(B)	Have never been restricted	Supreme Court has always ruled to expand civil rights
(C)	Supreme Court has changed the scope of Americans' civil liberties	Only applies to African Americans
(D)	Can be amended at the state level	Legislation, Supreme Court decisions, and constitutional amendments have expanded civil rights

5. The "right to privacy" established by some historically important Supreme Court cases is based primarily on a legal interpretation of

    (A) the Fourteenth Amendment's Due Process Clause
    (B) the Fourteenth Amendment's Equal Protection Clause
    (C) the Civil Rights Act of 1964
    (D) Title IX of the Education Amendments Act of 1972

6. Which of the following issues did the Supreme Court consider when deciding *Engel v. Vitale*?

    (A) Students' ability to protest in school
    (B) Students' freedom of speech in school
    (C) State-sponsored prayer in school
    (D) State-sponsored funding of religious schools

7. *Wisconsin v. Yoder* addressed which of the following provisions of the First Amendment?

   (A) Freedom of the Press
   (B) Freedom of Speech
   (C) Freedom of Assembly
   (D) Freedom of Religion

8. Which of the following did NOT advance the rights of African Americans?

   (A) The Thirteenth Amendment
   (B) The Fifteenth Amendment
   (C) The Nineteenth Amendment
   (D) The Civil Rights Act of 1875

Summary

o   It is very important to remember that the Bill of Rights protects Americans only from the federal government. It wasn't until the passage of the Fourteenth Amendment and the advocacy of the 20th-century Supreme Court that these freedoms were selectively incorporated to the states.

o   Know about freedom of speech, clear and present danger, and the preferred position doctrine.

o   Freedom of the press is protected by the ban on prior restraint, but has limits (as in the case of slander or libel).

o   The rights of the people to assemble generally can't be limited, though there are some exceptions to this rule.

o   The Constitution forbids the creation of an official religion through the establishment clause, but also prevents the government from infringing on religious freedom through the free exercise clause.

o   We have seen a steady expansion of the rights of the accused, particularly since the decisions of the Warren Court.

o   Rising from the disgrace of slavery and Jim Crow laws, the court has acted in the latter half of the 20th century to protect racial minorities from discrimination. Today, most controversy swirls around the issue of affirmative action and whether it constitutes a form of reverse racism and thus constitutes a violation of the Fourteenth Amendment.

REFLECT

Respond to the following questions:

- Of which content topics discussed in this chapter do you feel you have achieved sufficient understanding to answer multiple-choice questions correctly?

- Of which content topics discussed in this chapter do you feel you have achieved sufficient understanding to discuss them effectively in an essay?

- On which content topics discussed in this chapter do you feel you need more work before you can answer multiple-choice questions correctly?

- On which content topics discussed in this chapter do you feel you need more work before you can discuss them effectively in an essay?

- Which parts of this chapter are you going to re-review?

- Will you seek further help, outside of this book (such as from a teacher, tutor, or AP Students), on any of the content in this chapter—and, if so, on what content?

Chapter 7
American Political Ideologies and Beliefs

"Politics ought to be the part-time profession of every citizen who would protect the rights and privileges of free men."

— Dwight D. Eisenhower

Did You Know?

Differing opinions on key American cultural values such as individualism, equal opportunity, free enterprise, rule of law, and limited government impact the relationship that the federal government has with its citizens.

Want to Learn More?

Read more in Chapters 2 and 3 of Alexis de Tocqueville's *Democracy in America*, "The Origin of the Anglo-Americans" and "Social Condition of the Anglo-Americans."

CONCEPTS

- What is public opinion?
- What is the public agenda, and how is the agenda shaped?
- How is public opinion measured?
- What role does the media play in shaping public opinion?
- What effect does the media have on individual political beliefs and voting behavior?

Public opinion, simply put, is how people feel about things. Pollsters measure the public's opinion of everything from television programs to commercial products to political issues. Networks, companies, and politicians commission these polls because they seek the approval of the public.

Obviously, public opinion is not uniform. Even the most popular television shows attract a minority of all Americans. Furthermore, many programs are designed to receive favorable ratings from a specific subgroup of society rather than from the public at large. Networks, for example, seek high ratings from young, middle-class audiences, as these are the audiences most sought after by advertisers. Because advertisers are less interested in senior citizens, networks seek their approval less aggressively.

The same holds true for political issues. Most Americans—the **general public**—care more about the political issues that affect their day-to-day lives directly. A political issue does not have to interest the majority of Americans, then, to be considered important by politicians. If an issue is of enough importance to a smaller group—the **issue public**—to cause those voters to become more politically active, that issue may well become an important political issue. Furthermore, very few politicians seek the approval of the general public as a whole. With the exception of the president, all politicians have much smaller constituencies, and they measure the public opinion of these constituencies in order to appeal to them. Members of the House of Representatives, for example, are interested primarily in the concerns of their home districts, which are often quite different from the concerns of the general public.

CHARACTERISTICS OF PUBLIC OPINION

Those who measure public opinion are not just interested in the direction of public opinion—that is, how the public is feeling at a given moment. They also want to know how strongly the public feels and how likely people are to change their minds. That is why they try to gauge the following characteristics of public opinion:

- **Saliency.** The saliency of an issue is the degree to which it is important to a particular individual or group. For example, Social Security is an issue with high salience for senior citizens. Among young voters, Social Security has a much lower salience.

- **Intensity.** How strongly do people feel about a particular issue? When the intensity of a group's opinion is high, that group can wield political influence far beyond their numbers.

- **Stability.** Public opinion on issues changes over time. Some dimensions of public opinion, such as support for democracy and a controlled free-market economy, remain relatively stable. Others, like presidential approval ratings, can change quickly, as was the case during the last two years of George H. W. Bush's administration. During the Gulf War (January 1991), President Bush recorded the highest approval ratings of any president since 1945. Less than two years later, the majority of Americans showed their disapproval of his performance as president by voting against him.

In the United States, public opinion is measured regularly through elections. Elections measure public opinion indirectly, however, because votes for—or against—candidates can rarely be translated into clear and specific opinions. Referenda measure the public's opinion on specific issues (a **referendum** submits to popular vote to accept or reject a measure passed by a legislative body). Public opinion is measured most frequently and directly by **public opinion polls.**

POLLS MEASURE PUBLIC OPINION

Public opinion polls are designed to empirically determine public opinion by asking questions of a much smaller group. These polls are generally surveys conducted to measure the feelings and beliefs of a population. Pollsters achieve this through **random sampling**, a method that allows them to poll a representative cross-section of the public. When polling by phone, pollsters use a computer that dials numbers randomly. **Benchmark polls** are conducted by a campaign when a candidate initially announces their intention to run. These polls provide the campaign with baseline data to see if their chances of winning an election improve over time. **Tracking polls** are those that are performed multiple times with an identical sample in order to track changes in opinion. **Entrance polls** are conducted on Election Day as voters head

> **Polling Accuracy**
> When performed correctly, polls can measure the opinions of 300 million Americans—within about a 5% margin of error—by polling a mere 1,500 of them.

into the polling station to cast their vote. When conducting **exit polls** at polling places on election day, pollsters target voting districts that collectively represent the voting public and randomly poll voters who are leaving the voting place. This method discourages bias, which may occur if pollsters were to approach only those voters who seemed most friendly or eager to participate. **Stratified random sampling** is a variation of random sampling, in which the population is divided into subgroups and weighted based on demographic characteristics.

For a poll to accurately reflect public opinion, its questions must be carefully worded. A poll that asks, "Do you approve or disapprove of the death penalty?" would likely yield a very different response from one that asks, "Would you want the death penalty imposed on someone who killed your parents?" Most pollsters try to phrase questions objectively. Polls generally ask multiple-choice questions, which are closed-ended, as opposed to open-ended questions (such as, "Explain why you approve or disapprove of the death penalty"). Closed-ended questions yield results that are more easily quantifiable, providing a more accurate read of the direction and intensity of public opinion.

Even with those controls, polls cannot be 100% accurate. Polling organizations know how accurate their polls are and include this information with the poll results. The accuracy is measured as a sampling error and appears as a percentage with a plus and minus sign to the left (for example, ±4%). The **sampling error** tells how far off the poll results may be. Suppose a poll indicated that 60% of Americans favored the death penalty. If that poll had a sampling error of ±4%, the actual percentage of Americans favoring the death penalty could be anywhere between 56% and 64%. Generally, the more respondents a poll surveys, the lower the sampling error. The reliability and validity of polls have come into question over the past decade as they have failed to accurately predict election outcomes. For example, all the major national polls projected Hillary Clinton as the winner of the 2016 presidential election, but Donald Trump won the Electoral College.

The best-known poll is the Gallup poll. Many major newspapers and television networks conduct public opinion polls, as do academic and public interest institutions. Public opinion can also be measured through surveys distributed to the population or through smaller focus groups, in which researchers can discuss reactions to ideas or candidates in depth and gauge how the general public may react.

WHERE DOES PUBLIC OPINION COME FROM?

Public opinion is made up of the views of individuals, who develop their political attitudes through a process called **political socialization.** Why, and when, do they change? What factors influence a person's political beliefs?

The first factor that influences individual political beliefs is **family.** Most people eventually affiliate with the same political party as their parents. Children's political beliefs are also greatly affected by the moral and ethical values they learn from their parents. Also important is their **location**—people born in rural states may develop political views that are more socially conservative than those of city dwellers.

As children grow, other factors influence their political socialization. In **school**, they learn about history and government, and they are exposed to the political perspectives of teachers and peers. **Religious institutions** have a similar influence on many Americans. **Mass media,** such as television, radio, magazines, and the Internet, further inform political attitudes. In general, however, this is because most political issues have little direct impact on their day-to-day lives.

Despite what you may have heard, people do not become more conservative or liberal as they age. The political beliefs that people possess by early adulthood typically do not change much over the course of their lives. Generational differences exist, but they are ever-changing and contribute to the political socialization that, in turn, influences one's political ideology.

Those who progress to **higher education** often find themselves questioning their social and political assumptions for the first time. As a result, college can be a time of radical change in an individual's political beliefs. Studies have shown that students retain many of the political attitudes they acquire in college throughout their lives.

POLITICAL IDEOLOGIES

The terms *liberal* and *conservative* refer to the predominant ideologies in the United States. An **ideology** is a coherent set of thoughts and beliefs about politics and government.

The three most common political ideologies in the United States are the following:

- **Conservative**. Conservatives stress that individuals should be responsible for their own well-being and should not rely on government assistance. As a result, they tend to oppose government interference in the private sector. They also oppose most federal regulations, preferring that the market determine costs and acceptable business practices (*laissez-faire* economics). Social conservatives, who make up a powerful wing of the conservative population, do support government action on social issues. In a 2021 Gallup poll, 36% of Americans considered themselves to be conservatives.

- **Liberal**. Liberals believe that the government should be used in a limited way to remedy the social and economic injustices of the marketplace. They tend to support government regulation of the economy. They also support government efforts to redress past social injustices through programs such as affirmative action. Most liberals believe the government should strictly enforce the separation of church and state, and therefore oppose school-sponsored prayer and proposed bans on abortions, which they perceive as motivated by religious beliefs. In a 2021 Gallup poll, 25% of Americans considered themselves to be liberal.

- **Moderate (or Independent).** The beliefs of moderates do not constitute a coherent ideology. Instead, moderates view themselves as pragmatists who apply common sense rather than philosophical principles to political problems. A 2021 Gallup poll found that 37% of Americans considered themselves to be moderate.

Compared with citizens of other Western democracies, Americans have fewer main ideological groups. The many extreme political parties that exist in Europe, ranging from right-wing nationalists to left-leaning communists, are practically nonexistent in the United States. Furthermore, perhaps because of the paucity

Did You Know?
Due to globalization, the political culture of the United States has both influenced and been influenced by the values and beliefs of other countries.

For more information on the influence of globalization, check out Thomas Friedman's 2007 book, *The World Is Flat 3.0*, or Joseph Stiglitz's 2006 work, *Making Globalization Work*.

Did You Know?
Policy trends related to social issues reflect the success of either liberal or conservative ideologies in political parties. The way an individual perceives major historic events or policy changes influences the development of their political ideology. The way in which policy affects an individual's personal interests, the economy, social change, and the nation's growth also has a strong influence on the political ideology of an individual.

of viable groups, Americans readily vote outside of their self-professed political beliefs. In 2008, for example, 20% of self-identified conservative voters chose the more liberal Barack Obama over conservative Republican candidate John McCain because of the economic crisis and negative perception of Republican incumbent George W. Bush.

Americans who are strongly ideological tend to be the most politically active citizens. They are more likely than other Americans to join political organizations and participate in political activities, such as rallies and boycotts. One result of this phenomenon is that candidates in the presidential primaries must perform a balancing act. To win the primaries, they must first appeal to the more ideological party members. Then in the general elections, candidates must move back to the political center or risk alienating the general voting public.

See the next chapter for a more detailed explanation of political beliefs by party.

Determining Factors in Ideological and Political Behavior

Although there is no one-to-one correlation between people's backgrounds and their political beliefs, people who share certain traits tend to share political beliefs. Here are some of the factors that influence people's ideological and political attitudes.

- **Race/ethnicity.** Racial and ethnic groups who disproportionately populate the lower income levels tend to be more liberal than other Americans. Black and Hispanic people have been more likely than other Americans to support liberal social programs, for example. There are exceptions to these rules, however: Cuban Americans, for one, have tended to be conservative.

- **Religion.** Among the various religious groups in the United States, Jews and African American Protestants are generally the most liberal. Catholics also lean toward the political left, although many are conservative on social issues. Devout white Protestants tend to be more conservative. This is particularly true in the South, where white Protestants who attend church regularly are among the nation's strongest supporters of the Republican Party.

- **Gender.** Women tend to be more liberal than men. They are more likely to vote Democratic, more likely to support government social welfare programs, and less likely to support increases in military spending.

- **Income level.** Americans in higher income brackets tend to be more supportive of liberal goals such as racial and sexual equality. They also support greater international cooperation. However, they tend to be more fiscally conservative. Poorer Americans, conversely, are generally more conservative on all issues except those concerning social welfare.

Want to Know More?
To understand the ideological differences between the parties with regard to school vouchers, check out the Supreme Court case *Zelman v. Simmons-Harris* (2002).

To understand the differences among political ideologies about same-sex marriage, check out the Supreme Court case *Obergefell v. Hodges* (2015).

- **Region.** Regional differences arise from different economic and social interests. The ethnic and racial mix of the East Coast has made it the most liberal region of the country (making these "blue states"). In the more religious South, conservatism is predominant (making these "red states"). The West Coast, toward which many Americans continue to migrate, is the most polarized, with strong liberal and conservative contingencies scattered up and down the coast; however, this region has leaned more to the left in recent years. Liberals tend to congregate in cities; elsewhere, small town and more rural voters are generally conservative.

Red, Blue, Who?
On election maps, the color red is associated with Republicans (also called the GOP), and the color blue is associated with Democrats. So a state that is called a "purple state" is a mix of political party ideologies.

PUBLIC OPINION AND THE MASS MEDIA

The **news media** play an important role in the development of public opinion. News media include all of the following:

- news broadcasts on television (particularly 24-hour cable news networks), radio, and the Internet
- newspapers
- news magazines, such as *Time*
- magazine broadcast programs, such as *60 Minutes* and *20/20*
- newsmaker interview programs, such as *Meet the Press* and *The Daily Show* (which may be a comedy show, but has hosted many political guests and approached interviewing those guests seriously)
- political talk radio and podcasts
- websites, blogs, news aggregators, and online forums, such as *The Huffington Post, Drudge Report,* and *Politico*
- social media such as Meta, Instagram, Twitter, Tumblr, and Reddit

The Media and the Public Agenda

The most important role the media play is in setting the **public agenda.** By deciding which news stories to cover and which to ignore, and by returning to some stories night after night while allowing others to die after a few reports, the news media play an important part in determining the relative importance of political issues. This power of the media is limited by the public's inherent interest in a story, however. Prior to American involvement in Bosnia, constant coverage of the crisis there did little to raise public awareness of or interest in the story, because many Americans perceived the crisis as too remote to be of interest. In general, the process of setting the national agenda is a dynamic one. The media generally try to report stories that they believe will interest the public, and often there is a domino effect: as interest grows, coverage increases, and the story becomes more important.

These media provide most Americans with their most extensive exposure to politicians and the government. In many ways, they act as an intermediary between the people and the government, constantly questioning the motives and purposes of government actions and then reporting their findings to the public.

Throughout American history, public exposure to news media has consistently increased, both through higher literacy rates and through the expansion of news sources available in print, broadcast, and online. As a result, the media have played an increasingly significant role over the years in shaping public opinion.

Less clear is whether the media have the power to alter public opinion. It is generally believed that the media affect public opinion only when news coverage is extensive and is either predominantly negative or positive. For example, a constant barrage of negative images broadcast from Vietnam in the 1960s is credited with having turned many Americans against the war.

Conservative magazines, such as the *National Review,* are read almost exclusively by conservatives; liberal magazines, such as *The Nation,* are read primarily by liberals and progressives.

The news media can also alter public opinion when it is volatile: studies have demonstrated, for example, that public approval of the president is quite volatile and changes depending on whether news coverage of the president is positive or negative. In most other instances, however, the media do not greatly impact public opinion. This is in part because the news media cover many stories simultaneously, thus diluting their ability to influence public opinion on any single issue. It is also due in part to the fact that most Americans choose those news media that reinforce their political beliefs.

In addition to the news media, social media have become crucial tools for major grassroots political movements, both within the United States and abroad. Facebook, Twitter, Tumblr, Reddit, and other such social media sites can act as both a shaper and an indicator of public opinion, mostly with younger demographics (ages 18–25).

Are News Organizations Biased?

Critics from both ends of the political spectrum claim that the news media interject their political beliefs into their reports. It seems that not a day goes by without political pundits accusing Fox of being wildly conservative, and MSNBC of pushing a liberal agenda. Conservatives cite polls that have consistently shown that news reporters are more likely to hold liberal views and vote Democratic than are average Americans. Liberals point out that the major news media are owned by large, conservative companies. They argue that these companies exert pressure on the networks to downplay or ignore stories that reflect badly on the companies or the economic and political forces that support them.

Many studies have shown that there is less ideological bias in news reporting than is claimed by critics, either in the stories news organizations choose to report or in the way they report them. Over the course of American history, the news media have in fact grown markedly less biased. Most newspapers in the 18th and 19th centuries were openly partisan; today, many news organizations attempt to maintain journalistic integrity by remaining as objective as possible.

Commercial concerns reinforce this trend toward objectivity. Biased reporting may appeal strongly to one segment of the population, but it would just as surely alienate another segment. Seeking to offend the fewest possible audience members, most news organizations attempt to weed out bias and represent both sides of every story in their reports.

This does not mean, however, that the news media achieve complete objectivity, which is impossible. News organizations must make hundreds of decisions each day about what to report and how prominently to report it. Many local newspapers, for example, ignore all but the most major international stories, and not because they are not newsworthy but rather because their readers are generally uninterested in such stories. Network news broadcasts shy away from more complex stories, both because of time constraints and out of fear that they may bore viewers and listeners. This statement even applies to 24-hour news networks, which typically replay headlines throughout the day rather than discuss a larger variety of news stories.

Time and space constraints also result in bias in news reporting. Time and space concerns affect all news organizations, but they are most acutely felt by television news programs, which report up to 20 stories during their 18 minutes of broadcast time (some half-hour programs feature as many as 12 minutes of advertising!). News broadcasts increasingly use short sound bites to summarize information, with presidential candidates' sound bites decreasing in length from about 40 seconds (in 1968) to about 7.3 seconds today.

Finally, news reports can be biased by the sources that reporters use for their information. Reporters in Washington, D.C., must rely heavily on politicians and government sources for information, for example. The effect of this reliance is complicated. On one hand, reporters try to not offend their government sources with uncomplimentary reports, because they will need to return to those sources for future stories. Furthermore, there is the danger that reporters in Washington will become too close to the people and events they cover, resulting in bias. On the other hand, reporters must maintain their credibility and so must demonstrate their independence. They cannot consistently file favorable reports on the subjects they cover and expect to remain credible to the viewer. Moreover, surveys have demonstrated that reporters are more skeptical about the motives of politicians than average Americans are. This skepticism is reflected in their reporting. This may in part explain why public confidence in the government has decreased as the news media have grown more prominent.

Most modern politicians understand the power of the media and, accordingly, attempt to influence coverage. They stage events that yield appealing photographs (photo ops) and provide voluminous documented information in support of their positions (press releases). They plan appearances on shows with specific audience demographics that they are seeking, such as *The Daily Show* if they are seeking the youth vote. One famous photo op was President George W. Bush's speech aboard the *USS Abraham Lincoln* on May 1, 2003. A banner reading "Mission Accomplished" hung behind the president as he spoke, and it caused much controversy, as that was the final day of combat operations in Iraq. Many politicians felt that the banner was irresponsible and misleading, because casualties have continued for many years afterward. Attempts to manipulate media reports have grown more frequent and more sophisticated in recent years. Many politicians have studied the powerful way in which Ronald Reagan—a former actor—handled press coverage and have attempted to copy his successes.

The Audience Factor
A primary source of media bias is the media's need for immediate audience appeal.

CHAPTER 7 KEY TERMS

Public opinion
General public
Issue public
Saliency
Intensity
Stability
Referendum
Public opinion polls
Random sampling
Benchmark polls
Tracking polls
Entrance polls
Exit polls
Stratified random sampling

Sampling error
Political socialization
Family
Location
School
Religious institutions
Mass media
Higher education
Ideology
Conservative
Liberal
Moderate (Independent)
News media
Public agenda

Chapter 7 Drill

See Chapter 9 for answers and explanations.

Questions 1 and 2 refer to the chart below.

Percent of white American Christians who identify as

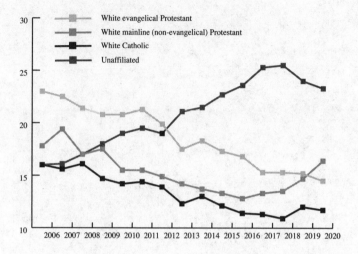

1. Which of the following describes a trend in the table above?

    (A) America's white population declined between 2006 and 2020.
    (B) The percent of white Americans who are unaffiliated with any religion was generally increasing from 2006 to 2020.
    (C) All religious affiliations increased from 2006 to 2020.
    (D) The number of American Christians declined from 2006 to 2020.

2. If the trends in the chart were to continue at the same rate, what is the best conclusion that could be drawn about the changing nature of political socialization in America?

    (A) Other religions than those popular with White Americans will become a dominant force in political socialization.
    (B) Fewer Americans will experience political socialization in a religious setting.
    (C) Political socialization will become obsolete.
    (D) Religion will become Americans' primary means of political socialization.

3. Which of the following is an accurate comparison between moderates and conservatives?

	Conservative	Moderate
(A)	Smallest voting bloc	Largest voting bloc
(B)	Back abortion rights	Rarely change their minds on political issues
(C)	Support affirmative action	Always vote the same way
(D)	Oppose government regulation	View themselves as pragmatists

4. Which of the following issues carries the most intensity with the American public?

    (A) Charter schools
    (B) Indian affairs
    (C) NASA's budget
    (D) Social Security

5. Which of the following is generally a factor in determining someone's ideological behavior?

    (A) Birth order
    (B) Sex
    (C) Sport preference
    (D) Age

6. In which of the following ways could a politician most likely generate positive media stories?

    (A) Change positions on a controversial issue
    (B) Appear in photographs with military veterans
    (C) Divorce a spouse with different political views
    (D) Solicit political donations from foreign governments

7. Which of the following is considered to have low stability in U.S. public opinion?

   (A) Presidential approval ratings
   (B) Support for an incumbent U.S. House Representative running unopposed
   (C) Support for Social Security benefits
   (D) U.S. Supreme Court approval ratings

8. Which of the following does the news media NOT play an integral role in?

   (A) Developing public opinion
   (B) Setting the public agenda
   (C) Providing Americans with their greatest exposure to government and politics
   (D) Measuring public opinion

Summary

o   Public opinion is measured by looking at saliency, intensity, and stability.

o   Data about what people think comes from polls, and many politicians base their decisions on polling data.

o   *Political socialization* is the term used to describe how people learn about politics as they grow and mature.

o   There are three basic political ideologies in America: conservative, liberal, and moderate.

o   Know which factors tend to lead to which ideologies. For example, a Black woman in Chicago is more likely to be liberal than a white man from the rural South.

o   The media plays a major role in the perception of government by placing certain policies and news events in the spotlight. This is also known as creating a public agenda.

REFLECT
Respond to the following questions:

- Of which content topics discussed in this chapter do you feel you have achieved sufficient understanding to answer multiple-choice questions correctly?

- Of which content topics discussed in this chapter do you feel you have achieved sufficient understanding to discuss them effectively in an essay?

- On which content topics discussed in this chapter do you feel you need more work before you can answer multiple-choice questions correctly?

- On which content topics discussed in this chapter do you feel you need more work before you can discuss them effectively in an essay?

- Which parts of this chapter are you going to re-review?

- Will you seek further help, outside of this book (such as from a teacher, tutor, or AP Students), on any of the content in this chapter—and, if so, on what content?

Chapter 8
Political Participation

"The only title in our democracy superior
to that of President is the title of citizen."
— Justice Louis D. Brandeis

Did You Know?
The Fifteenth, Seventeenth, Nineteenth, Twenty-Fourth, and Twenty-Sixth Amendments provided legal protections to citizens that enhanced the opportunity for political participation.

Concepts

- What are the different models of voting behavior?
- What coalitions make up the two main political parties in the United States?
- Why do third parties so often fail in U.S. politics?
- What effect has dealignment had on political parties?
- Are there serious policy differences between Democrats and Republicans?
- Who supports the two parties and why?
- How does the Constitution control special interests?
- How have interest groups helped to democratize the U.S. political system?
- Why are interest groups a threat to democracy?
- What role do interest groups play in setting the political agenda?
- What techniques do PACs use to get their messages across?
- How do interest groups achieve and exert their influence?

CITIZEN PARTICIPATION

In the previous chapter, we reviewed how individuals develop their political beliefs. Few political acts, however, are the work of a single person. Rather, most politically active people work within groups to achieve common political goals. The AP U.S. Government and Politics Exam expects you to know about the following types of linkage institutions: **political parties, interest groups, political action committees (PACs), 527 groups, elections,** and the **media.** This chapter reviews everything you need to know about the organization and activities of these groups.

Political Models of Voting Behavior

Sociologists and other academics have long analyzed voting behavior among populations. Due to the diverse beliefs and ideologies that exist, there are multiple models of voting behavior that theorize the reasons why an individual votes in a specific manner. For the AP U.S. Government and Politics Exam, you should know the following models:

Rational Choice—Rational choice voting is based on what is perceived to be in the citizen's individual interest.

Retrospective Voting—Retrospective voting involves the decision of whether a party or candidate in power should be reelected based on recent history and performance.

Prospective Voting—Prospective voting is based on the potential performance of a party or candidate should they be elected.

Party-line Voting—Party-line voting occurs when an individual votes for a candidate from one political party for all public offices.

POLITICAL PARTIES

As we've mentioned, few successful political accomplishments are the work of one person. More often, such a person joins with other like-minded individuals to form organizations that try to influence the outcomes of elections and legislative struggles. Political parties are unique among these groups in that they play a formal role in both of these processes. Although they are not mentioned in the Constitution, political parties became a mainstay of U.S. elections by the year 1800. Parties arose in the United States as a means of uniting those who shared political ideals, enabling them to elect like-minded representatives and pursue similar legislative goals. To those ends, parties endorse candidates for office and assist in their election efforts. In return for this support, parties expect candidates to remain loyal to goals defined by the party leadership.

The United States has two major political parties: Democrats and Republicans. This **two-party** or **bipartisan system** is reinforced by the nation's electoral system. U.S. election rules, which have been agreed upon by members of the two parties, also make it difficult for all but the two major parties to win a place on the ballot, further strengthening the two-party system.

No Partying
The framers of the Constitution disliked political parties and hoped to prevent them.

Party Characteristics

Don't forget these facts about political parties.

- Parties serve as intermediaries between the people and the government.
- Parties are made up of grassroots members, activist members, and leadership.
- Parties are organized to raise money, present positions on policy, and get their candidates elected to office.
- Parties were created outside of the Constitution—they are not mentioned in the document but were developed in the 1790s.
- Parties develop a **party platform**, which is a list of goals that outlines the party's positions on both issues and priorities.

Did You Know?
The structure of parties has been influenced by critical elections and consequent regional realignments, campaign finance law, and changes in communication and data management technology.

The major purpose of political parties is to get candidates elected to office. In the past, candidates were chosen by the party hierarchy, with little or no public input. However, since 1960, more states have passed laws requiring parties to select candidates through state-run **primary elections**. These primaries have reduced the power of political parties. Candidates must raise their own money for primaries, campaigning for their party's nomination with little to no support from the party itself. If the parties don't control the money, they can't control the candidates. This levels the playing field, but multiple candidates for the nomination can splinter the party membership.

Functions of Modern Political Parties

Political scientists identify three major subdivisions of political parties.

- **The party among the electorate.** Voters enroll in and identify with political parties. They generally vote for candidates who represent their party.

- **The party in government.** Government officials belong to political parties. They act together to pursue common goals, although regional and ideological differences sometimes subvert their efforts.

- **The party organization.** A group of people who are neither elected officials nor average voters, the party organization is made up of political professionals who recruit candidates and voters, organize campaign events, and raise money to promote the party.

Political parties perform all of the following functions:

- **Recruit and nominate candidates.** The parties are the major players in electoral politics. They seek candidates to run in their primary elections. They also create the rules by which candidates seek their nominations. In nearly all elections, nomination by one of the major parties is a prerequisite to victory. For example, in the 2008 Democratic primary, Barack Obama and Hillary Clinton continued to campaign until Obama had enough delegates to secure the nomination, at which point the Democratic Party formally announced him as their candidate.

- **Educate and mobilize voters.** Political parties fund propaganda campaigns to persuade voters to choose their candidates. They send mailings, hold rallies, and run advertisements. They target regions in which their support is strong and campaign to persuade voters in those regions to vote on election day.

- **Provide campaign funds and support.** The national parties have committees dedicated to raising funds for House and Senate campaigns. State parties also raise funds for candidates for both state and national offices. Although most candidates rely primarily on their own personal campaign support staff, they also need the help of the state or national party organizations.

- **Organize government activity.** Parties act as an organizing force in government. The House and Senate organize their leadership and committee systems strictly along party lines, as do state legislatures.

Did You Know?
Political parties are increasingly reliant on communication technology, including social media, and voter data management software to disseminate, control, and clarify political messages, improve outreach efforts, and increase voter mobilization.

- **Provide balance through opposition of two parties.** Each party serves as a check on the other by constantly watching for and exposing weakness and hypocrisy. The minority party (provided a single party controls both the White House and the Congress) performs the role of the *loyal opposition*, constantly critiquing the performance of the party in power.

- **Reduce conflict and tension in society.** The two-party system promotes compromise and negotiation in two ways: by encouraging parties to accommodate voters and encouraging voters to accept compromises in policy. The Republican Party, for example, includes both religious social conservatives and libertarians. To assemble winning coalitions, the party must somehow appease both groups. The groups, in turn, must be willing to compromise if they wish to prevent the Democrats from prevailing.

U.S. political parties are not hierarchical. The national party organization and each of the state and local organizations are largely autonomous and serve different functions; one does not necessarily take orders from the other.

Party committees are organized by geographic subdivisions. Locally, committees at the precinct, town, ward, and electoral district levels coordinate get-out-the-vote drives, door-to-door canvassing, and leaflet distribution. These party committees are staffed mostly by volunteers, and their work is largely concentrated around election time. The next largest geographic grouping is the county. County committees coordinate efforts in local elections and organize the efforts of committees on the precinct level. They also send representatives to each polling place to monitor voting procedures.

State committees raise money and provide volunteers to staff campaign events. They provide support to candidates for both state and national offices. National legislative elections, however, are also the responsibility of the powerful congressional district and senatorial committees. These committees, chaired by incumbents and staffed by professionals, are part of the national party organization. They are most likely to become involved in these legislative elections when the possibility exists of gaining or losing a seat. Because incumbents usually run for reelection and are often reelected easily, the congressional and senatorial committees are active in a minority of election efforts during each electoral cycle.

The national party plans the **national conventions** held every four years to nominate a presidential candidate. It sponsors polls to keep party members informed of public opinion and manages issue-oriented advertising and propaganda.

Did You Know?
A political party organization that often dominates politics in a particular region and relies heavily on patronage to both win votes and govern is known as a **political machine**.

Are Parties in Decline?

Some political scientists believe that the parties are no longer as powerful or as significant as they once were. Prior to 1968, one party typically controlled both the executive and legislative branches of government. Since that year, however, there have been only a few years of one-party control branches: 1977 to 1980, 1992 to 1994, 2003 to 2007, 2008 to 2010, and 2016 to 2018. (In 2021–2023, a 50-50 tie occurred in the Senate, resulting in VP Kamala Harris holding the tie-breaking vote.) Americans are voting a split ticket more frequently than ever before. They are more likely to consider the merits and positions of a particular candidate than to merely consider their party affiliation. As a result, no one party dominates government, and officials with different political agendas are elected to work together. As shown in the graph below, more and more Americans are identifying as independent rather than with a single political party.

Increasingly, modern candidates have taken control of their own election campaigns, relying less on party support than did past candidates. They are now able to appeal directly to the public through television and the Internet. This has left the parties—which once wielded great power over the electoral process—with less power. In their place, media consultants have become the chief movers and shakers in political campaigns.

U.S. Party Identification, Yearly Averages, 1988–2015

— % Republican   — % Independent   ····· % Democrat

Party Coalitions

Political parties consist of combinations of groups, which consist of combinations of individuals. The larger the **coalition**, the more likely the candidate will win. Party candidates and party positions on policy are designed to attract more groups of voters, putting together a winning military. A coalition is formed when these groups find common cause and temporarily work together to achieve a common goal.

In the presidential election of 2020, the Republican coalition included the following:

- social conservatives
- Christian conservatives
- libertarians
- opponents of affirmative action
- supporters of federal budget cuts, including to social welfare programs
- supporters of more restrictive immigration laws and enforcement
- skeptics of banks and large corporations (populists)
- rural dwellers

In the same election, the Democratic coalition included the following:

- economic and social liberals
- Socialists
- racial minority groups
- moderates on immigration, funding of the military, and crime laws
- environmentalists
- racial justice activists
- skeptics of American dominance of foreign affairs
- city dwellers

While there are always exceptions to the rule, the two parties tend to rely on these groups as a base of support. Regionally, it appears that the East and West Coasts and the upper Midwest are more Democratic, while the South and lower Midwest are more Republican.

Disaffected voters often switch political parties.

To learn about the latest ideological differences between the Democratic and Republican parties, consult the following resources:

Democratic Party Platform
https://democrats.org/where-we-stand/

Republican Party Platform
https://www.gop.com/about-our-party/

Ideological Differences Between the Parties

While there are general ideological differences between the two parties, there are also a number of similarities. Neither party, for example, questions the validity of the nation's capitalist economic system.

Although both parties tend to be centrist, there are nevertheless differences in the ways the two parties view the role of government. The greatest ideological differences are between the liberals in the Democratic Party and the conservatives in the Republican Party, the so-called **party bases.** While appealing to the independent centrist voter during election campaigns, each party counts on its base to get out and vote. Party leaders must use great care in choosing policy positions so they do not lose their party base. They must also avoid alienating the moderates of the party by taking extreme left or right positions.

Democrats Tend to Be...	Republicans Tend to Be...
Less disposed to spend on defense	More disposed to spend on defense
Less disposed to use vouchers, or other public funds, to enable certain students to attend private/charter/religious schools	More disposed to use vouchers for private or charter schools and to give governmental aid to religious schools
More disposed to spend money to advance social-welfare programs	Less disposed to spend money on social-welfare programs
More disposed to use government money for public education	Less disposed to use government money for public education
More disposed to grant tax relief to targeted programs such as those for the lower and middle classes	More disposed to grant tax relief to everyone, including the wealthy and corporations
Against private ownership of assault weapons and supportive of broader regulations on the ownership of firearms	Less disposed to regulate firearms
Support reproductive justice and the right to choose abortion	Oppose abortion rights
Support collective bargaining and unionization efforts	Oppose collective bargaining and support laws intended to limit the power of unions

Party Realignment

Party **realignment** occurs when the coalitions making up the two parties fall apart, such as when many of the groups that make up the majority party defect to the minority party. Realignments are very rare and usually occur as a result of some major traumatic event, such as an economic depression or a war. They are signaled by what is called a **critical election,** when a new party comes to dominate politics. Realignments occur over a period of time and show permanence. The New Deal coalition of the 1930s lasted for decades. There have been no realignments since the 1930s.

> ### Depression Politics
> The last realignment took place in 1932 as a result of the Great Depression, when the Republican Party became the minority party and the Democratic Party became the majority party, with overwhelming numbers of Democrats being elected to every branch of government at every level.

The trend today seems to be toward dealignment. **Dealignment** is usually a result of party members becoming disaffected as a result of some policy position taken by the party. These disaffected party members join no political party and vote for the candidate rather than the party they belong to. Since the 1960s, membership in the Democratic Party has declined significantly, while the number of Republicans has declined modestly. During the same time period, the number of voters self-identifying as independents has increased dramatically along with membership in third parties, such as the Democratic Socialists of America.

Third Parties

New parties are occasionally formed in the United States. Unless and until these parties reach the level of a major party, they are called third parties. Third parties form to represent constituencies that feel disenfranchised from both of the major parties. These so-called **splinter**, or **bolter**, **parties** usually unite around a feeling that the major parties are not responding to the demands of some segment of the electorate. The Reform Party, under whose banner Ross Perot ran for president in 1996, was an example of a splinter party whose constituency was fed up with "politics as usual."

Sometimes, third parties form to represent an ideology considered too radical by the mainstream parties. These **doctrinal parties** reject the prevailing attitudes and policies of the political system. The Socialist Party and Libertarian Party are examples. **Single-issue parties** are formed to promote one principle. The American Independent Party, which sponsored the segregationist candidacy of George C. Wallace in 1968, is an example. Third parties can have a major impact on elections, especially in tight races. The Green Party, which favors strict environmental policies, more government social programs, and controls over big business, ran Ralph Nader for president in 2000. Some analysts have suggested, based on voter patterns and polls, that if Nader had not run, Al Gore would have received a greater number of votes, which would have allowed him to win the election against George W. Bush.

**All For Many,
But All For One**

If you're curious, the two states that do not have this winner-take-all system are Maine and Nebraska, and both proportionately distribute their votes by congressional district. The 2008 presidential election between Barack Obama and John McCain was the first time Nebraska's electoral vote was split, and the 2016 presidential election between Donald Trump and Hillary Clinton was the first time Maine's electoral vote was split.

Third-party candidates should not be confused with **Independent candidates.** Independent candidates run without party affiliation. It is very difficult for Independent candidates to overcome the money and organization of the two major parties. Eugene McCarthy, an anti-Vietnam War candidate in 1968, and John Anderson, a fiscal conservative and social liberal in 1980, are two examples.

Why Third Parties Fail

The failure of third parties to elect presidential and other candidates to office is a direct result of an American political system designed to support only two major parties. National campaigns in countries using equal, single-member, plurality voting-district systems (like the United States) require huge sums of money and vast organizations. Third-party or independent candidates rarely have the name recognition or institutional support afforded by the major parties to win a majority of votes. Furthermore, the platform issues of third-parties are often incorporated into the party platforms of either the Republican or Democratic party, drawing away voters who want to support the candidate most likely to succeed. Also, in American presidential elections, almost all states have a winner-take-all system for the Electoral College (the candidate who receives the most votes, even if it is only by one, wins all of the votes in that state). Bush, for example, had 271 Electoral College votes to Gore's 266, but a candidate needs at least 270 to win. Because the losers get no electoral votes, the electoral count does not always accurately reflect the popular vote. During the 2000 presidential election (which featured the Florida voting controversy), Al Gore won the popular vote by about 500,000 votes nationwide, but George W. Bush was found to have won the Florida electorate, giving him all of Florida's 25 electoral votes and ultimately the presidency. Similarly, during the 2016 presidential election, Hillary Clinton won the popular vote by approximately 2.9 million votes, but Donald Trump won the Electoral College, winning him the presidential election.

For All, Even When All For None Politics

The purpose of an interest group is to advocate for a benefit that is in the best interests of its membership. The free rider problem, however, occurs when the beneficiaries of the interest group fail to participate in political action or give financial support. For instance, a professional organization will fight for the general goals of those in its profession, even those who are not formal members of the group. Those beneficiaries go along for a "free ride" because they reap the benefits of actions taken on their behalf, but do not share the burden of supporting the interest group level.

INTEREST GROUPS

Interest groups are organizations dedicated to a particular political goal or to a set of unified goals whose members educate voters and office holders about an issue, lobby on behalf of the issue, draft legislation, and mobilize members to work with legislators and government agencies to achieve their goals. Group members often share a common bond, either religious (Christian Coalition), racial (National Association for the Advancement of Colored People), or professional (American Medical Association). In other cases, they simply share a common interest, such as the environment (Sierra Club) or political reform (Common Cause). In any case, they are similar to political parties in that they try to influence the outcomes of elections and legislation. Unlike political parties, however, they do not nominate candidates, nor do they normally try to address a wide range of issues.

When interest groups try to influence legislators, we say they are **lobbying** for a bill or issue. The term originated with the historical practice of early lobbyists; they waited in the lobby of the capitol so they could catch legislators coming in and out of session. Today, most lobbyists are highly paid professionals. A number are former legislators, whose experience and friendships in the Capitol make them particularly effective.

There are literally thousands of interest groups in the United States. Most groups fall under one of the following categories:

- **Economic groups.** Economic groups are formed to promote and protect members' economic interests. They include peak business groups such as the U.S. Chamber of Commerce, which represents the interests of all businesspeople. Other groups represent specific trades and industries; among these are the American Farm Bureau Federation and the American Nuclear Energy Council. Labor groups such as the AFL-CIO and the United Auto Workers represent union members. Professional groups include the American Medical Association and the American Bar Association. Most economic groups have existed for a time and have developed strong ties with legislators and bureaucrats. They are also very large, highly influential, and extremely well-funded, and they either represent or employ large constituencies. As a result, they are usually the most powerful interest groups in Washington, D.C.

- **Public interest groups.** Public interest groups are nonprofit organizations that are generally organized around a well-defined set of public policy issues. Consumer groups usually work to promote safer products and more informative labeling; the most prominent of these groups is Public Citizen, founded by Ralph Nader. Environmental groups, such as the Sierra Club, advocate for the preservation of wildlife and wilderness areas. Religious groups such as the Christian Coalition attempt to influence public policy in such a way as to promote or protect their beliefs. Other groups promote causes such as women's rights, minority rights, and political reform. Single-issue groups like the National Rifle Association (NRA) and Mothers Against Drunk Driving (MADD) are often among the most powerful public interest groups because of the intensity of their supporters. Single-issue constituents are those more likely than other voters to use a single issue as a litmus test for candidates. Thus, a candidate who advocates gun control runs the risk of losing the votes of all three million NRA members.

- **Government interest groups.** Most states, many cities, and other localities maintain lobbying organizations in the nation's capital. A separate group represents the nation's governors, and yet another represents mayors. Most foreign governments and businesses lobby the government as well.

Did You Know?
The amount of influence an interest group has on policy-making can be negatively affected by the amount of access an interest group has to decision-makers and the amount of political and economic resources the interest group has.

How Interest Groups Influence Government

Interest groups use a number of tactics to disseminate information and persuade Congress, the president, the judiciary, and federal bureaucrats. Those tactics include the following:

- **Direct lobbying.** Representatives of the interest group meet privately with government officials to suggest legislation and to present arguments supporting their positions. Lobbyists are often the source of a great deal of information to young congress members who are trying to learn about new bills. Some would argue that the lobbyists need to give relatively good information to those congress members in order to maintain a good relationship with them; this way, they can lobby them again later on their issues.

- **Testifying before Congress.** Interest groups provide expert witnesses at committee hearings.

- **Socializing.** Social events in Washington, D.C., are often political events as well. Interest groups hold social functions and members attend other functions to meet and forge relationships with government officials.

- **Political donations.** Interest groups provide financial support to candidates and parties that champion their causes. Corporations, trade groups, and often unions do so by forming political action committees (PACs) and super PACs for that purpose.

- **Endorsements.** Many groups announce their support for specific candidates. Some groups rate legislators on the basis of their voting records; a high rating constitutes an implicit endorsement of that candidate.

- **Court action.** Interest groups file lawsuits or **class action suits** to protect and advance their interests. They will also submit *amicus curiae* (friend of the court) **briefs** in lawsuits to which they are not a party so that judges may consider their advice with respect to matters of law that directly affect the case in question.

- **Rallying their membership.** Public interest groups often engage in **grassroots campaigning** by contacting members and asking them to write, phone, or email their legislators in support of a particular program or piece of legislation. In addition, members may engage in demonstrations and rallies promoting their cause.

- **Propaganda.** Interest groups send out press releases and run advertisements promoting their views. Propaganda can take the form of television commercials, social media campaigns, and advertisements.

Did You Know?

Interest groups are among the many competing actors attempting to influence policy making. In addition to interest groups, professional organizations, social movements, and bureaucratic agencies vie to have their policy ideas adopted and implemented.

Limits on Lobbying

Several laws limit the scope of lobbyists' activities. Most are ineffective, but stronger efforts to regulate lobbying run the risk of violating the First Amendment right to free speech. The 1946 Federal Regulation of Lobbying Act was intended to allow the government to monitor lobbying activities by requiring lobbyists to register with the government and publicly disclose their salaries, expenses, and the nature of their activities in Washington, D.C.

Other laws prohibit, for limited amounts of time, certain lobbying activities by former government officials. These laws are meant to counteract the appearance of **influence peddling**, the practice of using personal friendships and inside information to get political advantage. Former House members must wait one year and former senators must wait two years before lobbying Congress directly, for example. However, they may lobby the executive branch immediately after leaving office. Some groups complain of a "revolving door" that pushes former federal employees into jobs as lobbyists and consultants. A limit similar to that of the former legislators also applies to former executive officials. It prevents them from lobbying for five years after they leave the agency that employed them. These limits were determined in *Buckley v. Valeo* (1976), the case that equated donations with free speech. In this ruling, the Supreme Court upheld federal limits on campaign contributions and ruled that donating money to influence elections is a form of constitutionally protected free speech.

Finally, federal laws prohibiting campaign contributions from corporations, unions, and trade associations can be sidestepped through the formation of a political action committee (PAC).

POLITICAL ACTION COMMITTEES (PACS) AND SUPER PACS

The 1974 **Federal Election Campaign Act (FECA)** allowed corporations, unions, and trade associations to form political action committees as a means of raising campaign funds. FECA set restrictions on contributors and contributions, and stipulated that corporate, union, and trade PACs must raise money from employees and members and may not simply draw it from their treasuries. Corporations, unions, and trade associations are not the only groups that form PACs. Many other interest groups form PACs to collect and distribute contributions, as do legislators (these are referred to as leadership PACs). After that change, the **Bipartisan Campaign Reform Act (BCRA) of 2002** (also known as the **McCain-Feingold Act**) further regulated campaign finance and PAC donations by prohibiting unregulated

Changes to Campaign Financing

In January of 2010, the Supreme Court changed many of the campaign finance rules in the case of *Citizens United v. Federal Election Commission*. The court ruled that corporations have a First Amendment right to expressly support political candidates for Congress and the White House. The ruling struck down restrictions that had prevented corporations from spending company money directly on campaign advertising right before an election. It is still important to learn how and why these groups function by reading the following sections.

Following the *Citizens United* decision, debates have increased over free speech and competitive and fair elections with regards to money and campaign finance. The Court's holding brought to the forefront the fact that people are hesitant to allow the wealthy to control the trajectory of American politics, but are similarly hesitant to restrict the individual liberties of a citizen to participate in the electoral process. While proponents of *Citizens United* believe the Court's holding was imperative to protect their political advertising, opponents have coined the phrases "Corporations aren't people" and "Money isn't speech" to show their disdain for the ruling.

contributions (soft money) to national political parties and limited the use of corporate and union money for ads discussing political issues within 60 days of a general election and 30 days of a primary.

Hard vs. Soft: We're Not Talking About Cheese

For the exam, you should be familiar with the terms "hard money" and "soft money." "Hard money" refers to tightly regulated contributions to candidates, while "soft money" refers to unregulated, unlimited contributions to political parties for general party-building activities such as get-out-the-vote drives, voter registration efforts, and ads that say "Vote for Democrats" or "Vote for Republicans." Potential uses of soft money were limited by Congress with the passage of the McCain-Feingold Act.

Then in 2010, in ***Citizens United v. Federal Election Commission***, the Supreme Court overturned BCRA's limits on PAC fundraising for "corporate independent expenditures." Under the terms of the *Citizens United* decision, PACs that donate to specific candidates must operate under limits on their contributors and their donations, but PACs that do not donate to specific candidates—as long as they do not directly coordinate with specific candidates—are not limited in their fundraising. In this context, political donations are considered free speech. These unlimited PACs have come to be known as **Super PACs** and are generally financed by the ultra-rich; however, because of disclosure laws affecting such Super PACs, it can be difficult to identify donors.

For regular PACs, donations from single-candidate PACs to individual candidates cannot exceed $3,300 ($5,000 for a multi-candidate PAC). Such PACs' donations to national political committees cannot exceed $15,000 from multi-candidate PACs and $41,300 from single-candidate PACs. Though Super PACs avoid limits by not directly or officially coordinating with specific candidates, the *Citizens United* decision is vague on what constitutes coordination.

527 GROUPS

A 527 group (named after the section of the tax code that allows such groups) is a tax-exempt organization that promotes a political agenda, although such a group cannot expressly advocate for or against a specific candidate. The term is generally used to refer to political organizations that are not regulated by the **FEC** (**Federal Election Commission**) and are not subject to the same contribution limits as PACs. They avoid regulation by the FEC because 527s are "political organizations" but are not registered as "political committees" subject to campaign finance law contribution limits. Sounds confusing, huh? The line between issue advocacy and candidate advocacy is a huge source of contention and disagreement. The BCRA changed **soft money** rules to make establishing new 527s a more attractive option than traditional PACs and allow outside organizations to circumvent the **hard money** limits of the BCRA. The *Citizens United* decision, however, makes Super PACs another viable alternative for avoiding such limits.

ELECTIONS

Concepts

- Does the media place too much emphasis on irrelevant issues in presidential campaigns?

- Why do incumbents win at such high rates?

- Why is voter turnout so low in the United States?

- What is the impact of primary elections, and who votes in them?

- Why do political parties have such a difficult time holding their coalitions together?

- Why are soft money contributions considered a threat to the election process?

- Why did the Supreme Court have a problem with the imposition of spending limits on PACs?

- Has the Federal Election Campaign Reform Act succeeded in fulfilling the intent of the legislation?

- What accounts for the so-called gender gap?

The federal government holds elections every two years. Each election gives voters the chance to select a new representative in the House of Representatives. Every other election allows them to vote for president. Each of a state's two seats in the Senate is contested every six years; as a result, state voters select a senator in two out of every three federal elections.

To cut expenses and to encourage voter turnout, states often hold their elections at the same time as federal elections. Thus, voters choose not only federal officials at election time, but also state legislators, judges, the governor, and local officials. They may also be asked to vote on referenda and state bond issues.

Thus, many officeholders are chosen and many issues are decided during each election. When the AP U.S. Government and Politics Exam asks about elections, however, it nearly always focuses on the presidential election. This section will do the same.

Did You Know?
Election administration is conducted at both the state and local level, and election law is a constitutionally afforded power given to the states.

Ranked-Choice Voting
A ranked-choice voting system (RCV) is an electoral system in which voters rank candidates by preference on their ballots. Maine and Alaska are currently the only two states that use RCV for statewide and federal general elections. Since 2021, New York City has used RCV in primary and special elections for local offices.

There is one exception to this rule. The AP U.S. Government and Politics Exam always asks at least one question about the **incumbent advantage.** Be sure you know the following two facts, as they will almost certainly be tested on the exam: (1) politicians who run for reelection win approximately 90% of the time; and (2) while incumbent senators have a tremendous electoral advantage, House incumbents have an even greater advantage. Senators must run statewide, and they almost always face a serious challenger. On the other hand, House members run in their home districts, where constituents are often overwhelmingly of one party due to **gerrymandering** (partisan redrawing of congressional district borders). In such races, victory in the primary election virtually guarantees victory in the general election. In fact, each year a number of House incumbents run for reelection unopposed.

THE ELECTION CYCLE

Elections consist of two phases: **nominations**, during which the parties choose their candidates for the general elections, and **general elections**, during which voters decide who will hold elective office.

The majority of states (39) use primary elections to select presidential nominees. All states use some form of primary election to select legislative and state nominees. These elections are usually held between early February and late spring of an election year, with the Iowa caucus and New Hampshire primary enjoying the coveted "first-in-the-nation" position. Each state sets its own rules for these elections, and there is considerable variation in primary procedures from state to state. There are several types of primaries.

- **Closed primary.** This is the most common type. In a closed primary, voting is restricted to registered members of a political party. Voters may vote only for candidates running for the nomination of their declared party. Democrats choose among the candidates for the Democratic nomination, while Republicans choose among Republican hopefuls.

- **Open primary.** In open primaries, voters may vote only in one party's primary, but they may vote in whichever party primary they choose. Voters select the party primary in which they wish to participate in the privacy of the voting booth. Critics argue that open primaries allow voters to sabotage their opponents' primaries by crossing party lines to vote for the candidate *least* likely to win the general election. This is likely to happen only when there are no close contests in one party, however.

- **Blanket primary.** Blanket primaries use the same procedure as that used in the general elections. In blanket primaries, voters may vote for one candidate per office of either party.

In primary voting for legislators and state officials, the candidate who receives a **plurality** (greatest number of votes, but not more than half the total votes cast) or majority (more than half) in each primary is declared the winner. Some states require the winner to receive a minimum percentage of the vote, however. If no candidate receives the required share of votes, a **runoff primary** is held between the top two. Runoffs occur most often when many challengers vie for an open office, especially when none of them are well known.

In primary elections for the presidency, voters also choose **delegates** pledged to a particular presidential candidate. Winning delegates attend their party's national convention. Some states select presidential convention delegates at **state caucuses** and **conventions.** This process begins with local meetings of party members, who select representatives to send to statewide party meetings. Compared with primaries, the state caucus and convention process usually attracts fewer participants. Those who participate tend to be more politically active and better informed than typical voters.

The Democratic Party uses a third method to choose some delegates to its national convention. It grants automatic delegate status to many elected party leaders, including congresspersons and important state leaders. These **superdelegates** generally support the front-runner. Critics complain that the superdelegates dilute the importance of the primary elections by making it easier for the party elite to control the nominating process. The Republican Party does not have superdelegates. To promote diversity within the delegate pool, the **McGovern-Fraser Commission** was created in 1968. It recommended that delegates be represented by the proportion of their population in each state.

General elections for federal office are held on the first Tuesday after the first Monday of November. Elections in which the president is chosen are called **presidential elections.** Those that occur between presidential elections are called **midterm elections.**

First Steps Toward Nomination

Nearly all elected officials first receive the endorsement, or nomination, of one of the two major parties. Nominees usually have extensive backgrounds in government. Some presidential candidates are current or former members of the Senate. Many have served as governors. Gubernatorial experience allows candidates to claim executive abilities, because governors serve many of the same government functions in their states as the president does in the federal government. Governors also have the advantage of being able to run as Washington outsiders, as opposed to senators, who usually have extensive federal experience (and whose congressional voting records are often used against them). At a time when public distrust of Washington is high, outsider status can be a significant benefit. Bill

Blanket Primary
This system at one time existed in Alaska, California, and Washington, but has since been struck down in those states by the Supreme Court. A form of this primary, the nonpartisan blanket primary, currently exists in Louisiana and Washington.

In 2018, the Democratic National Committee changed its rules regarding superdelegates. During a nominating convention, superdelegates do not vote for a nominee unless the first round of voting produces no winner.

Clinton, George W. Bush, and Donald Trump successfully exploited this factor in their presidential campaigns. Because Barack Obama had been a senator for only four years (as opposed to other candidates like Joe Biden, who had a 36-year tenure in 2008, or Rick Santorum, who had 16 years in 2012), he was also able to successfully campaign as an outsider in 2008.

On occasion, the major parties will pursue a candidate with little or no government experience. Such candidates are usually popular and well-respected figures, often from the military. World War II General Dwight Eisenhower was such a candidate in his successful 1952 campaign. More recently, the Republican nominee for the 2016 presidential race (and eventual winner of the Electoral College) was Donald Trump, a businessperson with no prior experience in government. Trump used his outsider status as a campaign selling point, which was successful with many voting demographics.

A presidential run is an all-consuming endeavor that must begin up to two years before the first primary. As a result, most candidates devote themselves to the effort full-time. Jimmy Carter and Ronald Reagan both left their governorships before running for the presidency; Bob Dole retired from the Senate in 1996 to commit himself more fully to his campaign. Others have remained in office and run successful campaigns. Bill Clinton and George W. Bush are two candidates who remained governors while successfully seeking their party's nomination. Chris Christie made his White House run while he remained governor of New Jersey, and numerous New Jersey newspapers called for his resignation, claiming that he had neglected his gubernatorial duties while campaigning. Presidents running for reelection and vice presidents seeking the presidency benefit from the prestige of their offices.

Those considering a run for the presidency must first seek support among the party organizations. They must especially seek the aid of influential donors to the party because elections are extremely expensive. Candidates spend much of the early stages of the nomination process meeting with potential donors, establishing PACs to raise funds (more about fundraising below), and campaigning for the endorsements of important political groups and leaders. This entire process is often referred to as *testing the waters*.

In the year before the first primaries, potential candidates attempt to increase their public profiles. They schedule public appearances and attempt to attract media coverage by taking stands on current issues and discussing the goals of their projected presidencies. Candidates are particularly vulnerable to the media during this period. Since the public knows little about most potential candidates, negative reports or media spin can quickly scuttle a campaign (for example, Newt Gingrich in 2012 or Ron DeSantis in 2024). As primary season begins, candidates try to raise as much money as possible and to garner as many votes in the primaries as possible, in an effort to win the nomination. Candidates who can't raise their own money and don't get enough votes are quickly forced out of the race. The candidates also begin to assemble campaign personnel—advisors, political consultants, public relations experts, speechwriters, fundraisers, lawyers, and office administrators—who will help manage the campaign.

Tick Tock
The most crucial decision a candidate makes is in relation to when they start campaigning. While candidates traditionally waited until after Labor Day the year before the election, to launch their candidacy, early announcements of candidacy are becoming increasingly necessary for candidates to both fundraise and develop a campaign infrastructure.

Elections and the Elite
Many campaigns fail when testing the waters, long before the public is ever aware of them, because of lack of interest among the political elite.

On occasion, wealthy candidates have attempted to run for the presidency without needing, or using, federal matching funds. Ross Perot in 1992 and Steve Forbes in 1996 used their own money to campaign, but both campaigns failed. Ross Perot's 1992 campaign spent more money than the Democratic and Republican candidates combined.

The following chart summarizes the nomination process.

Steps Toward Presidential Nomination

1 Approximately two years before the presidential election, candidates begin preparing for the first primary election, during which they will attempt to win the official nomination of their party.

Candidates seek support from party organizations.

Candidates campaign for the endorsements of political groups and leaders.

Candidates seek financial aid from donors and establish PACs to raise funds.

2 In the year before the first primaries, candidates attempt to increase their public profiles by scheduling public appearances in an effort to attract media coverage.

Candidates who don't raise enough money or receive enough votes are forced out of the race.

3 Candidates begin to assemble campaign personnel—advisors, political consultants, public relations experts, speechwriters, fundraisers, lawyers, and office administrators—to help manage the campaign.

4 Primary season begins in the presidential election year.

Endorse, Endorse, Of Course, Of Course
At some point during the campaign, candidates will likely pursue endorsements from other politicians and news organizations. This extra publicity can help them in all other steps. In presidential primaries, front-runners usually receive endorsements from former candidates who dropped out. These endorsements can then help the nominee during the general election.

Financing Campaigns

A successful presidential campaign requires much more than an appealing candidate. It needs a huge supporting staff, jets and buses, and the resources to hire consultants, pollsters, and advertising agencies. It should come as no surprise, then, that one of the most important skills a candidate can possess is the ability to raise money.

Presidential candidates who meet certain prerequisites may receive federal funding. Primary candidates who receive more than 10% of the vote in an election may apply for **federal matching funds.** These funds essentially double all campaign contributions of $250 and less by matching them. To receive matching funds, candidates must agree to obey federal spending limits (see sidebar to left). Any candidate who receives less than 10% of the vote in two consecutive primaries loses their eligibility for matching funds until they win more than 10% of the vote in another primary.

The federal government funds the general election campaigns of the two major presidential candidates, provided those candidates agree not to accept and spend other donations (an exception is made for up to $51,850 of the candidate's own money). The year 2004 was the first election in which both major party nominees declined public matching funds during the primaries. Independents do not receive federal funding for their campaigns. (In 2008, John McCain accepted matching funds while Barack Obama did not. In the subsequent 2012 race, neither Obama nor Mitt Romney accepted matching funds.) In the 2016 election, only one presidential contender sought and qualified for public financing (Martin O'Malley).

Despite attempts at campaign finance reform, the trend toward high levels of election spending has continued through the 1990s and into the first decade of the 21st century. In the 2004 election, George W. Bush raised $272.5 million and John Kerry raised $250.3 million. Both candidates refused matching funds to avoid all spending limits. This precedent-setting high, however, was swiftly broken in light of the ability for corporations and unions to now donate directly and without limits. The combined expenditures for the 2012 campaign that set Mitt Romney against Obama totaled over $7 billion dollars—just about 14 times as much in only eight years.

There is currently no public financing of congressional campaigns, and there are no spending limits for congressional candidates. There are, however, limits on the amounts that individuals and political committees may donate to candidates. These limits were revised by the Bipartisan Campaign Reform Act (BCRA) in 2002 and the table on the next page shows the limits for 2023–2024 federal elections.

Setting Limits

In 2024, the federal spending limit was $61.79 million for primary elections and $123.6 million for the general election. This is how much presidential candidates who receive public funding may spend on their campaigns.

	To a Candidate	To a National Party	To a Political Committee	Total per 2 Calendar Years
Individual may give	$3,300	$41,300	$10,000	no limit
Multi-candidate PAC may give	$5,000	$15,000	$5,000	no limit
Non-multi-candidate PAC committee may give	$3,300	$41,300	$10,000	no limit

Many Americans believe that the current campaign finance system has a corrupting effect on government, and a talking point among many of the candidates within the 2016 election was the fact that the public financing system was broken. Efforts to change the system, however, run into several obstacles. The Supreme Court ruled in *Buckley v. Valeo* (1976) that mandatory spending limits on campaigns violate candidates' First Amendment rights to free expression. Furthermore, the system currently benefits incumbents, in that the incumbent's job description is basically the stuff of reelections: meetings, events, talking to voters, photo ops, and so on. Accordingly, legislators are reluctant to make changes because changes would make their reelection more difficult. The permissible donations listed in the above table will change if campaign finance reform is enacted.

Primary Season

By January 1 of election year, candidates are campaigning widely among the public. From this point on, candidates participate in debates, campaign from state to state delivering their "stump speeches" (so called because campaigning is often referred to as "stumping"), and choreograph media events—in an effort to draw positive media coverage of their campaigns.

The earliest primaries (New Hampshire's is a prime example) provide a great boost to the campaigns of whoever wins, increasing the candidate's media exposure and making all-important fundraising chores easier. Major financial contributors usually desert the campaigns of the losers in early primaries. Furthermore, candidates who receive less than 10% of the vote in two successive primaries lose their eligibility for crucial federal matching funds. As a result, those who fare poorly in early primaries usually have to drop out of the race long before the majority of delegates have been selected.

Because early primaries are perceived to have grown increasingly important in recent years, many states have pushed forward the date of their primary elections. Many states even hold their primaries all on the same day in early March (called **Super Tuesday**). Large states such as New York and California have moved their primaries forward in hopes of having a greater influence on which candidates win the nominations. Political analysts refer to this strategy as **front-loading**, and the result has been to place increased pressure on candidates to succeed early. Critics argue that it unnecessarily forces voters to choose early in the election process, before they have gotten a chance to know the candidates well.

More Money, More Problems

The problems with campaign finance are easy to identify: dramatically rising costs to run a campaign, an increased dependence on PAC money, a decline in competitive challengers, and the ability of wealthy individuals to self-fund their campaigns. The American idea that any individual can run for office is more of a myth than a reality, and incumbent advantage will continue to dominate elections unless challengers can obtain financing.

Primary elections and state caucuses continue into late spring. In many recent elections, however, the party nominee has been decided long before the last elections. Mitt Romney's nomination in 2012 is an example of that very phenomenon.

National Conventions

After the primary season has ended, both parties hold national conventions to confirm their nominees. When no candidate has received the pledge of a majority of convention delegates, conventions decide who the nominee will be; such conventions are called **brokered conventions**. The parties have designed their primary systems to prevent brokered conventions, which can divide a party and cost it the election. The most recent brokered conventions were 1952 for Democrats (Adlai Stevenson) and 1948 for Republicans (Thomas Dewey) making them seem, at least for now, like historical relics.

One of the main purposes of a national convention, in fact, is to unify the party. Primary elections can damage each party, as candidates attack one another and thereby expose rifts within the party membership. Another main purpose of conventions is to make a show of party unity for political gain. Both parties' conventions are nationally televised and are widely covered by the news media. Not surprisingly, most of what occurs on the convention stage is choreographed to appeal to the party faithful and undecided voters watching at home.

That does not mean that conventions are placid affairs, however. Conventions are the site of many political negotiations, as different factions of the party attempt to win concessions in return for their full support during the general election. There are often intense battles over the party **platform**, a statement of purpose and party goals, which, ironically, has little concrete significance. The conventions also offer some political drama, as nominees sometimes wait until the convention to announce their choice of running mates.

The greatest impact conventions can have on general election results is negative. In 1968, for example, rioting outside the Democratic convention in Chicago created a bad impression among voters, especially when contrasted with the unified display at the Republican convention in Miami weeks later. In 1992, ultraconservatives were able to control key elements of the Republican convention. The image the convention created was one of an angry and activist party, which frightened voters and hurt President Bush's reelection campaign. Under normal circumstances, however, conventions usually help their candidates considerably. Polls taken immediately after conventions show the candidates' approval ratings up significantly. This rise in public approval is called a **post-convention bump**.

Nonetheless, it is important to note that national conventions have been altered dramatically in the last century. Until about mid-century, conventions and convention delegates actually selected and nominated the candidate. With the adoption of primary elections, conventions have been transformed into mere coronations, with the nominees generally being determined before the convention begins (as with Clinton and Trump in 2016).

Did You Know?

Candidates are faced with a dilemma about their stances when it comes to the nominating process. It's increasingly true that the most intensely conservative candidates receive the Republican Party's nomination or make it through the party's primary election. Similarly, Democratic candidates must appeal to the liberal wing of their party. Such movement toward the extremes has led to the polarization between parties and ideologies in the U.S.

The General Election and the Electoral College

The remaining candidates continue to campaign for the general election in much the same way as they campaigned during the primaries: holding rallies, participating in debates, running campaign advertisements, and pursuing positive media coverage. There are several key differences between the primaries and the general election. First, during the primaries, candidates run against members of their own party. Because primary candidates are often in general agreement about big-picture issues, their campaigns focus instead on the subtler differences between them. During the general elections, candidates often emphasize the general policy and philosophical differences between the two parties. Put simply, a candidate courts their political base during the primary season and then usually attempts to move toward the center in the general election to win undecided votes in hopes of securing the majority.

> Candidates planning their campaign strategies must consider the nature of the **Electoral College.** This institution was created by the framers of the Constitution as a means of insulating the government from the whims of a less-educated public. Critics feel this system is antiquated, but no one has successfully proposed an amendment to change it. Presidential elections therefore continue to be determined not by the final popular vote but by this institution. Each state is given a number of electors equal to the sum of its federal legislators (senators plus representatives). The winner of the presidential election in each state wins all of that state's electors[1] (which is why it is often referred to as a **winner-take-all system**).

The Electoral College places greater emphasis on election results in large states. Victory by a single vote in California wins a candidate all of that state's 55 electoral votes; a similar margin of victory in Vermont yields only three electoral votes. Despite the number of votes at stake in the large states, candidates will often devote the bulk of their time to "swing" states—areas in which polling indicates a close race. This is the reason that during the 2016 presidential election, states like Ohio, Colorado, and New Hampshire were inundated with political ads while large states, such as New York, California, and Texas, whose voters generally go with one party, were relatively quiet. Finally, candidates consider each other's electoral strategies in planning their campaigns. In 1968, the Democratic Party relied on the support of its Southern base. Republican Richard Nixon realized that his support there was weakening and campaigned aggressively in the region. Nixon's "Southern strategy" worked in enough Southern states to swing the election to the Republicans.

Did You Know?
A **faithless elector** is an elector who does not vote for their state's popular vote winner. Faithless electors have never changed the outcome of a presidential race, and historically change their vote to an independent or third-party candidate.

---

[1] The two exceptions are Maine and Nebraska, which give two electoral votes to the candidate who wins a plurality of the statewide vote, and one vote to the winner of each of the state's congressional districts. Maine has four electoral votes; Nebraska has five.

MEDIA INFLUENCE ON ELECTIONS

With approximately 240 million Americans of voting age, it is clear that candidates cannot come into direct contact with even a small portion of the electorate. Instead, they must rely on the media to get their political message across.

Modern Elections

The change in campaign finance and the growth of technology have led to a number of changes in the way campaigns are run. Due to the rising costs of running a campaign, candidates often spend a tremendous amount of time fundraising instead of talking to voters and developing policy. Such fundraising now primarily takes place in the digital arena through internet-based communication, social media, and online fundraising tools. In turn, grassroots campaigns have largely failed to gain traction as the dependence on professional consultants has risen.

- **News media** provide many voters with daily campaign information. While most news programs occasionally report on the candidates' positions on the issues, they concentrate on the candidates' standing in the polls, or the horse race aspect of the election. This is because news directors prefer information that can be communicated quickly and that changes regularly, such as public opinion poll results. In contrast, candidates' positions on issues are often complex. Furthermore, they rarely change. Therefore, news programs may report such information once during an election, but they do not report it repeatedly as they do with poll results. As a result, the attention of the network news audience is focused on the campaign game rather than on the candidates' political agendas.

- **Campaign advertisements** provide another, more controlled look at the candidates. Through advertising, candidates attempt to build a positive image with the public. In many cases, they also try to belittle their opponents through negative advertising. Negative advertising works best when the public knows little about a candidate. In 1988, for example, Democratic candidate Michael Dukakis was the subject of several effective negative advertisements. Although he led in the polls prior to the ads, Dukakis's support was weak, as most voters knew little about him. The negative advertisements were effective in destroying Dukakis's lead by portraying him as weak, incompetent, and soft on crime.

ELECTION DAY

Of the 240 million Americans of voting age, around 200 million are registered to vote. In the 2020 election, though, around 154.6 million actually turned out (higher than the 137.5 million who voted in the 2016 election). **Voter turnout** is low but trending upward for midterm elections: approximately 47.5% of all eligible voters participated in 2018 (an increase from 2014). American voter turnout rates have soared in recent elections, but are still behind those of many other countries. Uruguay, Turkey, Peru, Indonesia, and Argentina have extremely high voting rates.

Certain patterns are detectable in American voters' behavior. The likelihood that an individual will vote corresponds closely to their level of education: the more educated a person is, the more likely they are to vote. Age is also a factor. Turnout rates are highest among Americans over the age of 40, and lowest among those under the age of 20.

Voter turnout is also influenced in part by how close a race is. Voters are less likely to vote when they believe they know who will win the election. Such was the case in 1996, when many Americans were certain that Bill Clinton would be reelected. Remember, however, that many federal and state offices are up for grabs on election day. A closely contested race in any of those elections can be enough to motivate voters to participate. Voting rates were famously high for the 2020 presidential election, when many Americans were in crisis because of the Covid-19 pandemic and likely felt that Trump versus Biden was a crucially important election. Voter turnout can also be affected by various legislation. The National Voter Registration Act (1993), also known as The Motor Voter Act, made voting easier by allowing voter registration at the time someone applies for a driver's license. Conversely, the photo ID laws enacted in some areas at the state level depress voter turnout by requiring voters to show a photo ID before voting. These photo ID laws are controversial, with those in favor saying it reduces voter fraud and those opposed saying it decreases voting by impoverished Americans.

On election day, the media report not only election results but also the results of exit polls that break down the vote by age, gender, race, income level, region, and nearly every other demographic imaginable. They do so in an effort to determine the meaning of the results. Why did voters choose one candidate over another? How satisfied were voters with the choices presented to them? Were the voters sending a clear message—a **mandate**—or not? Winners search the results for evidence of a mandate. In 1992, Bill Clinton interpreted his victory as a mandate for a more active and progressive federal government. Several historic failures—on efforts to integrate gay people in the military and to establish nationalized health care—demonstrated that voter mandates are not always so clear. The voters' message has become more difficult to discern as **split-ticket voting**—voting for a presidential candidate of one party and legislators of the other—has grown more common.

> Split-ticket voting leads to **divided government**, when one party controls the Senate or House or both and the other controls the White House. An example of this comes from the composition of the government in 2015: following the 2014 elections, Republicans had House and Senate majorities, while Democrats controlled the White House. This can create policy **gridlock** because these two branches are often at odds with each other. Conversely, it can cause them to work together in the creation of moderate public policy. Lastly, it encourages party dealignment because voters do not align with their parties as uniformly as they once did.

Who Do You Think You/They Are?

Voting tends to be motivated by one or more of the following factors:

- **Rational**—A voter believes the candidate will support policies that further the voter's own personal interest.
- **Retrospective**—A voter chooses a candidate based on the candidate's political track record or that of the candidate's political party.
- **Prospective**—A voter chooses a candidate based on hopes of what that candidate may accomplish in the future.
- **Party-Line**—A voter selects all available candidates within a certain party, regardless of their individual merits.

POLICY MAKING: OBJECTIVES

Concepts

- Why do the poorest people in the United States have the least political power?
- What role does federalism play in the implementation of social welfare policy?
- Why is it so difficult to pass social welfare policy?
- Why are entitlement programs always a threat to the budget-making process?
- Why can it be said that the president is a secondary player when it comes to the economy?
- Why is it so difficult to write a budget for the United States?
- How can the president use the budget-making process to control his policy initiatives?

Want To Know More?

Interested in how ideology influences policy making? Check out "Ideology, Politics, and Deviance" from Seymour Martin Lipset's 1996 book *American Exceptionalism: A Double-Edged Sword.*

The process of public policy making consists of first deciding what the problem is and then deciding how to solve it. Policy making can have the following three purposes:

- **solving a social problem,** such as high crime rates, high unemployment, poverty among the aged, or teenage drinking
- **countering threats,** such as terrorism or war
- **pursuing an objective,** such as building a highway, exploring outer space, or finding a cure for cancer

Policy can be achieved by prohibiting certain kinds of behavior, such as polygamy, murder, assault, and robbery. It can also be achieved by protecting certain activities. Granting patents and copyrights to individuals for their intellectual property, protecting the environment, and setting rules for workplace safety are all examples. Policy can promote some social activity; giving tax deductions for donations to charities is an example. Policy can be achieved by providing direct benefits to citizens. These benefits may include building roads, libraries, or hospitals. Benefits can also take the form of individual government subsidies, student loans, and pensions for the elderly.

Policy making can be frustrating because it often depends on public opinion, which can be fickle and unpredictable. The **issue-attention cycle** requires policy makers to act quickly, before the public becomes bored and loses interest. Public complaints over high energy prices can cause a flurry of policy making. But when prices go down, the public forgets about it until the next time.

Policy making often involves trade-offs between competing goods. Finding additional energy resources may require access to pristine wildlife reserves. The risks to wildlife and the environment may be too high of a price to pay for the additional energy. Conservation, smaller cars, and alternative energy sources may be better solutions, but each will have its supporters and opponents.

Because policy making can have unforeseen results and can touch off bitter disputes, legislators often use **incrementalism**—the slow, step-by-step approach to making policy—or legislators may decide to use the policy of inaction, because taking no action is one way of making policy. Conflicts over health care reform and Social Security entitlements can result in simply maintaining the status quo (or not changing a policy).

Did You Know?
Public policies generated at any given time are a reflection of the attitudes, beliefs, and values of the citizens who participated in politics at that time.

POLICY MAKING: PROCESS

Policy making has five main steps, and each is influenced by politics.

1. **Defining the role of government** is the first step in solving social and economic problems. The political left sees a greater responsibility for government than the right, with the result that governments on the left are larger, more active, and more expensive than those on the right.

2. **Agenda setting** identifies social and economic problems, redefines them into political issues, and ranks them in order of importance. A citizen's socioeconomic status can determine which problems seem important and which don't. Poor people may rank job training high on the agenda, while the rich may rank tax cuts higher. When large numbers of people are affected, the concern will be ranked high. However, there are times when it is those with the most money who will have their issues placed high on the agenda. For example, large energy-producing corporations have a great deal of access to policy makers.

    Policy can try to address the concerns of opposing sides. Establishing environmental standards for oil exploration and refining tries to address the concerns of two constituencies: the environmentalists and the petroleum producers.

    A momentous event, such as a war, an oil embargo, or a collapsing stock market, may set the agenda. Issues such as universal health care, the war on drugs, or environmental concerns can resurface. Scholars can force issues into the agenda through research studies.

3. **Policy formulation and adoption** can be accomplished in a number of ways. Sometimes the most difficult method is the legislative process in Congress, while the easiest may be through the executive branch using executive orders from the president. Rules enacted by regulatory agencies or precedent-setting decisions by the Supreme Court are also sources of policy formulation and adoption. *Brown v. Board of Education* was certainly a policy-making decision.

4. **Policy implementation** puts the policy into effect by enforcement through the appropriate government agency. Timetables and rules for carrying out policies as well as anticipating problems are all part of policy implementation. Some of the major concerns of policy making are the unforeseen consequences. The "three-strike rule," intended to get career criminals off the streets by significantly increasing the penalty for a third conviction, has ended most plea-bargaining arrangements, causing more trials and overloaded courts, judges, and jails. The three-strike rule has turned out to be a much more expensive public policy than anticipated.

5. **Policy evaluation** is the final step. Does a policy work? Have unforeseen consequences caused other policy problems? Evaluation provides feedback to the policy makers, so that modifications can be made to better solve the problems. Evaluation may determine that the problem has been solved and that the policy can be terminated.

Obstacles to Policy Making

The United States is a pluralist democracy, with multiple centers of power for making policy. Those interested in affecting policy making concentrate their efforts at these many centers. Because the United States has a federal system of government, policy can be made at the local, state, and national levels. Separation of powers creates three policy-making centers: the executive, the legislative, and the judiciary. There is also the general bureaucracy, with its multiple policy-making centers. Trying to influence legislation, thousands of interest-group lobbyists, like jellyfish in the sea, descend upon these policy-making centers at all levels of government.

In their efforts to prevent tyranny and corruption, the framers created a policy-making nightmare by dispersing the power centers. Getting things done is cumbersome and frustrating. Multiple access points cause **policy fragmentation,** where many pieces of legislation deal with parts of policy problems but never deal with the entire problem.

Because so many agencies of government are involved, the drug war requires policy coordination. Interagency task forces try to iron out policy problems and conflicts between competing agencies, and Congress uses its oversight powers to change agency jurisdiction and give coherence to policy.

The War on Drugs has at least 75 congressional committees with some type of jurisdiction or oversight; local and state law enforcement agencies are involved, as well as the Army, Navy, Air Force, Coast Guard, Border Patrol, the Bureau of Citizenship and Immigration Services (formerly INS), customs service, DEA, and the FBI.

ECONOMIC POLICY

Of all the issues that face politicians, the economy is often the most important. Success or failure usually rests with the person the public perceives as responsible for the condition of the economy; and regardless of whether it is true, the electorate usually holds the president responsible. In 1992, the economy was in recession and George H. W. Bush was blamed. In 1996, the economy was booming, and Clinton was given credit and reelected.

Because of the importance of the economy in the eyes of the voters, it is in a politician's self-interest to make policies that will increase people's standard of living. The electorate looks to Washington to achieve this objective. For the policy-maker, the vexing question is how to achieve it.

Sound economic policy that achieves prosperity is probably the most elusive of all policies. There are many elements to the problem: inflation, deflation, interest rates, the supply of money in circulation, the profitability of corporations, foreign competition, international agreements, and consumer confidence, just to name a few. Complicating the problem are the various economic theories that drive policy decisions, and the various government agencies and institutions that make decisions affecting economic conditions.

Economic Theory

Capitalist free-market systems in which both government and private industry play a role are called **mixed economies.** Mixed free-market systems are characterized by both private and public (government) ownership of the means of production and distribution of goods and services. The price of goods and services is determined by the free-market interplay of supply and demand. The profits after taxes are kept by the owners.

Free-market economic systems are plagued by periods of prosperity followed by periods of economic contraction (decreased activity, economic downturn). Because the United States has a mixed free-market system, the major problem for policy makers is how to maintain prosperity and economic growth while reducing the impact of the inevitable economic contraction. In capitalist systems, the basic question is to what extent the government should intervene.

Laissez-faire economists believe that the government should never become involved in economic issues. They believe that the narrow pursuit of individual profit serves the broader interest of society. Central to laissez-faire economics is the belief that free markets are governed by the laws of nature and government should not interfere with those laws. In vogue with rugged individualists in the 19th century, laissez-faire economics was not a viable government policy option during the Great Depression of the 1930s.

Clinton's Economy
In 1992, Bill Clinton's informal campaign slogan was "it's the economy, stupid!" coined by political firebrand and Clinton strategist James Carville. It was a mantra that Carville recommended focusing on (as the nation endured a recession), and it helped Clinton win against incumbent George H. W. Bush.

Did You Know?
Conservatives tend to favor fewer regulations of the marketplace, libertarians tend to favor little to no regulation of the marketplace, and liberals tend to favor more governmental regulation of the marketplace.

Perhaps the most influential economist of the 20th century was John Maynard Keynes, an interventionist. **Keynesian economics**, on which FDR's New Deal was based, holds that the government can smooth out business cycles by influencing the amount of income individuals and businesses can spend on goods and services. Since the end of the Cold War, however, the United States has readopted laissez-faire economic policies.

Fiscal Policy

Fiscal policy refers to the government action of either lowering or raising taxes, which results in more or less consumer spending, or enacting of government spending programs, such as building highways or hospitals. Keynesians believe that during economic downturns, the government should spend money on projects to inject money into the economy. They are less worried about government deficit spending than about keeping the economy prosperous. A prosperous economy means a larger tax base, which will eventually correct deficit spending. In effect, the Keynesian school believes that when the economy is good, surplus taxes (money left over from tax revenues) should be saved to pay for the government spending that must take place during an economic downturn. Using this school of thought, the policy alternatives are obvious, but questions still remain. Should there be tax cuts? If so, how much, and who should get them? How much spending should the government engage in? How much **deficit spending** (funds raised by borrowing rather than taxation) should be allowed? The answers to these questions are extremely difficult, with major political consequences.

In the 1980s, the Reagan-Bush administration became the champion of the **supply-side** school of economic thought. The supply-siders take issue with supporters of Keynesian economics. Inflation is caused by too many dollars chasing too few goods. If the supply of goods is raised, the cost of the goods will decline. According to this theory, supply-siders argue that the government should cut taxes and spending on domestic programs to stimulate greater production.

Going along with supply-side theory, Congress in the 1980s enacted extensive tax cuts and reductions to social welfare programs, a policy later dubbed "Reaganomics." Inflation was brought under control, but huge yearly **budget deficits**, caused in part by a defense buildup, created a four-trillion-dollar debt. In the 1990s, budget surpluses began to shrink the deficit, but these gains were reversed as a result of policies enacted during the Bush and Obama administrations, particularly during the Great Recession. Tax cuts followed by rising costs associated with the War on Terrorism, the invasion and occupation of Afghanistan and Iraq, and government stimulus programs have resulted in record budget deficits. The most recent estimates of the Congressional Budget Office (CBO) have warned against increasingly large budget deficits. In 2020, the federal budget deficit hit an all-time high of $3.1 trillion, more than double the previous record, as the coronavirus pandemic shrank revenues and sent spending soaring.

Monetary Policy

Monetary policy refers to the process by which the government controls the supply of money in circulation and the supply of credit through the actions of the **Federal Reserve Board** (the Fed). The Fed can increase the amount of money in circulation by lowering interest rates. Rate reductions make borrowing money less expensive because interest on the money is low. This action usually inflates (expands) the economy, resulting in higher prices and wages. If the Fed raises interest rates, the impact on the economy will be deflationary, resulting in either more stable or lower prices or wages.

Monetary policy can be implemented by the Federal Reserve Board in three ways.

- By manipulating the **reserve requirement**, which raises or lowers the amount of money that banks are required to keep on hand. Raising the reserve shrinks the amount of money available for borrowing, which raises interest rates. Lowering the reserve will have the opposite effect, lowering interest rates.

- By manipulating the **discount rate**, which raises or lowers the interest banks pay to the Federal Reserve Banks for borrowing money. Lowering the discount rate will lower the interest rates for consumer loans. Raising the discount rate will raise the interest rates for consumer loans. The higher the rate, the less consumers will spend on purchases.

- By manipulating **open market operations**, the Federal Reserve buys and sells United States government bonds. People buy bonds because they have a better interest rate than savings accounts. When the Fed sells bonds, people withdraw money from banks to take advantage of the bond's higher interest rate. Because the bank has less to loan, consumer interest rates go up, which slows consumer spending and economic growth. When the Fed buys bonds, money flows back into the banks, which increases the money available for loans. With more money in the bank for consumers to borrow, interest rates are driven down. Lower interest rates mean more consumer spending, which increases economic growth.

Some economists believe that government should intervene only to manipulate the money supply, an idea championed by Milton Friedman. These monetarists believe that the money supply should be increased at a constant rate to accommodate economic growth. Monetarists do not believe that interest rate changes and manipulation of tax rates have much of an impact on economic conditions.

In the 1990s, the U.S. economy expanded without tax cuts, creating record employment levels with little inflation. Many gave the credit to the monetary policy of Alan Greenspan and the Federal Reserve.

The Tools of Economic Policy Making

The president receives advice on the state of the economy from the following departments and agencies:

- the Council of Economic Advisors
- the National Economic Council
- the Office of Management and Budget
- the Secretary of the Treasury

The president can influence the fiscal and monetary policies of these departments and agencies through his appointment power and policy **initiatives**. Remember that fiscal policy involves the budget, and monetary policy involves the money supply.

Fiscal Policy Making

The Director of the **Office of Management and Budget (OMB)** is responsible for initiating the budget process. The director meets with the president to discuss his policy initiatives. The state of the economy is discussed, centering on government revenue projections, which is the predicted income from taxes. Based on the president's priorities, some executive departments will receive more money than others. The OMB then writes the president's budget and submits it to Congress. Upon its arrival, the budget is sent to three committees. The **House Ways and Means Committee** deals with the taxing aspects of the budget. **Authorization committees** in both houses decide what programs Congress wants to fund. **Appropriations committees** in both houses then decide how much money to spend for those programs that have been authorized.

The budget process is complicated, politically divisive, and, in recent years, nearly impossible to conclude. The president's projected revenues and expenditures often conflict with those of Congress. Congress often simply does not trust the president's numbers, and conversely, the president does not trust Congress's. These yearly budget problems forced passage of the **Budget Reform Act of 1974**, which created the **Congressional Budget Office,** with budget committees in both the House and Senate. The congressional committees set their own revenue and spending levels. Negotiations then take place among the White House and the two houses of Congress in an effort to get one budget acceptable to everyone. Failure to achieve a budget by the beginning of the **fiscal year** could mean shutting down the government and sending employees home. When this occurs, budget stop-gap bills are passed to temporarily appropriate money to keep the government operating.

The **Budget Enforcement Act of 1990** was an effort to streamline the budget process and make it easier to arrive at a compromise budget. The law categorizes government expenditures as either mandatory or discretionary spending. **Mandatory spending** is required by law to fund programs such as the **entitlement programs,** Social Security, Medicare, veterans' pensions, and payment on the national debt. **Discretionary spending** programs, which are not required by law, include defense, education, highways, research grants, and all government operations. Discretionary programs are the primary targets for making cuts to balance the budget.

Shut It Down

The U.S. government experienced its longest shutdown—35 days—from December 2018 to January 2019. President Trump unsuccessfully tried to use the shutdown to gain funding for a U.S.-Mexico border wall.

TRADE POLICY

The United States is by far the richest nation in the world. The output of the economy of the state of California alone ranks among the top five nations in the world. The economic outputs of each of the three cities of Los Angeles, Chicago, and New York rank among the output of the top 20 nations. For better or for worse, the United States is the largest producer and consumer of products.

Foreign nations depend on the United States as a market for their products, as we depend on them for ours. The ratio of imported products to exported products is called the **balance of trade**. **Trade deficits** occur when imports exceed exports. Trade deficits cause wealth to flow from a nation. When nations face trade deficits, they often place restrictions on imported goods. The nation facing the restrictions can take retaliation by imposing high import taxes or unfair regulations on products, effectively keeping out foreign goods. Trade wars can result, stopping trade between countries. Trade surpluses are the result of more money flowing into a country than out. The oil-producing nations have huge amounts of money flowing into their treasuries and therefore have large trade surpluses when prices are high.

To promote trade, the United States signed the **General Agreement on Tariffs and Trade (GATT)**, which evolved into the World Trade Organization (WTO). The 125 members of the WTO account for 97% of the world's trade. The organization works to lower tariffs and quotas and reduce unfair trade practices.

In an effort to promote free trade between the United States, Canada, and Mexico, the three nations signed the **North American Free Trade Agreement (NAFTA)** in 1994, effectively removing import tariffs from one another's products. As an economic policy, NAFTA was controversial. It was opposed by United States industrial labor unions who feared that jobs would be lost to inexpensive Mexican labor. Others feared that the industrial capacity of the United States would be damaged because factories would move to Mexico, where environmental laws were not strictly enforced. NAFTA supporters claimed it would improve the U.S. economy and would also create jobs in Mexico, resulting in less undocumented immigration. Supporters also claimed that a richer Mexico would purchase more American goods. NAFTA proved to be something of a mixed blessing. Its passage led to cheaper labor (in Mexico) for many U.S. companies, and an increase in trade between the two countries. Nevertheless, many American jobs have undeniably been sent south of the border, and many Mexican farmers lost their land in a futile attempt to compete with American agribusinesses. At the insistence of President Trump, the three nations revised NAFTA in 2018, renaming the agreement the **United States-Mexico-Canada Agreement (USMCA).**

DOMESTIC POLICY

While economic policy is contentious, domestic policy is sometimes even more so because it gets to the very essence of the purposes of government. Liberals believe government has an obligation to provide for social welfare and to help those in need. Conservatives believe **social-welfare programs** are encroachments on individual liberties and responsibilities. They think these programs turn the government into an instrument used to create a permanent class of the underprivileged, dependent upon government handouts. Somewhere in between are the moderates, who believe government should provide opportunities and limited help during difficult times.

The 20th century has seen a dramatic change in the way society perceives the role of government in providing for the basic needs of people. Before the Great Depression, there were no government programs to help people who suffered from the hardships of old age, disabilities, unemployment, and poverty. So many people needed help in the 1930s that the government enacted programs to create jobs, provide housing, and feed the hungry. Later on, the **Great Society** programs of the Johnson administration expanded government welfare programs, but because of the expense and questions about their effectiveness, many of the Great Society programs were eliminated or scaled back during and after the Reagan administration.

Today there are two kinds of social-welfare programs.

- **Social insurance programs** are in reality national insurance programs into which employers and employees pay taxes. Because individuals pay into these programs, the public believes that the benefits derived from such programs have been earned. There seems to be little public debate over a citizen's "right" to Social Security.

- **Public assistance programs**, on the other hand, are not perceived as earned. These programs are something that a person must qualify for, and a government responsibility to help people in need. Recipients are not required to pay into the system to get something out. Public assistance is considered by some to be a "handout" to people who do not work. Because politicians understand this public perception, public policy initiatives from both parties have concentrated on forcing people on public assistance to either seek work or enter work-training programs.

Social Security

Social Security is an entitlement program mandated by law. The government must pay benefits to all people who meet the requirements of the program. Changing the law would require congressional action. Because the largest voting bloc of the electorate is made up of those nearing or at retirement age, there is little chance of major changes to the system, even though some experts warn that the Social Security trust fund will go bankrupt in the near future. Currently, entitlement programs account for the largest expense in the federal budget.

In its original form, Social Security provided benefits only to retired persons beginning at age 65.

The program has now been expanded to include four categories of persons.

- Retired workers and their survivors who are presently aged 65 and older receive monthly payments from the Social Security trust fund. To help maintain a recipient's standard of living, recipients are entitled to a **COLA (cost of living adjustment)** if the inflation rate exceeds 3%. COLAs put a strain on the ability of the trust fund to meet its obligations. Changes in the demographic composition of society are also putting a strain on the system. Society is aging, and the ratio of workers to retirees is declining. Because Social Security is a pay-as-you-go system, the money that is now paid into the system pays the present beneficiaries. As the ratio of workers to retirees continues to decline, workers will be faced with higher taxes to maintain the income of those who are retired.

- Insurance for Americans with disabilities provides monthly payments to those citizens who are permanently and totally disabled. This category includes those with learning disabilities and those dependent on drugs and alcohol.

- **Medicare** provides government assistance to people older than 65 for health care. For those retirees who pay an additional tax on their social security benefit, Medicare Part B will pay approximately 80% of their doctor's bills. The high and rising cost of health care has led some to question the solvency of this program, but recent reports note that it is more than able to cover 100% of its costs through at least 2030.

- **Medicaid** provides medical and health-related services for low-income parents, children, seniors, and people with disabilities. It is jointly funded by the states and federal government and is managed and run by the individual states.

- Temporary unemployment insurance for those out of work provides a weekly benefit, for a limited time. Each state government administers its own unemployment insurance program. Both the federal and state governments pay into a trust fund to provide the benefit. While states have traditionally set their own rules on the amount and duration of benefits, Congress has responded at the federal level to the recession that began in 2009 by helping states offer up to 99 weeks of benefits to the unemployed, significantly more than the previous standard of 26 weeks. In 2012, however, Congress imposed additional restrictions on those extended federal benefits, including a measure to gradually decrease the limit to 73 weeks. During the Covid-19 pandemic, the CARES Act of 2020 (signed by President Trump) and the American Rescue Plan Act of 2021 (signed by President Biden) extended unemployment assistance.

Social Welfare

No matter how well-intentioned the government has been, and no matter how much money has been spent, poverty has remained a perpetual problem for policy makers at both the state and federal levels. The first federal welfare programs were established by the Social Security Act in the 1930s. The largest and most controversial became known as Aid to Families with Dependent Children (AFDC).

All social welfare programs are designed to help targeted groups. Public assistance programs, known as welfare, target families whose total income falls below the federally determined minimum amount required to provide for the basic needs of a family. The present amount is approximately $17,000 for a family of four. The larger the family, the more income is required and the more money is paid out. Critics claim that welfare is an incentive for families to have more children. Further complicating matters are complaints from recipients about a system that is degrading because investigators, looking for welfare cheaters, are invading their privacy.

In addition to AFDC, the federal government has established **supplemental public assistance programs** (known as SSI) to help people with disabilities and the elderly who are living at or near the poverty level. To improve the diet and increase the buying power of the poor, the federal government also provides **SNAP benefits**, formerly known as food stamps. Recipients use government-provided debit cards to help pay for food. Both SSI and the food-stamp program are federal programs administered through local and state agencies.

In an effort to reduce the number of people living on public assistance, the **Welfare Reform Act** was passed in 1996. Under the law, social welfare programs are funded by both the state and federal governments, with the federal government contributing the greatest share in the form of block grants. Block grants are important because they allow states to experiment with new types of programs designed to get people off welfare and into work programs. The administration of programs (the distribution of cash payments) and the incentives for finding work and providing job training are left to the states. The intent of the law is to reduce the welfare rolls and force people to find work. This is accomplished by:

- abolishing Aid to Families with Dependent Children (AFDC), which has affected 22% of the families in the United States with children, and replacing it with Temporary Assistance for Needy Families (TANF)

- requiring adults to find work within two years or be cut off

- placing a lifetime limit of five years for welfare eligibility, although it is possible to get a waiver if a recipient is actively seeking work

- prohibiting undocumented immigrants from receiving assistance

The political debate over public assistance centers on two issues: who pays how much, and what is the fair standard to be used for the recipient? Both Democrats and Republicans have tried to reduce these programs. Cutting them, however, places more people at risk, reducing food stamp programs and school lunch programs, and causing increased hunger.

Health Care

One of the most vexing problems for policy makers is what to do about the high cost of health care. Americans spend more than 17% of the nation's **gross domestic product**, or **GDP** (the total of goods and services produced in a year), on health care. The United States has the most expensive health care system in the world, and it is the only fully industrialized nation without a national health care program. High costs have not guaranteed any longer life expectancy, nor better treatment than that found in other industrialized nations. Instead of a national program run by the government, most Americans have relied on various types of insurance programs to pay for health care costs. The premiums for these health care programs are paid by workers and employers. For many reasons, but primarily because of cost, 7.9% of the population, approximately 26 million people, were without health insurance in 2022.

As with other government programs, the electorate is divided on how to solve the two issues of universal health care and the burden of health care costs. Voters seem to want increased coverage, but there is little evidence to indicate they are willing to pay for it. The only taxes the American electorate seems willing to pay are the so-called "sin taxes"—still fairly unpopular in some circles—on alcohol and tobacco products, which will not generate enough revenues to provide increased coverage. Proposals for "anti-obesity" taxes on sugary drinks and sodas have been met with mixed reactions from the public. Another basic issue for which there is no consensus is whether health benefits should be a government or privately administered program. With little public consensus over the past two decades, reform has been extremely contentious.

High Costs
The average cost for health insurance programs is at least $5,000 per person per year and is rising faster than the cost of living.

An ill-fated attempt at health care reform was made in the first Clinton administration. The proposed policy called for universal coverage and strict cost controls. The policy would have required increased taxes coupled with cost-cutting limits on the types of medical procedures allowable. The lack of public consensus killed the proposal within a year.

The debate over health care continued during the 2000 presidential election. Both candidates agreed that something had to be done about both escalating costs and the increasing numbers of uninsured. The Democrats promoted a policy of a government-paid prescription drug program for senior citizens. The Republicans promoted a prescription-drug program run by insurance providers, but again there was no consensus.

The most significant health-care legislation in American history was signed into law by President Obama on March 23, 2010. The **Patient Protection and Affordable Health Care Act**, popularly known as Obamacare, was passed over the course of several months and it generated significant political debate and controversy. The law was celebrated by most Democrats, who touted it as the much-needed solution to the long-term flaws in the American health care system. Republicans and some independent voters criticized the law, claiming it was an expensive intrusion of the federal government into the public sector. The debate lasted until the midterm elections in November of 2010, when Republicans gained a large number of congressional seats partly as a result of voter discontent with the law.

The most important of the law's provisions allowed the federal government, beginning in 2014, to fine individuals who do not participate in an insurance program. This policy, known as the "individual mandate," has been the basis of many Republican criticisms of the law. The attorneys general of 28 states challenged this provision in the law in federal court, claiming that the Constitution prohibits Congress from taxing individuals for not purchasing a product (say, health insurance). However, the Supreme Court ruled that the individual mandate is constitutional in the 2012 case *National Federation of Independent Business v. Sebelius*.

Said individual mandate still exists today, but starting in 2019 there was no longer a federal penalty for non-compliance with the individual mandate. So technically, the law does still require most Americans to have some type of health insurance, but the IRS will not impose a penalty on people who don't comply with that requirement.

CHAPTER 8 KEY TERMS

Political parties

Interest groups

Political action committees (PACs)

527 groups

Elections

Media

Two-party system (bipartisan system)

Party platform

Primary elections

National conventions

Coalition

Party bases

Realignment

Critical election

Dealignment

Splinter parties (bolter parties)

Doctrinal parties

Single-issue parties

Independent candidates

Lobbying

Class action suits

Amicus curiae briefs

Grassroots campaigning

Influence peddling

Federal Election Campaign Act (FECA)

Bipartisan Campaign Reform Act (BRCA) of 2002 (McCain-Feingold Act)

Citizens United v. Federal Election Commission

Super PACs

Federal Election Commission (FEC)

Soft money

Hard money

Incumbent advantage

Gerrymandering

Nominations

General elections

Plurality

Runoff primary

Delegates

State caucuses

Conventions

Superdelegates

McGovern-Fraser Commission

Presidential elections

Midterm elections

Federal matching funds

Super Tuesday

Front-loading

Brokered conventions

Platform

Post-convention bump

Faithless elector

Electoral College

Winner-take-all system

Voter turnout

Mandate

Split-ticket voting

Divided government

Gridlock

Issue-attention cycle

Incrementalism

Policy fragmentation

Mixed economies

Laissez-faire

Keynesian economics

Fiscal policy

Deficit spending

Supply-side

Budget deficits

Monetary policy

Federal Reserve Board

Reserve requirement

Discount rate

Open market operations

Initiatives

Office of Management and Budget (OMB)

House Ways and Means Committee

Authorization committees

Appropriations committees

Budget Reform Act of 1974

Congressional Budget Office

Fiscal year

Budget Enforcement Act of 1990

Mandatory spending

Entitlement programs

Discretionary spending

Balance of trade

Trade deficits

General Agreement on Tariffs and
    Trade (GATT)

North American Free Trade Agreement
    (NAFTA)

United States-Mexico-Canada Agreement (USMCA)

Social-welfare programs

Great Society

Social Security

COLA (cost of living adjustment)

Medicare

Medicaid

Supplemental public assistance
    programs

SNAP benefits

Welfare Reform Act

Gross domestic product (GDP)

Patient Protection and Affordable
    Health Care Act

Chapter 8 Drill

See Chapter 9 for answers and explanations.

Question 1 refers to the passage below.

"However [political parties] may now and then answer popular ends, they are likely in the course of time and things, to become potent engines, by which cunning, ambitious, and unprincipled men will be enabled to subvert the power of the people and to usurp for themselves the reins of government, destroying afterwards the very engines which have lifted them to unjust dominion. Towards the preservation of your government, and the permanency of your present happy state, it is requisite, not only that you steadily discountenance irregular oppositions to its acknowledged authority, but also that you resist with care the spirit of innovation upon its principles, however specious the pretexts."

—George Washington, Farewell Address, 1796

1. Which of the following statements best reflects Washington's message in the passage?

    (A) Political parties are a natural part of American political life.
    (B) Political parties never work in the interests of the American people.
    (C) Political parties are run by moral people.
    (D) Political parties manipulate the government to ensure their grasp on power.

2. Which of the following is an accurate comparison between a political party and an interest group?

	Political Party	**Interest Group**
(A)	Organize government activity	Undergo realignment every few decades
(B)	Direct lobbying	Reduce conflict and tension in society
(C)	Nominate candidates for office	Make endorsements
(D)	Educate and mobilize voters	Help coordinate the campaign of a presidential candidate

3. Political Action Committees (PACs) allow unions and corporations to perform which of the following actions?

    (A) Run their own members for political office
    (B) Coordinate political activities not affiliated with a campaign
    (C) Have a voice in government
    (D) Sit down together to work out their differences

4. Which of the following describes an open Republican primary?

    (A) Only Republicans can vote.
    (B) Only Democrats can vote.
    (C) Only Republicans and Democrats can vote.
    (D) Only registered voters can vote.

5. At a nominating convention, which committee decides the positions that the political party will take?

    (A) Platform Committee
    (B) Credentials Committee
    (C) Rules Committee
    (D) Ideology Committee

6. Which of the following statements is true about presidential primaries?

    (A) All delegates in a primary are awarded to the winning candidate.
    (B) Voters in primaries all show up at the same time to discuss candidates and then vote.
    (C) Most states use primaries to award delegates to presidential candidates.
    (D) Voters in primaries choose representatives to vote for them.

7. Which of the following people would receive money from Social Security?

    (A) A worker retiring after 40 years
    (B) A foreign tourist injured on U.S. soil
    (C) A veteran working as a security guard
    (D) A family that is chronically poor

8. Which of the following terms describes a time when a nation's imports exceed its exports?

    (A) Trade deficit
    (B) Trade surplus
    (C) In default
    (D) Bankrupt

9. Which of the following programs is categorized as discretionary spending under the Budget Enforcement Act of 1990?

   (A) National debt payments
   (B) Social Security
   (C) Medicare
   (D) Education

10. An individual who votes in their perceived best interests is adhering to which of the following models of voter behavior?

   (A) Rational Choice Voting
   (B) Retrospective Voting
   (C) Prospective Voting
   (D) Party-line Voting

Summary

○ Though they are not mentioned in the Constitution, political parties have become an integral part of American government. They may embrace a wide spectrum of ideologies, but ultimately both parties share the same goal: to be elected by any means necessary.

○ American history has been marked by numerous third parties that have challenged the prevailing duopoly. If it is popular enough, a third party may influence the two major parties to adopt its ideas.

○ Parties serve many functions in American democracy: they recruit and fund candidates, educate voters, provide a loyal opposition, and run the government—all while mitigating societal tension.

○ Political parties often turn out to be broad coalitions of disparate ideologies and groups. The Republican Party, for example, blends libertarians who are hostile to government regulation with religious conservatives who want government to play a greater role in enforcing public morality.

○ Generally speaking, Democrats tend to be in favor of government regulation of industry, redistribution of government money to the poor, and social freedom. Republicans tend to want to empower business to free itself from government rules, encourage people to earn money with assistance from the state, and want more social and moral controls on society.

○ Interest groups are large organizations with strong policy goals, but they are different from political parties in that they do not change their ideologies. These groups try to control the political process by hiring lobbyists to influence legislators and by giving them money as well.

○ When labor unions or corporations want to fund candidates, they do so by forming Political Action Committees, or PACs. PACs and Super PACs, which provide a means to funnel money to a candidate of choice, are regulated by the Federal Election Commission (FEC).

○ 527 groups are not regulated by the FEC, and the nature of these groups is a source of great contention. They have become a way for organizations to avoid hard money limits, and their spending has ballooned in recent years, despite efforts to limit and regulate outside money in elections.

○ Elections consist of two phases: nominations and the general election. Most nominations are made through party primaries. These can be open, closed, or blanket.

o   Candidates need the backing of the major parties along with a compelling backstory before they can hope to make a strong campaign for national office.

o   Campaign finance was restricted by a complicated web of regulations defined by the election laws of the 1970s along with the 2002 Bipartisan Campaign Reform Act, but new laws were passed in 2010.

o   Before the general elections, the candidates need to win their party primaries, which often involves energizing the base. Later, candidates may have to repudiate some of the more radical statements they made to court primary voters in order to win more moderate voters in the general election.

o   Party nominees were originally selected at the nominating conventions, but now these conventions are symbolic coronations of the candidate who has already been selected through the primary process. Still, delegates assemble, cheer, and argue over the drafting of the party platform.

o   Presidential candidates must win each state's electors, which is done by getting a plurality of all the voters in that state. This method causes candidates to spend most of their time in "swing" or "battleground" states and can also result in the winner of the popular vote losing the election (as was the case with Al Gore in the election of 2000 and Hillary Clinton in 2016).

o   After all the voting is done, pollsters, the parties, and the media try their best to determine why the people voted the way they did. Exit polls and surveys are the tools used to decipher these factors.

o   Public policy is made when the government decides to take action to solve a societal problem, and consists of five steps:

1.   Defining the role of government
2.   Agenda setting
3.   Policy formulation
4.   Policy implementation
5.   Policy evaluation

o Economic policy has been one of the most important areas of public policy in American history. Policy makers have oscillated between supporting laissez-faire free market principles and redistributionist, interventionist policies.

o The United States has joined international trade organizations like the World Trade Organization (WTO) and the United States-Mexico-Canada Agreement (USMCA) in order to boost our commerce with the rest of the world. Nevertheless, we still use tariffs and subsidies to protect large swathes of our industry and agriculture.

o Before FDR, the federal government did not engage in much domestic policy making, but since that era we have seen the rise of programs like Social Security, Welfare (through Aid to Families with Dependent Children and new state-based systems), and Medicaid.

REFLECT

Respond to the following questions:

- Of which content topics discussed in this chapter do you feel you have achieved sufficient understanding to answer multiple-choice questions correctly?

- Of which content topics discussed in this chapter do you feel you have achieved sufficient understanding to discuss them effectively in an essay?

- On which content topics discussed in this chapter do you feel you need more work before you can answer multiple-choice questions correctly?

- On which content topics discussed in this chapter do you feel you need more work before you can discuss them effectively in an essay?

- Which parts of this chapter are you going to re-review?

- Will you seek further help, outside of this book (such as from a teacher, tutor, or AP Students), on any of the content in this chapter—and, if so, on what content?

Chapter 9
Chapter Drills:
Answers and
Explanations

CHAPTER 4 DRILL

1. **D** Choice (A) is incorrect as the excerpt does not describe the relationship between the national government and the states. Choice (B) is incorrect as the text clearly states that only Congress can declare war. Choice (C) is incorrect as the excerpt does not refer to Congress as being the sole governing body. Therefore, (D) is correct as the final sentence states that a majority of states must agree to major decisions.

2. **C** Choices (A) and (B) can be eliminated as the Articles gave more power to the states. Choice (D) can be eliminated as many of the powers of Congress in the Articles are identical to those granted to Congress by the Constitution. As a result, (C) is correct as the Articles created an inefficient government that could not meet the challenges facing the new nation.

3. **A** Choice (B) can be eliminated as the Connecticut Compromise refers to how states would be represented in Congress, not whether their enslaved people would count toward representation. Choice (C) can be eliminated as this compromise put a moratorium on the international slave trade. Choice (D) can be eliminated as the Bill of Rights does not mention slavery or congressional representation. Therefore, (A) is correct as the Three-Fifths Compromise counted each enslaved person as 3/5 of a person when determining a state's congressional representation.

4. **B** Choices (A) and (C) are incorrect as each one attributes elements of the New Jersey Plan to the Virginia Plan, and vice versa. Choice (D) is incorrect as the Virginia Plan first suggested the Electoral College as a method to elect the president. Therefore, (B) is correct as the Virginia Plan called for a bicameral legislature, while the New Jersey Plan called for a unicameral legislature.

5. **D** Federalism is a system under which the federal government shares power with the states. The system of checks and balances among the three branches of the federal government concerns the national government only, and not the states; eliminate (A). International treaties are the sole responsibility of the federal government, and do not relate to the states in any way, so (B) can also be eliminated. Washington, D.C., does have special constitutional status as the nation's capital and is governed by the federal government. However, it is not represented in Congress at the state level, so (C) doesn't really pertain to American federalism. Choice (D) must be the correct answer: the Tenth Amendment to the Constitution assigns to the states all powers not granted to the national government by the Constitution. It is instrumental in defining the relationship between the two levels of government, which is the essence of federalism.

6. **B** Choice (A) is incorrect as the Revolutionary War led to the overthrow of British rule. Choice (C) is incorrect as slavery had existed in the Americas for centuries before the founding of the United States. Choice (D) can be eliminated because Shays' Rebellion took place in Massachusetts. As a result, (B) is correct as after the national government put down the rebellion, elites realized a new national government was necessary to prevent future rebellions.

7. **D** This question requires that you know the differences between the enumerated, concurrent, and reserved powers granted by the Constitution. The enumerated powers of the Constitution include the powers to print money, declare war, regulate interstate commerce, regulate international trade, create treaties and engage in foreign policy, establish post offices, establish lower courts, establish rules of naturalization, establish copyright and patent laws, raise and support armed forces, and make all laws "necessary and proper" to carry out responsibilities. Accordingly, the only choice that is not an enumerated power is (D), the power to collect and levy taxes.

CHAPTER 5 DRILL

1. **A** Choice (B) is incorrect as nothing in the passage suggests a question concerning the reasons judges interpret the Constitution. Choice (C) is incorrect as Marshall is not asking how to do his job. Choice (D) is incorrect, as the passage says nothing about the specific steps and rituals involved when judges take office. Therefore, (A) is correct as "no rule for his government" suggests that the Constitution does not specifically describe the responsibilities of the Supreme Court.

2. **C** Choice (A) can be eliminated as *ex post facto* laws refer to applying laws to actions that took place before the laws were written. Choice (B) can be eliminated as judicial restraint refers to justices not injecting personal opinion or the national mood into their decisions. Choice (D) can be eliminated as *amicus curiae* briefs refer to letters written to the court by an interested party not directly involved with a case. As a result, (C) is correct. The passage, especially the final paragraph, affirms the principle of judicial review, the Supreme Court's ability to strike down unconstitutional laws.

3. **B** Choice (A) can be eliminated given that the president is the head of the executive branch and the checks-and-balances of the government would prevent them from also being the head of a legislative branch. Choice (C) can be eliminated as the president *pro tempore* is just below the official head of the Senate. Choice (D) can be eliminated because the chief whip is the *functional* head of the Senate, not the official head. This leaves the correct answer, (B); the vice president is the official head of the Senate, also known as the president of the Senate.

4. **D** Don't be tricked because one of the two options for a choice is correct. Both have to match. So for (A), it's true that the legislative branch handles the Library of Congress, but it's not true that the executive branch handles technology assessment (that, too, is handled by the legislative branch). Eliminate (A). Choice (B) is incorrect as the executive branch oversees the Department of Energy and the legislative branch oversees the Government Publishing Office. Choice (C) is incorrect as both departments fall under the control of the executive branch. Therefore, (D) is correct. The legislative branch oversees the GAO and the executive branch oversees Drug Control Policy.

5. **A** The modifying word in this question is *legislative*, which refers to Congress's power to pass laws. Choices (B), (C), and (D) are all powers of Congress, but they are not legislative. Therefore, (A) is correct as the power to tax and spend through legislation such as spending bills is one of the most important legislative powers possessed by Congress.

6. **C** Congressional districts are, as the question suggests, determined by the states, which should help you to eliminate both (A) and (B), given that it would be a violation of the Tenth Amendment for the federal government to determine districts for the House. Likewise, (D), which would take power away from the state and give it to a vague "commission," can also be ruled out. The correct answer, (C), describes the actual process—after a national census, the state legislatures or commissions draw congressional maps.

7. **A** Choice (C) is incorrect, as the Supreme Court has no say in the nomination or appointment of cabinet members. Choices (A), (B), and (D) all involve the president, which is correct, as the president nominates all cabinet members. Choice (D) can be eliminated as all cabinet members require confirmation. So can (B), as the House has no say in the appointment of cabinet members. Therefore, (A) is correct, as the president nominates cabinet members. The Senate interviews each candidate before voting.

8. **B** Here you need to understand the structure of the federal bureaucracy to identify the key players. Independent regulatory commissions have an inordinate amount of independence in their role of watchdogs over the federal government; eliminate (A). Independent executive agencies are generally run-of-the-mill bureaucracies with broad presidential oversight and an integral part of the bureaucratic structure; eliminate (C). Government corporations are hybrid public-private partnerships that provide services to Americans that could be provided by the private sector alone, and part of the bureaucratic structure; eliminate (D). Interest groups do have a tremendous influence on agency actions and policy implementation, but they are not a formal part of the bureaucratic structure. Accordingly, the correct answer is (B).

CHAPTER 6 DRILL

1. **C** For a Qualitative Analysis question, be very careful with choices that may be historically true or morally sound, but which do not match the passage itself. This applies even to implications; (A) and (D) can therefore be eliminated. Choice (B) is incorrect, as King does not make this claim. The correct answer, (C), matches what King says, which is that the legality or illegality of something does not make that thing inherently right or wrong.

2. **B** Choice (A) is more than a little extreme, and unsupported by the text; there's nothing to say that America was as bad as the other two nations mentioned. The focus of the passage is on the righteousness of certain laws. Martin Luther King Jr. isn't promoting himself; he is instead talking about the importance of nonviolent protest, so eliminate (C). King isn't trying to educate readers about Germany or Hungary; he's using them to make a point about his actions in America, so eliminate (D). This point about unjust laws is what is expressed in (B), so that is the correct answer.

3. **C**   Choice (A) can be eliminated; although *Powell* expanded defendants' right to legal representation, this right did not extend to all court cases. Choice (B) can be eliminated as *Betts* denied the right to counsel in certain circumstances. Choice (D) is incorrect as *Miranda* concerned informing defendants of their rights at the time of arrest. Therefore, (C) is correct: after *Gideon*, all defendants were allowed an attorney no matter the crime.

4. **A**   On a comparison question, you can look to eliminate options that use extreme language, because if you can find even one instance to the contrary, that means the choice is incorrect. That's certainly true for (B), as there are many cases in which the Supreme Court has ruled to restrict civil rights (e.g., *Plessy*, *Korematsu*). You can also eliminate (C), because civil rights are not limited to only one minority group. Finally, eliminate (D) because civil liberties cannot be amended at the state level. This leaves (A), which is correct: the Bill of Rights enshrines Americans' civil liberties, and the equal application of the law to all Americans is the foundation of civil rights.

5. **A**   A "right to privacy" is not explicitly named in the Constitution, but it has been cited in several important Supreme Court cases, most notably *Roe v. Wade* and *Griswold v. Connecticut*. In *Griswold*, the Supreme Court ruled that women have a "right to privacy" with their physicians, and legalized birth control throughout the United States. Civil rights, (C), and women's equal access to educational programs, (D), have more to do with equal rights than with notions of privacy, so eliminate those answers. Choices (A) and (B) are the closest, since the Fourteenth Amendment is, in fact, the legal justification for "right to privacy." Protection, (B), however, has more to do with citizens' equal treatment under the law, not privacy. That leaves choice (A) as the best answer. The court has interpreted the Due Process Clause to protect the right of privacy from state infringement, since "due process" rights may be violated by a state prying into medical decisions. This interpretation of the Due Process Clause has been the subject of controversy since its inception, but it remains the foundation of many legal decisions made in the 20th century.

6. **C**   During the 20th century, the Supreme Court took on many cases that affected students attending public schools. Choice (A) can be eliminated as *Tinker v. Des Moines* centered on the issue of student protest. Choice (B) can be eliminated as *Hazelwood School District v. Kuhlmeier* decided that schools can regulate students' speech in school. Choice (D) can be eliminated as *Lemon v. Kurtzman* decided that states cannot directly fund religious schools. Therefore, (C) is correct as *Engel v. Vitale* barred the practice of state-sponsored prayer in school.

7. **D**   *Wisconsin v. Yoder* pitted the state's Amish community against Wisconsin's compulsory education laws. Although the First Amendment was central to the case, (A), (B), and (C) were not at issue. As a result, (D) is correct as the Amish community successfully argued that their religious beliefs prompted them to remove their children from school after the eighth grade.

8. **C** The Thirteenth Amendment was ratified after the Civil War and made slavery illegal; that most certainly did advance the rights of African Americans, so eliminate (A). The Fifteenth Amendment banned laws that would prevent African Americans from voting on the basis of their race or if they were previously enslaved; eliminate (B). The Nineteenth Amendment granted women the right to vote, but it did not specifically advance the rights of African Americans. The Civil Rights Act of 1875 banned discrimination in public places, such as hotels, restaurants, and public transportation; eliminate (D). The correct answer is (C).

CHAPTER 7 DRILL

1. **B** Choice (A) is incorrect since the chart only measures religious affiliations, not the total white population. Choice (C) is incorrect since some affiliations decreased over time. Choice (D) is tempting, but the chart only measures white American Christians and only percentages, not raw numbers. As a result, (B) is correct, since the percent of unaffiliated Christians increased markedly during the time period measured.

2. **B** Choice (A) can be eliminated since "Other religions" are not measured in the chart and would likely be a small group compared to white Christians and unaffiliated Christians. Choice (C) can be eliminated since it sounds rather extreme, and the chart does not indicate anything about the future of political socialization as a whole. Choice (D) can be eliminated since the chart does not compare the impact of religion versus other means of political socialization. Therefore, (B) is correct: as more Americans become unaffiliated with a church denomination, they will experience political socialization in different ways.

3. **D** Remember that both sides of a comparison question must be correct, so if either is wrong, rule out that entire choice. For instance, conservatives are actually the largest voting bloc, so eliminate (A). Moderates often change their mind on political issues, so delete (B). Conservatives do not support affirmative action, so eliminate (C). Conservatives do oppose government regulation and moderates do view themselves as pragmatists, which makes (D) the correct answer.

4. **D** Remember that "intensity" refers to the strength of a feeling Americans, as a whole, have about an issue or topic. Some Americans have strong opinions about (A), (B), and (C); however, (D) is the best answer, as Social Security is an issue that the majority of Americans strongly support.

5. **B** Remember that many factors influence someone's ideological behavior. Choices (A) and (C) can be eliminated as they have no known effect on ideological behavior. Choice (D) can be eliminated as someone's ideological beliefs rarely change over time. As a result, (B) is correct, as men and women typically have differences of opinion regarding political ideology.

6. **B** It is possible for a politician to change their view, but whether that is seen as positive depends largely on how the public feels about the issue in question. The timing matters, too; during a campaign, changing positions can lead to attacks from one's opponent. For these reasons, eliminate (A). Many Americans do not approve of divorce, so you can also eliminate (C). Soliciting political donations from foreign governments is illegal, and unlikely to generate anything positive, so eliminate (D). This leaves (B), which is a fit, as appearing in photographs with military veterans suggests that the candidate is patriotic and supports veterans.

7. **A** Choices (B), (C), and (D) are incorrect: public opinion regarding incumbent U.S. House members, Social Security benefits, and the U.S. Supreme Court rarely go up or down except in the case of extreme circumstances. As a result, (A) is correct. Presidential public opinion often changes as a result of the president's decisions while in office.

8. **D** The news media plays a key role in developing public opinion through dispersing information via broadcast news, broadcast programming, print media, social media, political talk shows, the radio, the internet, and more; eliminate (A). The news media's most important role is in setting the public agenda, which it does by deciding which news stories to cover and the duration for which to cover such stories; in this sense, the media is in control of determining the relative importance of political issues. Eliminate (B). The news media also provides Americans with their greatest exposure to government and politics, acting as an intermediary between the people and the government as it reports on and questions their actions; eliminate (C). While the news media does influence public opinion, the media has no integral role in measuring public opinion. Thus, the correct answer is (D).

CHAPTER 8 DRILL

1. **D** Look to the passage, as you may be able to find answers to some of your questions there. Choice (A) can be eliminated as Washington does not approve of political parties. Choice (B) can be eliminated as Washington states that political parties sometimes work toward "popular ends." Choice (C) can be eliminated as Washington calls the men who run political parties "unprincipled." Washington warns that political parties will destroy the system that gave them power so that no one else can take power from them, which means that (D) is the correct answer.

2. **C** Remember that on comparison questions, you need to rule out only one of the two options for each incorrect choice. Interest groups do not undergo realignment every few decades, so you can eliminate (A). You can get rid of both (B) and (D) because they are flipped. Political parties do nominate candidates for office, and interest groups do endorse candidates they prefer to win, so (C) is the correct answer.

3. **B** Choice (A) can be eliminated, as PACs do not run their own candidates for office. Choice (C) can be eliminated, as PACs do not have a formal voice in government. Choice (D) can be eliminated as PACs do not function as arbiters in union/management corporate negotiations. Therefore, (B) is correct: PACs allow unions and corporations to funnel unlimited sums of money toward political activities not directly affiliated with a candidate.

4. **D** Pay close attention to the modifiers for a given scenario. You aren't being asked about any primary, or even any Republican primary—you're looking at an *open* Republican primary. These modifiers can help you to eliminate choices. Both (A) and (B) describe closed primaries, not open ones, so eliminate them. An open primary is one in which *any* registered voter can participate—not just Republicans or Democrats—and so (C) can also be eliminated. The correct answer is (D).

5. **A** Choices (B) and (C) are incorrect as these committees do not deal with a party's positions. The Credentials Committee decides if a delegate has voting privileges. The Rules Committee decides the all-important process of how delegates may vote during the primary (for example, whether they can change their vote after the first round of voting). Choice (D) is incorrect as there is no Ideology Committee. Choice (A) is correct, as the Platform Committee decides the positions the party will take over the next four years.

6. **C** Choice (A) is incorrect as states award delegates based on the proportion of the vote a candidate wins. Choice (B) is incorrect as this describes a caucus. Choice (D) is incorrect as this also describes a caucus. As a result, (C) is correct as the majority of states use the primary system to choose presidential candidates.

7. **A** Social security is a financial safety net for many Americans. Choice (B) is incorrect as foreign tourists do not qualify for Social Security benefits; foreigners who are permanent residents do qualify. Choice (C) is incorrect: although veterans receive many benefits from the government, a veteran who is employed does not qualify for Social Security benefits. Choice (D) is incorrect as chronic poverty does not qualify a family for Social Security. However, the family may qualify for other federal and state government benefits. Choice (A) is correct.

8. **A** Imports and exports have to do with trade, whereas defaults and bankruptcy have to do with not being able to pay debts and/or being broke, so eliminate (C) and (D). Between the two remaining choices, consider that a deficit means a loss and a surplus represents a gain. If a nation imports—buys—more than it exports—sells, then the nation has a trade deficit. Eliminate (B); the correct answer is (A).

9. **D** Discretionary spending is something that doesn't have a fixed amount that needs to be spent on it. Whether you remember the specifics of the Budget Enforcement Act or not, you should be able to identify the national debt, social security, and Medicare as mandatory, fixed payments; eliminate (A), (B), and (C). This means that (D) is the correct answer: education programs fall under discretionary spending.

10. **A** Rational choice voting is based on what is perceived to be in the citizen's individual interest; this is what the question asks you to identify. Retrospective voting involves the decision of whether a party or candidate in power should be reelected based on recent history and performance; eliminate (B). Prospective voting is based on the potential performance of a party or candidate should they be elected; eliminate (C). Party-line voting occurs when an individual votes for a candidate from one political party for all public offices; eliminate (D). Thus, the correct answer is (A).

Glossary

Scan the QR code below and register your book to access the digital flashcards of these key terms:

"9/11" The September 11, 2001 terrorist attacks on the World Trade Center and the Pentagon, leading to significant changes in U.S. domestic and foreign policies.

Adams, John The second U.S. president (1797–1801), a Federalist, and a key figure in the American Revolution, known for his role in drafting the Declaration of Independence.

affirmative action Government mandated programs that seek to create special employment opportunities for minorities, women, and other victims of past discrimination.

amendment Addition to the Constitution. Amendments require approval by two-thirds of both houses of Congress and three-quarters of the states. The first ten amendments make up the Bill of Rights.

***amicus curiae* briefs** "Friend of the court" briefs that qualified individuals or organizations file with lawsuits to which they are not a party, so the judge may consider their advice in respect to matters of law that directly affect the cases in question.

Anti-federalist Opponents of the U.S. Constitution during its ratification period, expressing concerns about a strong central government and advocating for the protection of individual and states' rights.

Article III of the U.S. Constitution Outlines the role of the judicial branch, establishing the Supreme Court and granting Congress the power to create lower federal courts, defining their jurisdictions.

Article V of the U.S. Constitution Describes the amendment process, allowing changes to the Constitution through proposal by two-thirds of Congress or state conventions and ratification by three-fourths of states.

Articles of Confederation The United States' first constitution. The government formed by the Articles of Confederation lasted from 1781 (two years before the end of the Revolutionary War) to 1789. The government under the Articles proved inadequate because it did not have the power to collect taxes from the states, nor could it regulate foreign trade to generate revenue from import and export tariffs.

assimilation The process by which individuals or groups adopt the customs, language, and culture of a dominant society, often associated with immigrants integrating into the prevailing societal norms.

***Baker v. Carr* (1962)** A landmark Supreme Court case that established the principle of "one person, one vote," requiring state legislative districts to be roughly equal in population.

bicameral legislature Consisting of two legislative houses. The United States has a bicameral legislature; its two houses are the House of Representatives and the Senate.

Bill of Rights First ten amendments to the U.S. Constitution. The Bill of Rights guarantees personal liberties and limits the powers of the government.

Bipartisan Campaign Reform Act (2002) Also known as the McCain-Feingold Act, this legislation aimed to regulate campaign financing by restricting soft money contributions and issue advocacy ads, influencing political advertising and financing practices.

block grants Federal money given to states with only general guidelines for its use. The states have the authority to decide how the money will be spent.

Brown v. Board of Education The 1954 case in which the Supreme Court overturned the "separate but equal" standard as it applied to segregation in education. In a 9-to-0 decision, the court ruled that "separate educational facilities are inherently unequal." "Separate but equal" had been the law of the land since the court had approved it in *Plessy v. Ferguson* (1896).

Brutus #1 A series of essays opposing the U.S. Constitution during its ratification, expressing Anti-Federalist concerns about a strong central government and potential abuses of power.

Budget and Impoundment Control Act (1974) Legislation enhancing congressional budgetary powers and limiting the president's ability to impound funds.

budget deficit Condition that arises when federal expenditures exceed revenues; in other words, when the government spends more money than it takes in.

budget resolution Set of budget guidelines that must pass both houses of Congress in identical form by April 15. The budget resolution guides government spending for the following fiscal year.

bully pulpit Term describing the president's influential platform to speak out and shape public opinion on important issues.

bureaucracy Administrative organization responsible for implementing government policies, often criticized for its complexity and perceived inefficiency.

cabinet Presidential advisory body composed of department heads, aiding in policy formulation and decision-making.

calendar assignments Congressional scheduling of bills for debate and voting.

campaign finance legislation Regulations and laws governing the funding of political campaigns to ensure transparency and prevent corruption.

Canvasing The practice of seeking voters' support through direct interaction, like door-to-door campaigning.

categorical grants Federal aid given to states with strings attached. To receive the money, the states must agree to adhere to federally mandated guidelines for spending it.

caucus Meeting of local party members for the purpose of choosing delegates to a national party convention. The term also refers to a meeting of the Democratic members of the House of Representatives.

census The process, mandated by the Constitution, by which the population of the United States is officially counted every ten years. Census data is then used to help distribute federal money and to reapportion congressional districts.

checks and balances   The system that prevents any branch of government from becoming too powerful by requiring the approval of more than one branch for all important acts.

Citizens United v. Federal Election Commission **(2010)**   Supreme Court case allowing corporations and unions greater influence in elections, stating that restricting their spending violates free speech.

civil liberties   Those protections against government power embodied in the Bill of Rights and similar legislation. Civil liberties include the right to free speech, free exercise of religion, and the right to a fair trial.

civil rights   Those protections against discrimination by the government and individuals. Civil rights are intended to prevent discrimination based on race, religion, gender, ethnicity, physical disabilities, or sexual orientation.

Civil Rights Act of 1964   Federal law that made segregation illegal in most public places, increased penalties and sentences for those convicted of discrimination in employment, and withheld federal aid from schools that discriminated on the basis of race or gender.

civil service system   Method of hiring federal employees based on merit rather than on political beliefs or allegiances. This system replaced the patronage system in the United States.

"clear and present danger" test   Interpretation by Justice Oliver Wendell Holmes which set limits on free speech if it presents a "clear and present danger" to the public or leads to illegal actions; for example, one cannot shout "Fire!" in a crowded theater if there is no fire.

Clinton, William Jefferson   42nd U.S. president (1993–2001), known for presiding over a period of economic prosperity but also facing impeachment proceedings when caught lying under oath. Clinton was not removed from office but was formally censured by Congress for his actions.

closed primary   Primary election in which voting is restricted to registered members of a political party.

cloture   A motion in the Senate to end debate, often used in the event of a filibuster. A cloture vote requires a three-fifths majority—60 ayes—of the Senate.

coalition   A combination of groups of people who work together to achieve a political goal. For example, the coalition of the Democratic Party is largely made up of urban dwellers on the coasts, minority groups, and young people. Coalitions also form among legislators who work together to advance or defeat a particular bill.

Commander-in-chief   The president's role as leader of all United States military forces. This is one of the executive powers authorized in the Constitution.

Commerce Clause   Constitutional provision granting Congress authority to regulate interstate and foreign trade.

compliance monitoring   Oversight to ensure that laws and regulations are followed.

concurrent powers   Constitutional powers shared by the federal and state governments.

conference committee Congressional committee that includes representatives of both houses of Congress. Their purpose is to settle differences between the House and Senate versions of bills that have been passed by their respective legislatures.

congressional district The geographically defined group of people on whose behalf a representative acts in the House of Representatives. Each state is divided into congressional districts of equal population, with larger states having more districts and representatives than small states. Congressional districts are reapportioned every ten years according to new census data.

congressional oversight One of Congress's most important tasks. In order to check the power of the executive branch, congressional committees investigate and evaluate the performance of corresponding executive agencies and departments.

conservative A political ideology that tends to favor traditional, restrained approaches to political issues. Most conservatives in the United States disapprove of excessive spending on social programs, abortion, affirmative action, and a large federal government. Conservatives are generally affiliated with the Republican Party.

constituents The people represented by elected officials in a specific district or state.

Constitution of the United States Fundamental law of the U.S., outlining the structure of the government and protecting individual rights.

constitutional convention An as of yet untried method by which the Constitution may be amended. To call a constitutional convention, two-thirds of all state legislatures must petition the federal government; not to be confused with the Constitutional Convention when the Constitution was written.

cooperative federalism Preeminent form of U.S. federalism since the passage of the Fourteenth Amendment. The Fourteenth Amendment initiated the long demise of dual federalism by providing the national government the means to enforce the rights of citizens against state infringement. The Progressive Era, the New Deal, and the Great Society all increased federal involvement in state government. The result is a system called cooperative federalism in which the national and state governments share many powers.

Court of Appeals Intermediate federal court reviewing decisions of district courts.

cruel and unusual punishment Eighth Amendment protection against excessively harsh or degrading punishments.

De Tocqueville, Alexis French political thinker known for his observations on American society in "Democracy in America."

death penalty Legal execution as a punishment for serious crimes, debated for its ethics and constitutionality.

Declaration of Independence Document proclaiming the U.S. colonies' independence from British rule in 1776.

defamation False spoken or written statements damaging a person's reputation.

Defense of Marriage Act (1996) Federal law defining marriage as between one man and one woman, later overturned by *Obergefell v. Hodges.*

delegate Representative who follows the will of constituents.

delegated powers Constitutional powers granted solely to the federal government.

Democratic Party One of the major U.S. political parties, generally supporting social equality and government intervention.

Department of Education Federal agency overseeing education policies and programs.

Department of Homeland Security Federal agency addressing domestic security and emergencies.

Department of Transportation Federal agency managing transportation policies and infrastructure.

Department of Veterans Affairs Federal agency providing services and benefits to military veterans.

Devolution Revolution Shift of power from the federal government to states and localities in the 1980s.

discretionary spending Non-mandatory government expenditures subject to annual budget decisions.

District Court Federal trial courts where cases are initially heard.

divided government A government in which the presidency is controlled by one party and Congress is controlled by the other. This has become a common occurrence in recent decades as voters have begun to act more independently of parties and increasingly vote split tickets.

***Dobbs* v. *Jackson Women's Health Organization* (2022)** A landmark Supreme Court case in which the court held that the U.S. Constitution does not grant a woman the right to abortion. This decision overruled both *Roe v. Wade* (1973) and *Planned Parenthood v. Casey* (1992), returning to individual states the power to regulate abortion.

DREAM Act Legislative proposal to address the status of undocumented immigrants brought to the U.S. as children. This act has not passed either house of Congress, despite being introduced several times.

dual federalism Form of U.S. federalism during the nation's early history. During this period, the federal and state governments remained separate and independent. What little contact most Americans had with government occurred on the state level, as the national government concerned itself primarily with international trade, construction of roads, harbors, and railways, and the distribution of public land in the West.

Due Process Clause Established legal procedures for the arrest and trial of an accused criminal.

Eighth Amendment Constitutional protection against cruel and unusual punishment.

electoral college Constitutionally established body created for the sole purpose of choosing the president and vice president. During general elections, voters choose a presidential ticket. The winner in each state usually receives all of that state's electoral votes in the Electoral College. A majority of electoral votes is required for victory in the Electoral College; if such a majority cannot be reached, the election result is determined by the House of Representatives.

elite democracy Political system wherein power is concentrated in the hands of a small, privileged group.

***Engel v. Vitale* (1962)** Supreme Court case prohibiting state-sponsored prayer in public schools.

entitlement programs Social insurance programs that allocate federal funds to all people who meet the conditions of the program. Social Security is the largest and most expensive entitlement program. Because these programs are a form of mandatory spending, it is incredibly difficult to cut funds to entitlement programs during the budgetary process.

enumerated powers Specific powers granted to Congress in the Constitution.

Environmental Protection Agency (EPA) Federal agency addressing environmental issues and regulations.

equal protection clause Fourteenth Amendment provision ensuring equal treatment under the law.

establishment clause Section of the Constitution that prohibits the government from designating one faith as the official religion of the United States.

exclusionary rule Rule that prohibits the use of illegally obtained evidence at trial. The Supreme Court has created several exceptions to the exclusionary rule, notably the objective good faith rule and the inevitable discovery rule.

exclusive powers Powers reserved for either the federal or the state governments.

executive agreements Presidential agreements made with foreign nations. Executive agreements have the same legal force as treaties but do not require the approval of the Senate.

executive branch The branch of government responsible for implementing and enforcing laws.

Executive Office of the President White House staff and agencies assisting the president in policy development.

executive orders Presidential directives with the force of law, used to manage the executive branch.

Federal Communications Commission (FCC) Agency regulating interstate communication by wire and radio in the U.S.

Federal Elections Commission (FEC) Federal agency overseeing campaign finance laws.

Federal Reserve Board Executive agency that is largely responsible for the formulation and implementation of monetary policy. By controlling the monetary supply, the Fed helps maintain a stable economy.

federalism   Term describing a system under which the national government and local governments (state governments, in the case of the United States) share powers. Other federal governments ratification. Canada, Switzerland, and Australia.

Federalist #10   James Madison's essay advocating for a large republic to prevent factionalism.

Federalist #51   James Madison's essay emphasizing the separation of powers and checks and balances.

Federalist #70   Alexander Hamilton's essay arguing for a strong executive branch.

Federalist #78 - Alexander Hamilton's essay discussing the role of the judiciary.

Federalist Papers, the   A series of essays written by James Madison, Alexander Hamilton, and John Jay to defend the Constitution and persuade Americans that it should be ratified. These documents presented the concerns and issues the framers faced as they created a blueprint for the new government.

Federalists   Supporters of the U.S. Constitution during its ratification.

Fifteenth Amendment (1870)   Prohibited states from denying voting rights to African Americans. Southern states circumvented the Fifteenth Amendment through literacy tests and poll taxes.

Fifth Amendment   Constitutional protection against self-incrimination and double jeopardy.

filibuster   A lengthy speech that halts all legislative action in the Senate. Filibusters are not possible in the House of Representatives because strict time limits govern all debates there.

First Amendment   Protects the rights of individuals against the government by guaranteeing the freedom of speech, the press, religion, and assembly.

fiscal policy   Government strategies influencing the economy through taxing and spending.

foreign policy   A government's strategy in dealing with other nations, encompassing diplomatic, economic, and military actions.

formal powers   Explicit powers granted by the Constitution to a governmental branch or official.

Fourteenth Amendment   Prevented the states from denying "due process of law" and "equal protection under the law" to citizens. The amendment was specifically aimed at protecting the rights of newly freed enslaved people. In the 20th century, the Supreme Court used the amendment to strike down state laws that violate the Bill of Rights.

Fourth Amendment (1868) Constitutional amendment ensuring equal protection under the law and due process.

Franklin, Benjamin   Founding Father, inventor, and diplomat; played a crucial role in drafting the Declaration of Independence.

free exercise clause   Part of the First Amendment protecting the right to practice one's religion freely.

free riders   Individuals benefiting from a group's actions without actively participating or contributing.

general election   Election held on the first Tuesday after the first Monday of November, during which voters elect officials.

gerrymandering The practice of drawing congressional district lines to benefit one party over the other.

***Gideon v. Wainwright* (1963)** Supreme Court case in which the court ruled that a defendant in a felony trial must be provided a lawyer free of charge if the defendant cannot afford one.

globalization The process of increased interconnectedness and interdependence among countries in terms of economics, culture, and politics.

Grand Committee Proposed by Benjamin Franklin during the Constitutional Convention, aimed at resolving disputes between large and small states.

Great (Connecticut) Compromise Settlement reached at the Constitutional Convention between large states and small states. The Great Compromise called for two legislative houses: one in which states were represented by their populations (favoring the large states) and one in which states received equal representation (favoring the small states).

gridlock Stalemate in government decision-making due to conflicting interests or opposing political parties.

***Griswold v. Connecticut* (1965)** Supreme Court decision in which the court ruled that the Constitution implicitly guarantees citizens' right to privacy.

Hamilton, Alexander Founding Father, author of Federalist Papers, and first Secretary of the Treasury.

Hatch Act (1939) A congressional law that forbade government officials from participating in partisan politics and protected government employees from being fired on partisan grounds; it was revised in 1993 to be less restrictive.

Hobbes, Thomas Political philosopher known for his social contract theory and pessimistic view of human nature.

"horse race" election coverage Media portrayal of elections emphasizing candidates' standings rather than substantive issues.

House of Representatives Lower house of U.S. Congress, in which representation is allocated to states in direct proportion to their population. The House of Representatives has sole power to initiate appropriations legislation.

House Rules Committee Determines the rules for debate of each bill, including whether the bill may be amended. This is the most powerful committee in the House. The Senate, which is smaller, has no rules for debate.

Hurricane Katrina 2005 catastrophic hurricane exposing government response challenges and social disparities.

Hyde Amendment of 1976 Legislation prohibiting federal funding for most abortions.

ideology A set of beliefs or ideas shaping political opinions and actions.

impeachment Process by which a president, judge, or other government official can be tried for high crimes and misdemeanors. Andrew Johnson, Bill Clinton, and Donald Trump were impeached but were found not guilty and were not removed from office.

implied powers Powers not explicitly stated in the Constitution but inferred to fulfill governmental duties.

incumbency advantage Electoral advantage held by sitting officeholders in seeking reelection.

informal powers Unwritten powers not specified in the Constitution but exercised by a government official.

initiative Process through which voters may propose new laws. One of several Progressive Era reforms that increased voters' power over government.

interest group Political group organized around a particular political goal or philosophy. Interest groups attempt to influence public policy through political action and donations to sympathetic candidates.

interstate commerce Trade and economic activities between states, regulated by Congress.

Iraq War Military conflict initiated in 2003, leading to the removal of Saddam Hussein.

iron triangle A network formed by the close working relationship among various interest groups, congressional committees, and executive agencies that enforce federal regulations. Working together, these groups can collectively exert a powerful influence over legislation and law enforcement.

issue networks Alliances of various interest groups and individuals advocating for specific policies.

Jefferson, Thomas Founding Father, principal author of the Declaration of Independence, and third U.S. president.

Johnson, Andrew Seventeenth U.S. president (1865–1869), faced challenges during the Reconstruction era, including impeachment.

Johnson, Lyndon B. Thirty-sixth U.S. president (1963–1969), known for civil rights and the "Great Society" anti-poverty programs.

joint committee Congressional committee composed of members of both houses of Congress, usually to investigate and research specific subjects.

judicial activism Term referring to the actions of a court that frequently strikes down or alters the acts of the executive and/or legislative branches.

judicial branch The branch of government responsible for interpreting laws, headed by the Supreme Court.

judicial restraint Term referring to the actions of a court that demonstrates an unwillingness to break with precedent or to overturn legislative and executive acts.

judicial review The power of the Supreme Court to declare laws and executive actions unconstitutional.

Keynesian economics Economic theory advocating government intervention in the economy, especially during economic downturns.

"lame duck" presidency A period when a president, nearing the end of their term, has reduced political influence.

legislative branch The branch of government responsible for making laws, consisting of Congress.

"Letter From a Birmingham Jail" Martin Luther King Jr.'s letter advocating civil disobedience and opposing racial segregation.

"Letters from a Federalist Farmer" Anti-Federalist essays expressing concerns about the Constitution's impact on individual rights.

libel False written statements harming a person's reputation.

liberal Descriptive of an ideology that tends to favor government spending on social programs, affirmative action, the legal right to abortion, and an active government. Liberals are generally affiliated with the Democratic Party.

libertarianism Political ideology emphasizing individual liberties and minimal government intervention.

life tenure The principle of serving in a position for one's lifetime, such as federal judges do.

limited government Principle of government that states that government powers must be confined to those allowed it by the nation's Constitution.

linkage institutions Organizations connecting citizens with government, such as political parties and the media.

Locke, John An English philosopher and Enlightenment thinker, he profoundly influenced political theory with his ideas on natural rights and the social contract. His work, including "Two Treatises of Government" (1690), emphasized the role of government in protecting individual rights, shaped democratic principles, and inspired the U.S. Declaration of Independence.

logrolling The practice of exchanging political favors or support.

Madison, James Founding Father, author of Federalist Papers, and fourth U.S. president.

mandates Clear instructions or commands, often given to elected officials.

mandatory spending Government expenditures required by law, typically entitlement programs.

Marbury v. Madison **(1803)** Supreme Court decision that established the principle of judicial review.

marijuana, legalization of As of November 2023, a total of 24 states have passed measures legalizing marijuana for recreational use: Alaska, Arizona, California, Colorado, Connecticut, Delaware, Illinois, Maine, Maryland, Massachusetts, Michigan, Minnesota, Missouri, Montana, Nevada, New Jersey, New Mexico, New York, Ohio, Oregon, Rhode Island, Vermont, Virginia, and Washington (plus Guam, Northern Mariana Islands, U.S. Virgin Islands, and District of Columbia). It's also decriminalized in 7: Hawaii, Louisiana, Mississippi, Nebraska, New Hampshire, North Carolina, and North Dakota.

Marshall, Thurgood First African American Supreme Court Justice, played a key role in civil rights cases.

Mayflower Compact (1620) Considered the first written set of laws in America, it was an agreement among the Pilgrims, setting principles for self-government in the Plymouth colony.

McCulloch v. Maryland **(1819)** Supreme Court case affirming the federal government's implied powers.

McDonald v. Chicago **(2010)** Supreme Court case affirming an individual's right to bear arms.

midterm elections Congressional elections held between presidential elections.

Milliken v. Bradley (1974)
Supreme Court case addressing desegregation in public schools.

minimum wage laws
Government-set minimum wages to ensure fair compensation for workers.

Miranda v. Arizona (1966)
Supreme Court case in which the court ruled that, upon arrest, a suspect must be advised of the right to remain silent and the right to consult with a lawyer.

Montesquieu, Baron de   a French political philosopher of the Enlightenment: proposed the separation of governmental powers into legislative, executive, and judicial branches. His influential work, "The Spirit of the Laws" (1748), profoundly shaped the concept of checks and balances in constitutional governance, influencing the framers of the U.S. Constitution.

Morse v. Frederick (2007)
Supreme Court case addressing student free speech rights.

multiculturalism   Recognition and promotion of diverse cultural perspectives within a society.

national convention   Occasion at which a political party officially announces its presidential nominee and reveals its party platform for the next four years.

National Minimum Drinking Age Act of 1984   Federal law setting the legal drinking age at 21 to reduce drunk driving incidents.

National Organization for Women (NOW)   Feminist political group formed in 1967 to promote legislative change. NOW lobbied for the failed Equal Rights Amendment to the Constitution.

National Recovery Act of 1933   Part of FDR's New Deal, aimed at economic recovery during the Great Depression through industry regulations.

natural rights   Fundamental rights inherent to individuals, often cited in the Declaration of Independence.

naturalization   The legal process by which non-citizens become U.S. citizens.

Necessary and Proper Clause
Constitutional provision granting Congress the authority to make laws required for executing its powers.

New Deal   President Franklin Roosevelt's comprehensive set of programs and policies addressing economic challenges during the Great Depression in the 1930s.

New York Times v. United States (1971)   Supreme Court case protecting the press's right to publish classified information in the public interest.

Nineteenth Amendment (1920)
Granted voting rights to women.

Ninth Amendment   Constitutional provision affirming that rights not specifically listed are retained by the people.

Nixon, Richard   37th U.S. president (1969–1974), known for ending the Vietnam War and for resigning amid the Watergate scandal.

No Child Left Behind Act (2001)
Education reform legislation emphasizing standardized testing and accountability.

nomination   Endorsement to run for office by a political party.

Obergefell v. Hodges (2015)
Supreme Court case legalizing same-sex marriage across the United States.

obscenity Material offensive to accepted standards of decency, not protected by the First Amendment.

O'Connor, Sandra Day First female Supreme Court Justice, appointed by Ronald Reagan in 1981.

Omnibus Budget Reconciliation Act of 1985 Legislation addressing federal budget matters through reconciliation.

open primary Primary election in which voters may vote in whichever party primary they choose, though they must select that party before entering the voting booth.

original jurisdiction Term used to describe a court's power to initially try a case. Courts in which cases are first heard are those with original jurisdiction in the case. By contrast, appellate courts hear challenges to earlier court decisions.

override The Constitutional power of Congress to supersede a president's veto by a two-thirds majority in both houses. Such a vote is difficult to achieve, however, so overrides are fairly rare.

participatory democracy System wherein citizens actively engage in decision-making and policy development.

partisanship Strong allegiance to a political party, often influencing one's views and actions.

Patriot Act (2001) Act passed in response to the terrorist attacks of September 11, 2001, granting broad police authority to the federal, state, and local governments to interdict, prosecute, and convict suspected terrorists.

patronage system The political practice of trading government jobs and preferences for political and financial support. President Andrew Jackson was the first to be widely accused of using the spoils system to reward political friends and supporters. Ended with the Pendleton Act in 1883.

Pendleton Civil Service Act (1883) Legislation establishing a merit-based system for federal employment.

Personal Responsibility and Work Opportunity Act of 1996 Welfare reform legislation promoting work and self-sufficiency.

phone banking Campaign strategy involving volunteers making calls to voters to promote candidates or issues.

***Pierce v. Society of Sisters* (1925)** Supreme Court case affirming parental rights in education.

***Planned Parenthood v. Casey* (1992)** Supreme Court case upholding abortion rights while allowing some state regulations.

platform Statement of purpose and policy objectives drafted and approved by political parties at their national conventions. Party platforms rarely exert much influence on day-to-day politics.

pluralist democracy System wherein various interest groups compete for influence in policymaking.

pocket veto If the president fails to approve a bill passed during the last 10 days of a congressional session, the bill does not become law.

polarization Increasing ideological distance and division between political parties and voters.

policy agenda A set of issues and priorities government officials focus on, influenced by public concerns.

policy implementation   The process by which executive departments and agencies put legislation into practice. Agencies are often allowed a degree of freedom to interpret legislation as they write guidelines to enact and enforce the law.

political action committee (PAC)   The fundraising apparatus of interest groups. Donations to and contributions from PACs are regulated by federal law. PACs contribute heavily to the reelection campaigns of representatives and senators sympathetic to the PACs' political agendas.

political party   Group of people with common political goals, which hopes to influence policy through the election process. Parties run candidates for office who represent the political agenda of party members. They therefore serve as an institutional link between the electorate and politicians.

political socialization   Process by which individuals acquire their political beliefs and values.

poll, benchmark   Initial survey to gauge public opinion before a campaign.

poll, exit   Survey of voters leaving polling places to understand their choices.

poll, opinion   Surveys measuring public attitudes and preferences on various issues.

poll, tracking   Continuous surveying over time to monitor changes in public opinion.

polling methodology   Techniques and procedures used to conduct public opinion polls.

popular sovereignty   Concept that political power resides with the people.

pork-barrel legislation   Budget items proposed by legislators to benefit constituents in their home states or districts. Such expenditures are sometimes unnecessary but are passed anyway because they are politically beneficial.

"power of the purse"   Congressional authority over government spending and taxation.

precedent   Legal decision serving as a reference for future similar cases.

primary elections   Form of election held by the majority of states, during which voters select the nominees for political parties. Winners of primary elections appear on the ballot during the general election.

prior restraint   Censorship of news material before it is made public.

pro-choice movement   Advocacy for the legal right to choose abortion.

progressive income tax   A progressive tax increases tax rates for people with higher incomes. Those citizens at the poverty level, for example, may pay few or no taxes. Middle-class citizens may be taxed at a slightly higher rate, while the wealthy are taxed at the highest rates. The goal of a progressive tax is to allow those with greater need to keep more of what they earn while harvesting the majority of revenue from higher income taxpayers.

pro-life movement   Advocacy against abortion, supporting the sanctity of life.

prospective voting   Decision-making based on a candidate's future promises and policies.

ratification   Formal approval of a constitutional amendment or treaty.

rational choice voting   Voting based on self-interest and personal values.

Reagan, Ronald   40th U.S. president (1981–1989), known for conservative policies and the end of the Cold War.

realignment   Occurs when a party undergoes a major shift in its electoral base and political agenda. The groups of people composing the party coalition may split up, resulting in a vastly different party. Realignments are rare and tend to be signaled by a critical election.

redistricting   Process by which congressional districts are redrawn to reflect population changes reported by census data. Each district must have an equal number of residents. Redistricting typically occurs with reapportionment, a process in which seats are redistributed among states in the House. States may lose or gain seats during reapportionment, but the total House membership remains 435.

Reed v. Reed (1971)   Supreme Court case establishing gender-based discrimination as unconstitutional.

Regents of the University of California v. Bakke (1978)   Supreme Court case on affirmative action in college admissions.

regulatory agency   Executive agency responsible for enforcing laws pertaining to a certain industry. The agency writes guidelines for the industry, such as safety codes, and enforces them through methods such as inspection.

Religious Freedom Restoration Act of 1993   Legislation protecting religious freedom from government interference.

representative democracy   Form of government under which citizens vote for delegates who in turn represent citizens' interests within the government. In contrast, a direct democracy requires all citizens to vote on all government issues. The United States is a representative democracy.

Republican Party   One of the two major U.S. political parties, generally supporting conservative principles.

republicanism   Political philosophy emphasizing civic virtue and the common good.

reserved powers   Constitutional powers that belong solely to the states. According to the Tenth Amendment, these powers include any that the Constitution does not either specifically grant the national government or deny the state governments.

retrospective voting   Decision-making based on an assessment of an incumbent's past performance.

revenue sharing   Distribution of federal funds to state and local governments.

rider amendment   Unrelated provision added to a legislative bill.

Roe v. Wade (1973)   Supreme Court case legalizing abortion in all fifty states, later overturned by *Dobbs* v. *Jackson Women's Health Organization* (2022).

Roosevelt, Franklin Delano   32nd U.S. president (1933–1945), implemented New Deal programs during the Great Depression.

sampling error   Margin of error in public opinion polls. Most polls are accurate within a margin of ±4%.

Schenck v. United States **(1919)**
Supreme Court case involving
limits on free speech rights. The
Schenck case established the "clear
and present danger" principle in
determining what type of speech
could be restricted.

search warrant Document issued
by the courts to allow the police to
search private property. To obtain a
warrant, the police must go before
a judge and explain (1) where they
want to search and (2) what they
are looking for. A search warrant
also limits where the police may
search and what they may take as
evidence (Fourth Amendment).

Second Amendment Constitutional
provision ensuring the right to bear
arms.

**Securities and Exchange Commission
(SEC)** U.S. agency regulating
securities markets to protect
investors.

selective incorporation Process
by which the Supreme Court has
selectively applied the Fourteenth
Amendment to state law.

Senate Upper house of Congress, in
which each state has two senators.
The Senate has the sole power to
approve cabinet, ambassadorial,
and federal judicial appointments.
International treaties must receive
two-thirds approval from the Senate.

senate confirmation Approval
process for presidential appointees
by the U.S. Senate.

"separate but equal" Legal doctrine
allowing racial segregation as long
as facilities are considered equal;
nullified by *Brown v. Board of
Education* and the Civil Rights Act
of 1964.

separation of powers The system that
prevents any branch of government
from becoming too powerful by
dividing important tasks among
the three branches. Also called the
system of checks and balances.

Seventeenth Amendment
Amendment establishing the direct
election of U.S. Senators by the
people.

Shaw v. Reno **(1993)** Supreme Court
case addressing racial gerrymandering
in congressional districts.

Shay's Rebellion 1786–1787
uprising in Massachusetts against
economic injustices and state taxes,
highlighting the weaknesses of the
Articles of Confederation.

signing statement A president's
written comment when signing a
bill into law, often expressing their
interpretation or concerns.

Sixteenth Amendment (1913)
Authorized Congress to impose and
collect federal income taxes.

Sixth Amendment Constitutional
provision guaranteeing the right to
a fair and speedy trial.

slander False spoken statements
damaging a person's reputation.

social contract The theoretical
agreement wherein individuals give
up some freedoms for government
protection and order.

soft money Political donations made
to parties for the purpose of general
party maintenance and support,
such as get-out-the-vote campaigns,
issue advocacy, and advertisements
that promote the party (but
not individual candidates). Soft
money contributions to political
parties were banned in 2002 by
the Bipartisan Campaign Reform
Act (BCRA) (also known as the
McCain-Feingold Bill).

Speaker of the House Individual chosen by members of the majority party in the House of Representatives to preside over its sessions.

split-ticket voting Choosing candidates from different parties for offices listed on the same ballot. Voters have been more inclined to vote a split ticket in recent decades. This trend has led to divided government.

stare decisis Legal principle wherein courts follow precedents in decision-making.

"state of nature" Philosophical concept imagining human existence without government influence.

State of the Union address Annual presidential speech updating Congress on the nation's condition and outlining priorities.

straight-ticket voting Casting votes for all candidates of a single political party in an election.

super PAC A type of political action committee that does not have donation limits but cannot donate directly to a specific candidate.

supply-side economics Economic theory advocating tax cuts to stimulate business investment and economic growth.

Supremacy Clause Section of the Constitution that requires conflicts between federal and state law to be resolved in favor of federal law. State constitutions and laws that violate the U.S. Constitution, federal laws, or international treaties can be invalidated through the supremacy clause.

Supreme Court Highest court in the United States. The only federal court specifically mentioned in the U.S. Constitution.

Swann v. Charlotte-Mecklenburg Board of Education (1970) Supreme Court case supporting busing to achieve school desegregation.

third-party candidates Candidates from political parties other than the two major parties.

Three-Fifths Compromise Agreement reached at the Constitutional Convention between Southern and Northern states. The South wanted enslaved people counted among the population for voting purposes but not for tax purposes; the North wanted the exact opposite. Both sides agreed that three-fifths of a state's enslaved-person population would be counted toward both congressional apportionment and taxation.

"time, place, and manner" Constitutional provisions allowing states to regulate aspects of elections.

Tinker v. Des Moines (1969) Supreme Court case affirming students' First Amendment rights in schools.

Title II Section of the Civil Rights Act of 1964 addressing public accommodations.

Title VII Section of the Civil Rights Act of 1964 prohibiting workplace discrimination.

Title IX Legislation prohibiting gender discrimination in federally funded education programs.

Transportation Safety Administration (TSA) U.S. agency ensuring transportation security, especially in airports.

treaty Formal agreement between countries, requiring Senate approval.

trustee   Representative who uses personal judgment rather than following constituents' preferences.

Twenty-Fourth Amendment (1964)   Outlawed poll taxes, which had been used to prevent the poor from voting.

Twenty-Second Amendment (1951)   Limited the number of years an individual may serve as president. According to the Twenty-Second Amendment, a president may be elected no more than twice.

Twenty-Sixth Amendment (1971)   Lowered the voting age from 21 to 18.

***United States v. Lopez* (1995)**   Supreme Court case limiting Congress's authority under the Commerce Clause.

***United States v. Morrison* (2000)**   Supreme Court ruling that held that parts of the Violence Against Women Act of 1994 were unconstitutional because they exceeded the powers granted to Congress under the Commerce Clause and the Equal Protection Clause.

***United States v. Nixon* (1974)**   Supreme Court case compelling the release of Watergate-related tapes.

USA Freedom Act (2015)   Legislation modifying and limiting the scope of government surveillance programs allowed by the Patriot Act.

veto   The power held by chief executives (such as the president or governors) to reject acts of the legislature. A presidential veto can be overridden by a two-thirds majority vote of both houses of Congress.

Vice-President   The second-highest-ranking official in the U.S. government, presiding over the Senate.

Vietnam War   Conflict (1955–1975) between North and South Vietnam, involving the U.S. in the fight against communism.

Violence Against Women Act (1994)   Legislation addressing domestic violence and gender-based crimes.

voter identification laws   Regulations requiring specific identification to vote.

Voting Rights Act of 1965   Federal law that increased government supervision of local election practices, suspended the use of literacy tests to prevent people from voting, and expanded government efforts to register voters. The Voting Rights Act of 1970 permanently banned literacy tests.

Washington, George   Founding Father and first U.S. president (1789–1797).

***West Virginia Board of Education v. Barnette* (1943)**   Supreme Court case protecting students' right to refuse to salute the flag.

whip   Party official responsible for ensuring party discipline and vote counting.

"winner-take-all" voting districts   Electoral system wherein the candidate with the most votes wins all the electoral votes.

***Wisconsin v. Yoder* (1972)**   Supreme Court case allowing Amish exemption from compulsory education laws.

The Constitution of the United States of America

Note: Text in *italics* indicates that a section of the Constitution is no longer in effect.

Preamble

We the people of the United States, in order to form a more perfect union, establish justice, insure domestic tranquility, provide for the common defense, promote the general welfare, and secure the blessings of liberty to ourselves and our posterity, do ordain and establish this Constitution for the United States of America.

Article I

Section 1. All legislative powers herein granted shall be vested in a Congress of the United States, which shall consist of a Senate and House of Representatives.

Section 2. The House of Representatives shall be composed of members chosen every second year by the people of the several states, and the electors in each state shall have the qualifications requisite for electors of the most numerous branch of the state legislature.

No person shall be a Representative who shall not have attained to the age of twenty-five years, and been seven years a citizen of the United States, and who shall not, when elected, be an inhabitant of that state in which he shall be chosen.

Representatives *and direct taxes*[1] shall be apportioned among the several states which may be included within this union, according to their respective numbers, *which shall be determined by adding to the whole number of free persons, including those bound to service for a term of years, and excluding Indians not taxed, three-fifths of all other Persons.*[2] The actual Enumeration shall be made within three years after the first meeting of the Congress of the United States, and within every subsequent term of ten years[3], in such manner as they shall by law direct. The number of Representatives shall not exceed one for every thirty thousand, but each state shall have at least one Representative; and until such enumeration shall be made, the state of New Hampshire shall be entitled to choose three, Massachusetts eight, Rhode Island and Providence Plantations one, Connecticut five, New York six, New Jersey four, Pennsylvania eight, Delaware one, Maryland six, Virginia ten, North Carolina five, South Carolina five, and Georgia three.

When vacancies happen in the Representation from any state, the executive authority[4] thereof shall issue writs of election to fill such vacancies. The House of Representatives shall choose their speaker and other officers; and shall have the sole power of impeachment.

Section 3. The Senate of the United States shall be composed of two Senators from each state, *chosen by the legislature thereof*[5], for six years; and each Senator shall have one vote.

Immediately after they shall be assembled in consequence of the first election, they shall be divided as equally as may be into three classes. The seats of the Senators of the first class shall be vacated at the expiration of the second year, of the second class at the expiration of the fourth year, and the third class at the expiration of the sixth year,[6] so that one third may be chosen every second year; *and if vacancies happen by resignation, or otherwise, during the recess of the legislature of any state, the executive thereof may make temporary appointments until the next meeting of the legislature, which shall then fill such vacancies.*[7]

No person shall be a Senator who shall not have attained to the age of thirty years, and been nine years a citizen of the United States and who shall not, when elected, be an inhabitant of that state for which he shall be chosen. The vice president of the United States shall be President of the Senate, but shall have no vote, unless they be equally divided. The Senate shall choose their other officers, and also a President *pro tempore*[8], in the absence of the vice president, or when he shall exercise the office of President of the United States. The Senate shall have the sole power to try all impeachments. When sitting for that purpose, they shall be on oath or affirmation. When the President of the United States is tried, the Chief Justice shall preside: And no person shall be convicted without the concurrence of two thirds of the members present.

Judgment in cases of impeachment shall not extend further than to removal from office, and disqualification to hold and enjoy any office of honor, trust or profit under the United States: but the party convicted shall nevertheless be liable and subject to indictment, trial, judgment and punishment, according to law.

Section 4. The times, places and manner of holding elections for Senators and Representatives, shall be prescribed in each state by the legislature thereof; but the Congress may at any time by law make or alter such regulations, except as to the places of choosing Senators.

The Congress shall assemble at least once in every year, *and such meeting shall be on the first Monday in December*[9], unless they shall by law appoint a different day.

Section 5. Each House shall be the judge of the elections, returns and qualifications of its own members, and a majority of each shall constitute a quorum[10] to do business; but a smaller number may adjourn from day to day, and may be authorized to compel the attendance of absent members, in such manner, and under such penalties as each House may provide.

Each House may determine the rules of its proceedings, punish its members for disorderly behavior, and, with the concurrence of two thirds, expel a member.

Each House shall keep a journal of its proceedings, and from time to time publish the same, excepting such parts as may in their judgment require secrecy; and the yeas and nays of the members of either House on any question shall, at the desire of one fifth of those present, be entered on the journal.

Neither House, during the session of Congress, shall, without the consent of the other, adjourn for more than three days, nor to any other place than that in which the two Houses shall be sitting.

Section 6. The Senators and Representatives shall receive a compensation for their services, to be ascertained by law, and paid out of the treasury of the United States. They shall in all cases, except treason, felony and breach of the peace, be privileged from arrest during their attendance at the session of their respective Houses, and in going to and returning from the same; and for any speech or debate in either House, they shall not be questioned in any other place.

No Senator or Representative shall, during the time for which he was elected, be appointed to any civil office under the authority of the United States, which shall have been created, or the emoluments[11] whereof shall have been increased during such time: and no person holding any office under the United States, shall be a member of either House during his continuance in office.[12]

Section 7. All bills for raising revenue shall originate in the House of Representatives; but the Senate may propose or concur with amendments as on other Bills.

Every bill which shall have passed the House of Representatives and the Senate, shall, before it become a law, be presented to the President of the United States; if he approve he shall sign it, but if not he shall return it[13], with his objections to that House in which it shall have originated, who shall enter the objections at large on their journal, and proceed to reconsider it. If after such reconsideration two thirds of that House shall agree to pass the bill, it shall be sent, together with the objections, to the other House, by which it shall likewise be reconsidered, and if approved by two thirds of that House, it shall become a law[14]. But in all such cases the votes of both Houses shall be determined by yeas and nays, and the names of the persons voting for and against the bill shall be entered on the journal of each House respectively. If any bill shall not be returned by the President within ten days (Sundays excepted) after it shall have been presented to him, the same shall be a law, in like manner as if he had signed it, unless the Congress by their adjournment prevent its return[15], in which case it shall not be a law.

Every order, resolution, or vote to which the concurrence of the Senate and House of Representatives may be necessary (except on a question of adjournment) shall be presented to the President of the United States; and before the same shall take effect, shall be approved by him, or being disapproved by him, shall be repassed by two thirds of the Senate and House of Representatives, according to the rules and limitations prescribed in the case of a bill.

Section 8. The Congress shall have power to lay and collect taxes, duties, imposts and excises, to pay the debts and provide for the common defense and general welfare of the United States; but all duties, imposts and excises shall be uniform throughout the United States;

- To borrow money on the credit of the United States;
- To regulate commerce with foreign nations, and among the several states, and with the Indian tribes;
- To establish a uniform rule of naturalization, and uniform laws on the subject of bankruptcies throughout the United States;
- To coin money, regulate the value thereof, and of foreign coin, and fix the standard of weights and measures;
- To provide for the punishment of counterfeiting the securities and current coin of the United States;
- To establish post offices and post roads;
- To promote the progress of science and useful arts, by securing for limited times to authors and inventors the exclusive right to their respective writings and discoveries;
- To constitute tribunals inferior to the Supreme Court;
- To define and punish piracies and felonies committed on the high seas, and offenses against the law of nations;
- To declare war, grant letters of marque and reprisal[16], and make rules concerning captures on land and water;
- To raise and support armies, but no appropriation of money to that use shall be for a longer term than two years;
- To provide and maintain a navy;
- To make rules for the government and regulation of the land and naval forces;
- To provide for calling forth the militia to execute the laws of the union, suppress insurrections and repel invasions;

- To provide for organizing, arming, and disciplining the militia, and for governing such part of them as may be employed in the service of the United States, reserving to the states respectively, the appointment of the officers, and the authority of training the militia according to the discipline prescribed by Congress;
- To exercise exclusive legislation in all cases whatsoever, over such District (not exceeding ten miles square) as may, by cession of particular states, and the acceptance of Congress, become the seat of the government of the United States[17], and to exercise like authority over all places purchased by the consent of the legislature of the state in which the same shall be, for the erection of forts, magazines, arsenals, dockyards, and other needful buildings; and
- To make all laws which shall be necessary and proper for carrying into execution the foregoing powers, and all other powers vested by this Constitution in the government of the United States, or in any department or officer thereof.[18]

Section 9. *The migration or importation of such persons as any of the states now existing shall think proper to admit, shall not be prohibited by the Congress prior to the year one thousand eight hundred and eight, but a tax or duty may be imposed on such importation, not exceeding ten dollars for each person.*[19]

The privilege of the writ of habeas corpus[20] *shall not be suspended, unless when in cases of rebellion or invasion the public safety may require it.*

- No bill of attainder[21] or *ex post facto* law[22] shall be passed.
- *No capitation, or other direct, tax shall be laid, unless in proportion to the census or enumeration herein before directed to be taken.*[23]
- No tax or duty shall be laid on articles exported from any state.
- No preference shall be given by any regulation of commerce or revenue to the ports of one state over those of another: nor shall vessels bound to, or from, one state, be obliged to enter, clear or pay duties in another.
- No money shall be drawn from the treasury, but in consequence of appropriations made by law; and a regular statement and account of receipts and expenditures of all public money shall be published from time to time.
- No title of nobility shall be granted by the United States: and no person holding any office of profit or trust under them, shall, without the consent of the Congress, accept of any present, emolument, office, or title, of any kind whatever, from any king, prince, or foreign state.

Section 10. No state shall enter into any treaty, alliance, or confederation; grant letters of marque and reprisal; coin money; emit bills of credit; make anything but gold and silver coin a tender in payment of debts; pass any bill of attainder, *ex post facto* law, or law impairing the obligation of contracts, or grant any title of nobility.

No state shall, without the consent of the Congress, lay any imposts or duties on imports or exports, except what may be absolutely necessary for executing its inspection laws; and the net produce of all duties and imposts, laid by any state on imports or exports, shall be for the use of the treasury of the United States; and all such laws shall be subject to the revision and control of the Congress.

No state shall, without the consent of Congress, lay any duty of tonnage, keep troops, or ships of war in time of peace, enter into any agreement or compact with another state, or with a foreign power, or engage in war, unless actually invaded, or in such imminent danger as will not admit of delay.

Article II

Section 1. The executive power shall be vested in a President of the United States of America. He shall hold his office during the term of four years, and, together with the vice president, chosen for the same term, be elected, as follows:

Each state shall appoint, in such manner as the Legislature thereof may direct, a number of electors, equal to the whole number of Senators and Representatives to which the State may be entitled in the Congress: but no Senator or Representative, or person holding an office of trust or profit under the United States, shall be appointed an elector.

The electors shall meet in their respective states, and vote by ballot for two persons, of whom one at least shall not be an inhabitant of the same state with themselves. And they shall make a list of all the persons voted for, and of the number of votes for each; which list they shall sign and certify, and transmit sealed to the seat of the government of the United States, directed to the President of the Senate. The President of the Senate shall, in the presence of the Senate and House of Representatives, open all the certificates, and the votes shall then be counted. The person having the greatest number of votes shall be the President, if such number be a majority of the whole number of electors appointed; and if there be more than one who have such majority, and have an equal number of votes, then the House of Representatives shall immediately choose by ballot one of them for President; and if no person have a majority, then from the five highest on the list the said House shall in like manner choose the President. But in choosing the President, the votes shall be taken by States, the representation from each state having one vote; a quorum for this purpose shall consist of a member or members from two thirds of the states, and a majority of all the states shall be necessary to a choice. In every case, after the choice of the President, the person having the greatest number of votes of the electors shall be the vice president. But if there should remain two or more who have equal votes, the Senate shall choose from them by ballot the vice president.[24]

The Congress may determine the time of choosing the electors, and the day on which they shall give their votes; which day shall be the same throughout the United States.

No person except a natural born citizen, or a citizen of the United States at the time of the adoption of this Constitution[25], shall be eligible to the office of President; neither shall any person be eligible to that office who shall not have attained to the age of thirty five years, and been fourteen years a resident within the United States.

In case of the removal of the President from office, or of his death, resignation, or inability to discharge the powers and duties of the said office, the same shall devolve on the vice president, and the Congress may by law provide for the case of removal, death, resignation or inability, both of the President and vice president, declaring what officer shall then act as President, and such officer shall act accordingly, until the disability be removed, or a President shall be elected.[26]

The President shall, at stated times, receive for his services, a compensation, which shall neither be increased nor diminished during the period for which he shall have been elected, and he shall not receive within that period any other emolument[27] from the United States, or any of them.

Before he enter on the execution of his office, he shall take the following oath or affirmation: "I do solemnly swear (or affirm) that I will faithfully execute the office of President of the United States, and will to the best of my ability, preserve, protect and defend the Constitution of the United States."

Section 2. The President shall be commander in chief of the Army and Navy of the United States, and of the militia of the several states, when called into the actual service of the United States; he may require the opinion, in writing, of the principal officer in each of the executive departments, upon any subject relating to the duties of their respective offices, and he shall have power to grant reprieves and pardons for offenses against the United States, except in cases of impeachment.

He shall have power, by and with the advice and consent of the Senate[28], to make treaties, provided two thirds of the Senators present concur; and he shall nominate, and by and with the advice and consent of the Senate, shall appoint ambassadors, other public ministers and consuls, judges of the Supreme Court, and all other officers of the United States, whose appointments are not herein otherwise provided for, and which shall be established by law: but the Congress may by law vest the appointment of such inferior officers, as they think proper, in the President alone, in the courts of law, or in the heads of departments.

The President shall have power to fill up all vacancies that may happen during the recess of the Senate, by granting commissions which shall expire at the end of their next session.

Section 3. He shall from time to time give to the Congress information of the state of the union, and recommend to their consideration such measures as he shall judge necessary and expedient; he may, on extraordinary occasions, convene both Houses, or either of them, and in case of disagreement between them, with respect to the time of adjournment, he may adjourn them to such time as he shall think proper; he shall receive ambassadors and other public ministers; he shall take care that the laws be faithfully executed, and shall commission all the officers of the United States.

Section 4. The President, vice president and all civil officers of the United States, shall be removed from office on impeachment for, and conviction of, treason, bribery, or other high crimes and misdemeanors.

Article III

Section 1. The judicial power of the United States, shall be vested in one Supreme Court, and in such inferior courts as the Congress may from time to time ordain and establish. The judges, both of the supreme and inferior courts, shall hold their offices during good behavior, and shall, at stated times, receive for their services, a compensation, which shall not be diminished during their continuance in office.

Section 2. The judicial power shall extend to all cases, in law and equity, arising under this Constitution, the laws of the United States, and treaties made, or which shall be made, under their authority; to all cases affecting ambassadors, other public ministers and consuls; to all cases of admiralty and maritime jurisdiction; to controversies to which the United States shall be a party; to controversies between two or more states; between a state and citizens of another state[29]; between citizens of different states; between citizens of the same state claiming lands under grants of different states, and between a state, or the citizens thereof, and foreign states, citizens or subjects.

In all cases affecting ambassadors, other public ministers and consuls, and those in which a state shall be party, the Supreme Court shall have original jurisdiction. In all the other cases before mentioned, the Supreme Court shall have appellate jurisdiction, both as to law and fact, with such exceptions, and under such regulations as the Congress shall make.

The trial of all crimes, except in cases of impeachment, shall be by jury; and such trial shall be held in the state where the said crimes shall have been committed; but when not committed within any state, the trial shall be at such place or places as the Congress may by law have directed.

Section 3. Treason against the United States, shall consist only in levying war against them, or in adhering to their enemies, giving them aid and comfort. No person shall be convicted of treason unless on the testimony of two witnesses to the same overt act, or on confession in open court.

The Congress shall have power to declare the punishment of treason, but no attainder of treason shall work corruption of blood, or forfeiture except during the life of the person attainted.[30]

Article IV

Section 1. Full faith and credit shall be given in each state to the public acts, records, and judicial proceedings of every other state.[31] And the Congress may by general laws prescribe the manner in which such acts, records, and proceedings shall be proved, and the effect thereof.

Section 2. The citizens of each state shall be entitled to all privileges and immunities of citizens in the several states.

A person charged in any state with treason, felony, or other crime, who shall flee from justice, and be found in another state, shall on demand of the executive authority of the state from which he fled, be delivered up, to be removed to the state having jurisdiction of the crime.[32]

No person held to service or labor in one state, under the laws thereof, escaping into another, shall, in consequence of any law or regulation therein, be discharged from such service or labor, but shall be delivered up on claim of the party to whom such service or labor may be due.[33]

Section 3. New states may be admitted by the Congress into this union; but no new states shall be formed or erected within the jurisdiction of any other state; nor any state be formed by the junction of two or more states, or parts of states, without the consent of the legislatures of the states concerned as well as of the Congress.

The Congress shall have power to dispose of and make all needful rules and regulations respecting the territory or other property belonging to the United States; and nothing in this Constitution shall be so construed as to prejudice any claims of the United States, or of any particular state.

Section 4. The United States shall guarantee to every state in this union a Republican form of government, and shall protect each of them against invasion; and on application of the legislature, or of the executive (when the legislature cannot be convened) against domestic violence.

Article V

The Congress, whenever two thirds of both houses shall deem it necessary, shall propose amendments to this Constitution, or, on the application of the legislatures of two thirds of the several states, shall call a convention for proposing amendments, which, in either case, shall be valid to all intents and purposes, as part of this Constitution, when ratified by the legislatures of three fourths of the several states, or by conventions in three-fourths thereof, as the one or the other mode of ratification may be proposed by the Congress; provided that no amendment which may be made prior to the year one thousand eight hundred and eight shall in any manner affect the first and fourth clauses in the ninth section of the first article; and that no state, without its consent, shall be deprived of its equal suffrage in the Senate.

Article VI

All debts contracted and engagements entered into, before the adoption of this Constitution, shall be as valid against the United States under this Constitution, as under the Confederation.

This Constitution, and the laws of the United States which shall be made in pursuance thereof; and all treaties made, or which shall be made, under the authority of the United States, shall be the supreme law of the land[34]; and the judges in every state shall be bound thereby, anything in the Constitution or laws of any State to the contrary notwithstanding.

The Senators and Representatives before mentioned, and the members of the several state legislatures, and all executive and judicial officers, both of the United States and of the several states, shall be bound by oath or affirmation, to support this Constitution; but no religious test shall ever be required as a qualification to any office or public trust under the United States.

Article VII

The ratification of the conventions of nine states, shall be sufficient for the establishment of this Constitution between the states so ratifying the same.

Done in convention by the unanimous consent of the states present the seventeenth day of September in the year of our Lord one thousand seven hundred and eighty seven and of the independence of the United States of America the twelfth. In witness whereof We have hereunto subscribed our Names,

Signed:

G. Washington—President, and 38 representatives of the states

Amendments to the Constitution

[Note: Amendments I through X are collectively known as the "Bill of Rights."]

Amendment I (1791)

Congress shall make no law respecting an establishment of religion, or prohibiting the free exercise thereof [35]; or abridging the freedom of speech, or of the press; or the right of the people peaceably to assemble, and to petition the government for a redress of grievances.

Amendment II (1791)

A well regulated militia, being necessary to the security of a free state, the right of the people to keep and bear arms, shall not be infringed.

Amendment III (1791)

No soldier shall, in time of peace be quartered in any house, without the consent of the owner, nor in time of war, but in a manner to be prescribed by law.

Amendment IV (1791)

The right of the people to be secure in their persons, houses, papers, and effects, against unreasonable searches and seizures, shall not be violated, and no warrants shall issue, but upon probable cause, supported by oath or affirmation, and particularly describing the place to be searched, and the persons or things to be seized.

Amendment V (1791)

No person shall be held to answer for a capital[36], or otherwise infamous crime[37], unless on a presentment or indictment of a grand jury, except in cases arising in the land or naval forces, or in the militia, when in actual service in time of war or public danger; nor shall any person be subject for the same offense to be twice put in jeopardy of life or limb[38]; nor shall be compelled in any criminal case to be a witness against himself, nor be deprived of life, liberty, or property, without due process of law; nor shall private property be taken for public use, without just compensation.

Amendment VI (1791)

In all criminal prosecutions, the accused shall enjoy the right to a speedy and public trial, by an impartial jury of the state and district wherein the crime shall have been committed, which district shall have been previously ascertained by law, and to be informed of the nature and cause of the accusation; to be confronted with the witnesses against him; to have compulsory process for obtaining witnesses in his favor, and to have the assistance of counsel for his defense.

Amendment VII (1791)

In suits at common law, where the value in controversy shall exceed twenty dollars, the right of trial by jury shall be preserved, and no fact tried by a jury, shall be otherwise reexamined in any court of the United States, than according to the rules of the common law.

Amendment VIII (1791)

Excessive bail shall not be required, nor excessive fines imposed, nor cruel and unusual punishments inflicted.

Amendment IX (1791)

The enumeration in the Constitution, of certain rights, shall not be construed to deny or disparage others retained by the people.

Amendment X (1791)

The powers not delegated to the United States by the Constitution, nor prohibited by it to the states, are reserved to the states respectively, or to the people.

Amendment XI (1795)

The judicial power of the United States shall not be construed to extend to any suit in law or equity, commenced or prosecuted against one of the United States by citizens of another state, or by citizens or subjects of any foreign state.

Amendment XII (1804)

The electors shall meet in their respective states and vote by ballot for President and vice president, one of whom, at least, shall not be an inhabitant of the same state with themselves; they shall name in their ballots the person voted for as President, and in distinct ballots the person voted for as vice president, and they shall make distinct lists of all persons voted for as President, and of all persons voted for as vice president, and of the number of votes for each, which lists they shall sign and certify, and transmit sealed to the seat of the government of the United States, directed to the President of the Senate.

The President of the Senate shall, in the presence of the Senate and House of Representatives, open all the certificates and the votes shall then be counted; the person having the greatest number of votes for President, shall be the President, if such number be a majority of the whole number of electors appointed; and if no person have such majority, then from the persons having the highest numbers not exceeding three on the list of those voted for as President, the House of Representatives shall choose immediately, by ballot, the President. But in choosing the President, the votes shall be taken by states, the representation from each state having one vote; a quorum for this purpose shall consist of a member or members from two-thirds of the states, and a majority of all the states shall be necessary to a choice. And if the House of Representatives shall not choose a President whenever the right of choice shall devolve upon them, *before the fourth day of March next following*[39], then the vice president shall act as President, as in the case of the death or other constitutional disability of the President.

The person having the greatest number of votes as vice president, shall be the vice president, if such number be a majority of the whole number of electors appointed, and if no person have a majority, then from the two highest numbers on the list, the Senate shall choose the vice president; a quorum for the purpose shall consist of two-thirds of the whole number of Senators, and a majority of the whole number shall be necessary to a choice. But no person constitutionally ineligible to the office of President shall be eligible to that of vice president of the United States.

Amendment XIII (1865)

Section 1. Neither slavery nor involuntary servitude, except as a punishment for crime whereof the party shall have been duly convicted, shall exist within the United States, or any place subject to their jurisdiction.

Section 2. Congress shall have power to enforce this article by appropriate legislation.

Amendment XIV (1868)

Section 1. All persons born or naturalized in the United States, and subject to the jurisdiction thereof, are citizens of the United States and of the state wherein they reside.[40] No state shall make or enforce any law which shall abridge the privileges or immunities of citizens of the United States; nor shall any state deprive any person of life, liberty, or property, without due process of law; nor deny to any person within its jurisdiction the equal protection of the laws.

Section 2. Representatives shall be apportioned among the several states according to their respective numbers, counting the whole number of persons in each state[41], excluding Indians not taxed. But when the right to vote at any election for the choice of electors for President and vice president of the United States, Representatives in Congress, the executive and judicial officers of a state, or the members of the legislature thereof, is denied to any of the *male* inhabitants of such state, being *twenty-one* years of age, and citizens of the United States, or in any way abridged, except for participation in rebellion, or other crime, the basis of representation therein shall be reduced in the proportion which the number of such *male* citizens shall bear to the whole number of male citizens *twenty-one* years of age in such state.[42]

Section 3. No person shall be a Senator or Representative in Congress, or elector of President and vice president, or hold any office, civil or military, under the United States, or under any state, who, having previously taken an oath, as a member of Congress, or as an officer of the United States, or as a member of any state legislature, or as an executive or judicial officer of any state, to support the Constitution of the United States, shall have engaged in insurrection or rebellion against the same, or given aid or comfort to the enemies thereof. But Congress may by a vote of two-thirds of each House, remove such disability.

Section 4. The validity of the public debt of the United States, authorized by law, including debts incurred for payment of pensions and bounties for services in suppressing insurrection or rebellion, shall not be questioned. But neither the United States nor any state shall assume or pay any debt or obligation incurred in aid of insurrection or rebellion against the United States, or any claim for the loss or emancipation of any enslaved person; but all such debts, obligations and claims shall be held illegal and void.

Section 5. The Congress shall have power to enforce, by appropriate legislation, the provisions of this article.

Amendment XV (1870)

Section 1. The right of citizens of the United States to vote shall not be denied or abridged by the United States or by any state on account of race, color, or previous condition of servitude.

Section 2. The Congress shall have power to enforce this article by appropriate legislation.

Amendment XVI (1913)

The Congress shall have power to lay and collect taxes on incomes, from whatever source derived, without apportionment among the several states, and without regard to any census of enumeration.

Amendment XVII (1913)

The Senate of the United States shall be composed of two Senators from each state, elected by the people thereof, for six years; and each Senator shall have one vote. The electors in each state shall have the qualifications requisite for electors of the most numerous branch of the state legislatures.

When vacancies happen in the representation of any state in the Senate, the executive authority of such state shall issue writs of election to fill such vacancies: Provided, that the legislature of any state may empower the executive thereof to make temporary appointments until the people fill the vacancies by election as the legislature may direct.

This amendment shall not be so construed as to affect the election or term of any Senator chosen before it becomes valid as part of the Constitution.

Amendment XVIII (1919)

Section 1. After one year from the ratification of this article the manufacture, sale, or transportation of intoxicating liquors within, the importation thereof into, or the exportation thereof from the United States and all territory subject to the jurisdiction thereof for beverage purposes is hereby prohibited.

Section 2. The Congress and the several states shall have concurrent power to enforce this article by appropriate legislation.

Section 3. This article shall be inoperative unless it shall have been ratified as an amendment to the Constitution by the legislatures of the several states, as provided in the Constitution, within seven years from the date of the submission hereof to the states by the Congress.[43]

Amendment XIX (1920)

Section 1. The right of citizens of the United States to vote shall not be denied or abridged by the United States or by any state on account of sex.

Section 2. The Congress shall have power to enforce this article by appropriate legislation.

Amendment XX (1933)

Section 1. The terms of the President and vice president shall end at noon on the twentieth day of January, and the terms of Senators and Representatives at noon on the third day of January, of the years in which such terms would have ended if this article had not been ratified; and the terms of their successors shall then begin.[44]

Section 2. The Congress shall assemble at least once in every year, and such meeting shall begin at noon on the third day of January, unless they shall by law appoint a different day.

Section 3. If, at the time fixed for the beginning of the term of the President, the President elect[45] shall have died, the vice president elect shall become President. If a President shall not have been chosen before the time fixed for the beginning of his term, or if the President elect shall have failed to qualify, then the vice president elect shall act as President until a President shall have qualified; and the Congress may by law provide for the case wherein neither a President elect nor a vice president elect shall have qualified, declaring who shall then act as President, or the manner in which one who is to act shall be selected, and such person shall act accordingly until a President or vice president shall have qualified.

Section 4. The Congress may by law provide for the case of the death of any of the persons from whom the House of Representatives may choose a President whenever the right of choice shall have devolved upon them, and for the case of the death of any of the persons from whom the Senate may choose a vice president whenever the right of choice shall have devolved upon them.

Section 5. Sections 1 and 2 shall take effect on the fifteenth day of October following the ratification of this article.

Section 6. This article shall be inoperative unless it shall have been ratified as an amendment to the Constitution by the legislatures of three-fourths of the several states within seven years from the date of its submission.

Amendment XXI (1933)

Section 1. The eighteenth article of amendment to the Constitution of the United States is hereby repealed.

Section 2. The transportation or importation into any state, territory, or possession of the United States for delivery or use therein of intoxicating liquors, in violation of the laws thereof, is hereby prohibited.[46]

Section 3. This article shall be inoperative unless it shall have been ratified as an amendment to the Constitution by conventions in the several states, as provided in the Constitution, within seven years from the date of the submission hereof to the states by the Congress.

Amendment XXII (1951)

Section 1. No person shall be elected to the office of the President more than twice, and no person who has held the office of President, or acted as President, for more than two years of a term to which some other person was elected President shall be elected to the office of the President more than once. But this article shall not apply to any person holding the office of President when this article was proposed by the Congress, and shall not prevent any person who may be holding the office of President, or acting as President, during the term within which this article becomes operative from holding the office of President or acting as President during the remainder of such term.

Section 2. This article shall be inoperative unless it shall have been ratified as an amendment to the Constitution by the legislatures of three-fourths of the several states within seven years from the date of its submission to the states by the Congress.

Amendment XXIII (1961)[47]

Section 1. The District constituting the seat of government of the United States shall appoint in such manner as the Congress may direct:

A number of electors of President and vice president equal to the whole number of Senators and Representatives in Congress to which the District would be entitled if it were a state, but in no event more than the least populous state; they shall be in addition to those appointed by the states, but they shall be considered, for the purposes of the election of President and vice president, to be electors appointed by a state; and they shall meet in the District and perform such duties as provided by the twelfth article of amendment.

Section 2. The Congress shall have power to enforce this article by appropriate legislation.

Amendment XXIV (1964)

Section 1. The right of citizens of the United States to vote in any primary or other election for President or vice president, for electors for President or vice president, or for Senator or Representative in Congress, shall not be denied or abridged by the United States or any state by reason of failure to pay any poll tax or other tax.

Section 2. The Congress shall have power to enforce this article by appropriate legislation.

Amendment XXV (1967)

Section 1. In case of the removal of the President from office or of his death or resignation, the vice president shall become President.

Section 2. Whenever there is a vacancy in the office of the vice president, the President shall nominate a vice president who shall take office upon confirmation by a majority vote of both Houses of Congress.

Section 3. Whenever the President transmits to the President pro tempore of the Senate and the Speaker of the House of Representatives his written declaration that he is unable to discharge the powers and duties of his office, and until he transmits to them a written declaration to the contrary, such powers and duties shall be discharged by the vice president as Acting President.

Section 4. Whenever the vice president and a majority of either the principal officers of the executive departments or of such other body as Congress may by law provide, transmit to the President pro tempore of the Senate and the Speaker of the House of Representatives their written declaration that the President is unable to discharge the powers and duties of his office, the vice president shall immediately assume the powers and duties of the office as Acting President.

Thereafter, when the President transmits to the President pro tempore of the Senate and the Speaker of the House of Representatives his written declaration that no inability exists, he shall resume the powers and duties of his office unless the vice president and a majority of either the principal officers of the executive department or of such other body as Congress may by law provide, transmit within four days to the President pro tempore of the Senate and the Speaker of the House of Representatives their written declaration that the President is unable to discharge the powers and duties of his office. Thereupon Congress shall decide the issue, assembling within forty-eight hours for that purpose if not in session. If the Congress, within twenty-one days after receipt of the latter written declaration, or, if Congress is not in session, within twenty-one days after Congress is required to assemble, determines by two-thirds vote of both Houses that the President is unable to discharge the powers and duties of his office, the vice president shall continue to discharge the same as Acting President; otherwise, the President shall resume the powers and duties of his office.

Amendment XXVI (1971)

Section 1. The right of citizens of the United States, who are 18 years of age or older, to vote, shall not be denied or abridged by the United States or any state on account of age.

Section 2. The Congress shall have the power to enforce this article by appropriate legislation.

Amendment XXVII (1992)

No law, varying the compensation for the services of the Senators and Representatives, shall take effect, until an election of Representatives shall have intervened.

Notes

[1] This clause says that the government may assess taxes on the states only on the basis of population. Amendment XVI changed this by allowing the government to tax individuals' incomes.

[2] *Other persons* meant enslaved people. Amendment XIII abolished slavery, and Amendment XIV nullified the *three-fifths* clause.

[3] This is the clause that requires a national census every 10 years. The census is taken to apportion congressional representation; it is also used by Congress to decide how to distribute federal funding.

[4] The *executive authority* of a state is the governor.

[5] Amendment XVII changed this; senators are now elected by state voters, not by the state legislature.

[6] This section applied only to the first two Senates, to guarantee senatorial elections every two years from the beginning of the Republic.

[7] Amendment XVII changed this by allowing the governor to make such temporary appointments.

[8] The president *pro tempore* presides over the Senate when the vice president is not present.

[9] Amendment XX changed this date to January 3.

[10] *Quorum* means the minimum number of people required for the legislature to act. In other words, the Senate cannot begin a session unless at least 51 members are in attendance. Once a session has begun, however, the senators may leave the floor.

[11] *Emoluments* means payments.

[12] A congressperson cannot hold a second government job. This is a central component of the *separation of powers* within the U.S. government.

[13] The president's veto power.

[14] Congress can override a presidential veto with a two-thirds vote in both houses.

[15] This is called a *pocket veto* by the president. He does not return the bill to Congress, but because Congress has adjourned, the bill does not become law. Congress must then repass the bill in its next session to force the president to consider it again.

[16] *Letters of marque and reprisal* allow private citizens to arm their boats so that they can attack enemy ships. In other words, Congress has the power to license private navies (called *privateers*). Given the circumstances of modern warfare, the chances that Congress will ever again exercise this power are pretty small.

[17] This section refers to the District of Columbia (Washington, D.C.).

[18] This is the elastic clause.

[19] This section prohibited Congress from outlawing the importation of enslaved people until the year 1808. In 1808, Congress did in fact outlaw the import of enslaved people.

[20] A *writ of habeas corpus* is used by a defendant to appear before a judge, who determines whether the government has the right to hold the defendant as a prisoner. A defendant's right to a writ of *habeas corpus* is what prevents the government from arresting and imprisoning people without just cause.

[21] A *bill of attainder* is a law that finds an individual guilty of a capital offense (usually treason). Because it denies an individual's right to a fair trial, it is prohibited by the Constitution.

[22] An *ex post facto* law is one that declares an action a crime retroactively.

[23] Amendment XVI negated this section by altering Congress's power to impose taxes.

[24] Amendment XII overrides this section of the Constitution.

[25] This clause was inserted to provide for the first presidents, who as colonists had been born British subjects.

[26] This entire paragraph was modified by Amendments XX and XXV.

[27] *Emolument* means payment.

[28] This paragraph enumerates several key features of the system of *checks and balances*.

[29] Amendment XI prohibits an individual from using the federal courts to sue a state other than her state of residence.

[30] This paragraph says that if Congress finds a person guilty of treason, it may punish that person but not his heirs.

[31] States must accept the actions of one anothers' governments. Every state must accept every other state's driver's licenses, marriage licenses, legal decisions, and so on.

[32] The process described in this section is called *extradition*.

[33] This section refers to escaped enslaved people. It was nullified by Amendment XIII.

[34] This means that federal law takes priority when federal law and state law conflict. In *McCulloch v. Maryland*, Chief Justice Marshall interpreted this to mean that the federal government could nullify laws that contradicted federal law.

[35] *Free exercise* means the freedom to practice whatever religion you choose.

[36] A *capital* crime is one punishable by death.

[37] An *otherwise infamous crime* is one that is considered serious enough to be punishable by imprisonment.

[38] This is the *double jeopardy* clause. A person cannot be tried again if a court finds him not guilty in a prior trial.

[39] Amendment XX changed this date to January 20th.

[40] This sentence grants citizenship to the former enslaved people.

[41] This sentence overrides the *three-fifths* clause in the body of the Constitution.

[42] This section grants voting rights only to males over the age of 21. Amendment XIX extended voting rights to women; Amendment XXVI lowered the voting age to 18.

[43] Amendment XVIII was repealed by Amendment XXI.

[44] This amendment shortened the amount of time that a president serves after he has been voted out of office.

[45] *President elect* refers to someone who has been elected president but has not yet taken the oath of office. Whenever the presidency changes hands by election, there is a president elect between Election Day and Inaugural Day.

[46] Amendment XXI repealed prohibition but it did not prohibit state and local governments from imposing prohibition. This section makes it a federal crime to transport liquor to a dry county (area in which alcoholic beverages are prohibited).

[47] This amendment gave residents of the District of Columbia the right to vote for president.

Part VI
Additional
Practice Tests

- Practice Test 2
- Practice Test 2: Answers and Explanations
- Practice Test 3
- Practice Test 3: Answers and Explanations
- Practice Test 4
- Practice Test 4: Answers and Explanations

Practice Test 2

Completely darken bubbles with a No. 2 pencil. If you make a mistake, be sure to erase mark completely. Erase all stray marks.

1. YOUR NAME:
(Print)
Last   First   M.I.

SIGNATURE: _____ DATE: ___ / ___ / ___

HOME ADDRESS: _____
(Print)
Number and Street

_____
City   State   Zip Code

PHONE NO. : _____
(Print)

5. YOUR NAME

First 4 letters of last name				FIRST INIT	MID INIT
Ⓐ	Ⓐ	Ⓐ	Ⓐ	Ⓐ	Ⓐ
Ⓑ	Ⓑ	Ⓑ	Ⓑ	Ⓑ	Ⓑ
Ⓒ	Ⓒ	Ⓒ	Ⓒ	Ⓒ	Ⓒ
Ⓓ	Ⓓ	Ⓓ	Ⓓ	Ⓓ	Ⓓ
Ⓔ	Ⓔ	Ⓔ	Ⓔ	Ⓔ	Ⓔ
Ⓕ	Ⓕ	Ⓕ	Ⓕ	Ⓕ	Ⓕ
Ⓖ	Ⓖ	Ⓖ	Ⓖ	Ⓖ	Ⓖ
Ⓗ	Ⓗ	Ⓗ	Ⓗ	Ⓗ	Ⓗ
Ⓘ	Ⓘ	Ⓘ	Ⓘ	Ⓘ	Ⓘ
Ⓙ	Ⓙ	Ⓙ	Ⓙ	Ⓙ	Ⓙ
Ⓚ	Ⓚ	Ⓚ	Ⓚ	Ⓚ	Ⓚ
Ⓛ	Ⓛ	Ⓛ	Ⓛ	Ⓛ	Ⓛ
Ⓜ	Ⓜ	Ⓜ	Ⓜ	Ⓜ	Ⓜ
Ⓝ	Ⓝ	Ⓝ	Ⓝ	Ⓝ	Ⓝ
Ⓞ	Ⓞ	Ⓞ	Ⓞ	Ⓞ	Ⓞ
Ⓟ	Ⓟ	Ⓟ	Ⓟ	Ⓟ	Ⓟ
Ⓠ	Ⓠ	Ⓠ	Ⓠ	Ⓠ	Ⓠ
Ⓡ	Ⓡ	Ⓡ	Ⓡ	Ⓡ	Ⓡ
Ⓢ	Ⓢ	Ⓢ	Ⓢ	Ⓢ	Ⓢ
Ⓣ	Ⓣ	Ⓣ	Ⓣ	Ⓣ	Ⓣ
Ⓤ	Ⓤ	Ⓤ	Ⓤ	Ⓤ	Ⓤ
Ⓥ	Ⓥ	Ⓥ	Ⓥ	Ⓥ	Ⓥ
Ⓦ	Ⓦ	Ⓦ	Ⓦ	Ⓦ	Ⓦ
Ⓧ	Ⓧ	Ⓧ	Ⓧ	Ⓧ	Ⓧ
Ⓨ	Ⓨ	Ⓨ	Ⓨ	Ⓨ	Ⓨ
Ⓩ	Ⓩ	Ⓩ	Ⓩ	Ⓩ	Ⓩ

IMPORTANT: Please fill in these boxes exactly as shown on the back cover of your test book.

2. TEST FORM

3. TEST CODE   **4. REGISTRATION NUMBER**

⓪	Ⓐ	⓪	⓪	⓪	⓪	⓪	⓪	⓪	⓪	⓪	⓪
①	Ⓑ	①	①	①	①	①	①	①	①	①	①
②	Ⓒ	②	②	②	②	②	②	②	②	②	②
③	Ⓓ	③	③	③	③	③	③	③	③	③	③
④	Ⓔ	④	④	④	④	④	④	④	④	④	④
⑤	Ⓕ	⑤	⑤	⑤	⑤	⑤	⑤	⑤	⑤	⑤	⑤
⑥	Ⓖ	⑥	⑥	⑥	⑥	⑥	⑥	⑥	⑥	⑥	⑥
⑦		⑦	⑦	⑦	⑦	⑦	⑦	⑦	⑦	⑦	⑦
⑧		⑧	⑧	⑧	⑧	⑧	⑧	⑧	⑧	⑧	⑧
⑨		⑨	⑨	⑨	⑨	⑨	⑨	⑨	⑨	⑨	⑨

The Princeton Review®

© The Princeton Review, Inc.
FORM NO. 00001-PR

6. DATE OF BIRTH

Month	Day		Year	
◯ JAN				
◯ FEB				
◯ MAR	⓪	⓪	⓪	⓪
◯ APR	①	①	①	①
◯ MAY	②	②	②	②
◯ JUN	③	③	③	③
◯ JUL		④	④	④
◯ AUG		⑤	⑤	⑤
◯ SEP		⑥	⑥	⑥
◯ OCT		⑦	⑦	⑦
◯ NOV		⑧	⑧	⑧
◯ DEC		⑨	⑨	⑨

Section ① Start with number 1 for each new section.
If a section has fewer questions than answer spaces, leave the extra answer spaces blank.

1. Ⓐ Ⓑ Ⓒ Ⓓ
2. Ⓐ Ⓑ Ⓒ Ⓓ
3. Ⓐ Ⓑ Ⓒ Ⓓ
4. Ⓐ Ⓑ Ⓒ Ⓓ
5. Ⓐ Ⓑ Ⓒ Ⓓ
6. Ⓐ Ⓑ Ⓒ Ⓓ
7. Ⓐ Ⓑ Ⓒ Ⓓ
8. Ⓐ Ⓑ Ⓒ Ⓓ
9. Ⓐ Ⓑ Ⓒ Ⓓ
10. Ⓐ Ⓑ Ⓒ Ⓓ
11. Ⓐ Ⓑ Ⓒ Ⓓ
12. Ⓐ Ⓑ Ⓒ Ⓓ
13. Ⓐ Ⓑ Ⓒ Ⓓ
14. Ⓐ Ⓑ Ⓒ Ⓓ
15. Ⓐ Ⓑ Ⓒ Ⓓ

16. Ⓐ Ⓑ Ⓒ Ⓓ
17. Ⓐ Ⓑ Ⓒ Ⓓ
18. Ⓐ Ⓑ Ⓒ Ⓓ
19. Ⓐ Ⓑ Ⓒ Ⓓ
20. Ⓐ Ⓑ Ⓒ Ⓓ
21. Ⓐ Ⓑ Ⓒ Ⓓ
22. Ⓐ Ⓑ Ⓒ Ⓓ
23. Ⓐ Ⓑ Ⓒ Ⓓ
24. Ⓐ Ⓑ Ⓒ Ⓓ
25. Ⓐ Ⓑ Ⓒ Ⓓ
26. Ⓐ Ⓑ Ⓒ Ⓓ
27. Ⓐ Ⓑ Ⓒ Ⓓ
28. Ⓐ Ⓑ Ⓒ Ⓓ
29. Ⓐ Ⓑ Ⓒ Ⓓ
30. Ⓐ Ⓑ Ⓒ Ⓓ

31. Ⓐ Ⓑ Ⓒ Ⓓ
32. Ⓐ Ⓑ Ⓒ Ⓓ
33. Ⓐ Ⓑ Ⓒ Ⓓ
34. Ⓐ Ⓑ Ⓒ Ⓓ
35. Ⓐ Ⓑ Ⓒ Ⓓ
36. Ⓐ Ⓑ Ⓒ Ⓓ
37. Ⓐ Ⓑ Ⓒ Ⓓ
38. Ⓐ Ⓑ Ⓒ Ⓓ
39. Ⓐ Ⓑ Ⓒ Ⓓ
40. Ⓐ Ⓑ Ⓒ Ⓓ
41. Ⓐ Ⓑ Ⓒ Ⓓ
42. Ⓐ Ⓑ Ⓒ Ⓓ
43. Ⓐ Ⓑ Ⓒ Ⓓ
44. Ⓐ Ⓑ Ⓒ Ⓓ
45. Ⓐ Ⓑ Ⓒ Ⓓ

46. Ⓐ Ⓑ Ⓒ Ⓓ
47. Ⓐ Ⓑ Ⓒ Ⓓ
48. Ⓐ Ⓑ Ⓒ Ⓓ
49. Ⓐ Ⓑ Ⓒ Ⓓ
50. Ⓐ Ⓑ Ⓒ Ⓓ
51. Ⓐ Ⓑ Ⓒ Ⓓ
52. Ⓐ Ⓑ Ⓒ Ⓓ
53. Ⓐ Ⓑ Ⓒ Ⓓ
54. Ⓐ Ⓑ Ⓒ Ⓓ
55. Ⓐ Ⓑ Ⓒ Ⓓ

The Exam

AP® U.S. Government and Politics Exam

SECTION I: Multiple-Choice Questions

DO NOT OPEN THIS BOOKLET UNTIL YOU ARE TOLD TO DO SO.

At a Glance

Total Time
80 minutes
Number of Questions
55
Percent of Total Grade
50%
Writing Instrument
Pencil required

Instructions

Section I of this examination contains 55 multiple-choice questions. Fill in only the ovals for numbers 1 through 55 on your answer sheet.

Indicate all of your answers to the multiple-choice questions on the answer sheet. No credit will be given for anything written in this exam booklet, but you may use the booklet for notes or scratch work. After you have decided which of the suggested answers is best, completely fill in the corresponding oval on the answer sheet. Give only one answer to each question. If you change an answer, be sure that the previous mark is erased completely. Here is a sample question and answer.

Sample Question   Sample Answer

Chicago is a
(A) state
(B) city
(C) country
(D) continent

Use your time effectively, working as quickly as you can without losing accuracy. Do not spend too much time on any one question. Go on to other questions and come back to the ones you have not answered if you have time. It is not expected that everyone will know the answers to all the multiple-choice questions.

About Guessing

Many candidates wonder whether or not to guess the answers to questions about which they are not certain. Multiple-choice scores are based on the number of questions answered correctly. Points are not deducted for incorrect answers, and no points are awarded for unanswered questions. Because points are not deducted for incorrect answers, you are encouraged to answer all multiple-choice questions. On any questions you do not know the answer to, you should eliminate as many choices as you can, and then select the best answer among the remaining choices.

GO ON TO THE NEXT PAGE.

UNITED STATES GOVERNMENT AND POLITICS

Section I

Time—80 minutes

55 Questions

Directions: Each of the questions or incomplete statements below is followed by four suggested answers or completions. Select the one that is best in each case and then fill in the corresponding oval on the answer sheet.

Questions 1 and 2 refer to the graph below.

Number of Viewers of the State of the Union Addresses from 1993 to 2018 (in millions)

Source: Statista, © 2018.

1. Which of the following statements best reflects a trend in the graph above?

   (A) Republican presidents receive fewer viewers during their State of the Union addresses.
   (B) Since 1993, the State of the Union has fallen in importance in American political life.
   (C) For presidents serving multiple terms, viewership typically peaks within the first term.
   (D) Americans watch the State of the Union in higher numbers during an economic recession.

2. Based on the information in the bar graph, which of the following is true about the State of the Union?

   (A) While a president's first State of the Union may be their best chance to connect with the nation, actual viewership can be influenced by other factors.
   (B) The State of the Union is no longer an effective method for presidents to communicate with the American people.
   (C) A president should announce broad policy goals during his or her final two State of the Union addresses.
   (D) Broadcasting the State of the Union has little to no effect on a president's policy proposals.

Questions 3 and 4 refer to the graph below.

Presidential Vetoes and Bills Passed in Congress

Sources: www.Senate.gov, www.Congress.gov

3. Which of the following best describes a trend in the graph above?

   (A) The number of presidential vetoes rose dramatically in the 1990s.
   (B) The number of vetoes matched the number of passed bills in 1975.
   (C) Presidents are more likely to veto bills in years when Congress passes fewer bills.
   (D) More bills were vetoed between 1945 and 1960 than in any subsequent 15-year period.

4. Which of the following most likely explains why, between 1953 and 1993, Republican presidents issued more vetoes than their Democratic counterparts?

   (A) Republican presidents use the veto to enact their policies.
   (B) Congress was very unproductive during this time period.
   (C) Republican presidents were highly unpopular.
   (D) The Democratic Party controlled both houses of Congress for almost the entire period.

GO ON TO THE NEXT PAGE.

Questions 5 and 6 refer to the cartoon below.

Source: Mike Keefe, InToon.com

5. Which of the following statements describes the message in the political cartoon?

   (A) The National Security Agency is an American intelligence agency.
   (B) American citizens are furious that the government is spying on them.
   (C) Government actions violate protections enshrined in the Constitution.
   (D) Stopping government surveillance would not repair civil liberties.

6. A lawyer arguing against the government actions as depicted by the political cartoon would invoke which constitutional amendment?

   (A) Third Amendment
   (B) Fourth Amendment
   (C) Fifth Amendment
   (D) Eighth Amendment

Questions 7 and 8 refer to the graph below.

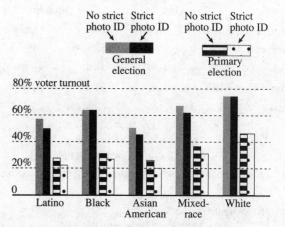

Source: "Voter Identification Laws and the Suppression of Minority Votes," *The Journal of Politics*.

7. Based on the information in the bar graph, which of the following is the most likely implication of photo ID requirements on voter turnout?

   (A) White voters turn out in fewer numbers in states that require approved ID.
   (B) Mixed-race Americans vote in higher numbers than white Americans.
   (C) Compared to white voters, voters of other races are less likely to have approved ID.
   (D) Black Americans are the least likely group to vote in primary elections.

8. Based on the information in the graph, why would opponents of voter ID laws argue that these laws violate the Voting Rights Act of 1965?

   (A) Voter ID laws affect the voting patterns of all races.
   (B) Voter ID laws do not protect elections against fraudulent votes.
   (C) Voter ID laws result in a disproportionate decrease in minority turnout during elections.
   (D) Voter ID laws are just another form of literacy tests or poll taxes.

GO ON TO THE NEXT PAGE.

Questions 9 and 10 refer to the table below.

**Opinions on Support for Congressional
Gun Control Measures**

Region	Men		Women	
	Favor	Oppose	Favor	Oppose
Northeast	56%	33%	58%	33%
Midwest	41%	48%	39%	49%
South	31%	56%	31%	57%
West	65%	26%	64%	27%

9. Based on the information in the table, which of the following categories has the largest difference in opinion?

   (A) Women from the Midwest
   (B) Men from the South
   (C) Women from the Northeast
   (D) Men from the West

10. Which of the following is an accurate conclusion based on the data in the table and your understanding of the impact of culture on public attitudes?

    (A) There are more guns in the West than in other parts of the country.
    (B) All women grow up with identical beliefs about gun control.
    (C) The region where one lives affects one's political socialization.
    (D) Gun ownership is a topic that Congress should address with legislation.

Questions 11–13 refer to the passage below.

In San Francisco a few weeks ago, I saw demonstrators carrying signs reading: "Lose in Vietnam, bring the boys home."

Well, one of the strengths of our free society is that any American has a right to reach that conclusion and to advocate that point of view. But as President of the United States, I would be untrue to my oath of office if I allowed the policy of this Nation to be dictated by the minority who hold that point of view and who try to impose it on the Nation by mounting demonstrations in the street.

For almost 200 years, the policy of this Nation has been made under our Constitution by those leaders in the Congress and the White House elected by all of the people. If a vocal minority, however fervent its cause, prevails over reason and the will of the majority, this Nation has no future as a free society.

—President Richard Nixon, "Silent Majority" Speech, 1969

11. Which of the following statements best summarizes President Nixon's message in the passage above?

    (A) People protesting the Vietnam war should not have the right to do so.
    (B) A political minority is always incorrect.
    (C) A single-interest group does not always represent the will of the people.
    (D) Protesting undermines the military effort in Vietnam.

12. Which statement best describes why President Nixon is giving this speech?

    (A) To connect with the Americans who are not protesting the Vietnam War
    (B) To appeal to the Americans who are protesting the Vietnam War
    (C) To campaign for the presidency
    (D) To convince the American people to keep supporting the war effort

13. Which of the following is a reasonable assumption to make about the demonstrators?

    (A) They wish to overthrow the government.
    (B) They wish for the government to change its policies.
    (C) They wish that President Nixon would not pander to them.
    (D) They wish to create a tyranny of the minority.

GO ON TO THE NEXT PAGE.

Questions 14–17 refer to the passage below.

When the legislative and executive powers are united in the same person, or in the same body of magistrates, there can be no liberty; because apprehensions may arise, lest the same monarch or senate should enact tyrannical laws, to execute them in a tyrannical manner.

Again, there is no liberty, if the judiciary power be not separated from the legislative and executive. Were it joined with the legislative, the life and liberty of the subject would be exposed to arbitrary control; for the judge would be then the legislator. Were it joined to the executive power, the judge might behave with violence and oppression. There would be an end of everything, were the same man, or the same body, whether of the nobles or of the people, to exercise those three powers, that of enacting laws, that of executing the public resolutions, and of trying the causes of individuals.

—Baron de Montesquieu, *The Spirit of the Laws*, 1748

14. Which of the following statements best summarizes the passage?

    (A) The separation of powers helps ensure liberty.
    (B) The separation of powers ensures domestic tranquility and international peace.
    (C) People, after experiencing a dictator's oppression, will rise up in protest.
    (D) Governments in which one person wields legislative, executive, and judicial power are always corrupt.

15. How did James Madison expand on Montesquieu's ideas when he wrote Federalist No. 51?

    (A) He argued that three branches of government, each with the ability to limit the power of the other two, would best serve the United States.
    (B) He wrote a draft of the Constitution that incorporated Montesquieu's ideas.
    (C) He proposed a new way to separate the branches of government.
    (D) He studied the fates of different governments that had attempted to separate government power.

16. Which of the following events best reflects Montesquieu's ideas in action?

    (A) The passage of the Affordable Health Care Act
    (B) Vice President Lyndon Johnson becoming president after the assassination of President John Kennedy
    (C) Supreme Court justices attending the annual State of the Union address
    (D) The impeachment of President Clinton

17. Based on the text, which of the following statements would the author most likely agree with?

    (A) Conflict between the branches of government is expected in a healthy democracy.
    (B) Conflict between the branches of government slows down the government's functions.
    (C) The different branches of government should not know what the other branches are doing.
    (D) The different branches of government should always cooperate with one another.

GO ON TO THE NEXT PAGE.

Questions 18 and 19 refer to the table below.

Party Affiliation in the United States Based on Educational Attainment

Highest Level of Educational Attainment	Males		Females	
	Republicans	**Democrats**	**Republicans**	**Democrats**
Grade School	12%	85%	13%	87%
High School Diploma	13%	80%	21%	72%
Vocational Degree	24%	72%	28%	58%
College Degree	36%	64%	36%	52%
Master's Degree	49%	51%	30%	61%
Doctoral Degree	56%	34%	19%	70%

18. Which of the following statements does the above table support?

   (A) Women whose highest educational level is a master's degree are more likely to identify as Republicans as compared to all other groups.
   (B) Men who have attained a doctoral degree are more likely to identify as Democrats than are those with only a college degree.
   (C) Women whose highest level of education is grade school and men whose highest level of education is high school are equally likely to identify as Republicans.
   (D) Women who have attained a doctoral degree are the most reliable group of Democratic women voters.

19. Based on the information in the table and your understanding of political ideology, male voters with college degrees (no post-graduate degree) would be most likely to support which of the following policies?

   (A) The United States should expand its military budget.
   (B) Congress should increase spending on social welfare programs.
   (C) The Supreme Court should overturn *Brown v. Board of Education.*
   (D) The Justice Department should more harshly prosecute drug users.

GO ON TO THE NEXT PAGE.

Questions 20 and 21 refer to the table below.

INDEPENDENT VOTERS AND PRESIDENTIAL ELECTIONS (1980–2012)				
Percent of Independents Voting for Candidates, by Party				
	2000	**2004**	**2008**	**2012**
Democratic	44.3	52.4	51.1	42.3
Republican	48.6	47.5	48.5	50.1
Percent of Popular Vote Won, by Party (Incumbents' results in parentheses)				
Democratic	48.4	48.3	52.9	(51.1)
Republican	47.9	(50.7)	45.7	47.2
Other	*	*	*	*

*No third-party candidate won more than 5% of the popular vote in these elections.

20. The table above supports which of the following statements about independent voters during presidential elections?

    (A) Compared to other voters, Independents are more likely to vote for the challenger when a president runs for reelection.
    (B) The independent vote generally aligns with the popular vote.
    (C) The unpredictability of the independent voters is why politicians do not try to attract them.
    (D) Republicans have won a plurality of independent votes whenever there was a viable third-party candidate.

21. Based on the information in the table, which of the following statements is the likeliest explanation for the voting decisions of the independent voters from 2000 to 2012?

    (A) Almost all independent voters felt there was not a viable alternative to the candidates from the traditional two-party system.
    (B) The Republican and Democratic parties fielded the strongest candidates in these elections.
    (C) The third-party candidates were extremely charismatic.
    (D) Changes in election law gave independent voters more options at the ballot box.

GO ON TO THE NEXT PAGE.

Questions 22 and 23 refer to the table below.

			U.S. Citizens							
All races		**Total Population**	**Total Citizen Population**	**Reported registered**		**Reported not registered**		**No response to registration[1]**	
				Number	**Percent**	**Number**	**Percent**	**Number**	**Percent**
Both Sexes	Total 18 years and over	245,502	224,059	157,596	70.3	32,622	14.6	33,841	15.1
	18 to 24 years	29,320	26,913	14,905	55.4	6,650	24.7	5,358	19.9
	25 to 44 years	83,698	72,610	48,629	67.0	12,467	17.2	11,514	15.9
	45 to 64 years	83,799	77,544	57,394	74.0	9,063	11.7	11,087	14.3
	65 to 74 years	28,832	27,839	21,908	78.7	2,502	9.0	3,429	12.3
	75 years and over	19,852	19,154	14,759	77.1	1,941	10.1	2,454	12.8
Men	Total 18 years and over	118,488	107,554	73,761	68.6	17,068	15.9	16,724	15.5
	18 to 24 years	14,822	13,530	7,200	53.2	3,579	26.5	2,752	20.3
	25 to 44 years	41,264	35,431	22,718	64.1	6,733	19.0	5,980	16.9
	45 to 64 years	40,642	37,516	27,229	72.6	4,853	12.9	5,434	14.5
	65 to 74 years	13,428	13,018	10,245	78.7	1,211	9.3	1,561	12.0
	75 years and over	8,333	8,059	6,369	79.0	692	8.6	997	12.4
Women	Total 18 years and over	127,013	116,505	83,835	72.0	15,553	13.3	17,117	14.7
	18 to 24 years	14,498	13,382	7,706	57.6	3,070	22.9	2,606	19.5
	25 to 44 years	42,435	37,178	25,911	69.7	5,734	15.4	5,533	14.9
	45 to 64 years	43,157	40,028	30,165	75.4	4,210	10.5	5,653	14.1
	65 to 74 years	15,404	14,821	11,663	78.7	1,291	8.7	1,868	12.6
	75 years and over	11,519	11,095	8,390	75.6	1,249	11.3	1,456	13.1

Reported Voting and Registration, by Race, Hispanic Origin, Sex, and Age, for the United States: November 2016 (in thousands)

[1]"No response to registration" includes those who were not asked if they were registered as well as those who responded 'Don't know' and 'Refused.'

22. Which of the following is an accurate statement about the information in the table?

(A) Based on those who disclosed registration status, women are more likely to be registered voters than men.

(B) There are approximately 20,000 adults living in the United States who are not citizens.

(C) As men and women age, they are less likely to be registered voters.

(D) Men tend to live longer lives than women.

23. Which of the following is a likely implication of the data provided above?

(A) Age plays little role in whether men or women are politically active.

(B) Male registered voters between the ages of 18 and 24 are the most valuable voting bloc for presidential candidates.

(C) For presidential elections, a significant percentage of the otherwise eligible population remains unregistered to vote.

(D) Millions of Americans cannot vote for various reasons.

GO ON TO THE NEXT PAGE.

24. Which of the following was a belief of the Federalists during the Constitutional Convention of 1787?

    (A) The legislative branch should have a Senate.
    (B) The federal government should be stronger than state governments.
    (C) The slave trade was a necessary institution.
    (D) A small republic was the best form the United States could take.

25. Which of the following businesses would most likely be directly affected by Congressional legislation based upon the powers in the commerce clause?

    (A) A French bakery that plans to export croissants to New Jersey
    (B) A workshop in rural Tennessee that repairs tractors for local farmers
    (C) A service center in Oakland, California, that provides tune-ups to the city's police cars
    (D) A restaurant in Kansas that plans to build three more restaurants throughout the state

26. Federalism is a principle of government in which

    (A) power is shared between the national government and the state governments
    (B) states have equal representation in the national government
    (C) individual liberties are guaranteed by a Bill of Rights
    (D) legislative, executive, and judicial powers are separated

27. According to the Constitution, who determines voter eligibility requirements?

    (A) The president
    (B) Congress
    (C) State legislatures
    (D) The Supreme Court

28. Which of the following best describes the balance the Supreme Court has struck between the establishment clause and the free exercise clause?

    (A) Freedom of speech is protected except in certain situations, such as yelling "fire" in a crowded theater.
    (B) Once a church has been recognized by the federal government, its tax-exempt status can never be revoked.
    (C) Once Congress has created an administrative agency, that agency can be dissolved only by a constitutional amendment.
    (D) State-sponsored prayer during school hours is prohibited, but voluntary prayer by student groups before school is allowed.

29. In which of the following cases did the Supreme Court decision strike down the "separate but equal" doctrine of state-sponsored racial segregation?

    (A) *Brown v. Board of Education* (1954)
    (B) *Baker v. Carr* (1961)
    (C) *McCulloch v. Maryland* (1819)
    (D) *Shaw v. Reno* (1993)

30. Which of the following scenarios reflects a conservative political belief?

    (A) A state passes a law to protect an endangered species.
    (B) A city hall makes its restrooms gender neutral.
    (C) A person waits five days before receiving a gun they purchased.
    (D) A new military base opens in a rural community, providing jobs to residents.

31. Which of the following scenarios is an example of political socialization?

    (A) Working on a group project in math class
    (B) Playing high school football
    (C) Watching the evening news with family
    (D) Joining a fiction book club

32. Which of the following statements about political action committees (PACs) is most accurate?

    (A) They cannot legally funnel donations directly to political candidates.
    (B) Their activities are not regulated by the Federal Election Commission (FEC).
    (C) Their activities are limited to national presidential elections.
    (D) They raise money to influence federal, state, and local elections.

33. The American Civil Liberties Union (ACLU), the National Association of Women Lawyers (NAWL), and the American Federation of Labor and Congress of Industrial Organizations (AFL-CIO) collaborating to block Samuel Alito's 2006 nomination to the Supreme Court is an example of

    (A) realignment
    (B) coalition building
    (C) logrolling
    (D) non-commitment

GO ON TO THE NEXT PAGE.

34. Which of the following statements about the House of Representatives is true?

    (A) All revenue bills must originate in the Senate before moving to the House.
    (B) Representation in the House is allocated equally among the states, while representation in the Senate is allocated proportional to population.
    (C) The Speaker of the House wields less power than the president *pro tempore* of the Senate.
    (D) The House has a Committee on Ways and Means, while the Senate does not.

35. Which of the following statements best characterizes cooperative federalism?

    (A) The executive and legislative branches working on legislation together
    (B) The federal government granting power over a policy area to the states
    (C) Governments working with businesses to address an issue
    (D) State and federal governments working on the same issue

36. The attorney general is the head of which of the following entities?

    (A) The Senate Judiciary Committee
    (B) The Department of Justice
    (C) The Department of State
    (D) The Judge Advocate General's Corps

37. Which of the following situations is an example of logrolling?

    (A) Giving up one's political position to win a short-term victory
    (B) Changing the shape of congressional districts to favor one party
    (C) Gaining federal funding for one's home district
    (D) Agreeing to vote on a bill in exchange for a vote on another bill

38. The Voting Rights Act of 1965 has had which of the following effects?

    (A) States have been prohibited from establishing voter identification requirements.
    (B) Voters must now pass literacy tests before voting.
    (C) Voting participation for racial minority voters has increased.
    (D) The voting age was lowered from 21 to 18.

39. In *Brown v. Board of Education* (1954), the Supreme Court based its decision on which provision of the Fourteenth Amendment?

    (A) Automatic citizenship for persons born in the United States
    (B) Equal protection under the law
    (C) Overturning the Three-Fifths Compromise
    (D) Refusal of compensation for freed enslaved people

40. How did *New York Times Co. v. United States* (1971) affect the interpretation of the First Amendment?

    (A) It shielded newspapers from government lawsuits.
    (B) It limited the government's power to interfere with the press.
    (C) It codified the process of gaining a restraining order against a newspaper.
    (D) It changed what the government could and could not classify as Top Secret.

41. One of Representative Jones's stated goals when running for office was to increase the feelings of political efficacy among his constituents. Once he is elected, which of the following would best describe an effort to meet that goal?

    (A) Going after special interest groups
    (B) Hosting periodic town halls in his district and using the feedback to pursue relevant policies
    (C) Investigating how checks and balances can be strengthened
    (D) Holding town halls to persuade voters to support a piece of legislation

42. Which of the following is most likely to lead to a decrease in political knowledge among Americans?

    (A) A media outlet that reports only one point of view
    (B) A media outlet that routinely interviews candidates
    (C) A media outlet that protects its sources
    (D) A media outlet that summarizes the day's news events

GO ON TO THE NEXT PAGE.

43. Which of the following is an accurate comparison of the Articles of Confederation and the Constitution?

	The Articles of Confederation	Constitution
(A)	Bicameral legislative branch	Unicameral legislative branch
(B)	Term limits for legislative branch	No term limits for legislative branch
(C)	Forbids *ex post facto* laws	Does not forbid *ex post facto* laws
(D)	The Supreme Court settles disputes between states	Congress settles disputes between states

44. Which of the following accurately compares the roles of the Federal Elections Commission (FEC) and Securities and Exchange Commission (SEC)?

	FEC	SEC
(A)	Enforce campaign finance law	Promote an orderly and fair stock market
(B)	Oversee the nation's infrastructure	Enforce environmental regulations
(C)	Enforce civil rights legislation regarding elections	Protect the nation from external threats
(D)	Regulate the banking industry	Set education policy at the federal level

45. Which of the following is an accurate comparison of the two court cases?

	Gideon v. Wainwright (1963)	*Wisconsin v. Yoder* (1972)
(A)	Police officers have to inform people under arrest of their constitutional rights	Upheld states' mandatory vaccination laws for school attendance
(B)	Guaranteed right to an attorney for all criminal cases	Established a constitutional right to privacy
(C)	Guaranteed access to contraception	Struck down municipal laws restricting gun ownership
(D)	Incorporated the Sixth Amendment to the states	Allowed for religious exemptions to states' compulsory education laws

46. Which of the following is an accurate comparison between presidential general election voters and the Electoral College in a presidential election?

	Presidential General Election Voters	The Electoral College
(A)	Have to register in their state of residence	Like the president, must be over the age of 35
(B)	A candidate must win the popular vote to win the presidency	Chosen by a state legislature or other organization
(C)	Candidates campaign to them	Has the final say of who becomes president
(D)	Must follow rules regarding whom to vote for	A candidate must win a majority of Electoral College votes to win the presidency

47. Which of the following is an accurate comparison between conservative and liberal beliefs?

	Conservative	Liberal
(A)	Favor increasing access to abortion	Favor restricting access to abortion
(B)	Promote reduced military spending	Promote increased military spending
(C)	Favor expansion of immigration	Favor restriction of immigration
(D)	Believe in limited regulation of business	Believe in increased regulation of business

48. Which of the following statements best expresses a core value concerning the government's role in Americans' daily lives?

(A) The government should promote equality of opportunity.

(B) The government should promote equality of outcome.

(C) The government should promote both equality of outcome and equality of opportunity.

(D) The government should promote neither equality of outcome nor equality of opportunity.

GO ON TO THE NEXT PAGE.

49. Which of the following activities are interest groups barred from taking part in?

    (A) Sending lawmakers to educational seminars
    (B) Giving tangible gifts to lawmakers
    (C) Providing research to government officials
    (D) Staging protests and boycotts

50. Which of the following defines an open primary election?

    (A) Voters select the winner by caucus instead of by individual ballots.
    (B) The election results are not binding.
    (C) Any registered voter may participate, regardless of party affiliation.
    (D) Voters may register to vote on the day of the election.

51. Which of the following statements accurately describes the legal impact of *United States v. Lopez* (1996)?

    (A) Congress gained expanded power over the states.
    (B) The Supreme Court completely redefined federalism as a concept.
    (C) The Supreme Court put limitations on Congress's use of the commerce clause to justify legislation.
    (D) For the first time, states could pass gun control legislation.

52. Which of the following is an example of an implied power of Congress?

    (A) Passing laws regulating interstate trade
    (B) Raising the debt limit every year
    (C) Overseeing executive branch agencies
    (D) Declaring war on Japan in 1941

53. Which of the following would occur if Congress were to pass legislation and declare a recess, and the president took no action on the bill within ten days of its passage?

    (A) A line-item veto
    (B) A pocket veto
    (C) An adjournment
    (D) A writ of *certiorari*

54. Which of the following statements best describes the purpose of gerrymandering?

    (A) To increase the control voters have over their elected officials
    (B) To influence elections by drawing boundary lines to increase or decrease the influence of some voters
    (C) To put all racial minorities into a single district
    (D) To equally divide a state's congressional districts by size

55. Which of the following statements outlines a key weakness of the Articles of Confederation?

    (A) Free residents of each state were given "all the privileges and immunities of free citizens in the several states."
    (B) Individual states had to negotiate with one another concerning interstate commerce.
    (C) Governmental departments oversaw foreign affairs, armed conflict, shipping, and government spending.
    (D) Canada was given the right to become part of the United States at any time.

STOP
END OF SECTION I
IF YOU FINISH BEFORE TIME IS CALLED, YOU MAY CHECK YOUR WORK ON THIS SECTION.
DO NOT GO ON TO SECTION II UNTIL YOU ARE TOLD TO DO SO.

UNITED STATES GOVERNMENT AND POLITICS

Section II

Time—1 hour and 40 minutes

<u>Directions:</u> You have 1 hour and 40 minutes to answer all four of the following questions. It is suggested that you spend approximately 20 minutes each on Questions 1, 2, and 3 and 40 minutes on Question 4. Unless directions indicate otherwise, respond to all parts of all four questions. In your response, use substantive examples where appropriate. It is recommended that you take a few minutes to plan each answer. You may plan your answers in this Questions booklet, but no credit will be given for notes written in this booklet. You will earn credit only for what you write in the Free Response booklet.

1. "Current and former executives with the pharmaceutical distributors that are accused of flooding communities with powerful prescription painkillers have been summoned to testify before Congress about their role in the U.S. opioid epidemic....The pharmaceutical executives are expected to face tough questions under oath about why their companies pumped so many highly addictive pain pills into West Virginia and other states, fueling what has become the deadliest drug crisis in U.S. history."

   "Drug executives to testify before Congress about their role in U.S. opioid crisis," *The Washington Post,* 2018

   After reading the scenario, respond to A, B, and C below:

   (A) Describe a power Congress could use to address the comments outlined in the scenario.

   (B) In the context of the scenario, explain how the use of the congressional power described in Part A can be affected by its interaction with the Supreme Court.

   (C) In the context of the scenario, explain the responsibilities of states like West Virginia as described under the Tenth Amendment.

GO ON TO THE NEXT PAGE.

Apportionment of the U.S. House of Representatives
Based on the 2020 Census

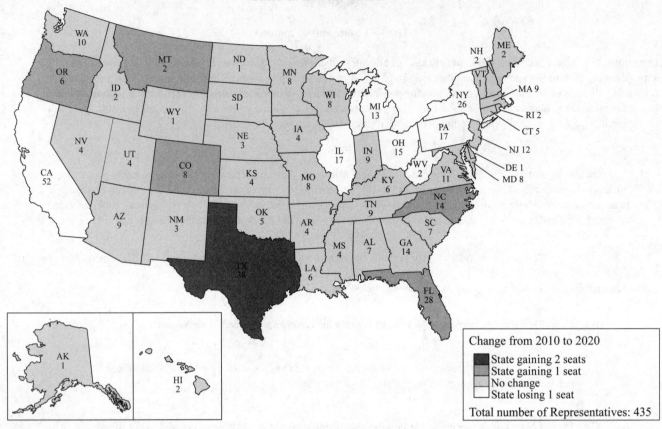

Change from 2010 to 2020

- State gaining 2 seats
- State gaining 1 seat
- No change
- State losing 1 seat

Total number of Representatives: 435

2. Use the graphic above to answer the questions.

(A) Identify the state that gained the most seats through congressional apportionment in 2020.

(B) Describe a trend based on how congressional apportionment shifted in 2020.

(C) Explain how the changes in congressional apportionment over time, as shown in the information graphic, reflect one principle set forth in Article I of the Constitution.

GO ON TO THE NEXT PAGE.

3. In the summer of 1964, Clarence Brandenburg—an Ohio resident and Ku Klux Klan leader—organized a Klan rally where he and other Klan members espoused hate speech against African Americans, Jewish Americans, and the U.S. government's efforts to enact civil rights legislation. Brandenburg was arrested after making calls for a KKK march on Washington, D.C. Ohio charged him with advocating violence, although he had made no specific threats.

In the ensuing case, *Brandenburg v. Ohio* (1969), the Supreme Court unanimously ruled that Brandenburg's comment during the KKK rally did not suggest that Brandenburg or fellow KKK members were about to commit any "imminent lawless action." Since then, *Brandenburg* has been the litmus test used by law enforcement and the courts to determine whether or not to arrest individuals who speak or write inflammatory speech.

   (A) Identify the constitutional clause that is common to both *Brandenburg v. Ohio* (1969) and *Schenck v. United States* (1919).

   (B) Based on the constitutional clause in Part A, explain why the court found differently in *Brandenburg v. Ohio* than it did in *Schenck v. United States*.

   (C) Describe an action that local governments who disagree with the holding in *Brandenburg v. Ohio* could take to limit its impact in their communities.

GO ON TO THE NEXT PAGE.

4. Develop an argument that explains which of the three forms of action taken by the federal government—constitutional amendments, Supreme Court rulings, or legislation—has best ensured the civil rights of minorities and historically repressed groups.

In your essay, you must:

- Articulate a defensible claim or thesis that responds to the prompt and establishes a line of reasoning.

- Support your claim with at least TWO pieces of accurate and relevant information:
  - At least ONE piece of evidence must be from one of the following foundational documents:
    - Federalist No. 10
    - The Declaration of Independence
    - "Letter from a Birmingham Jail" (MLK)
  - Use a second piece of evidence from another foundational document from the list or from your study of civil rights.

- Use reasoning to explain why your evidence supports your claim/thesis.

- Respond to an opposing or alternative perspective using refutation, concession, or rebuttal.

END OF EXAMINATION

Practice Test 2: Answers and Explanations

PRACTICE TEST 2 ANSWER KEY

1.	C	29.	A
2.	A	30.	D
3.	D	31.	C
4.	D	32.	D
5.	C	33.	B
6.	B	34.	D
7.	C	35.	D
8.	C	36.	B
9.	D	37.	D
10.	C	38.	C
11.	C	39.	B
12.	A	40.	B
13.	B	41.	B
14.	A	42.	A
15.	A	43.	B
16.	D	44.	A
17.	A	45.	D
18.	C	46.	C
19.	B	47.	D
20.	A	48.	A
21.	A	49.	B
22.	A	50.	C
23.	C	51.	C
24.	B	52.	C
25.	A	53.	B
26.	A	54.	B
27.	C	55.	B
28.	D		

Once you have checked your answers, return to page 4 and respond to the Reflect questions.

PRACTICE TEST 2 ANSWERS AND EXPLANATIONS

Section I: Multiple Choice

1. **C** The graph shows the number of Americans who watched the president's State of the Union address between 1993 and 2018. Choice (A) can be eliminated as some addresses given by Republican presidents (2002 and 2003, for example) were watched by more Americans than some addresses given by Democratic presidents (2000 and 2016, for example). Choice (B) can be eliminated as viewership has gone up and down since 1993. Choice (D) can be eliminated: although viewership peaked during the height of the Great Recession (2009–2011), larger peaks occurred in prior years when war, rather than recession, made Americans watch in greater numbers. The correct answer is (C) because for the two-term presidents, the highest-rated addresses occurred in their first terms, as happened in 1993 for Clinton, 2003 for Bush, and 2009 for Obama.

2. **A** Choice (B) can be eliminated as millions of Americans still watch the State of the Union address. Choice (C) can be eliminated as the fewest number of viewers tune in to a president's final two State of the Union addresses. Choice (D) is incorrect as the president can use the State of the Union as a way to measure the public's reaction to policy goals. Accordingly, (A) is the correct answer because the highest number of viewers usually tune in to a president's first State of the Union, but Bush's State of the Union in 2003 was an exception, since its ratings were higher than those of his first State of the Union in 2001. This abnormality was due to the ongoing War on Terror and imminent invasion of Iraq.

3. **D** The graph compares the number of bills passed by Congress between 1945 and 2016 with the number of presidential vetoes issued during that same time frame. Choice (A) can be eliminated as the number of vetoes fell throughout the first half of the 1990s before making a slight rebound. Choice (B) can be eliminated: although the two lines in the graph touch, they correspond with different axes and, therefore, do not represent the same number. Choice (C) can be eliminated as it describes a relationship that is the opposite of what the graph portrays. Therefore, (D) is correct as the graph supports this statement.

4. **D** Choice (A) is incorrect as the graph gives no information concerning Republican presidents' policies. Choice (B) is incorrect: although the number of bills passed by Congress lessened over time, Congress still passed tens of thousands of bills into law. Choice (C) is incorrect as the graph does not provide information on the popularity of Republican presidents. Therefore, (D) is correct as the bills passed by a Democratic Congress would not align with a Republican president's policy agenda, increasing the number of vetoes.

5. **C** The cartoon portrays the National Security Agency spying on American citizens. Choice (A) can be eliminated: although someone can infer this fact by examining the political cartoon, the cartoon concerns what the agency does rather than what the agency is. Choice (B) can be eliminated as the citizens either are aware of the NSA's actions and ignoring it or don't know about it and are still calm. Choice (D) can be eliminated as the cartoon does not portray the surveillance stopping. Therefore, (C) is correct as spying on American citizens damages civil liberties enshrined in the Constitution.

6. **B**   Choice (A) is incorrect as the cartoon does not depict American soldiers. Choice (C) is incorrect as neither of the American citizens depicted in the cartoon is on trial. Choice (D) is incorrect as the American citizens depicted in the cartoon are not being punished for a crime. Therefore, (B) is correct as the government's action, recording Americans' conversations without a warrant, violates the Fourth Amendment's protections against unreasonable search and seizure.

7. **C**   The table depicts voter turnout of different races in states with and without voter ID laws. Choice (A) is incorrect as white voter turnout does not decrease in states with voter ID laws. Choice (B) is incorrect as mixed-race voters turn out in lower numbers than white Americans. Choice (D) is incorrect as Asian Americans and Latinos vote in fewer numbers than Black Americans. Therefore, (C) is correct as minority voter turnout drops off more than does white voter turnout in states with voter ID laws.

8. **C**   Choice (A) is incorrect as voting ID laws do not affect the voting patterns of white Americans. Choice (B) is incorrect as the graph does not provide information regarding fraudulent voting. Choice (D) is incorrect as the graph does not make that argument. The only valid argument an opponent could make is (C), that voter ID laws most negatively affect groups that the Voting Rights Act of 1965 was passed to protect.

9. **D**   The table depicts Americans' opinions on gun control based on sex and region of the country. Choice (A) has a difference in opinion of 10% (compare 39% and 49% for women in the Midwest). Choice (B) has a difference in opinion of 25%. Choice (C) also has a difference in opinion of 25%. Choice (D) has a difference in opinion of 39%. Choice (D) has the greatest difference, so it is the correct answer.

10. **C**   Choice (A) is incorrect as the graph does not provide information about the number of guns throughout the United States. Choice (B) is incorrect as the opinions of women on gun control are not identical throughout the country. Choice (D) is incorrect as the survey did not ask Americans about the steps Congress should take. As a result, (C) is correct as the region where one lives is a more reliable predictor of gun support than gender is.

11. **C**   The quote conveys President Nixon's opinion of Americans protesting the Vietnam War. Choice (A) is incorrect as Nixon praises the First Amendment. Choice (B) is incorrect as Nixon does not directly or indirectly make such a strong assertion. Choice (D) is incorrect as Nixon does not make the connection between the protestors and America's military effort in Vietnam. Choice (C) is correct as Nixon makes the point that a small but loud interest group will not influence American policy concerning the war.

12. **A**   Choice (B) can be eliminated as Nixon talks about the protesters in the third person. Choice (C) can be eliminated as Nixon does not address his reelection campaign for president. Choice (D) can be eliminated as Nixon does not directly address the war effort. As a result, (A) is correct as Nixon is addressing the "silent majority," the group of Americans who are not protesting the Vietnam War.

13. **B**   Choice (A) can be eliminated as Nixon describes the protesters' beliefs in the first sentence. Choice (C) can be eliminated as Nixon does not pander to the protesters in his speech. Choice (D) is incorrect as that is not the protesters' intention, despite Nixon's claim. As a result, (B) is correct as the protesters want the government to end the war and bring the troops home.

14. **A** In *The Spirit of the Laws*, Baron de Montesquieu laid out his ideas for a just government. In this passage, he addresses the dangers of combining legislative and executive power in the same person or group. Choice (B) is incorrect as Montesquieu does not speak of international relations. Choice (C) is incorrect as the passage does not address people's reactions to tyranny. Choice (D) is incorrect as Montesquieu does not make this broad assumption: he states that tyranny *can* happen in the situation he describes. Accordingly, the correct answer is (A) as "there can be no liberty" in a nation where the executive and legislative branches are the same person or group.

15. **A** Choice (B) is incorrect as a proposed draft of the Constitution had already been written when Madison wrote Federalist No. 51. Choice (C) is incorrect as Madison does not propose a way to separate government power different from that in the then-proposed Constitution. Choice (D) is incorrect as Madison did not compare different governments throughout history in Federalist No. 51. As a result, (A) is correct as Madison argues the benefits of how the separation of powers will prevent the tyranny Montesquieu describes in *The Spirit of the Laws*.

16. **D** Choice (A) is incorrect as the legislative and executive branches cooperated on the passage of the Affordable Care Act. Choice (B) is incorrect as the scenario deals exclusively with the executive branch. Choice (C) is incorrect as the scenario does not describe conflict or cooperation between two branches of government. Therefore, (D) is correct as the impeachment of President Clinton in 1998 is an example of the legislative branch checking the power of the executive branch.

17. **A** Choice (B) is incorrect as Montesquieu does not discuss how the separation of powers affects the speed at which a government operates. Choice (C) is incorrect as Montesquieu does not bring up this idea in his text. Choice (D) is incorrect as it contradicts Montesquieu's main point. Therefore, (A) is correct as conflict between branches of government shows that no one faction or group has complete control.

18. **C** The table reports on political party affiliation classified by respondents' level of education and gender. Choices (A) and (B) are incorrect as both are contradicted by the table. Choice (D) is incorrect as women with only a grade school education are the most reliable Democratic voters. As a result, (C) is correct as 13% of women who have completed only grade school and 13% of men who have completed only high school identify as Republicans.

19. **B** According to the data, roughly 2/3 (64%) of males with college degrees are Democrats. Choice (A) is incorrect since most Democrats would tend to believe that military spending is already adequate, or perhaps should even be cut. Choice (C) is incorrect since very few Americans would support the racial segregation of schools outlawed by *Brown*. Choice (D) is incorrect since most Democrats support lighter sentences for drug users. Therefore, (B) is correct since most Democrats support increased spending on social welfare programs.

20. **A** The charts display the preferences of independent voters alongside the popular vote for the presidential elections between 2000 and 2012. Choice (B) is incorrect as the preferences of independent voters often do not align with the popular vote. Choice (C) is incorrect as the chart does not report on the campaign practices of politicians running for president. Choice (D) is incorrect as, from 2000 to 2012, no viable third-party candidate attracted more than 5% of the popular vote.

Therefore, (A) is correct because in 2004 and 2012, independent voters were more likely to vote for the challenger than for the incumbent.

21. **A** Choice (B) is incorrect as the chart does not describe the candidates' strengths during these presidential elections. Choice (C) is incorrect as no third-party candidate gained more than 5% of the vote. Choice (D) is incorrect as the chart does not provide information about changes in election law. As a result, (A) best explains why independent voters voted the way they did: they had no other option besides the candidates from the traditional two-party system.

22. **A** The table presents data on registered voters in the United States broken down by sex and age. Choice (B) is incorrect because the data is presented in thousands; the actual number is closer to 20,000,000. Choice (C) is incorrect as the number of registered voters rises and falls as men and women age. Choice (D) is incorrect as the chart does not provide data regarding the lifespans of men and women. Therefore, (A) is correct as approximately 10,000,000 more American women reported being registered to vote than American men.

23. **C** Choice (A) is incorrect since, as people age, their likelihood of voting changes. Choice (B) is incorrect as male registered voters between the ages of 18 and 24 are not the largest voting bloc. Choice (D) is incorrect as the graph does not display information regarding barriers to voting. As a result, (C) is correct as the data shows that a large number of Americans eligible to vote in presidential elections had not registered.

24. **B** After the drafting of the Constitution in 1787, Federalists and Anti-Federalists argued about the role of the federal government in a series of writings known as the *Federalist* and *Anti-Federalist Papers*. Choice (A) is incorrect because it is incomplete, as the failures of the Articles of Confederation had already shown the limitations of a unitary legislative branch. Choice (C) is incorrect as Federalists were not known for their defense of slavery. Choice (D) is incorrect as Anti-Federalists favored a small republic. Therefore, (B) is correct as the primary tenet of Federalist beliefs is that the power of the federal government should supersede that of the state governments.

25. **A** The interstate commerce clause gives Congress the power to regulate interstate and foreign trade. Choices (B), (C), and (D) all deal with businesses that work exclusively in one state, making them intrastate commerce. As a result, (A) is correct. If a French bakery wants to export its croissants to the United States, Congress can regulate their import through the commerce clause.

26. **A** In addition to the Bill of Rights, the Constitution laid the framework for federalism in the United States. Choice (B) is incorrect as states do not have equal representation in the House of Representatives. Choice (C) is incorrect as federalism does not deal with individual liberty. Choice (D) is incorrect as this answer deals with the relationship between the three branches of the federal government, also known as the separation of powers, not federalism. Therefore, (A) is correct as it accurately describes the principle of federalism.

27. **C** Voter eligibility requirements concern the regulations surrounding who is eligible to vote in an election. Choice (A) is incorrect as the president has no role in this process. Although Congress has passed constitutional amendments expanding voting rights, (B) is incorrect as determining

voter eligibility is not one of Congress's powers. Choice (D) is incorrect as the Supreme Court can only interpret the constitutionality of laws regarding voter eligibility, not create them. As a result, (C) is correct as the Constitution allows states to set voter eligibility requirements as long as these requirements do not violate the Constitution.

28. **D** The establishment clause bans the federal government from recognizing a state religion, and the free-exercise clause allows Americans to observe (or not) the religion of their choice. Choice (A) is incorrect as the scenario does not involve either clause. Choice (B) is incorrect as religious institutions can lose their tax-exempt status. Choice (C) is incorrect as the scenario does not involve either clause. Therefore, (D) is correct as a public school cannot force students to pray, but students still have the right to do so on their own.

29. **A** "Separate but equal" refers to a Supreme Court ruling that upheld state-sponsored segregation, mainly in the American South in the century after the Civil War. Choice (B) is incorrect because *Baker v. Carr* expanded the judiciary's power concerning legislative redistricting cases. Choice (C) is incorrect as *McCulloch v. Maryland* dealt with Congress's implied powers. Choice (D) is incorrect as *Shaw v. Reno* gave the courts greater authority to oversee states' compliance with the Voting Rights Act of 1965. "Separate but equal" was ultimately struck down in *Brown v. Board of Education*, so the correct answer is (A).

30. **D** The majority of conservative political beliefs center on the concepts of small government, a strong military, and minimal government interference in citizens' lives. Choice (A) can be eliminated as this law would interfere with private property and business. Choice (B) can be eliminated as conservatives might see it as an attempt to redefine gender. Choice (C) is incorrect as it would be viewed as an infringement on citizens' Second Amendment rights. Therefore, (D) is correct as conservatives support a strong military.

31. **C** "Political socialization" refers to how people's political views develop over time. Choices (A), (B), and (D) are incorrect; although they are "social" activities, none of them is one of the primary causes of political socialization. As a result, (C) is the best answer because consuming media causes people to develop and later change their political views.

32. **D** In recent years, PACs have raised billions of dollars to influence elections throughout the United States. Choice (A) is incorrect as some PACs can donate directly to political candidates (only Super PACs cannot). Choice (B) is incorrect as the FEC does regulate PACs. Choice (C) is incorrect as PACs raise money to support state and local candidates, as well. Therefore, (D) is correct as PACs attempt to influence elections at every level of government.

33. **B** In 2006, many liberal groups collaborated in an attempt to block the nomination of Samuel Alito to the Supreme Court. Choice (A) is incorrect as realignment refers to a group changing its beliefs over time. Choice (C) is incorrect as these groups did not exchange favors. Choice (D) is incorrect as these groups were committed to the cause of blocking Alito. As a result, (B) is correct as the groups built a united coalition of resistance against Congress confirming Alito to the Supreme Court.

34.   **D**   As laid out in the Constitution, the House of Representatives and Senate have different responsibilities and powers. Choice (A) is incorrect as all revenue bills must originate in the House. Choice (B) is incorrect as the opposite is true. Choice (C) is incorrect as the president *pro tempore* of the Senate has very little power compared to the Speaker of the House. Therefore, (D) is correct as the House Committee on Ways and Means creates revenue bills, a task the Constitution delegated to the House of Representatives.

35.   **D**   Cooperative federalism refers to cooperation between the federal government and one or more state governments. Choice (A) can be eliminated as the scenario takes place within the federal government. Choice (B) can be eliminated as the scenario involves only the actions of the federal government. Choice (C) can be eliminated as private businesses do not represent their states. As a result, (D) is correct as the scenario includes both the state and federal governments working together.

36.   **B**   The attorney general is the federal government's most powerful lawyer. Choice (A) can be eliminated as the attorney general is not a member of Congress. Choice (C) can be eliminated as the secretary of state leads the State Department. Choice (D) can be eliminated as the JAG Corps is a branch of the military and not the civilian government. Therefore, (B) is correct as the attorney general leads the Department of Justice.

37.   **D**   Logrolling refers to two or more politicians exchanging political favors. Choice (A) is incorrect as it involves only one politician. Choice (B) is incorrect as the scenario refers to gerrymandering. Choice (C) is incorrect as the scenario refers to pork-barrel spending. Therefore, (D) is correct as the scenario accurately describes logrolling.

38.   **C**   The Voting Rights Act of 1965 was a landmark piece of legislation that strengthened voting rights in the United States. Choice (A) is incorrect as states still have the power to establish voter identification requirements, as long as these requirements do not violate the Constitution. Choice (B) is incorrect as the law banned literacy tests. Choice (D) is incorrect as the Twenty-Sixth Amendment lowered the nationwide voting age from 21 to 18. As a result, (C) is correct: since the law's passage, millions of minority voters have been able to vote without hindrance.

39.   **B**   The Fourteenth Amendment played a crucial role when the Supreme Court decided *Brown v. Board of Education* in 1954. Choice (A) is incorrect as the court case did not hinge on the issue of Americans' citizenship. Choice (C) is incorrect as the case did not deal with states' representation in Congress. Choice (D) is incorrect as the case was about school access, not compensation for slavery. Therefore, (B) is correct as the Supreme Court ruled that segregation violated the Fourteenth Amendment's guarantee of equal protection under the law.

40.   **B**   *New York Times Co. v. United States* was a landmark case that involved *The New York Times's* publication of the Pentagon Papers, government documents that detailed the history of the United States' post-WWII involvement in Vietnam. Choice (A) is incorrect as the ruling did not interfere with the government's right to sue. Choice (C) is incorrect as the ruling did not change the legal process of obtaining a restraining order. Choice (D) is incorrect as the Supreme Court cannot interfere with what the Executive or Legislative Branches classify as Top Secret. As a result, (B) is correct as the Supreme Court struck down the concept of "prior restraint," the government suppressing news stories.

41. **B** "Political efficacy" refers to the concept of the public's trust in their government and a belief that their voices are heard by those in power. Choice (A) can be eliminated as special interest groups are not political institutions. Choice (C) can be eliminated as this scenario does not involve the public. Choice (D) can be eliminated as Representative Jones is persuading voters on an issue; the voters themselves have little to no say. Therefore, (B) is correct as holding town halls where people could ask questions and give feedback would raise their political efficacy—their faith and trust in government.

42. **A** Americans get their news from many different media outlets. Choice (B) can be eliminated as interviews reveal the beliefs of political candidates. Choice (C) can be eliminated as journalists protecting sources has been a long-established journalistic practice. Choice (D) can be eliminated as all media sources summarize the day's news events in some way or form. As a result, (A) is correct as reporting only one point of view can have the effect of decreasing political knowledge and politically radicalizing people.

43. **B** The Articles of Confederation was the first attempt by America's founders to bind the states together into a single country. Its failures and limitations led to the writing of the Constitution in 1787. Choices (A), (C), and (D) can be eliminated as the statements for each choice would need to be switched for them to be correct. Therefore, (B) is correct as the Articles of Confederation set term limits for members of Congress. The Constitution sets no such limits.

44. **A** The Federal Election Commission (FEC) and Securities and Exchange Commission (SEC) are two critical regulatory agencies within the executive branch. Choice (B) is incorrect as the Environmental Protection Agency oversees environmental protections. Choice (C) is incorrect as the Justice Department enforces civil rights legislation. The Department of Homeland Security helps protect the nation against external threats. Choice (D) is incorrect as the Department of Education sets educational policy at the federal level. As a result, (A) is correct as the FEC enforces campaign finance law and the SEC promotes an orderly and fair stock market.

45. **D** *Gideon v. Wainwright* and *Wisconsin v. Yoder* were two landmark cases that expanded individuals' rights. Choice (A) is incorrect as another Supreme Court case, *Miranda v. Arizona,* required police officers to inform the people they arrest of their constitutional rights. Choice (B) is incorrect as *Griswold v. Connecticut* (1965) established a constitutional right to privacy. Choice (C) is incorrect because *Griswold* allowed people to buy contraception and *McDonald v. Chicago* struck down municipal laws restricting gun ownership. Therefore, (D) is correct: the statements accurately describe *Gideon* and *Wisconsin*.

46. **C** Presidential general election voters and the Electoral College both cast votes in a presidential election. Choice (A) is incorrect as there is no rule on how old an elector must be. Choice (B) is incorrect as the popular vote does not always coincide with the winner of a presidential election. Choice (D) is incorrect as general election voters do not have to follow rules regarding whom to vote for; electors have rules regarding voting and can face fines or other consequences in their home states if their vote does not reflect the popular vote. As a result, (C) is correct as presidential candidates appeal directly to voters and the Electoral College makes the final determination of who becomes president.

47.   **D**   In the United States, there is often a large gap between conservative and liberal political beliefs. Choices (A), (B), and (C) can be eliminated as the statements would need to be switched to be correct. Therefore, (D) is correct as conservatives believe in limited regulation of business, and liberals support greater regulation of business.

48.   **A**   The core value concerning the government's role in Americans' daily lives is influenced by both the actions of citizens and the government. Choices (B) and (C) are incorrect as "equality of outcome" suggests a Communist form of government. Choice (D) is incorrect as various civil rights movements suggest that Americans are deeply invested in the concept of "equality of opportunity." As a result, (A) is correct as Americans' civil liberties and the government's respect for civil rights suggest that the government should ensure equality of opportunity.

49.   **B**   Interest groups such as PACs play a significant role in electing candidates to office. Choices (A), (C), and (D) can be eliminated as these scenarios are all legal activities interest groups perform. As a result, (B) is correct as tangible gifts constitute bribery.

50.   **C**   Primaries are a valuable tool political parties use to select their best candidates for the general election. As in the general election, voters select the candidate through voting at the ballot box. Choice (A) is incorrect as a caucus is a separate method of selecting a candidate. Choice (B) is incorrect as the results of an open primary are binding. Choice (D) is incorrect as open primaries do not necessitate that voters be allowed to register on the day of the primary. Therefore, (C) is correct as any registered voter may participate in an open primary; during closed primaries, only voters registered with a specific political party may participate.

51.   **C**   *United States v. Lopez* (1996) was a landmark case regarding the federal government's ability to make public schools gun-free zones. Choice (A) can be eliminated as Congress lost power due to the court's ruling. Choice (B) is incorrect as the court's ruling did not redefine federalism between the federal government and states. Choice (D) is incorrect as states had always had the right to pass gun control legislation that did not infringe on the Second Amendment. As a result, (C) is correct as the court ruled that Congress could not use the commerce clause to justify gun control legislation on a national level.

52.   **C**   The necessary and proper clause in the Constitution gives Congress implied powers—powers that Congress uses to accomplish its expressed powers. Choices (A), (B), and (D) are incorrect as regulating trade, borrowing money, and declaring war are all expressed powers. Therefore, (C) is correct as overseeing executive branch agencies is not an expressed power mentioned in the Constitution.

53.   **B**   There are specific rules regarding how a president may or may not approve of a bill passed by Congress. Choice (A) is incorrect as line-item vetoes refer to a president vetoing only part of a bill; the Supreme Court ruled this practice unconstitutional in the mid-1990s. Choice (C) is incorrect as adjournment is a term used in a jury trial. Choice (D) is incorrect as a writ of *certiorari* is an appeal to the Supreme Court to take up a case. As a result, (B) is correct as a pocket veto refers to how a president's inaction on a passed bill can have the same effect as a regular veto; in recent years, Congress never takes a recess within 10 days of passing a bill to make it impossible for a president to use the pocket veto.

54. **B** Gerrymandering is an attempt by one political party to redraw a state's congressional districts to their advantage. Choice (A) is incorrect as gerrymandering reduces voters' influence in elections. Choice (C) is incorrect: although gerrymandering has been used as a tool to reduce the importance of the minority vote, that is not its explicit intent. Choice (D) is incorrect as gerrymandered districts are not all the same size. Therefore, (B) is correct as the purpose of gerrymandering is to isolate members of certain populations to ensure a desired electoral outcome.

55. **B** The Articles of Confederation was the nation's first attempt to bind the states together. It had many flaws, which led to the creation of the Constitution in 1787. Choices (A) and (C) can be eliminated as these ideas were later incorporated into the Constitution. Choice (D) can be eliminated as preapproving Canada for statehood did not negatively affect how the federal government and states interacted. As a result, (B) is correct: since states had to negotiate with one another regarding commerce, multiple sets of laws slowed down commerce between the states, weakening the nation as a whole.

Section II: Free Response

Remember that you need to answer all four free-response questions in 1 hour and 40 minutes, so you do not have time to waste, nor can you skip any questions. Nevertheless, you should take time to brainstorm some ideas and to organize what you come up with before you start to write each response. Otherwise, your responses will probably be incomplete, disorganized, or both.

You should take about 20 minutes each for Questions 1, 2, and 3 and about 40 minutes for Question 4. Make sure you read each question carefully and respond directly to each of its components in your response. The questions are about broad issues, but they ask for specific information. A general free response that fails to address specific concerns raised by the question will not earn a high score. Your replies to Questions 1–3 should be brief and to the point. The information on the next few pages represents what you should consider before writing a concise answer.

Question 1

(A)   Describe a power Congress could use to address the comments outlined in the scenario.

Some of the powers that Congress could use include:

- Interstate commerce clause: Congress could invoke this to regulate the interstate transport of legal narcotics through appropriate legislation, thus reducing the number of pain pills that enter West Virginia.

- Subpoenas: Congress could use these to force pharmaceutical executives to testify and provide evidence of how they are addressing the problem.

(B)   In the context of the scenario, explain how the use of the congressional power described in Part A can be affected by its interaction with the Supreme Court.

- Interstate commerce clause: The pharmaceutical distributors could sue the federal government, taking the case to the Supreme Court. As with *Gonzales v. Raich,* the Supreme Court can reinterpret Congress's power concerning the commerce clause.

- Subpoenas: An executive could refuse to testify or provide evidence, at which point the Supreme Court would need to become involved.

(C)   In the context of the scenario, explain the responsibilities of states like West Virginia as described under the Tenth Amendment.

The Tenth Amendment gives states like West Virginia the power to regulate their healthcare industries. The amendment dictates that it is the state's ultimate responsibility to address the issue of painkiller abuse. A way that West Virginia could do this is by regulating opioid prescriptions once the pills have entered the state. This action would not violate the interstate commerce clause, as the state would not attempt to interfere with the number of pills that cross state lines.

Question 2

(A)   Identify the state that gained the most seats through congressional apportionment in 2020.

- Texas (TX) gained the most seats through congressional apportionment.

(B)   Describe a trend based on how congressional apportionment shifted in 2020.

- Large numbers of Americans moved to Texas, Florida, Oregon, Montana, Colorado, and North Carolina between 2010 and 2020.

- Large numbers of Americans left California, Illinois, Michigan, Ohio, West Virginia, Pennsylvania, and New York during this time.

(C)   Explain how the changes in congressional apportionment over time, as shown in the information graphic, reflect one principle set forth in Article I of the Constitution.

- One principle from Article I the changes reflect is the requirement to modify congressional apportionment every 10 years based on the results of the national census.

Question 3

(A)   Identify the constitutional clause that is common to both *Brandenburg v. Ohio* (1969) and *Schenck v. United States* (1919).

- The First Amendment is relevant to both cases as both defendants were charged with making anti-government speech.

(B)   Based on the constitutional clause in Part A, explain why the court found differently in *Brandenburg v. Ohio* than it did in *Schenck v. United States*.

- *Schenck* was prompted by the first Red Scare—an attempt to suppress Communists in the United States. The court did not apply this or any other political agenda against inflammatory speech during *Brandenburg*.

(C)   Describe an action that local governments who disagree with the holding in *Brandenburg v. Ohio* could take to limit its impact in their communities.

- A local government could deny the KKK or similar group a permit to march or have a large public gathering. Also, a local government could also put on its own events that encourage racial equality and integration.

Question 4

Develop an argument that explains which of the three forms of action taken by the federal government—constitutional amendments, Supreme Court rulings, or legislation—has best ensured the civil rights of minorities and historically repressed groups.

Articulate a defensible claim.

Constitutional amendments have best ensured the rights of minorities and historically repressed groups.

Support your claim.

- In his "Letter from a Birmingham Jail," MLK spoke out against legislation at the state level suppressing African Americans. This reasoning implies that at the time of the letter's writing, legislation was more of a hindrance than a help in ensuring civil rights.

- The group of white Americans suppressing the civil rights of minorities constitutes a political faction as defined by Madison's Federalist No. 10. A strong central government, backed by a Constitution, can suppress factions that infringe on citizens' rights.

- The Thirteenth, Fourteenth, and Fifteenth Amendments to the Constitution were the first steps to ensuring civil rights for minorities. In the 20th century, the Nineteenth, Twenty-Fourth, and Twenty-Sixth expanded these rights for African Americans, and did the same for women and young Americans.

- Madison's Federalist No. 51 argues that a strong federal government can protect against a "tyranny of the majority" that existed within states that passed laws King and other civil rights leaders were fighting against.

- Some Supreme Court rulings, such as *Plessy v. Ferguson*, *Korematsu v. U.S.*, and *Buck v. Bell*, have restricted the civil rights of minority groups.

Use reasoning.

- Constitutional amendments make the most significant impact on how the state and federal governments interact with citizens.

- Since the writing of the Constitution, the United States has repealed only one constitutional amendment. This fact implies that constitutional amendments have greater lasting power than legislation or Supreme Court decisions.

- Both federal and state governments base their legislation on what the Constitution and its amendments allow. The Supreme Court bases its decisions on constitutional provisions, as well.

Respond to an opposing perspective.

- **Opposing Perspective:** Historically oppressed groups and other minorities needed immediate change to improve their lives; Congress and the states sometimes require years to draft and adopt constitutional amendments.

- **Response (Refutation):** Constitutional amendments give the federal government broad powers to carry them out. The legislation and Supreme Court decisions associated with the civil rights movements in the 20th century stem from the civil rights constitutional amendments adopted in the 19th century.

- **Opposing Perspective:** From the passage of the Thirteenth, Fourteenth, and Fifteenth Amendments until the mid-20th century, many states subverted the constitutional protections for minorities and other historically repressed groups.

- **Response (Concession):** At the time, the amendments did not take into account how states might subvert them. Only in later amendments, such as the Twenty-Fourth Amendment banning poll taxes, were these oversights remedied.

HOW TO SCORE PRACTICE TEST 2

Section I: Multiple Choice

_____ × 1.0000 = _____
Number of Correct   Weighted
(out of 55)   Section I Score
         (Do not round)

The following conversion chart provides only a rough estimate, as scoring ranges may vary from administration to administration. Check your online Student Tools for possible updates.

Section II: Free Response

Question 1   _____ × 4.5833 = _____
             (out of 3)   (Do not round)

Question 2   _____ × 3.4375 = _____
             (out of 4)   (Do not round)

Question 3   _____ × 3.4375 = _____
             (out of 4)   (Do not round)

Question 4   _____ × 2.2917 = _____
             (out of 6)   (Do not round)

Sum   = _____
         Weighted Section II
         Score (Do not round)

AP Score Conversion Chart U.S. Government and Politics

Composite Score Range	AP Score
83–110	5
72–82	4
56–71	3
38–55	2
0–37	1

Composite Score

_____ + _____ = _____
Weighted   Weighted   Composite Score
Section I Score   Section II Score   (Round to nearest
                                            whole number)

Practice Test 3

The Princeton Review®

Completely darken bubbles with a No. 2 pencil. If you make a mistake, be sure to erase mark completely. Erase all stray marks.

1. YOUR NAME:
(Print)   Last   First   M.I.

SIGNATURE: _____   **DATE:** ___/___/___

HOME ADDRESS: _____
(Print)   Number and Street

          City   State   Zip Code

PHONE NO. : _____
(Print)

IMPORTANT: Please fill in these boxes exactly as shown on the back cover of your test book.

2. TEST FORM

3. TEST CODE   4. REGISTRATION NUMBER

5. YOUR NAME

First 4 letters of last name				FIRST INIT	MID INIT
Ⓐ	Ⓐ	Ⓐ	Ⓐ	Ⓐ	Ⓐ
Ⓑ	Ⓑ	Ⓑ	Ⓑ	Ⓑ	Ⓑ
Ⓒ	Ⓒ	Ⓒ	Ⓒ	Ⓒ	Ⓒ
Ⓓ	Ⓓ	Ⓓ	Ⓓ	Ⓓ	Ⓓ
Ⓔ	Ⓔ	Ⓔ	Ⓔ	Ⓔ	Ⓔ
Ⓕ	Ⓕ	Ⓕ	Ⓕ	Ⓕ	Ⓕ
Ⓖ	Ⓖ	Ⓖ	Ⓖ	Ⓖ	Ⓖ
Ⓗ	Ⓗ	Ⓗ	Ⓗ	Ⓗ	Ⓗ
Ⓘ	Ⓘ	Ⓘ	Ⓘ	Ⓘ	Ⓘ
Ⓙ	Ⓙ	Ⓙ	Ⓙ	Ⓙ	Ⓙ
Ⓚ	Ⓚ	Ⓚ	Ⓚ	Ⓚ	Ⓚ
Ⓛ	Ⓛ	Ⓛ	Ⓛ	Ⓛ	Ⓛ
Ⓜ	Ⓜ	Ⓜ	Ⓜ	Ⓜ	Ⓜ
Ⓝ	Ⓝ	Ⓝ	Ⓝ	Ⓝ	Ⓝ
Ⓞ	Ⓞ	Ⓞ	Ⓞ	Ⓞ	Ⓞ
Ⓟ	Ⓟ	Ⓟ	Ⓟ	Ⓟ	Ⓟ
Ⓠ	Ⓠ	Ⓠ	Ⓠ	Ⓠ	Ⓠ
Ⓡ	Ⓡ	Ⓡ	Ⓡ	Ⓡ	Ⓡ
Ⓢ	Ⓢ	Ⓢ	Ⓢ	Ⓢ	Ⓢ
Ⓣ	Ⓣ	Ⓣ	Ⓣ	Ⓣ	Ⓣ
Ⓤ	Ⓤ	Ⓤ	Ⓤ	Ⓤ	Ⓤ
Ⓥ	Ⓥ	Ⓥ	Ⓥ	Ⓥ	Ⓥ
Ⓦ	Ⓦ	Ⓦ	Ⓦ	Ⓦ	Ⓦ
Ⓧ	Ⓧ	Ⓧ	Ⓧ	Ⓧ	Ⓧ
Ⓨ	Ⓨ	Ⓨ	Ⓨ	Ⓨ	Ⓨ
Ⓩ	Ⓩ	Ⓩ	Ⓩ	Ⓩ	Ⓩ

6. DATE OF BIRTH

Month	Day		Year	
◯ JAN				
◯ FEB				
◯ MAR	⓪	⓪	⓪	⓪
◯ APR	①	①	①	①
◯ MAY	②	②	②	②
◯ JUN	③	③	③	③
◯ JUL		④	④	④
◯ AUG		⑤	⑤	⑤
◯ SEP		⑥	⑥	⑥
◯ OCT		⑦	⑦	⑦
◯ NOV		⑧	⑧	⑧
◯ DEC		⑨	⑨	⑨

Test Code columns: Ⓐ Ⓑ Ⓒ Ⓓ Ⓔ Ⓕ Ⓖ and digits ⓪①②③④⑤⑥⑦⑧⑨

The Princeton Review®
© The Princeton Review, Inc.
FORM NO. 00001-PR

Section 1

Start with number 1 for each new section.
If a section has fewer questions than answer spaces, leave the extra answer spaces blank.

1. Ⓐ Ⓑ Ⓒ Ⓓ
2. Ⓐ Ⓑ Ⓒ Ⓓ
3. Ⓐ Ⓑ Ⓒ Ⓓ
4. Ⓐ Ⓑ Ⓒ Ⓓ
5. Ⓐ Ⓑ Ⓒ Ⓓ
6. Ⓐ Ⓑ Ⓒ Ⓓ
7. Ⓐ Ⓑ Ⓒ Ⓓ
8. Ⓐ Ⓑ Ⓒ Ⓓ
9. Ⓐ Ⓑ Ⓒ Ⓓ
10. Ⓐ Ⓑ Ⓒ Ⓓ
11. Ⓐ Ⓑ Ⓒ Ⓓ
12. Ⓐ Ⓑ Ⓒ Ⓓ
13. Ⓐ Ⓑ Ⓒ Ⓓ
14. Ⓐ Ⓑ Ⓒ Ⓓ
15. Ⓐ Ⓑ Ⓒ Ⓓ

16. Ⓐ Ⓑ Ⓒ Ⓓ
17. Ⓐ Ⓑ Ⓒ Ⓓ
18. Ⓐ Ⓑ Ⓒ Ⓓ
19. Ⓐ Ⓑ Ⓒ Ⓓ
20. Ⓐ Ⓑ Ⓒ Ⓓ
21. Ⓐ Ⓑ Ⓒ Ⓓ
22. Ⓐ Ⓑ Ⓒ Ⓓ
23. Ⓐ Ⓑ Ⓒ Ⓓ
24. Ⓐ Ⓑ Ⓒ Ⓓ
25. Ⓐ Ⓑ Ⓒ Ⓓ
26. Ⓐ Ⓑ Ⓒ Ⓓ
27. Ⓐ Ⓑ Ⓒ Ⓓ
28. Ⓐ Ⓑ Ⓒ Ⓓ
29. Ⓐ Ⓑ Ⓒ Ⓓ
30. Ⓐ Ⓑ Ⓒ Ⓓ

31. Ⓐ Ⓑ Ⓒ Ⓓ
32. Ⓐ Ⓑ Ⓒ Ⓓ
33. Ⓐ Ⓑ Ⓒ Ⓓ
34. Ⓐ Ⓑ Ⓒ Ⓓ
35. Ⓐ Ⓑ Ⓒ Ⓓ
36. Ⓐ Ⓑ Ⓒ Ⓓ
37. Ⓐ Ⓑ Ⓒ Ⓓ
38. Ⓐ Ⓑ Ⓒ Ⓓ
39. Ⓐ Ⓑ Ⓒ Ⓓ
40. Ⓐ Ⓑ Ⓒ Ⓓ
41. Ⓐ Ⓑ Ⓒ Ⓓ
42. Ⓐ Ⓑ Ⓒ Ⓓ
43. Ⓐ Ⓑ Ⓒ Ⓓ
44. Ⓐ Ⓑ Ⓒ Ⓓ
45. Ⓐ Ⓑ Ⓒ Ⓓ

46. Ⓐ Ⓑ Ⓒ Ⓓ
47. Ⓐ Ⓑ Ⓒ Ⓓ
48. Ⓐ Ⓑ Ⓒ Ⓓ
49. Ⓐ Ⓑ Ⓒ Ⓓ
50. Ⓐ Ⓑ Ⓒ Ⓓ
51. Ⓐ Ⓑ Ⓒ Ⓓ
52. Ⓐ Ⓑ Ⓒ Ⓓ
53. Ⓐ Ⓑ Ⓒ Ⓓ
54. Ⓐ Ⓑ Ⓒ Ⓓ
55. Ⓐ Ⓑ Ⓒ Ⓓ

AP® U.S. Government and Politics Exam

SECTION I: Multiple-Choice Questions

DO NOT OPEN THIS BOOKLET UNTIL YOU ARE TOLD TO DO SO.

At a Glance

Total Time
80 minutes
Number of Questions
55
Percent of Total Grade
50%
Writing Instrument
Pencil required

Instructions

Section I of this examination contains 55 multiple-choice questions. Fill in only the ovals for numbers 1 through 55 on your answer sheet.

Indicate all of your answers to the multiple-choice questions on the answer sheet. No credit will be given for anything written in this exam booklet, but you may use the booklet for notes or scratch work. After you have decided which of the suggested answers is best, completely fill in the corresponding oval on the answer sheet. Give only one answer to each question. If you change an answer, be sure that the previous mark is erased completely. Here is a sample question and answer.

Sample Question   Sample Answer

Chicago is a   Ⓐ ● Ⓒ Ⓓ
(A) state
(B) city
(C) country
(D) continent

Use your time effectively, working as quickly as you can without losing accuracy. Do not spend too much time on any one question. Go on to other questions and come back to the ones you have not answered if you have time. It is not expected that everyone will know the answers to all the multiple-choice questions.

About Guessing

Many candidates wonder whether or not to guess the answers to questions about which they are not certain. Multiple-choice scores are based on the number of questions answered correctly. Points are not deducted for incorrect answers, and no points are awarded for unanswered questions. Because points are not deducted for incorrect answers, you are encouraged to answer all multiple-choice questions. On any questions you do not know the answer to, you should eliminate as many choices as you can, and then select the best answer among the remaining choices.

GO ON TO THE NEXT PAGE.

UNITED STATES GOVERNMENT AND POLITICS

Section I

Time—80 minutes

55 Questions

<u>Directions</u>: Each of the questions or incomplete statements below is followed by four suggested answers or completions. Select the one that is best in each case and then fill in the corresponding oval on the answer sheet.

Questions 1 and 2 refer to the graphics.

% of registered voters who identify as...

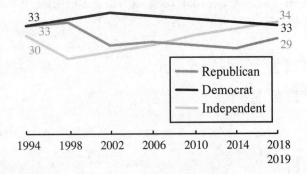

% of registered voters who identify as/lean toward...

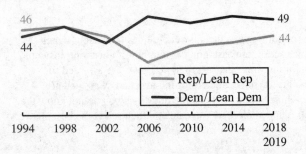

1. Which of the following statements can be supported by the charts?

   (A) From 1994–2019, the majority of registered voters in the United States identified as independents.

   (B) The percent of registered voters who identified as Republican was smaller in 2000 than in any other year from 1994–2019.

   (C) A larger share of the electorate identified as Republican or leaned toward Republican in 2008 than in 2000

   (D) A larger share of the electorate identified as Democrats or leaned toward Democrat in 2008 than in 2000.

2. Which of the following was the most likely consequence of the political trends in party identification depicted in the charts?

   (A) After the mid-term election of 2002, Democrats gained control of Congress.

   (B) In the mid-term election of 1994, Democrats lost control of Congress, a sign that independent voters were leaning Republican at that time.

   (C) Throughout the history of the United States, independent voters have had little influence on national politics.

   (D) When Texas Governor George W. Bush ran for president in 2000, he won the election due to a large increase in Republican voters.

Notes: Based on registered voters. Due to smaller sample sizes in 2018 and 2019, the data from these years has been combined. "Don't know" responses not shown.
Source: Pew Research Center, Washington DC.

GO ON TO THE NEXT PAGE.

Questions 3 and 4 refer to the table.

Federal Domestic Assistance Programs (FDAP)				
Year	Total FDAP Grants (Billions of $)	FDAP Grants as a Percentage of State and Municipal Budgets	Department of Health and Human Services Grants (Part of FDAP)	
			Grants (Billions of $)	As a Percentage of FDAP Grants
1972	195.3	14.6	35.1	18.0
1982	182.1	22.0	30.0	16.5
1992	175.8	30.8	37.1	21.1
2002	380.7	19.8	108.3	28.4
2012	512.4	25.0	156.2	30.5

3. Which of the following conclusions can be drawn from the data in the table?

   (A) FDAP grants comprised a larger share of state and municipal budgets in 1972 than in 1992.
   (B) The amount of money allocated for FDAP grants increased from 1972 to 1992.
   (C) The share of FDAP grants allocated to the Department of Health and Human Services increased between 1982 and 2012.
   (D) The amount of money allocated for FDAP grants decreased from 1972 to 2012.

4. Which of the following is a type of financial assistance that could be included in FDAP grants based on the trends in the table above and your own knowledge?

   (A) A block grant intended for community development
   (B) A program that allows for the use of National Parks for scientific research
   (C) The dissemination of consumer information through a federal agency
   (D) The recruitment and hiring of federal agency personnel

Questions 5 and 6 refer to the graph.

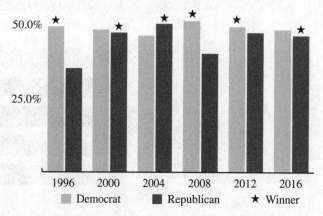

Popular Vote Summary for the U.S. Presidential Elections (% of recorded votes)

5. Which of the following conclusions regarding voting laws and behavior can best be supported by the information in the graph?

   (A) Voters in states that favored the Republican candidate in 2000 did not support the Republican candidate in 2004.
   (B) Voters in the states that have the largest populations were more likely to vote Democratic than Republican.
   (C) After Republican George W. Bush won the presidential election of 2000, voters were unsatisfied with his first term in office.
   (D) In two elections from 1996 to 2016, the Electoral College awarded the presidency to the candidate with fewer votes.

6. Which of the following conclusions about the 2000 and 2004 election results is most easily proven based on the information from the graph?

   (A) In 2004, Republican George W. Bush won the popular vote in all the states where he won in 2000.
   (B) The Democratic popular vote increased from 2000 to 2004.
   (C) Smaller states were more likely to vote Republican in 2004 than in 2000.
   (D) In 2004, Republican George W. Bush won the popular vote due to higher voter turnout than in 2000.

GO ON TO THE NEXT PAGE.

Questions 7 and 8 refer to the graph.

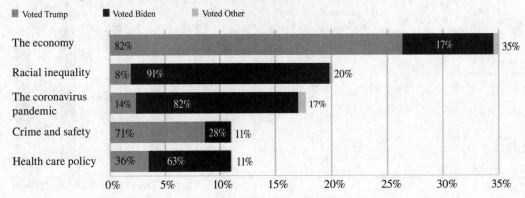

% of voters saying the following issue mattered most when deciding whom they voted for in the 2020 election*

Voted Trump Voted Biden Voted Other

Issue		
The economy	82%	17% 35%
Racial inequality	8% 91%	20%
The coronavirus pandemic	14% 82%	17%
Crime and safety	71% 28%	11%
Health care policy	36% 63%	11%

0% 5% 10% 15% 20% 25% 30% 35%

*Preliminary results from exit polls based on interviews of 15,590 voters.
Source: Edison Research via the New York Times
**In 2020, Donald Trump was the Republican candidate for U.S. President and Joseph Biden
was the Democratic candidate.

7. Based on the data shown in the graph, which of the following conclusions about the 2020 election is most supported?

   (A) Hispanic voters were more likely to vote Republican than they were Democratic.
   (B) The plurality of voters in the East voted Republican.
   (C) The percentage of voters who prioritized concern over the coronavirus pandemic was higher than that of voters who prioritized the economy.
   (D) Voters who prioritized racial and health issues were more likely to vote Democratic than Republican.

8. Which of the following can be inferred from the results shown in the graph?

   (A) Concern about health care policy makes people more likely to vote Republican.
   (B) Less-educated Americans are dependable Republican voters.
   (C) Political priorities have a dramatic effect on voting behavior.
   (D) Someone's race does not affect their voting behavior.

GO ON TO THE NEXT PAGE.

Questions 9 and 10 refer to the graph.

Public Approval for U.S. Presidents, 1953 to 2015
% approving of president's job performance, by party

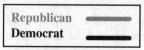
Republican
Democrat

9. Which of the following statements regarding approval ratings can be concluded from the graph?

(A) Carter consistently received higher approval ratings than Johnson.
(B) Nixon's approval ratings dropped continuously throughout his presidency.
(C) Reagan had a higher approval rating at the beginning of his presidency than he did at the end.
(D) George W. Bush received higher approval ratings from Republicans than Obama did throughout his term of office.

10. Which of the following could best explain the trend in the approval ratings for George W. Bush as shown in the graph?

(A) Although national unity was high after the terrorist attacks of September 11, 2001, the subsequent Iraq War, Afghanistan War, and downturn of the economy began to negatively affect public opinion thereafter.
(B) *Time* magazine named George W. Bush as its Person of the Year for both 2000 and 2004.
(C) Responding to a 2008 poll about whether history would rate George W. Bush as the worst president ever, 50% said "No," 41% said "Yes," and 9% were unsure.
(D) The presidential election of 2000 was a controversial one, since George W. Bush did not win the majority of the popular vote.

GO ON TO THE NEXT PAGE.

Questions 11–14 refer to the passage below.

"It is insisted, indeed, that this constitution must be received, be it ever so imperfect. If it has its defects, it is said, they can be best amended when they are experienced. But remember, when the people once part with power, they can seldom or never resume it again but by force. Many instances can be produced in which the people have voluntarily increased the powers of their rulers; but few, if any, in which rulers have willingly abridged their authority. This is a sufficient reason to induce you to be careful, in the first instance, how you deposit the powers of government."

—Brutus, Brutus No. 1 (1787)

11. Which of the following statements best summarizes the argument made in this excerpt?

    (A) The Constitution allows for the unlimited use of state power to further the interests of society as a whole.
    (B) An effective constitution should favor a strong state and guarantee civil liberties for all.
    (C) Governmental power is inevitably harmful.
    (D) The people should be cautious when ceding power to the government.

12. Which of the following constitutional amendments would limit the power of a national government as described in Brutus's argument?

    (A) The Third Amendment
    (B) The Fifth Amendment
    (C) The Seventh Amendment
    (D) The Tenth Amendment

13. Opponents of Brutus's view would have ideas most similar to those in which of the following texts?

    (A) Federalist No. 10
    (B) The Articles of Confederation
    (C) The Declaration of Independence
    (D) "Letter from a Birmingham Jail"

14. Which of the following modern-day groups would be most likely to disagree with the ideas presented in Brutus No. 1?

    (A) Libertarians
    (B) Liberal Democrats
    (C) Conservatives
    (D) Republicans

GO ON TO THE NEXT PAGE.

Questions 15–17 refer to the passage below.

"It is clear that corporations seek to use campaign contributions to gain government contracts, but despite anecdotes, whether they succeed has been largely ignored in academic studies… I [believe] campaign contributions may influence contracting and [there is a] relationship between the donation of campaign contributions and the receipt of government contracts for a sample of firms politically active between 1979 and 2006. The analysis shows that even after controlling for past contracts and other factors, companies that contributed more money to federal candidates subsequently received more contracts."

—Christopher Witko, *Journal of Public Administration Research and Theory,* October 2011

15. Which of the following statements best summarizes Witko's argument?

    (A) For at least twenty-five years, big corporations were illegally making campaign contributions to federal candidates in exchange for government contracts.

    (B) There has been a noticeable correlation between campaign contributions and the attainment of federal government contracts by some corporations.

    (C) Federal candidates for public office have sought to secure contracts with corporations in exchange for campaign contributions.

    (D) Despite anecdotes, many corporations have been unsuccessful in their bids to exchange campaign contributions for government contracts.

16. Which of the following pieces of legislation, constitutional amendment, or case law would best serve to limit the harmful effects of the phenomenon described in Witko's argument?

    (A) Federal Election Campaign Act of 1974
    (B) The Bipartisan Campaign Reform Act of 2002
    (C) *Citizens United v. Federal Election Commission* (2010)
    (D) The Fifteenth Amendment

17. A debate over the practices described in Witko's argument would most likely revolve around which two competing principles?

    (A) Free speech versus fair elections
    (B) Campaign fundraising versus undue corporate influence
    (C) Soft money versus PACs
    (D) Individual rights versus corporate interests

GO ON TO THE NEXT PAGE.

Questions 18 and 19 refer to the map below.

Number of Electoral College Votes by State

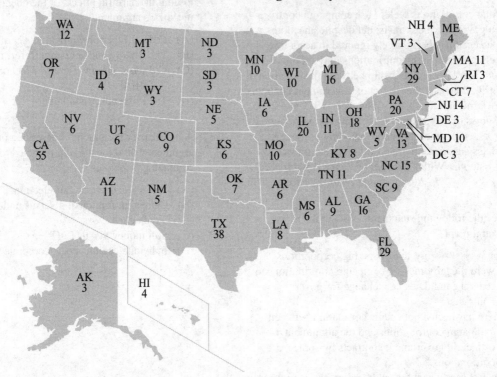

18. Based on the distribution of the Electoral College shown in the map, which of the following would be a good strategy for presidential candidates seeking to win a general election?

   (A) Avoid battleground states and focus their campaigns on "safe" states

   (B) Campaign more heavily in states with large populations

   (C) Spend more television advertising money in the Plains States

   (D) Campaign extensively in states that heavily favor one party over the other

19. Which of the following statements best explains the differences in the distribution of electoral votes across the country?

   (A) The number of electoral votes is equal in number to that state's combined total of U.S. senators and representatives.

   (B) The number of electoral votes is determined by the geographical size of each state.

   (C) The number of electoral votes is proportionate to the size of each state's legislative body.

   (D) The Constitution specifically mandates the number of electoral votes granted to each state, and this number cannot be changed.

GO ON TO THE NEXT PAGE.

Questions 20 and 21 refer to the cartoon below.

20. Which of the following best describes the message in the political cartoon?

(A) Legal protections for U.S. corporations have undermined the fairness of the judicial system.

(B) The equal protection clause empowers corporations to override the rights of individual citizens.

(C) Although the equal protection clause is viewed with suspicion by many citizens, it does not influence how judges treat corporations in legal disputes.

(D) The equal protection clause in the Constitution has often been used by judges to protect the interests of corporations instead of individual citizens.

21. Someone who wished to dispute the message expressed in the cartoon might point to which of the following Supreme Court cases to support their critique?

(A) *Brown v. Board of Education* (1954)

(B) *Engel v. Vitale* (1962)

(C) *New York Times Co. v. United States* (1971)

(D) *Shaw v. Reno* (1993)

GO ON TO THE NEXT PAGE.

Questions 22 and 23 refer to the chart.

Federal Judges Appointed by Recent Presidents, by Gender

■ Percent male judges   ■ Percent female judges

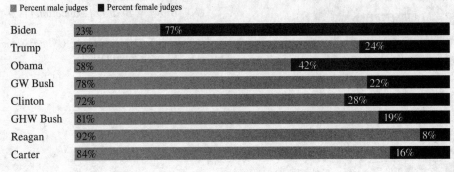

Biden	23% 77%
Trump	76% 24%
Obama	58% 42%
GW Bush	78% 22%
Clinton	72% 28%
GHW Bush	81% 19%
Reagan	92% 8%
Carter	84% 16%

Chart: Disha Raychaudhuri, REUTERS
Source: American Bar Association 2022 Profile of the Legal Profession

Federal Judges Appointed by Recent Presidents, by Race and Ethnicity

■ Percent of judges

White	78.4%
Black	11%
Hispanic	7.7%
Asian American	3.8%
Mixed race or ethnicity	1.3%
Native American	0.4%

Chart: Disha Raychaudhuri, REUTERS
Note: Numbers do not add up 100 because categories overlap. Data is accurate as of July 1, 2022.
Source: American Bar Association 2022 Profile of the Legal Profession

22. Which of the following conclusions can be drawn from the charts?

(A) Reagan, the Bushes, and Trump have appointed a higher percentage of women to the judiciary than the other presidents combined.

(B) Carter, Clinton, Obama, and Biden have appointed a higher percentage of males to the judiciary than the other presidents combined.

(C) President Clinton made more judicial appointments than President Reagan.

(D) President Biden has appointed the highest percentage of women to the judiciary.

23. Based on the charts and your own knowledge, which of the following claims would an advocate for affirmative action most likely make?

(A) If judges are selected in part by racial group, they better represent the citizenry's diverse interests by mirroring the racial diversity of citizens across the nation.

(B) The Constitution is colorblind and thus lifetime appointments of judges should be made without consideration to the candidate's race.

(C) A judge's race, gender, or disability has no influence on the legal decisions that judge may make.

(D) Since a judge's race or gender may have a negative influence on their legal opinions, caution should be used when selecting candidates for lifetime appointments.

GO ON TO THE NEXT PAGE.

24. Which of the following statements is true of voters in federal, state, and local elections?

    (A) Voter turnout is higher in midterm elections than it is in presidential elections.
    (B) Voters lacking party affiliation tend to vote more regularly than those with strong party affiliation.
    (C) Young adults are more likely to vote than senior citizens.
    (D) Individuals are less likely to vote when they believe they know which candidate will win an election.

25. A presidential veto would most likely be overturned in which of the following situations?

    (A) Approximately 30% of the senators and representatives are members of the presidential political party.
    (B) The majority of American citizens support the proposed legislation.
    (C) The chief justice of the Supreme Court was appointed by the president.
    (D) The president's successful reelection campaign advocated bipartisanship.

26. Which of the following is generally understood to be the purpose of the Tenth Amendment to the Constitution?

    (A) It allows for trial by jury in common-law cases.
    (B) It grants voting rights to all American women.
    (C) It lowers the legal voting age from 21 to 18.
    (D) It reserves powers to the states.

27. An appeal to the Supreme Court is called a "petition for a *writ of certiorari*." Which of the following is the Supreme Court's most likely response to such a petition?

    (A) It will refuse to hear the appeal.
    (B) It will declare a mistrial.
    (C) It will order a lower court to retry the case.
    (D) It will rule in favor of the defendant.

28. Which of the following principles is realized when the federal government provides most of the funding to a project in which multiple levels of government work together?

    (A) Confederation
    (B) Fiscal federalism
    (C) Grant-based funding
    (D) Dual federalism

29. A representative has just joined the Rules Committee. With which of the following will she most likely be involved?

    (A) Determining both the rules of the House and conditions for legislative process
    (B) Managing the Library of Congress
    (C) Taking jurisdiction over fisheries and wildlife
    (D) Ruling on the ethics of behavior in the House

30. Which of the following represents a historical trend of the constitutional commerce clause?

    (A) An increase in the release of detainees from prison following unlawful arrest
    (B) Increased funding of the military
    (C) A general increase in the power of the federal government
    (D) An increase in vetoes of legislative bills of attainder

31. Which of the following is the most accurate description of how each of the two main political parties of the United States is organized?

    (A) Each party has a presence at the national level only.
    (B) Each party has centralized national leadership, while state and local parties have very little power.
    (C) Each party has relatively independent organizations that exist at all levels of government.
    (D) Party leadership is hierarchical, so that decisions are dispersed from the national level to the state and local levels.

GO ON TO THE NEXT PAGE.

32. Which of the following laws or court cases served to grant citizenship to freed enslaved people?

    (A) *Brown v. Board of Education* decision
    (B) Missouri Compromise
    (C) Jim Crow laws
    (D) Fourteenth Amendment

33. The president solely chooses the staff for which of the following?

    (A) Peace Corps
    (B) White House Office
    (C) Senate Committee on Appropriations
    (D) House Committee on Foreign Affairs

34. Which of the following processes best exemplifies the principle of federalism in the United States government?

    (A) Amending the United States Constitution
    (B) Imposing export taxes
    (C) Spending treasury money without the passage of an appropriations bill
    (D) Granting titles of nobility

35. Which of the following statements about voting populations is most accurate?

    (A) Individuals are less likely to vote in a closely contested race.
    (B) Voters are more likely to vote at age 18 than they are at age 65.
    (C) An individual with a graduate degree is more likely to vote than an individual who has only a high school diploma.
    (D) Affluent individuals are less likely to vote than impoverished individuals.

36. The majority of state legislatures do which of the following?

    (A) Redraw congressional district boundaries
    (B) Elect a new state governor
    (C) Evaluate the physical accessibility of polling venues
    (D) Decide where to construct new elementary schools

37. While redistricting for congressional representation, a group of Republican politicians decides to split the voters in an urban area among several suburban districts. In the next election, Republican candidates win in all the affected districts. Which of the following best explains the reason for these results?

    (A) The districts ran their elections a week earlier than was customary in the past.
    (B) Local newspapers in the urban district ran editorials that were biased against Democrat candidates.
    (C) As a result of the most recent census data, the number of candidates for the House of Representatives had been reapportioned.
    (D) The suburban districts were gerrymandered to ensure a Republican majority in the new districts.

38. The First Amendment to the Constitution protects which of the following rights of American citizens?

    (A) To petition the government for a redress of grievances
    (B) The right to keep and bear arms
    (C) The lack of obligation to quarter soldiers in times of war
    (D) Protection from cruel and unusual punishment

39. Although Maryland was originally settled by Catholics, Catholicism is not its official state religion because this would be a violation of which portion of the Constitution?

    (A) The establishment clause
    (B) The Nineteenth Amendment
    (C) The inevitable discovery rule
    (D) The Seventh Amendment

GO ON TO THE NEXT PAGE.

40. Which of the following is a method that lobbyists commonly use to try to endear themselves to legislators?

   (A) The lobbyist may spread negative propaganda about the legislator to the opposing political party.
   (B) The lobbyist may publicly endorse candidates for office that may challenge the legislator in a midterm election.
   (C) The lobbyist may socialize with the legislator at informal gatherings.
   (D) The lobbyist may attempt to acquire corporate campaign donations for the legislator.

41. Which of the following best describes a block grant?

   (A) Money provided to individuals to fund research projects
   (B) Funds with few restrictions that are provided to state or local governments for general purpose use
   (C) Funds distributed among states according to a set formula
   (D) Money that can be used only for a specific purpose

42. Which of the following practices became illegal only after the Voting Rights Act of 1965?

   (A) Barring women from voting
   (B) Race-based discrimination in the workplace
   (C) Barring racial minorities from voting
   (D) Using literacy tests at voting centers

43. Which of the following is an accurate comparison of civil rights and civil liberties?

	Civil Rights	Civil Liberties
(A)	Are affirmed by the equal protection clause	Are affirmed by the due process clause
(B)	Are enshrined in the Constitution	Were nullified by the Civil Rights Act of 1964
(C)	Extend only to minorities who need protection	Are granted to all U.S. citizens regardless of race, national origin, religion, or sex
(D)	Are protected by the Fourth Amendment	Are ensured by the USA Patriot Act

44. Which of the following is an accurate comparison of the Fourth Amendment and the Fifth Amendment?

	Fourth Amendment	Fifth Amendment
(A)	The individual right to bear arms	Freedom from self-incrimination
(B)	Prohibits government collection of digital metadata	Prohibits double jeopardy
(C)	Rarely challenged in state courts	Often challenged in Supreme Court cases
(D)	Allows for government seizure of property	Allows for government seizure of real estate

45. Which of the following is an accurate comparison of the powers of Congress and the powers of the president?

	Congress	The President
(A)	Passes a federal budget	Collects taxes
(B)	Members' service is not term-limited	Is limited to serve no more than two terms of office
(C)	Declares war	Confirms Supreme Court nominees
(D)	Signs Executive Orders	Has veto power

GO ON TO THE NEXT PAGE.

46. Which of the following is an accurate comparison of the two court cases?

	Baker v. Carr (1961)	*Shaw v. Reno* (1993)
(A)	"One person, one vote"	Restricted racial gerrymandering
(B)	Prohibited redistricting in Southern states	Prohibited gerrymandering
(C)	Enabled courts to intervene in congressional redistricting	Ended court interference in congressional redistricting
(D)	Ruled that redistricting based solely on race was unconstitutional	Ruled that redistricting must comply with the Civil Rights Act of 1965

47. Which of the following is an accurate comparison of the Speaker of the House and the President of the Senate?

	Speaker of the House	**President of the Senate**
(A)	Can initiate the legislative process by proposing bills	Cannot initiate the legislative process by proposing bills
(B)	Serves a six-year term	Serves a two-year term
(C)	Regularly participates in floor debates	Rarely participates in floor debates
(D)	Assumes the presidency if both the president and vice president die or otherwise become disqualified from serving in office	Is also the vice president of the United States

48. Which of the following cases established the precedent that a municipality could not restrict Americans' Second Amendment Rights?

(A) *Baker v. Carr* (1962)
(B) *Gideon v. Wainwright* (1963)
(C) *United States v. Lopez* (1995)
(D) *McDonald v. Chicago* (2010)

49. A president wishes to reduce the number of inmates in federal prisons. Which of the following is a power mandated by the Constitution that the president could use to accomplish this?

(A) Ratifying a treaty
(B) Overriding a legislative veto
(C) Granting reprieves and pardons
(D) Formally declaring war upon an enemy nation

50. Which of the following is an example of "horse race journalism"?

(A) A news story focuses on a politician's scandals rather than achievements.
(B) A news anchor reports an event before the station's rivals.
(C) A reporter announces which candidate leads in a public opinion poll.
(D) A newspaper editor prints stories about long-term political developments.

51. Which of the following is a direct result of an electoral system that features single-member districts?

(A) Only two major parties can successfully be supported.
(B) National campaigns can be conducted without incurring great expense.
(C) Third parties can be as successful as the two major political parties can.
(D) Each political party tends to focus its campaign on a single issue.

52. Which of the following is true under the system of checks and balances?

(A) The president's nominees must be approved by the House of Representatives before taking office.
(B) Two-thirds of the Senate must approve treaties negotiated by the president.
(C) The president can override a congressional veto and pass laws.
(D) Congress cannot override a presidential veto.

GO ON TO THE NEXT PAGE.

53. What is true about the majority of Supreme Court justices?

    (A) They are appointed by presidents of the same political party.
    (B) They have no prior judicial experience.
    (C) They switch party affiliation during their term.
    (D) They stay on the court for only a decade.

54. Which of the following is required under federal election laws?

    (A) In an area that has a substantial community of non-English speakers, voters must be provided with ballots in their native language.
    (B) In an electoral district that has historically low voter turnout, polling places must be open for longer than eight hours.
    (C) In a state with a budget deficit, a tax must be collected from each voter to pay for the cost of the election.
    (D) In a region with racial diversity, congressional district lines must be drawn to guarantee that at least one elected congressperson be of a racial minority.

55. Which of the following best articulates an argument made by James Madison in Federalist No. 10?

    (A) Honest politicians can prevent factions from developing.
    (B) Factions are more likely to occur in large republics than in small ones.
    (C) The negative effects of factionalism can be reduced by a republican government.
    (D) Free elections are the people's best defense against factionalism.

STOP
END OF SECTION I
IF YOU FINISH BEFORE TIME IS CALLED, YOU MAY CHECK YOUR WORK ON THIS SECTION.
DO NOT GO ON TO SECTION II UNTIL YOU ARE TOLD TO DO SO.

UNITED STATES GOVERNMENT AND POLITICS

SECTION II

Time—1 hour and 40 minutes

<u>Directions:</u> You have 1 hour and 40 minutes to answer all four of the following questions. It is suggested that you spend approximately 20 minutes each on Questions 1, 2, and 3 and 40 minutes on Question 4. Unless directions indicate otherwise, respond to all parts of all four questions. In your response, use substantive examples where appropriate. It is recommended that you take a few minutes to plan each answer. You may plan your answers in this Questions booklet, but no credit will be given for notes written in this booklet. You will only earn credit for what you write in the Free Response booklet.

1. "The effects on the federal budget of the aging population and rapidly growing health care costs are already apparent over the ten-year horizon—especially for Social Security and Medicare—and will grow in size beyond the baseline period. Unless laws governing fiscal policy are changed—that is, spending for large benefit programs is reduced, increases in revenues are implemented, or some combination of those approaches is adopted—debt will rise sharply relative to GDP (Gross Domestic Product) after 2027."

"The Budget and Economic Outlook: 2017 to 2027"—Congressional Budget Office

After reading the scenario, respond to A, B, and C below:

(A) Explain one cause for the trend described in the scenario.

(B) Describe a power Congress or the president could use to reverse the trend outlined in the quote.

(C) Explain how the power you identified in Part B could be affected by linkage institutions.

GO ON TO THE NEXT PAGE.

Voter Turnout and Registration, Presidential Elections 2000–2020 (in percent)

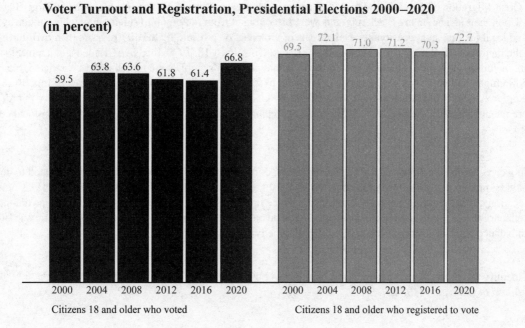

Source: U.S. Census Bureau, Current Population Survey, November supplement 2000 to 2020

2. Use the graph above and your own knowledge of U.S. politics to answer A, B, and C.

(A) Identify one four-year shift on the graph in which the percentage of voter turnout increased and explain one possible cause of that shift.

(B) Identify one four-year shift on the graph in which the percentage of voter turnout decreased and explain one possible cause of that shift.

(C) Describe a similarity or difference between voter turnout during midterm elections and voter turnout for presidential elections and identify a possible cause of this similarity or difference.

GO ON TO THE NEXT PAGE.

3. During the Great Migration of the early and mid-20th century, the greater Detroit, Michigan, area gained a large Black population. Upon their arrival, many Black migrants were discouraged from moving into suburban neighborhoods by various economic and legal factors, and occasionally even threats of violence. As a result, by the 1970s, more than two-thirds of students in the metropolitan Detroit school system were Black. On August 18, 1970, the NAACP filed suit against the state of Michigan, including Governor William Milliken, arguing that although schools were not officially segregated, the city of Detroit and Michigan had unfairly allowed racial segregation in schools by failing to take action against it. Initially, a district court judge ordered the city of Detroit to transport students by buses to schools outside of their home territory in order to achieve more racial balance in their schools. Milliken and company appealed the decision, citing the need for local control of education.

In the ensuing case, *Milliken v. Bradley* (1974), the Supreme Court ruled that school districts were not obligated to desegregate unless it could be proven that the segregation occurred as a result of racist intent on the part of the districts. The Court noted that desegregation did not require "any particular racial balance in each 'school, grade or classroom.'" Perhaps the most significant effect of the case was its implication that planned busing of students into neighboring school districts in order to create racial balance was not always necessary in order to remedy segregation.

    (A)   Identify the constitutional clause that is common to both *Milliken v. Bradley* (1974) and *Brown v. Board of Education* (1954).

    (B)   Based on the constitutional clause identified in Part A, explain why the facts of *Brown v. Board of Education* led to a different holding than the holding in *Milliken v. Bradley*.

    (C)   Explain what long-term effect the holding in *Milliken v. Bradley* may have had on public schools in the United States.

GO ON TO THE NEXT PAGE.

4. Develop an argument that explains whether a two-party system effectively prevents one faction or political party from gaining complete control of government.

In your essay, you must:

- Articulate a defensible claim or thesis that responds to the prompt and establishes a line of reasoning.
- Support your claim with at least TWO pieces of accurate and relevant information:
  - At least ONE piece of evidence must be from one of the following foundational documents:
    - U.S. Constitution
    - Federalist No. 10
    - Federalist No. 51
  - Use a second piece of evidence from another foundational document from the list or your study of the electoral process.
- Use reasoning to explain why your evidence supports your claim/thesis.
- Respond to an opposing or alternative perspective using refutation, concession, or rebuttal.

END OF EXAMINATION

Practice Test 3: Answers and Explanations

PRACTICE TEST 3 ANSWER KEY

1.	D	29.	A
2.	B	30.	C
3.	C	31.	C
4.	A	32.	D
5.	D	33.	B
6.	D	34.	A
7.	D	35.	C
8.	C	36.	A
9.	D	37.	D
10.	A	38.	A
11.	D	39.	A
12.	D	40.	C
13.	A	41.	B
14.	B	42.	D
15.	B	43.	A
16.	B	44.	D
17.	B	45.	B
18.	B	46.	A
19.	A	47.	D
20.	D	48.	D
21.	A	49.	C
22.	D	50.	C
23.	A	51.	A
24.	D	52.	B
25.	A	53.	A
26.	D	54.	A
27.	A	55.	C
28.	B		

Once you have checked your answers, return to page 4 and respond to the Reflect questions.

PRACTICE TEST 3 ANSWERS AND EXPLANATIONS

Section I: Multiple Choice

1. **D** Choice (A) is incorrect because only 34% or less of registered voters have ever identified as Independents; more than 50% would be required in order to qualify as a majority. Choice (B) is incorrect because the charts show that fewer voters identified as Republicans in the years from 2010 on as compared with 2000. (Note that this answer would've been wrong had *any* of the other years had a higher percentage.) Choice (C) is incorrect because the second chart shows that the percentage of voters who identified as Republican or leaned toward Republican decreased from 2000 to 2008. Then, in the other direction, (D) is correct because the second chart shows that the percentage of voters who identified as Democrat or leaned toward Democrat increased from 2000 to 2008.

2. **B** The charts show a general trend toward a lower proportion of Republican and Republican-leaning voters, with a higher percentage identifying as Independent or leaning Democrat. The number of Democrat leaners increases throughout the time period depicted, with a noticeable uptick after 2002. Given their statistical tie with Republicans in 2002, however, Democrats would have been unlikely to gain control of Congress, so (A) can be eliminated. Choice (C) makes a broad and sweeping statement that is unsupported by the charts and is unlikely to be true, since Independents have, at times, been the deciding factor in a close election. Choice (D) may look tempting since Bush did win the presidential election of 2000. However, we do not see evidence in the charts that there was a "large increase" in Republican voters at that time. By contrast, the correct answer, (B), speaks directly to a trend that is supported by the charts. It explains the slight difference in numbers who "identified" as Democrats or Republicans (top chart) versus those who "leaned" Democrat or Republican (bottom chart) in 1994.

3. **C** Choice (A) is incorrect because FDAP grants comprised 30.8% of state and municipal budgets in 1992, compared with 14.6% in 1972. Choice (B) is incorrect because FDAP grants decreased from $195.3 million in 1972 to $175.8 million in 1992. Eliminate (D), since the total amount of FDAP grants was $195.3 billion in 1972 and $512.4 billion in 2012. Choice (C) is correct because grants to the Department of Health and Human Services (HHS) increased from 16.5% of FDAP grants to 30.5% of FDAP grants between 1982 and 2012.

4. **A** Federal Domestic Assistance can take various forms. The key to this question is that it is asking for "financial" assistance. Choices (B) and (C) describe nonfinancial means of aid, while (D) is unrelated to the question. Only a block grant, (A), would constitute cash for a social program.

5. **D** Eliminate (A) because voters in states that favored the Republican candidate in 2000 most likely did support the Republican candidate in 2004, since the Republican candidate received more votes overall in 2004. Choice (B) can be eliminated since there is no evidence in the chart about the sizes of the individual states and how they voted. Eliminate (C) because there is no evidence in the chart regarding voter satisfaction. Choice (D) is correct because in both 2000 and 2016, the Republican candidate won the election despite having received fewer popular votes than the Democrat. Only the Electoral College system, which awards state electoral votes, could explain this disparity.

6. **D** Be careful to consider all of the answer choices before you select one. Choice (A) is not supported by the graph simply because individual states are not represented on the graph. Choice (B) is not supported by the graph because the Democratic votes increased slightly between 2000 and 2004. The graph does not support (C) because it does not indicate anything about the size of states and their voting behaviors. Choice (D) is supported by the graph because the number of Democrat votes was roughly the same in 2000 and 2004, while the number of Republican votes increased. An increase in voter turnout could explain this disparity.

7. **D** Choices (A) and (B) are incorrect because there is no data in the chart about Hispanic voters or voters from a particular region of the country. Choice (C) is incorrect, since, according to the percentages on the right side of each bar, only 17% of voters prioritized the coronavirus epidemic as their key concern, while 35% prioritized the economy. Accordingly, the correct answer is (D) because voters who prioritized racial concerns, coronavirus, and health care supported the Democratic candidate, Biden, at a rate of 91%, 82%, and 63%, respectively.

8. **C** Choice (A) is incorrect: according to the chart, voters who prioritized health care policy voted in larger percentages for Biden, the Democrat. Choice (B) is incorrect since education is unrelated to the issues measured in the chart. Choice (D) is incorrect because all races are unique in their voting behavior. You can infer that race plays a large role in how someone will vote, especially since those who care most about racial issues voted overwhelmingly for Biden. As a result, (C) is correct. Each category of issues produced dramatically different results in voting behavior.

9. **D** Read the data carefully and make comparisons as necessary. Eliminate (A) because Carter's approval ratings were mostly lower than Johnson's for both Democrats and Republicans. Choice (B) can be eliminated because Nixon's Republican approval rating rating briefly spiked in the middle of his presidency. Eliminate (C) because Reagan's approval ratings actually improved as his presidency progressed. Choice (D) is the best, since George W. Bush received an approximate approval rating of over 85% in 2000/2001, whereas Obama's approval rating from Republicans tended to decrease as his presidency went on.

10. **A** The table shows a clear and consistent trend: public approval ratings for George W. Bush declined throughout the early 2000s. What could explain both the high approval numbers in 2001 and the low approval numbers in 2008? Choice (B) could explain the former, but not the latter, so eliminate it. Choice (C) is ambiguous, since it indicates that the country was divided on the question of George W. Bush, but does not explain why. Choice (D) is true, but it would not explain Bush's high approval numbers in 2001. That leaves (A). The events of 9/11, the state of the national economy, and the results of the wars in Iraq and Afghanistan would explain President Bush's generally declining approval ratings throughout his presidency.

11. **D** Brutus states that "when the people once part with power, they can seldom or never resume it again but by force" and that they should "be careful, in the first instance, how you deposit the powers of government," which indicates that Brutus is an Anti-Federalist who would favor a government with limited power. Choices (A) and (B) are the opposite of this idea. Choice (C) may look tempting, but it is too extreme. Choice (D) is the closest to Brutus's argument.

12. **D** Choice (A) can be eliminated because the Third Amendment states that "no soldier shall, in time of peace be quartered in any house, without the consent of the owner, nor in time of war, but in a manner to be prescribed by law." Brutus does not suggest that a liberal state would allow or require the quartering of soldiers, an archaic practice. The Fifth Amendment, (B), protects against self-incrimination and is not relevant to Brutus's argument. Choice (C) is likewise irrelevant, since the Seventh Amendment allows for trial by jury in common-law cases. The Tenth Amendment states that any powers not given to the federal government by the Constitution are reserved to the states, thus curtailing the power of that government, so the best answer is (D).

13. **A** Anti-Federalist writings, including Brutus No. 1, emphasized the benefits of a small republic and warned against a large, centralized government. Since Brutus warns against a central government with too much power, opponents of his view would favor a piece of writing that advocates for a strong centralized government. The Articles of Confederation did not confer much power to Washington, and were favored by Anti-Federalists, so eliminate (B). The Declaration of Independence, (C), would have been favored by everyone except loyalists to the king. Because "Letter from a Birmingham Jail" is concerned with civil rights for disenfranchised members of society, it is unrelated to Brutus's argument, also ruling out (D). Madison's arguments in Federalist No. 10 focused on the superiority of a large republic in order to stave off factionalism, so choose (A).

14. **B** Brutus is warning people against the dangers of ceding too much power to a central government. Eliminate (A), since libertarians would share this view. Eliminate (C) and (D) as well, since conservatives and Republicans do favor a small, limited form of government and have not opposed checks and balances. That leaves (B): liberal Democrats would favor a strong central government as an effective means of accomplishing their political goals.

15. **B** According to Witko's research, "[there is a] relationship between the donation of campaign contributions and the receipt of government contracts for a sample of firms politically active between 1979 and 2006" and "companies that contributed more money to federal candidates subsequently received more contracts." Use those quotes to answer the question, and eliminate choices that exaggerate or contradict Witko's words, such as (A), which makes an extreme claim of illegality that isn't supported by the passage, or (D), which is the opposite of what Witko is saying. Don't be fooled by familiar-seeming choices; although Witko discusses contracts, they're sought by corporations, not federal candidates, which rules out (C). Choice (B) is the best paraphrase of his statements.

16. **B** The Federal Election Campaign Act, (A), was signed in 1974, but considering that the activities Witko speaks of still occurred from 1979 to 2006, it wasn't effective in curbing those effects. *Citizens United v. Federal Election Commission,* (C), is the opposite of the correct answer, since it ruled that political spending by corporations is a protected form of speech under the First Amendment and would tend to allow for some possible pay-for-play mentioned by Witko. The Fifteenth Amendment, (D), pertains to voting rights, not campaign finance. That leaves (B), and, in fact, the Bipartisan Campaign Reform Act of 2002 has attempted to limit campaign contributions by corporations by requiring them to set up PACs, rather than making unlimited contributions directly to candidates.

17. **B** On the one hand, federal candidates for elected office have a need to raise money for their campaigns. On the other hand, corporations may seek to gain influence by making contributions to these candidates. Although campaign contributions are deemed to represent "free speech" by the Supreme Court, Witko's arguments are not obviously pertinent to fair elections, so eliminate (A). Choice (C) may look tempting because it relates to campaign finance, but neither of these things is present in Witko's argument. Choice (D) is a close second, but Witko does not directly address the issue of individual rights. Choice (B) adheres the most closely to the subject of Witko's statements.

18. **B** Choices (A) and (D) are incorrect because candidates campaign more heavily in battleground states (those that do not favor either candidate) in an effort to win their electoral votes, rather than in states the candidates think they'll surely win ("safe" states that strongly support them) or lose (states that strongly support the opponent). Eliminate (C) because television advertising is not more valuable to candidates in the Plains States than elsewhere. The number of electoral votes a state has is equal to the number of senators and representatives from that state. Accordingly, states with larger populations, such as New York, have more electoral votes than states with smaller populations, such as Hawaii. Furthermore, most states have "winner-take-all" rules regarding electoral votes: this means that the candidate who wins the popular vote in a state receives all of that state's electoral votes. Therefore, during the general election, candidates tend to campaign in states with large populations in an attempt to garner a windfall of electoral votes. Choose (B).

19. **A** Use both the graphic and your knowledge of electoral votes to answer this question. You can eliminate (B) because the map clearly shows that approximately equally sized states may have a drastically different number of votes. You can also eliminate (C) because the state legislative body is irrelevant. You can also eliminate (D), as the number of electoral votes allotted to each state does change, and isn't mandated by the Constitution. This leaves the correct answer, (A), which rightly identifies that each state has a number of electors equal to the sum of its federal legislators (senators and representatives).

20. **D** The cartoon depicts a judge with gavel in hand, standing in a rainstorm with an umbrella marked "Equal Protection" to protect "U.S. Corporations," while a group of citizens looks on in frustration, unprotected from the rain by the judge's umbrella. The judge seems to be looking at the crowd of citizens with scorn. Choice (A) makes an overly broad statement by casting doubt on the fairness of the judicial system as a whole. Choice (B) is likewise too extreme since there is no evidence that corporations are overriding the rights of individuals. Choice (C) must be incorrect since the judge is using the equal protection clause to protect corporations. This leaves (D), which is best supported by the cartoon: the judge's so-called Equal Protection umbrella shields corporations from the rain, but not the citizen onlookers.

21. **A** An opponent of this cartoon would have to find an example of a case that shows the opposite of what the cartoon claims, in other words, a situation in which the equal protection clause was used to protect the rights of individuals. Use POE to rule out any case that does not use the Fourteenth Amendment to support the advancement of equality. Choice (B), *Engel v. Vitale*, is not a good match since it pertains to the establishment clause, prohibiting public school sponsorship of religious activities. *New York Times Co. v. United States* bolstered freedom of the press, so eliminate (C), and *Shaw v. Reno* pertains to legislative redistricting, so also get rid of (D). This leaves *Brown v. Board of Education*, (A), as the best choice, since it used the equal protection clause of the Fourteenth Amendment to ban segregation in schools,

arguing that minority children deserved equal protection under the law. As this did not concern the rights of corporations, it would serve as an effective critique of the cartoon's message.

22. **D** Choices (A) and (B) are incorrect because women comprised only 8%, 19%, 22%, and 24% of Reagan, GHW Bush, GW Bush, and Trump appointments, respectively; on the other hand, women comprised 16%, 28%, 42%, and 77% of the remaining presidents' appointments. Choice (C) is unsupported because we do not know President Clinton's total number of appointments, only the breakdown by gender. Choice (D) is correct because 77% of President Biden's appointments have been women, the highest percentage of all the presidents shown.

23. **A** Advocates for affirmative action support the hiring of certain minority groups and women with the purpose of creating more diversity in positions of power or leadership. Choices (B) and (D) contradict this notion. Choice (C) may look tempting, but, if true, would not explain why it is desirable to choose candidates on the basis of their race or gender. Choice (A) is best supported by the table and the philosophy behind affirmative action. According to the second chart, white judges far outnumber racial minorities, which an advocate for affirmative action may interpret as necessitating a deliberate manipulation of the racial makeup of judges in order to provide adequate representation to minority groups.

24. **D** Individuals are actually *less* likely to vote when they believe they know who will win an election, so (D) is the best choice. The other choices do not accurately reflect voting behavior in the United States and therefore can be eliminated.

25. **A** Look at each scenario. Rule out the ones that are irrelevant or impractical, and then evaluate which of any that remain would *most likely* result in the overturning of a veto. In this case, both (C) and (D) are unrelated to presidential vetoes and can be cut. Now, for (B), it's true that Congress might consider overriding a veto if the public were openly opposed to it. However, this would still require Congress to reach a two-thirds majority, which is likely to occur only if a single party has a strong majority in each house. That scenario is described by (A), because if 30% of senators and representatives are in the president's party, then about 70% are not, and that makes (A) the best answer.

26. **D** If you can't remember the Tenth Amendment, try to eliminate any choices that you know correspond to a different amendment. Choice (A) is the Seventh Amendment, (B) is the Nineteenth, and (C) is the Twenty-Sixth. The Tenth Amendment states that any powers not given to the federal government by the Constitution remain with the states, so the best answer is (D).

27. **A** Choice (B) can be eliminated because the Supreme Court rarely declares a mistrial. Choice (D) is incorrect because the Supreme Court hears the arguments of both sides without favoring either one. Choice (A) is correct for two main reasons: the Supreme Court will not grant appeal until all legal options in the lower appellate courts have been attempted, and the Supreme Court usually agrees with the lower court decision. (Choice (C) is incorrect because of this agreement.)

28. **B** Federalism is the principle that the federal government shares power with state and local governments. Choice (A) is incorrect because a confederation is a loose association of relatively independent states; in such a system, most power is left to the states and the cooperation described in the question is unlikely. Eliminate (C) because grants do not necessarily require collaboration with the federal government. The

theory of dual federalism, popular in the early history of the United States, is that the national and state governments operate largely independently from each other. Since this is not what's described in the question, eliminate (D). Fiscal, or cooperative, federalism occurs when all three levels of government work together on a project and the funds come from the federal government, so (B) is the best choice.

29. **A**   If you don't remember the specifics, try to eliminate any tasks that you know fall under the responsibilities of a different committee. Choice (B) describes the role of the House Administration Committee, (C) corresponds to the Natural Resources Committee, and (D) matches the Ethics Committee. The Rules Committee sets the conditions for debate and amendment of most legislation, so choose (A).

30. **C**   The commerce clause (Article 1, Section 8, Clause 3) of the Constitution gives the federal government the power to regulate interstate commerce. Choice (A) is incorrect because the judicial branch is responsible for releasing detainees following unlawful arrest. Choice (B) is incorrect because this is a power granted to Congress by other clauses in Article 1, Section 8. Choice (D) is incorrect because Article 1, Section 9 prohibits Congress from passing bills of attainder. It is fair to say that the commerce clause has been used to increase the power of the national government, (C).

31. **C**   Political parties have organizations at the national, state, and local levels, so eliminate (A). They are not, however, organized in a way in which all power is enshrined at the national level, whose decisions are issued to the state and local levels, so eliminate (B) and (D). Instead, a political party is something of a hodgepodge of organizations at the national, state, and local levels. These organizations operate largely independently of each other, so (C) is the best choice.

32. **D**   Prior to the Civil War, the Supreme Court ruled that African Americans could not become U.S. citizens and that Congress could not prohibit slavery in the territories. The decision overturned the Missouri Compromise, which prohibited slavery in certain territories, so eliminate (B). *Brown* ended school segregation long after freed enslaved people were granted citizenship, so eliminate (A). Jim Crow laws were those passed by Southern states to restrict African Americans' freedoms after the Civil War, so eliminate (C). Choice (D) is correct because the Fourteenth Amendment granted African Americans citizenship.

33. **B**   Note the use of the word *chooses* and not *nominates* in the question stem. Someone nominated, like the director of the Peace Corps, (A), must still be confirmed by the Senate. Eliminate (C) and (D), since party conference members select Senate and House committee members prior to the start of a new Congress. The Reorganization Plan 1 of 1939 and Executive Order 8248 allow the president to select the staff for the White House Office; this makes (B) the best answer. The president has the ability to both organize and staff the White House Office as they desire.

34. **A**   Choices (B), (C), and (D) can be eliminated because the Constitution prohibits the federal government from engaging in each of these acts. Under federalism, both national and local governments hold power; certain powers are exclusive to the national government, others exist solely for use by the states, and still others are shared by the two. The process of amending the Constitution illustrates this sharing of power, making (A) the best answer.

35. **C** Choice (A) can be eliminated because individuals are more likely to vote in a tight race. Eliminate (B) because younger voters are less likely to vote than older voters. Choice (D) can be eliminated because wealthy individuals are more likely to vote than economically disadvantaged individuals. Education plays a significant role in voter turnout: the more educated an individual, the more likely they will vote in an election, so (C) is the best choice.

36. **A** If you can't identify the correct answer, try to eliminate the choices that you know aren't performed by state legislatures. Choice (B) can be eliminated because eligible voters in each state are responsible for electing the state governors. Eliminate (C) because the U.S. Department of Justice is authorized by the Americans with Disabilities Act to be responsible for evaluating the physical accessibility of polling venues. Choice (D) can be eliminated because school districts decide whether or not to construct new schools. This leaves the correct answer, (A): following the release of census data every 10 years, the congressional districts are redrawn. In most states, the state legislature performs this task.

37. **D** Choice (A) can be eliminated because changing the date of an election would not favor one party's candidates over another. Eliminate (B) since the bias of one district's media would not explain the overall election results, nor do we know what political biases may have existed in other newspapers, or in those same newspapers in prior elections. Choice (C) can be eliminated because reapportionment refers to the process by which census data is used to redraw congressional districts and redistribute seats among states in the House of Representatives. It has no impact on voter behavior. The practice of drawing congressional district lines in an attempt to give one party a benefit over another is referred to as gerrymandering, so (D) is the best answer. If the urban voters were Democrats, distributing their votes over largely Republican suburban districts would dilute their collective impact and allow for Republican majorities to decide the elections.

38. **A** Eliminate (B) because the Second Amendment states that a "well regulated militia, being necessary to the security of a free state, the right of the people to keep and bear arms, shall not be infringed." Choice (C) can be eliminated because the Third Amendment states that "no soldier shall, in time of peace be quartered in any house, without the consent of the owner, nor in time of war, but in a manner to be prescribed by law." Eliminate (D) because the Eighth Amendment states that "excessive bail shall not be required, nor excessive fines imposed, nor cruel and unusual punishments inflicted." According to the Constitution, the First Amendment, (A), states that "Congress shall make no law respecting an establishment of religion, or prohibiting the free exercise thereof; or abridging the freedom of speech, or of the press; or the right of the people to peaceably assemble, and to petition the government for a redress of grievances."

39. **A** Choice (B) can be eliminated because the Nineteenth Amendment granted women the right to vote. Eliminate (C) because the inevitable discovery rule allows the use of illegally acquired evidence if a court agrees the evidence would have eventually been gathered by legal means. Choice (D) can be eliminated because the Seventh Amendment provides individuals with the right to a jury trial in civil cases. The establishment clause prevents the government from forming a state religion, so choose (A).

40. **C** Since the question is asking about how a lobbyist might try to endear him or herself to a legislator (that is, attempt to befriend or find common cause with), eliminate (A) and (B). These actions would be antagonistic to the legislator, not persuasive. While lobbyists and interest groups are allowed to provide financial support for a candidate, corporations, trade groups, and unions are forbidden by law to do so; instead, a corporation must form a political action committee (PAC) in order to make donations. Eliminate (D). Choice (C) is the best. Lobbyists can legally influence legislators through soft means, such as through informal socializing (e.g., buying them lunch).

41. **B** Eliminate (A), (C), and (D) because those answers represent project, formula, and categorical grants, respectively. A block grant, (B), is a large amount of money provided by the federal government to state or local governments with only general guidelines regarding its use. Aside from the overall guidelines, state and local governments have the power to decide the best way in which to spend the grant money.

42. **D** Eliminate (A), (B), and (C) because those changes occurred with the passage of the Nineteenth Amendment, the Civil Rights Act, and the Fifteenth Amendment, respectively. The Voting Rights Act of 1965 gave federal officials the power to register voters, suspended literacy tests, and prohibited states from altering voting procedures without federal permission, so choose (D).

43. **A** Civil liberties deal with the fundamental freedoms of all Americans, protecting citizens from undue restrictions. Civil rights ensure that equal protection under the law is available to all, so that no groups find themselves disenfranchised. Eliminate (B), since civil liberties do not conflict with civil rights. Choice (C) is incorrect since civil rights should be granted to all. Choice (D) is wrong on both counts since the Fourth Amendment is more pertinent to civil liberties (the prohibition of unlawful search and seizure), and the USA Patriot Act allows for certain collections of private information by the government. Choice (A) is the best answer: the equal protection and due process clauses in the Fourteenth Amendment have been used to defend civil rights and civil liberties, respectively.

44. **D** The Fourth Amendment to the United States Constitution prohibits unreasonable searches and seizures, while the Fifth Amendment protects individuals from being compelled to be witnesses against themselves in criminal cases, provides for a grand jury, protects against double jeopardy, and allows for eminent domain. Eliminate (A), since the Second, not the Fourth, Amendment protects the right to bear arms. Choice (B) is incorrect because the Fourth Amendment does not specifically prohibit government collection of digital metadata, as the technology did not exist during the Amendment's writing. Choice (C) is not true on either count. Choice (D) is the best: according to the Fourth Amendment, government can seize property for "lawful" reasons such as evidence collection or civil forfeiture. Likewise, the Fifth Amendment does allow for eminent domain seizure of real estate, as long as just compensation is provided in return.

45. **B** This question is testing you on the separation of powers delineated in the Constitution. Choice (A) is wrong since the Congress and the Treasury collect taxes, not the president. Choice (C) is incorrect because the president nominates Supreme Court justices, while the Senate confirms them. Choice (D) is wrong, given that the president signs executive orders, not Congress. That leaves (B); presidents are term-limited, whereas members of Congress are not.

46.　**A**　Both of these Supreme Court cases deal with congressional redistricting but have some important differences. *Baker v. Carr* opened the door to equal protection challenges to redistricting and established the "one person, one vote" doctrine, holding that each individual had to be weighted equally in legislative apportionment. Pay close attention to the extremes used: you can eliminate (B) because redistricting wasn't prohibited in Southern states. Also focus on whether the categories apply: *Shaw v. Reno*, not *Baker v. Carr,* had to do with gerrymandering based on racial grounds, so eliminate (D). Choice (A) is the best match.

47.　**D**　The Speaker of the House, an office established by the Constitution, is the presiding officer of the U.S. House of Representatives. The Speaker neither initiates legislation nor personally participates in debates, so eliminate (A) and (C). Choice (B) reverses the correct term length of each congressional body. That leaves (D) as the correct answer. The Speaker of the House is next in the line of presidential succession behind the vice president, and the vice president is also the president of the Senate, able to cast a tie-breaking vote in that body, if necessary.

48.　**D**　If you're unsure of the answer, try to rule out the cases that you are familiar with but that don't match this scenario. Eliminate (A) because *Baker v. Carr* did not concern guns but rather the judiciary's ability to interfere with congressional redistricting. Eliminate (B) because *Gideon v. Wainwright* ruled that states have to provide lawyers to defendants in criminal cases. Eliminate (C) because even though *United States v. Lopez* concerned guns, the ruling limited the federal government's power on gun control, not municipalities' ability to regulate gun ownership. In *McDonald v. Chicago,* the court ruled that the cities could not restrict gun ownership, so choose (D).

49.　**C**　Since the president only has the power to negotiate treaties, which must be ratified by two-thirds of the Senate and cannot supersede a congressional veto override, (A) and (B) can be eliminated. While the president is the commander in chief of the armed forces and can deploy troops, only Congress has the power to declare war, so eliminate (D). Choice (C) is the only answer that represents a true power of the presidency.

50.　**C**　"Horse race journalism" refers to the media practice of focusing its reports on how candidates fare relative to each other in public opinion polls rather than on substantive issues in the campaigns. This makes (C) the best answer. The other choices are incorrect because they are not about campaigns. Even if these other choices took place during a campaign, they would still be incorrect because they do not draw attention to the relative positions of the candidates in the polls.

51.　**A**　Choice (B) is incorrect because national campaigns require a great deal of money to plan and implement, regardless of the electoral system. Choice (C) can be eliminated because a third party that receives 10% of the votes in every district, for example, does not receive 10% of the seats in the legislature; such a party would receive no representation. The House of Representatives and many state legislatures are based on a system of single-member districts. This system leads to the creation of large parties that try to appeal to a wide voting base to win as many votes as possible; therefore, eliminate (D). Choice (A) is the best answer.

52.   **B**   Choice (A) is false, as the confirmation of nominees is part of the Senate's (not the House's) "advice and consent" power, found in Article II, Section 2 of the Constitution. Likewise, only Congress can pass laws, and only the president can veto laws. Congress can override this veto with a two-thirds majority, which rules out (D), but the president cannot override the Congress's presidential veto, so (C) is also out. This leaves (B), which correctly states that two-thirds of the Senate must approve a treaty.

53.   **A**   Pay attention to the extremes in this question, which talks about what is true for the *majority* of justices, not one or two of them. The majority of Supreme Court justices have had some prior judicial experience, which rules out (B). While some Supreme Court justices do switch party affiliation during their term, most justices remain loyal to their original parties, so eliminate (C). Choice (D) is incorrect because the average tenure of a Supreme Court justice is 16 years. Presidents appoint Supreme Court justices with political views similar to their own: therefore, (A) is the best answer.

54.   **A**   Subsequent amendments to the Voting Rights Act of 1965 have aimed to protect language minority groups. To protect minority groups from being denied the right to vote based solely on language, federal election laws require that, in areas where more than 5% of the voting population belongs to a single language minority, election materials be provided in that minority's preferred language. The other answer choices are not true and, in some cases, as with the poll tax suggested by (C), are specifically illegal based on federal election laws.

55.   **C**   Recall that in *The Federalist Papers*, Alexander Hamilton, James Madison, and John Jay argued in favor of states ratifying the Constitution. Rule out choices that are at odds with this, such as (B). Beware also of extremes like (A): factions can emerge even when politicians are honest. Also note that while (D) may be something the founders believed, it is off-topic for this question; it isn't what was argued in Federalist No. 10. The correct answer is (C), as James Madison argued that the federal government would protect individual liberties better than states and that a republican system of government would prevent a majority from oppressing a minority.

Section II: Free Response

Remember that you need to answer all four free-response questions in 1 hour and 40 minutes, so you do not have time to waste, nor can you skip any questions. Nevertheless, you should take time to brainstorm some ideas and to organize what you come up with before you start to write each response. Otherwise, your responses will probably be incomplete, disorganized, or both.

You should take about 20 minutes each for Questions 1, 2, and 3 and about 40 minutes for Question 4. Make sure you read each question carefully and respond directly to each of its components in your response. The questions are about broad issues, but they ask for specific information. A general free response that fails to address specific concerns raised by the question will not earn a high score. Your replies to Questions 1–3 should be brief and to the point. The information below represents what you should consider before writing a concise answer.

Question 1

(A)   Explain one cause for the trend described in the scenario.

Begin by identifying the trend, which is that spending by Social Security and Health and Human Services has increased dramatically during the past few decades, and, according to the Congressional Budget Office (CBO) report, will continue to increase until 2027.

Any one of the following can be used to explain a cause for that trend:

* The senior citizen population has been steadily increasing throughout the past few decades due to better medical care, more active lifestyles in older populations, and a general increase in the U.S. population. Seniors collect Social Security payments for longer periods of time than in generations past. The increased senior population led to higher enrollment in Medicare, which provides government-funded medical insurance for seniors. Since Medicare is a social insurance program funded by the U.S. government, higher enrollment in the program resulted in a rise in its cost, and the agency's budget ate up a higher percentage of the national budget. In fact, almost half of the U.S. budget is devoted to mandatory spending such as Social Security, Medicare, and Medicaid.

* Health care costs are rising in the United States. Medicare and Medicaid costs are directly tied to the cost of medicine in private systems. These costs, dictated by market forces, are predicted to continue to climb into the near future.

* Medicaid, a health-benefits program designed to support low-income Americans, was dramatically expanded after the passage of the Affordable Care Act (ACA) in 2010. This has resulted in a larger number of people being enrolled in the program, which ensures the long-term trend from the CBO's report.

(B)   Describe a power Congress or the president could use to reverse the trend outlined in the quote.

Remember that the CBO report mentions not only higher costs in the Social Security and Medicare/Medicaid sectors, but also revenue concerns. Possible answers include:

* Raising federal income tax rates and/or limiting federal income tax deductions
* Reducing Social Security and/or Medicare payments to high-income seniors
* Raising the eligibility age for Social Security
* Reducing Medicare eligibility and/or qualified benefits
* Reducing other budget expenditures, such as defense

Also bear in mind that presidents are responsible for submitting budgets to Congress for approval, so these two entities are directly responsible for any imbalances in spending and revenues. They are the sole channel for implementing change in either category. In addition, federal agencies cannot spend money unless funds are authorized by the House and Senate Appropriations Committees. Appropriations bills must then be signed by the president in order to give federal agencies the legal authority to spend.

(C)   Explain how the power you identified in Part B could be affected by linkage institutions.

"Linkage institutions" are channels that allow individuals to communicate their preferences to policy makers. This can include a variety of groups: political parties, interest groups, and the media. Even elections can serve to "link" the electorate to their representatives.

In general, Democrats and liberals tend to favor generous spending for Social Security and Medicare, although they may favor cutting these benefits for certain high-income citizens. Republicans and Libertarians generally support low taxes and restricted spending. Therefore, linkage institutions will influence Congress and the president in ways that correspond to their ideology. Linkage institutions can influence budgetary issues in the following ways:

- When presidents or members of Congress propose budgetary changes, nonprofit think tanks such as the Center on Budget and Policy Priorities or the Bipartisan Policy Center can evaluate these proposals and provide their endorsement (or criticism).

- Some organizations, such as the American Enterprise Institute, the Center for American Progress, the Economic Policy Institute, The Heritage Foundation, and the Roosevelt Institute Campus Network create their own budget plans and policy proposals to attempt to influence Congress.

- Specific interest groups such as the American Association of Retired People (AARP) lobby Congress to ensure that any changes to Social Security and Medicare align with their members' interests.

- Politicians often campaign by discussing specific issues relevant to Social Security and other entitlement spending. In states with high numbers of senior voters, such as Florida, representatives know that policy decisions must align with their electorate's interests.

Question 2

(A)   Identify one four-year shift on the graph in which the percentage of voter turnout increased and explain one possible cause of that shift.

Answers will vary depending on which time period you choose, but both of them are acceptable, so go with whichever you feel most comfortable describing. The following are some appropriate reasons.

- The 2004 turnout was high because of significant events that occurred between 2001 and 2004, including the September 11, 2001 terrorist attacks and the American invasions of Afghanistan and Iraq.

- Possible reasons for the high voter turnout in 2020 might include the ease of early voting and voting by mail, concerns about the coronavirus pandemic and the economy, and increased political polarization.

(B)   Identify one four-year shift on the graph in which the percentage of voter turnout decreased and explain one possible cause of that shift.

Again, the answers will vary depending on which time period you choose. Some appropriate reasons are as follows:

- Some Democrats who had supported Hillary Clinton's candidacy in 2008 may have been discouraged by her loss of the nomination and may have stayed home on Election Day.

- Black voters who had turned out in large numbers to vote for Barack Obama in 2008 may have been more apathetic in 2012, assuming that he would be reelected or perhaps disenchanted with his presidency.

- In 2016, many voters disliked both Hillary Clinton and Donald Trump and may simply have chosen not to vote that year.

(C)   Describe a similarity or difference between voter turnout during midterm elections and voter turnout for presidential elections and identify a possible cause of this similarity or difference.

Some acceptable answers include the following:

- lower media attention/interest for midterm elections
- many congressional candidates run unopposed
- fewer citizens are aware of midterm elections
- midterm elections are viewed as less important than presidential elections

Be sure to identify a reason and also explain it. For instance, if you chose the reason that many congressional candidates run unopposed, then the explanation could be that some citizens wouldn't take the time to vote when the outcome of the race is certain.

Question 3

This type of question describes a Supreme Court case that may or may not be familiar to you and asks you to compare or contrast it with a Supreme Court case that you should have studied in some depth in your AP Government class. To be successful with this type of question, you must be prepared to know the basic facts of all the required Supreme Court cases.

Here we are given a description of *Milliken v. Bradley*. In this case, the Supreme Court ruled that Detroit schools did not have to take drastic measures to desegregate. At first glance, it appears to contradict *Brown v. Board of Education*, which ordered the prompt desegregation of Southern schools in the 1950s, but *Milliken* was 20 years after *Brown*. What are the similarities and what are the differences?

(A)   Identify the constitutional clause that is common to both *Milliken v. Bradley* (1974) and *Brown v. Board of Education* (1954).

Both cases revolve around the Fourteenth Amendment's equal protection clause. *Brown* found that racial segregation was a violation of the equal protection clause. This ruling paved the way for school integration, but it did not specify an actual method for doing this effectively.

(B)   Based on the constitutional clause identified in Part A, explain why the facts of *Brown v. Board of Education* led to a different holding than the holding in *Milliken v. Bradley*.

Milliken applies to a city in which the schools were never required by law to be segregated, and, in fact, there were significant numbers of white students attending Detroit schools in the 1970s. This is in sharp contrast to the Southern schools of the pre-Civil Rights era that were deliberately segregated in order to achieve racial separation.

For years after the *Brown v. Board of Education* decision, however, some school districts were either forced or chose to counteract historical segregation by transporting students outside of their geographic areas in order to attend other schools. This practice was known as "busing" and was an attempt to achieve more racial balance in the classroom. In the 1971 case *Swann v. Charlotte-Mecklenburg Board of Education,* the Supreme Court ruled that forced busing was a legitimate way to desegregate schools. No doubt civil rights activists in Detroit may have thought that they could rightly demand busing in order to move some of their students into suburban school districts. After the *Milliken* decision, however, it was clear that busing would be required only in places where segregation had been deliberately implemented in the past.

(C)   Explain what long-term effect the holding in *Milliken v. Bradley* may have had on public schools in the United States.

The most visibly positive effect is that the deliberate segregation of schools is no longer a legal practice; some Southern schools now have roughly equal numbers of Black and white students, along with members of other races and various nationalities. *Milliken v. Bradley* held that schools need not engage in busing in order to deliberately distribute students to schools outside of their home neighborhoods. The effects of this you may have discussed could be similar to one of the following:

- Experts note that a kind of natural re-segregation may be occurring in many cities. According to the Civil Rights Project at Harvard University, re-segregation of U.S. public schools started in the late 1980s. The proportion of Black students at majority-white schools is at a level comparable to the 1960s.

- A majority of both white and Black families opposed the busing schemes of the 1970s, mainly on the grounds that it weakened local community ties. Furthermore, urban busing schemes may have accelerated "white flight" whereby white families moved out of urban school districts entirely, thereby exacerbating segregation in schools. One effect of Milliken v. Bradley was to tamp down community conflicts around busing.

- A focus on racial desegregation may create the misconception that mostly Black schools are incapable of success without the influence of white students. Some Black activists now promote the idea of largely Black schools in order to foster group cohesion and autonomy.

- In the early 1970s, some parents who opposed busing may have enrolled their children in private schools, leading to a possible "brain drain" in metropolitan school districts. After *Milliken*, this practice may have waned.

Question 4

Articulate a defensible claim.

Develop an argument that explains whether a two-party system effectively prevents one faction or political party from gaining complete control of government.

Support your claim.

Remember that you must use TWO pieces of information, one from the list of foundational documents, and another from either that same list, or from your own studies. Here's a breakdown of the three given documents, and a few other possibilities:

The Constitution

- If you are taking an "anti-two-party" stance in this essay, the U.S. Constitution would be a primary source of evidence. It does not mention political parties at all, which strongly suggests that the founders did not intend for political parties to be the sole means of maintaining a balance of power. Rather, the Constitution seeks to maintain equilibrium through the three branches of government and checks and balances, a system which does not depend on party affiliation. In fact, one could argue that the judicial branch functions most effectively when its members are nonpartisan.

Federalist No. 10

- This document could be used to support either a pro- or anti-party stance. In Federalist No. 10, James Madison warns of the dangers of political factions. On the other hand, he also acknowledges that political factions are inevitable. He concludes that American federalism, as embodied in the Constitution, checks the dangers of factions through the separation of powers, making it difficult for a faction to control the entire governing process. According to Madison, so many different regional and economic agendas are represented in federal and state government that it would be impossible for any single group to gain undue control or disrupt the entire system.

Federalist No. 51

- Federalist No. 51 advocates for checks and balances in government and separation of powers. One of its most important ideas is the oft-quoted phrase, "Ambition must be made to counteract ambition." Madison discusses at great length the issue of political factions and the potential for the oppression of the minority by the majority. He recognizes that factions will always be present and that the remedy for this is to have a diversity of interest groups so that no one faction can seize absolute power. This document would work well for an anti-two-party essay, although passages could be used to support the pro-party stance, as well.

Other Documents

Federalist No. 9

- In this document, Madison advocates for a large republic as a means to combat factionalism. It could be argued that a two-party system works in a large republic such as the United States. Madison argues that smaller groups devolve into "an infinity of little, jealous, clashing tumultuous commonwealths."

Washington's Farewell Address

- George Washington was not a member of any political party at the time of his presidency. As outlined in his Farewell Address, he hoped that political parties would not be formed, fearing infighting and political gridlock.

Use reasoning.

- *Pro:* Two political parties serve as checks against each other's power. If politicians are herded into two opposing camps, they are less likely to form coalitions that could dominate politics for years. Dynasties and dictators would be unlikely to hold power for any length of time under this system.

- *Con:* Political parties are not mandated by the Constitution, and many Founding Fathers were suspicious of them. Having only two political parties makes it virtually impossible for other, less powerful, political actors to have a voice. If the two parties cooperate in crucial matters, over time the two parties become so similar that they do not truly represent two different ideologies. They are "two wings on the same bird," so to speak, leading to protracted rule by a small elite.

Respond to an opposing perspective.

The two-party system in the United States has meant that two major political parties, currently the Democrats and Republicans, dominate the government. Whichever party holds the presidency and a majority in Congress is often thought of as the governing party while the minority party waits in the wings, likely to gain power in the next election cycle. Nearly all elected officials, both on the federal and state levels of government, belong to one of the two major parties. Although it is theoretically possible for third-party candidates to win elections, they rarely do. This is due to both winner-take-all election rules and the public perception that only two political parties have any chance of success. Within the two major parties, there are often liberal and conservative wings that exert influence with varying degrees of success.

In this essay prompt, you are being asked to decide whether a two-party system effectively prevents one faction or political party from gaining complete control of government. On the one hand, the two parties may serve as foils, balancing out any extremists that may seek to seize power. On the other hand, only *two* parties may lead to a concentration of power in the hands of a few, crowding out alternative solutions to problems and the representation of minority political opinions.

If you choose to argue that the two-party system does effectively prevent one faction or political party from gaining complete control of government, then you might cite some of the following arguments:

Opposing perspective: Two parties are not diverse enough. More than two would ensure that no one group gains too much power.

Response (Refutation): With the exceptions of the now-defunct Democratic-Republican Party of the early 19th century and the four-term reign of Franklin Delano Roosevelt, no party has ever been able to control the presidency for more than three terms. This would appear to support the idea that two-party systems encourage a fair balance of power.

Opposing perspective: The two parties are too extreme in their political views.

Response (Refutation): Since there are only two parties, politicians must take a centrist approach to politics in order to appeal to a broad swath of voters, thus preventing the rise of more radical factions.

Opposing perspective: The Founding Fathers warned against factionalism.

Response (Refutation): Although Hamilton and Madison make warning statements against political parties in *The Federalist Papers*, both ended up being core leaders in the First Party System: the Federalists and the Democratic-Republicans (Anti-Federalists).

Opposing perspective: The two political parties do not curb each other's power effectively.

Response (Refutation): Since the two parties often have control of different branches of the government (Executive and Legislative), they serve to counteract each other's power in the following ways:

- Congress can override the president's veto. But, on the other hand, Congress needs at least two-thirds of the votes in the House and the Senate in order to override a presidential veto.

- The president can nominate Supreme Court justices who could potentially strike down congressional legislation, BUT the Senate has the option to deny confirmation of a Supreme Court nominee. The Senate holds confirmation hearings for all Supreme Court nominees, and the Senate can deny the president's nominee a seat on the Supreme Court if they have a simple majority (51 votes) to defeat the nomination. (This scenario happened in 1987, when conservative Robert Bork's Supreme Court nomination was defeated in the Democratic-controlled Senate, 58–42.)

If you choose to argue that the two-party system does not effectively prevent one faction or political party from gaining complete control of government, then you might cite some of the following arguments:

Opposing perspective: Two parties prevent any one political ideology from permanently taking root.

Response (Refutation): Since there are only two parties, they are more apt to cooperate with each other in ways that make certain "factions," such as business, banking, or powerful interest groups, dominant. The two parties often promote very similar views on a particular issue, despite rhetoric that may differ somewhat.

Opposing perspective: There have always been two parties in American politics.

Response (Refutation): A two-party system has led to voter apathy, since there are fewer choices. This has led to poor voter turnout, especially in midterm elections. Many of the founders did not intend for American politics to be partisan. Political parties are not mentioned in the Constitution, President Washington was not a member of a party, and he warned of the dangers of political parties in his Farewell Address.

Opposing perspective: Having only one party would lead to a dictatorship.

Response (Refutation): Between 1815 and 1825, the Era of Good Feelings marked a time when there was only one major political party, the Democratic-Republicans. Like Washington, President James Monroe strove to downplay partisanship in making his nominations, with the ultimate goal of national unity and the elimination of parties altogether. He was unsuccessful, but the Monroe administration did not lead to some rash seizure of power. To the contrary, the federal government was very stable during this time.

HOW TO SCORE PRACTICE TEST 3

Section I: Multiple Choice

_____ × 1.0000 = _____
Number of Correct   Weighted
(out of 55)   Section I Score
                                 (Do not round)

Section II: Free Response

Question 1   _____ × 4.5833 = _____
                   (out of 3)   (Do not round)

Question 2   _____ × 3.4375 = _____
                   (out of 4)   (Do not round)

Question 3   _____ × 3.4375 = _____
                   (out of 4)   (Do not round)

Question 4   _____ × 2.2917 = _____
                   (out of 6)   (Do not round)

Sum   = _____
        Weighted Section II
        Score (Do not round)

The following conversion chart provides only a rough estimate, as scoring ranges may vary from administration to administration. Check your online Student Tools for possible updates.

AP Score Conversion Chart U.S. Government and Politics

Composite Score Range	AP Score
83–110	5
72–82	4
56–71	3
38–55	2
0–37	1

Composite Score

_____ + _____ = _____
   Weighted   Weighted   Composite Score
Section I Score   Section II Score   (Round to nearest
                                        whole number)

Practice Test 4

Completely darken bubbles with a No. 2 pencil. If you make a mistake, be sure to erase mark completely. Erase all stray marks.

1. YOUR NAME:
(Print) _____
　　　　Last　　　　　　First　　　　　　M.I.

SIGNATURE: _____ DATE: ___/___/___

HOME ADDRESS: _____
(Print)　　　　　　　　Number and Street

_____
　　　　City　　　　　　State　　　　Zip Code

PHONE NO. : _____
(Print)

IMPORTANT: Please fill in these boxes exactly as shown on the back cover of your test book.

2. TEST FORM
_____

6. DATE OF BIRTH

Month	Day		Year	
○ JAN				
○ FEB				
○ MAR	⓪	⓪	⓪	⓪
○ APR	①	①	①	①
○ MAY	②	②	②	②
○ JUN	③	③	③	③
○ JUL		④	④	④
○ AUG		⑤	⑤	⑤
○ SEP		⑥	⑥	⑥
○ OCT		⑦	⑦	⑦
○ NOV		⑧	⑧	⑧
○ DEC		⑨	⑨	⑨

3. TEST CODE

⓪	Ⓐ	⓪	⓪	⓪	⓪
①	Ⓑ	①	①	①	①
②	Ⓒ	②	②	②	②
③	Ⓓ	③	③	③	③
④	Ⓔ	④	④	④	④
⑤	Ⓕ	⑤	⑤	⑤	⑤
⑥	Ⓖ	⑥	⑥	⑥	⑥
⑦		⑦	⑦	⑦	⑦
⑧		⑧	⑧	⑧	⑧
⑨		⑨	⑨	⑨	⑨

4. REGISTRATION NUMBER

⓪	⓪	⓪	⓪	⓪	⓪
①	①	①	①	①	①
②	②	②	②	②	②
③	③	③	③	③	③
④	④	④	④	④	④
⑤	⑤	⑤	⑤	⑤	⑤
⑥	⑥	⑥	⑥	⑥	⑥
⑦	⑦	⑦	⑦	⑦	⑦
⑧	⑧	⑧	⑧	⑧	⑧
⑨	⑨	⑨	⑨	⑨	⑨

The Princeton Review®

© The Princeton Review, Inc.
FORM NO. 00001-PR

5. YOUR NAME

First 4 letters of last name				FIRST INIT	MID INIT
Ⓐ	Ⓐ	Ⓐ	Ⓐ	Ⓐ	Ⓐ
Ⓑ	Ⓑ	Ⓑ	Ⓑ	Ⓑ	Ⓑ
Ⓒ	Ⓒ	Ⓒ	Ⓒ	Ⓒ	Ⓒ
Ⓓ	Ⓓ	Ⓓ	Ⓓ	Ⓓ	Ⓓ
Ⓔ	Ⓔ	Ⓔ	Ⓔ	Ⓔ	Ⓔ
Ⓕ	Ⓕ	Ⓕ	Ⓕ	Ⓕ	Ⓕ
Ⓖ	Ⓖ	Ⓖ	Ⓖ	Ⓖ	Ⓖ
Ⓗ	Ⓗ	Ⓗ	Ⓗ	Ⓗ	Ⓗ
Ⓘ	Ⓘ	Ⓘ	Ⓘ	Ⓘ	Ⓘ
Ⓙ	Ⓙ	Ⓙ	Ⓙ	Ⓙ	Ⓙ
Ⓚ	Ⓚ	Ⓚ	Ⓚ	Ⓚ	Ⓚ
Ⓛ	Ⓛ	Ⓛ	Ⓛ	Ⓛ	Ⓛ
Ⓜ	Ⓜ	Ⓜ	Ⓜ	Ⓜ	Ⓜ
Ⓝ	Ⓝ	Ⓝ	Ⓝ	Ⓝ	Ⓝ
Ⓞ	Ⓞ	Ⓞ	Ⓞ	Ⓞ	Ⓞ
Ⓟ	Ⓟ	Ⓟ	Ⓟ	Ⓟ	Ⓟ
Ⓠ	Ⓠ	Ⓠ	Ⓠ	Ⓠ	Ⓠ
Ⓡ	Ⓡ	Ⓡ	Ⓡ	Ⓡ	Ⓡ
Ⓢ	Ⓢ	Ⓢ	Ⓢ	Ⓢ	Ⓢ
Ⓣ	Ⓣ	Ⓣ	Ⓣ	Ⓣ	Ⓣ
Ⓤ	Ⓤ	Ⓤ	Ⓤ	Ⓤ	Ⓤ
Ⓥ	Ⓥ	Ⓥ	Ⓥ	Ⓥ	Ⓥ
Ⓦ	Ⓦ	Ⓦ	Ⓦ	Ⓦ	Ⓦ
Ⓧ	Ⓧ	Ⓧ	Ⓧ	Ⓧ	Ⓧ
Ⓨ	Ⓨ	Ⓨ	Ⓨ	Ⓨ	Ⓨ
Ⓩ	Ⓩ	Ⓩ	Ⓩ	Ⓩ	Ⓩ

Section ①

Start with number 1 for each new section.
If a section has fewer questions than answer spaces, leave the extra answer spaces blank.

1. Ⓐ Ⓑ Ⓒ Ⓓ
2. Ⓐ Ⓑ Ⓒ Ⓓ
3. Ⓐ Ⓑ Ⓒ Ⓓ
4. Ⓐ Ⓑ Ⓒ Ⓓ
5. Ⓐ Ⓑ Ⓒ Ⓓ
6. Ⓐ Ⓑ Ⓒ Ⓓ
7. Ⓐ Ⓑ Ⓒ Ⓓ
8. Ⓐ Ⓑ Ⓒ Ⓓ
9. Ⓐ Ⓑ Ⓒ Ⓓ
10. Ⓐ Ⓑ Ⓒ Ⓓ
11. Ⓐ Ⓑ Ⓒ Ⓓ
12. Ⓐ Ⓑ Ⓒ Ⓓ
13. Ⓐ Ⓑ Ⓒ Ⓓ
14. Ⓐ Ⓑ Ⓒ Ⓓ
15. Ⓐ Ⓑ Ⓒ Ⓓ

16. Ⓐ Ⓑ Ⓒ Ⓓ
17. Ⓐ Ⓑ Ⓒ Ⓓ
18. Ⓐ Ⓑ Ⓒ Ⓓ
19. Ⓐ Ⓑ Ⓒ Ⓓ
20. Ⓐ Ⓑ Ⓒ Ⓓ
21. Ⓐ Ⓑ Ⓒ Ⓓ
22. Ⓐ Ⓑ Ⓒ Ⓓ
23. Ⓐ Ⓑ Ⓒ Ⓓ
24. Ⓐ Ⓑ Ⓒ Ⓓ
25. Ⓐ Ⓑ Ⓒ Ⓓ
26. Ⓐ Ⓑ Ⓒ Ⓓ
27. Ⓐ Ⓑ Ⓒ Ⓓ
28. Ⓐ Ⓑ Ⓒ Ⓓ
29. Ⓐ Ⓑ Ⓒ Ⓓ
30. Ⓐ Ⓑ Ⓒ Ⓓ

31. Ⓐ Ⓑ Ⓒ Ⓓ
32. Ⓐ Ⓑ Ⓒ Ⓓ
33. Ⓐ Ⓑ Ⓒ Ⓓ
34. Ⓐ Ⓑ Ⓒ Ⓓ
35. Ⓐ Ⓑ Ⓒ Ⓓ
36. Ⓐ Ⓑ Ⓒ Ⓓ
37. Ⓐ Ⓑ Ⓒ Ⓓ
38. Ⓐ Ⓑ Ⓒ Ⓓ
39. Ⓐ Ⓑ Ⓒ Ⓓ
40. Ⓐ Ⓑ Ⓒ Ⓓ
41. Ⓐ Ⓑ Ⓒ Ⓓ
42. Ⓐ Ⓑ Ⓒ Ⓓ
43. Ⓐ Ⓑ Ⓒ Ⓓ
44. Ⓐ Ⓑ Ⓒ Ⓓ
45. Ⓐ Ⓑ Ⓒ Ⓓ

46. Ⓐ Ⓑ Ⓒ Ⓓ
47. Ⓐ Ⓑ Ⓒ Ⓓ
48. Ⓐ Ⓑ Ⓒ Ⓓ
49. Ⓐ Ⓑ Ⓒ Ⓓ
50. Ⓐ Ⓑ Ⓒ Ⓓ
51. Ⓐ Ⓑ Ⓒ Ⓓ
52. Ⓐ Ⓑ Ⓒ Ⓓ
53. Ⓐ Ⓑ Ⓒ Ⓓ
54. Ⓐ Ⓑ Ⓒ Ⓓ
55. Ⓐ Ⓑ Ⓒ Ⓓ

AP® U.S. Government and Politics Exam

DO NOT OPEN THIS BOOKLET UNTIL YOU ARE TOLD TO DO SO.

At a Glance

Total Time
80 minutes
Number of Questions
55
Percent of Total Grade
50%
Writing Instrument
Pencil required

Instructions

Section I of this examination contains 55 multiple-choice questions. Fill in only the ovals for numbers 1 through 55 on your answer sheet.

Indicate all of your answers to the multiple-choice questions on the answer sheet. No credit will be given for anything written in this exam booklet, but you may use the booklet for notes or scratch work. After you have decided which of the suggested answers is best, completely fill in the corresponding oval on the answer sheet. Give only one answer to each question. If you change an answer, be sure that the previous mark is erased completely. Here is a sample question and answer.

Sample Question   Sample Answer

Chicago is a   Ⓐ ● Ⓒ Ⓓ
(A) state
(B) city
(C) country
(D) continent

Use your time effectively, working as quickly as you can without losing accuracy. Do not spend too much time on any one question. Go on to other questions and come back to the ones you have not answered if you have time. It is not expected that everyone will know the answers to all the multiple-choice questions.

About Guessing

Many candidates wonder whether or not to guess the answers to questions about which they are not certain. Multiple-choice scores are based on the number of questions answered correctly. Points are not deducted for incorrect answers, and no points are awarded for unanswered questions. Because points are not deducted for incorrect answers, you are encouraged to answer all multiple-choice questions. On any questions you do not know the answer to, you should eliminate as many choices as you can, and then select the best answer among the remaining choices.

GO ON TO THE NEXT PAGE.

UNITED STATES GOVERNMENT AND POLITICS

Section I

Time—80 minutes

55 Questions

<u>Directions</u>: Each of the questions or incomplete statements below is followed by four suggested answers or completions. Select the one that is best in each case and then fill in the corresponding oval on the answer sheet.

Questions 1 and 2 refer to the graph below.

Rise of the Filibuster

Cloture motions filed per legislative session

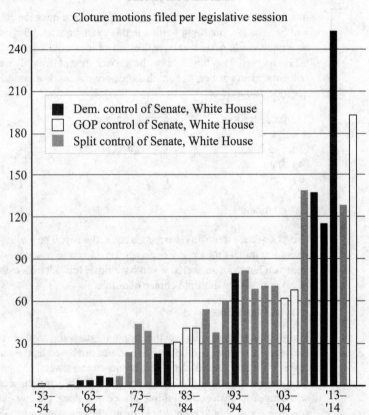

1. Based on the information in the bar graph, which of the following statements is true?

   (A) Democratic senators rarely filibuster when there is a Democratic president.
   (B) The trend in filibuster use changed dramatically in the mid-2000s.
   (C) Before the 1970s, senators were barred from using the filibuster more than a certain number of times per year.
   (D) The number of filibusters plummets when the same party controls the White House and Senate.

2. Which of the following scenarios best explains the trend in the graph?

   (A) Presidents have become less effective since the 1970s.
   (B) The number of far-right and far-left senators has decreased since the 1970s.
   (C) The number of far-right and far-left senators has increased since the 1970s.
   (D) The number of bills the Senate considers each year has increased.

GO ON TO THE NEXT PAGE.

Questions 3 and 4 refer to the table below.

Reported Rates of Voting	
Annual Family Income	**Voted Percent**
Less than $20,000	51.9
$20,000 to $29,999	56.3
$30,000 to $39,999	62.2
$40,000 to $49,999	64.7
$50,000 to $74,999	70.9
$75,000 to $99,999	76.4
$100,000 and over	79.8
Income not reported	49.0

3. Which of the following statements about the table is true?

   (A) There is no correlation between income and voter turnout.
   (B) There is a direct correlation between income and voter turnout.
   (C) There is an inverse correlation between income and voter turnout.
   (D) The largest group of eligible voters are those who make more than $100,000 per year.

4. Which of the following policies would help raise the voting participation rate for low-income working voters in America?

   (A) Make election day a national holiday.
   (B) Give Americans who vote a small tax deduction.
   (C) Strengthen voter ID laws.
   (D) Ensure that presidential candidates visit every state.

GO ON TO THE NEXT PAGE.

Questions 5 and 6 refer to the graph below.

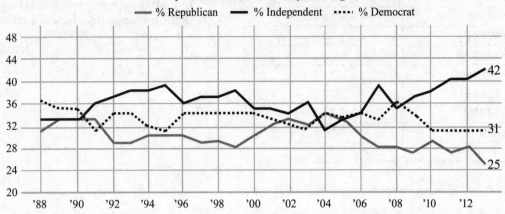

U.S. Party Identification, Yearly Averages, 1988–2013

—— % Republican ——— % Independent ∙∙∙∙∙ % Democrat

Source: Gallup, based on multiple-day polls conducted by telephone.

5. Which of the following statements about the graph is true?

   (A) Democrats were more popular than Republicans in 2003.
   (B) The number of Republicans and Democrats rose between 1988 and 2012.
   (C) The number of Republicans rose throughout the 1990s.
   (D) Independents were the only group to show positive growth between 1988 and 2012.

6. Based on how the poll was conducted, which of the following scenarios may have skewed the results?

   (A) If someone polled did not pick up the first time, the pollster called back later.
   (B) The pollster called Americans living in rural and urban areas in each state.
   (C) The pollster called people who only used landline telephones.
   (D) The pollster collected data from 10,000 people.

GO ON TO THE NEXT PAGE.

Questions 7 and 8 refer to the map below.

Federal Spending Throughout the Continental United States

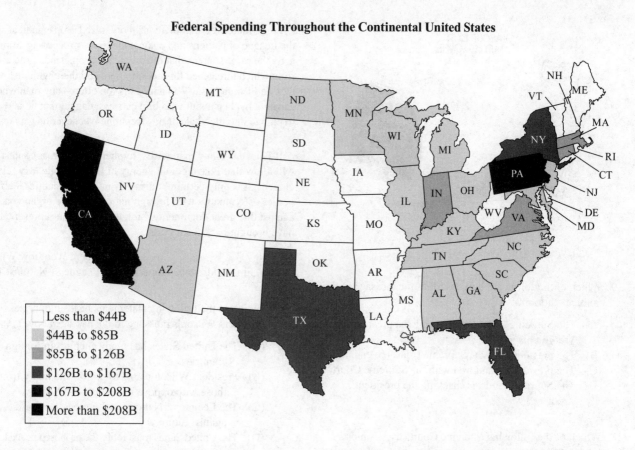

Legend:
- Less than $44B
- $44B to $85B
- $85B to $126B
- $126B to $167B
- $167B to $208B
- More than $208B

7. Which of the following is an accurate statement about the information in the map?

   (A) The Midwest receives the bulk of federal dollars.
   (B) States with many military bases receive more federal dollars than states with few military bases.
   (C) Federal spending tends to be higher in coastal states.
   (D) Federal spending is equal in every state.

8. Which of the following individuals has the most power to change the information portrayed on the map?

   (A) The president of the United States
   (B) The chair of the House Appropriations Committee
   (C) The chief justice of the Supreme Court
   (D) The Senate majority leader

GO ON TO THE NEXT PAGE.

Questions 9 and 10 refer to the political cartoon below.

9. Which of the following best describes the message in the political cartoon?

 (A) The Supreme Court is preventing the president from doing his job.
 (B) The president and the Supreme Court are enemies.
 (C) The president is annoyed with the Supreme Court.
 (D) The Supreme Court is checking the president's power.

10. Which of the following Supreme Court cases is most relevant to the topic of the cartoon?

 (A) *Marbury v. Madison* (1803)
 (B) *McCulloch v. Maryland* (1819)
 (C) *Schenck v. United States* (1919)
 (D) *Shaw v. Reno* (1993)

Questions 11–13 refer to the passage below.

I find, moreover, that there is an organized propaganda against the League of Nations and against the treaty proceeding from exactly the same sources that the organized propaganda proceeded from which threatened this country here and there with disloyalty, and I want to say—I cannot say too often—any man who carries a hyphen about with him carries a dagger that he is ready to plunge into the vitals of this Republic whenever he gets ready.

If I can catch any man with a hyphen in this great contest I will know that I have got an enemy of the Republic. My fellow citizens, it is only certain bodies of foreign sympathies, certain bodies of sympathy with foreign nations that are organized against this great document which the American representatives have brought back from Paris.

—President Woodrow Wilson,
Final address in support of the League of Nations, 1919

11. Which of the following statements best summarizes President Wilson's message in the passage above?

 (A) The United States has many enemies in foreign countries.
 (B) President Wilson wants to protect the treaty from those who oppose it.
 (C) The League of Nations will protect the world against future wars.
 (D) The United States must ratify the proposed peace treaty.

12. Which statement best explains why President Wilson is giving this speech?

 (A) The majority of foreign nations do not approve of the treaty.
 (B) American citizens do not realize how destructive World War I was.
 (C) American veterans have spoken in favor of the treaty.
 (D) The majority of the Senate does not approve of the treaty.

13. Based on the text, which of the following statements would the author most likely agree with?

 (A) Those who obstruct the ratification of the treaty work against America's interest.
 (B) The treaty requires further examination before the United States decides whether to join the League of Nations.
 (C) American citizens need to understand the economic benefits that come with joining the League of Nations.
 (D) People with hyphenated names are enemies of the state.

GO ON TO THE NEXT PAGE.

Questions 14–17 refer to the passage below.

But this nation is now in competition with malignant forces of evil who are using every instrument at their command to empty the minds of their subjects and fill those minds with slogans, determination and faith in the future. If we go on as we are, we are protecting the mind of the American public from any real contact with the menacing world that squeezes in upon us. We are engaged in a great experiment to discover whether a free public opinion can devise and direct methods of managing the affairs of the nation. We may fail. But we are handicapping ourselves needlessly…

We are currently wealthy, fat, comfortable and complacent. We have currently a built-in allergy to unpleasant or disturbing information. Our mass media reflect this. But unless we get up off our fat surpluses and recognize that television in the main is being used to distract, delude, amuse and insulate us, then television and those who finance it, those who look at it and those who work at it, may see a totally different picture too late…

This instrument can teach, it can illuminate; yes, and it can even inspire. But it can do so only to the extent that humans are determined to use it to those ends. Otherwise it is merely wires and lights in a box. There is a great and perhaps decisive battle to be fought against ignorance, intolerance and indifference. This weapon of television could be useful.

—Edward R. Murrow, Speech to the Radio-Television News Directors Association and Foundation, 1958

14. Which of the following statements best summarizes the author's message in the passage above?

   (A) Television is a refuge that Americans need to protect themselves against harsh truths.
   (B) The American people have no idea how companies are using television to delude them.
   (C) It is unknown whether television could be used as a tool to inform the public.
   (D) As it stands, television is being used as a toy, but it could be so much more.

15. Which of the following is a reasonable assumption to make about the author?

   (A) He is deeply concerned about the gullibility of the American people.
   (B) He wants to make television solely an educational tool.
   (C) He is deeply concerned about how television will impact the nation.
   (D) He feels that nothing on television should be fictitious or dishonest.

16. Which of the following reflects how modern political media coverage acts to "distract, delude, amuse and insulate us"?

   (A) Election night coverage
   (B) "Horse race" journalism during presidential campaigns
   (C) Televised presidential debates
   (D) Networks uncovering political scandals

17. With which of the following events would the author most likely disagree?

   (A) No longer requiring radio and television stations to present both sides on controversial issues
   (B) The Supreme Court's decision in *Citizens United v. FEC*
   (C) The creation of 24-hour news networks
   (D) The use of social media as a form of news dissemination

GO ON TO THE NEXT PAGE.

Questions 18 and 19 refer to the passages below.

The equality arguments for abortion rights come in two varieties. A leading proponent of one variety… is Professor Reva Siegel. She argues that we cannot explain prolife states' policies in terms of their professed concern for fetal life alone. Those policies also reflect invidious motivations, like stereotypes about women's "proper" role as mothers before all else. Other equal-protection arguments, including Professor Jack Balkin's, focus less on motivation than on impact. They suggest that prolife states impose burdens on women they would never tolerate on men. Either way, the idea is that abortion bans—viewed together with prolife states' other policies—reflect or impose sexist double standards.

Harvard Journal of Law & Public Policy, June 2022

The right to life under the Constitution is not debatable but even many in the pro-life movement have accepted that it is. Abortion takes the life of a person without due process… When pro-lifers say we want *Roe v. Wade* overturned so that each state can decide the fate of their preborn, we deny babies… constitutional protection.

Rebecca Hagelin, The Washington Times, February 2019

18. Which of the following Amendments to the Constitution could be used to defend both of the positions described in the quotes above?

(A) The First Amendment
(B) The Fourth Amendment
(C) The Tenth Amendment
(D) The Fourteenth Amendment

19. How might an opponent of abortion rights respond to the arguments put forth in the Harvard Journal quote?

(A) Abortion is causing the birth rate to plummet in the United States, leading to unsustainable economic problems for future generations.
(B) Banning abortion is not an attempt to control women's lives, but rather to elevate the rights of the unborn to their rightful place under the Constitution.
(C) Polls show that younger Americans' attitudes on abortion are changing; thus, banning abortion in all fifty states would accurately represent modern public opinion on this issue.
(D) Access to abortion in the United States has expanded in the past fifty years, not contracted.

GO ON TO THE NEXT PAGE.

Questions 20 and 21 refer to the graph below.

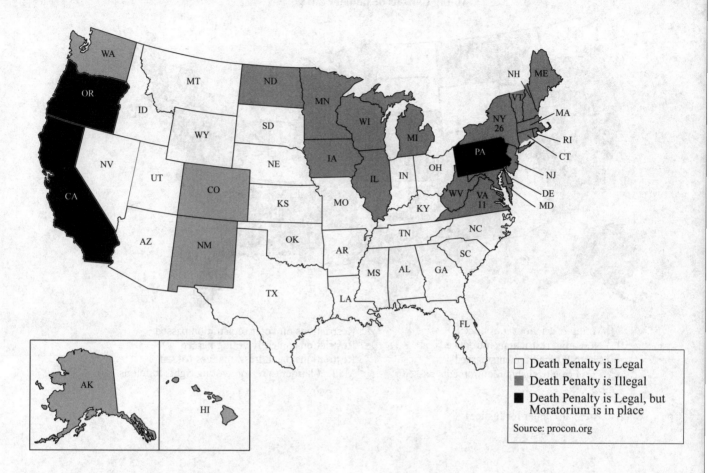

Death Penalty is Legal

Death Penalty is Illegal

Death Penalty is Legal, but Moratorium is in place

Source: procon.org

20. Which of the following statements does the data in the graphic support?

(A) The number of executions in the United States is lower than it has been in the past.

(B) Executions are on an upward trend in Southern and Rocky Mountain states.

(C) States that have banned the death penalty outnumber states in which the death penalty is legal.

(D) States that tend to vote for Democratic presidential candidates in nationwide elections are more likely to have a ban or moratorium on the death penalty as compared with states that vote reliably Republican.

21. Why did the Supreme Court impose a brief national moratorium on the death penalty in the 1970s?

(A) The Supreme Court sought to ban the use of the death penalty for partisan political reasons.

(B) Governors at the time were pardoning hundreds of condemned inmates, leading to the release of dangerous criminals and a subsequent increase in violent crime.

(C) Some states had methods of execution that were deemed to violate the Eighth Amendment's ban on "cruel and unusual punishment."

(D) States were refusing to adopt more humane execution methods, despite federal laws requiring them to do so.

GO ON TO THE NEXT PAGE.

Questions 22 and 23 refer to the map below.

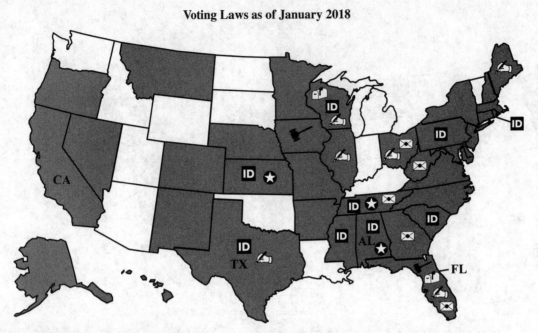

Voting Laws as of January 2018

■ Voting restrictions introduced
□ No voting restrictions introduced
ID Photo ID requirements passed
★ Proof of citizenship requirements passed

✍ Restrictions on voter registration passed
✉ Restrictions on early voting passed
Restrictions on address changes passed
Made it harder to restore voting rights to felons

Source: Brennan Center for Justice

22. Which of the following statements does the map's data best support?

(A) Texas voters must prove citizenship when they go to the polls.
(B) California adopted new voting restrictions.
(C) Alabama voters have new restrictions on early voting.
(D) Florida ex-convicts may not be able to vote.

23. Which of the following is a possible negative consequence for residents living in a state that passed one or more voting restrictions?

(A) Residents could rest assured that no voter fraud would occur in their states.
(B) Every voter was affected by their state's new law(s).
(C) Many once-eligible voters were turned away at the polls on election day.
(D) It took longer to fill out a ballot on election day.

GO ON TO THE NEXT PAGE.

24. Which of the following acts of the Confederation, later affirmed by the first American Congress, established a method of admitting new states into the United States?

    (A) The Pendleton Act
    (B) The Three-Fifths Compromise
    (C) The New Jersey Plan
    (D) The Northwest Ordinance

25. Which of the following Supreme Court cases was a victory against prior restraint?

    (A) *Schenck v. United States* (1919)
    (B) *New York Times Co. v. United States* (1971)
    (C) *Engel v. Vitale* (1962)
    (D) *Tinker v. Des Moines* (1969)

26. Which action would a Keynesian economist most favor?

    (A) An increase in domestic government spending
    (B) No change in domestic government spending
    (C) Tax cuts
    (D) An increase in prime interest rates

27. Which of the following best describes an iron triangle?

    (A) An agreement between the secretaries of state, defense, and treasury
    (B) The union of the army, navy, and air force
    (C) Another name for the three branches of government
    (D) A policy-making group made of a committee of Congress, an interest group, and a bureaucratic agency

28. Which of the following actions includes an example of logrolling?

    (A) Representative Smith helps pass a bill that brings government spending to his home district.
    (B) Representatives Smith and Adams have a heated debate on the House floor.
    (C) Representatives Smith and Adams agree to vote on each other's bills.
    (D) Representative Smith speaks at a fundraiser for the upcoming general election.

29. The Tenth Amendment affects the relationship between which of the following groups?

    (A) States and other states
    (B) States and foreign nations
    (C) States and private businesses
    (D) States and the federal government

30. A conservative would most likely agree with which of the following policies?

    (A) Expansion of the social safety net
    (B) More open borders to allow immigration
    (C) A robust military defense budget
    (D) Restrictions on gun ownership

31. Which of the following describes the structure of the Democratic and Republican parties?

    (A) A group of small, independent political parties
    (B) An organization that only helps candidates running for Congress or the presidency
    (C) An organization that works to elect candidates at all levels of government
    (D) A decentralized group of different ideological beliefs

32. Which of the following describes an original feature of the Senate not present in the 21st century?

    (A) State legislatures elected senators.
    (B) Senators could serve only two terms.
    (C) Senators did not play a role in declaring war.
    (D) The Supreme Court could impeach senators.

33. Which of the following programs makes up the largest percentage of the national budget?

    (A) Defense spending
    (B) Entitlements
    (C) Education
    (D) Debt payments

GO ON TO THE NEXT PAGE.

34. James Madison argued which of the following points in Federalist No. 10?

    (A) A strong, single executive can act quickly and decisively when the nation is under threat.
    (B) A Bill of Rights must exist to protect American citizens from the abuses of power by the federal government.
    (C) The abuses of power by King George III led to the United States breaking away from Great Britain.
    (D) Dividing power among different branches of government reduces the problems of factionalism.

35. The Constitution's establishment clause affects the relationship between which of the following groups?

    (A) The federal government and states
    (B) The states and racial minorities
    (C) The federal government and religion
    (D) The states and their residents

36. Which of the following scenarios describes a budget deficit?

    (A) The federal government spends $600 billion on defense each year.
    (B) The federal government raises tariffs by 15%.
    (C) The federal government borrows $150 billion to cover its expenses.
    (D) The federal government increases the currency supply.

37. If the president does not approve of a bill, what is their only option to stop the legislation if Congress has veto-proof majority?

    (A) They can use the pocket veto.
    (B) They can veto the bill.
    (C) They can send the bill back with proposed revisions.
    (D) They can call a conference committee.

38. The Supreme Court used which provision of the First Amendment when deciding *Wisconsin v. Yoder* (1972)?

    (A) Freedom of speech
    (B) Freedom of religion
    (C) Freedom of the press
    (D) Freedom of assembly

39. Which of the following describes a negative consequence of a state being the last to hold a presidential primary?

    (A) The party conventions may have already taken place.
    (B) There may be long lines to vote on primary election day.
    (C) The state may receive considerable news coverage.
    (D) One candidate may have already won a majority of delegates.

40. The National Security Council (NSC) performs which of the following duties?

    (A) Advises the president concerning foreign policy matters
    (B) Administers the federal government's programs related to space exploration
    (C) Protects the environment from human-made pollution
    (D) Screens new immigrants coming into the country

41. Which of the following scenarios involves a *writ of certiorari*?

    (A) An interest group writes a letter to the Supreme Court in favor of one side of a case.
    (B) The Supreme Court issues a ruling on a case.
    (C) The Supreme Court brings a case up from a lower court in order to review it.
    (D) A case makes its way through lower courts before finally reaching the Supreme Court.

42. Students learning about government and civics in school is an example of which of the following?

    (A) General public
    (B) Political socialization
    (C) Public agenda
    (D) Public opinion

GO ON TO THE NEXT PAGE.

43. Which of the following is an accurate comparison of the impact of *McCulloch v. Maryland* (1819) and *United States v. Lopez* (1995)?

	McCulloch v. Maryland **(1819)**	*United States v. Lopez* **(1995)**
(A)	Expanded federal power	Expanded state power
(B)	Expanded state power	Expanded federal power
(C)	Narrowed Congress's implied powers	A win for gun control activists
(D)	Dismantled the Second Bank of the United States	Restricted Congress's use of the commerce clause as justification for legislation

44. Which of the following is an accurate comparison of the enumerated and implied powers of Congress?

	Enumerated Powers	**Implied Powers**
(A)	Declaring war	Raising and supporting an army and navy
(B)	Raising revenue	Creating antipollution laws
(C)	Establishing national parks	Setting a federal minimum wage
(D)	Coining money	Paying debts

45. Which of the following is an accurate comparison of the Civil Rights Act of 1964 and the Voting Rights Act of 1965?

	The Civil Rights Act of 1964	**The Voting Rights Act of 1965**
(A)	Barred sex discrimination in education programs receiving federal funding	Required certain states and jurisdictions to receive preclearance by the federal government to change voting laws
(B)	Gave Congress expanded powers to end school segregation	Banned literacy tests for voting
(C)	Barred discrimination in public accommodations	Barred school segregation
(D)	Enacted to strengthen the Fifteenth Amendment	Barred employers from discriminating on the basis of race

46. Which of the following is an accurate comparison of the beliefs held by Liberals and Libertarians?

	Liberals	**Libertarians**
(A)	Unlikely to defend Medicare	No government interference in private property
(B)	Support low taxes for businesses	Support government welfare programs
(C)	Support progressive tax structure	Champion personal responsibility
(D)	Likely to support prayer in school	Fiscally conservative and socially liberal

47. Which of the following is an accurate comparison of the impact of the Bipartisan Campaign Reform Act of 2002 and *Citizens United v. Federal Election Commission* (2010)?

	Bipartisan Campaign Reform Act of 2002	*Citizens United v. Federal Election Commission* (2010)
(A)	Barred political advertising by corporations and labor groups within 60 days of general election	Banned unlimited political spending by corporations and labor groups
(B)	Required corporations to donate to both political parties	Made candidates release names of donors to the FEC
(C)	Controlled spending on political campaigns	Banned foreign-owned corporations from participating in political spending
(D)	Limited "soft money" donations	Authorized unlimited political spending by corporations and labor groups

GO ON TO THE NEXT PAGE.

48. Which of the following lobbying activities is illegal?

    (A) Running attack adds against a piece of legislation
    (B) Giving cash gifts to a senator
    (C) Paying private citizens to protest in the streets
    (D) Buying an expensive lunch for a group of influential House members

49. Which of the following scenarios includes an example of selective incorporation?

    (A) A state creates its own system of courts.
    (B) A state and federal government both pay for a road construction project.
    (C) People cannot espouse hate speech that advocates specific violence against a person.
    (D) Defendants in all criminal trials must have an attorney.

50. If the Supreme Court strikes down a law passed by Congress, what action can Congress take to overturn the decision?

    (A) Pass the same law again
    (B) Begin drafting a constitutional amendment
    (C) Appeal to the states to pass similar laws at the state level
    (D) Have the president impeach Supreme Court justices hostile to the law

51. The works of Baron de Montesquieu influenced which aspect of the American government?

    (A) Separation of powers
    (B) A strong executive
    (C) The number of Supreme Court justices
    (D) A bicameral legislature

52. Which of the following scenarios describes an exit poll?

    (A) A pollster asking voters whom they plan to vote for one week before the election
    (B) A pollster asking voters whom they plan to vote for just before voters enter the polls
    (C) A pollster asking voters whom they voted for just after voters have cast their ballot
    (D) A pollster asking voters whom they voted for one week after the election

53. Which of the following scenarios illustrates a legal form of affirmative action?

    (A) A university that sets racial quotas when making admissions decisions
    (B) A company that hires only African Americans
    (C) A university that considers race when making admissions decisions
    (D) A company that hires applicants only from minority groups

54. Which of the following events led to a realignment of the Democratic and Republican parties?

    (A) The end of the Cold War
    (B) The Great Recession
    (C) The Civil Rights Movement
    (D) The election of Ronald Reagan

55. A Supreme Court nominee who pledges to use *stare decisis* when ruling on a case will likely do which of the following when considering a case?

    (A) Base their decision on the Constitution
    (B) Base their decision on personal preference
    (C) Base their decision on the national mood
    (D) Base their decision on legal precedent

STOP
END OF SECTION I

IF YOU FINISH BEFORE TIME IS CALLED, YOU MAY CHECK YOUR WORK ON THIS SECTION.
DO NOT GO ON TO SECTION II UNTIL YOU ARE TOLD TO DO SO.

UNITED STATES GOVERNMENT AND POLITICS

SECTION II

Time—1 hour and 40 minutes

<u>Directions:</u> You have 1 hour and 40 minutes to answer all four of the following questions. It is suggested that you spend approximately 20 minutes each on Questions 1, 2, and 3 and 40 minutes on Question 4. Unless directions indicate otherwise, respond to all parts of all four questions. In your response, use substantive examples where appropriate. It is recommended that you take a few minutes to plan each answer. You may plan your answers in this Questions booklet, but no credit will be given for notes written in this booklet. You will only earn credit for what you write in the Free Response booklet.

1. Rep. Jenniffer González-Colón (R) filed a bill on Wednesday that would pave the way for the island to become a state no later than January 2021. The measure . . . fulfills the promises of González-Colón and Puerto Rico Gov. Ricardo Rosselló, who campaigned on a statehood platform and said statehood is a civil rights issue for Puerto Ricans. . . .

   Rep. José E. Serrano (D-N.Y.), who was born in Puerto Rico, said that if it wasn't clear that "Puerto Rico is in a colonial relationship with the United States, look at what happened after Hurricane Maria . . . they are an afterthought."

   —"Puerto Rico pushes for statehood, calling it a civil rights issue," *The Washington Post,* 2018

   (A) Describe a power Congress could use to address the comments outlined in the scenario.

   (B) In the context of the scenario, explain how the use of congressional power described in Part A can be affected by Congress's interaction with interest groups.

   (C) In the context of the scenario, explain the responsibilities of the federal government as prescribed by the Constitution.

GO ON TO THE NEXT PAGE.

Federal Outlays by Category FY 1962–FY 2017

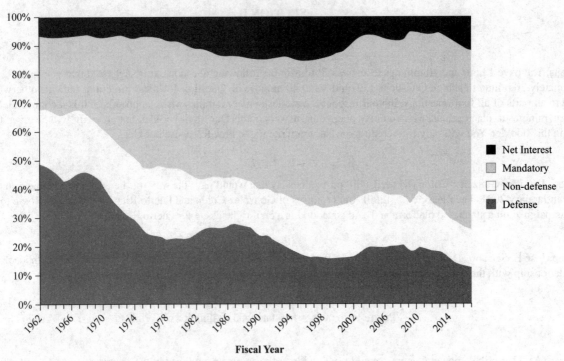

Fiscal Year

Source: OMB Historical Table 8.1—Fiscal Year 2013

2. Use the graph above and your own knowledge to answer Parts A, B, and C.

   (A) Between 1962 and 2017, in which category did federal spending decrease the most as a percentage of the national budget?

   (B) Describe a trend in the data and draw a conclusion about how it reflects a change in federal priorities over time.

   (C) Explain how federal spending as shown in the chart relates to the adoption of entitlement programs.

GO ON TO THE NEXT PAGE.

3. In the late 1980s, the Michigan State Legislature passed the Michigan Campaign Finance Act. The law stipulated that unless corporations set up a fund specifically for campaign activities, they could not participate in political spending. The Michigan Chamber of Commerce took the state government to court over the law.

In the ensuing case, *Austin v. Michigan Chamber of Commerce* (1990), the Supreme Court ruled in a 6-3 decision that the Michigan law did not violate Michigan corporations' rights. The Court cited that Michigan was rightfully trying to hinder a "type of corruption in the political arena: the corrosive and distorting effects of immense aggregations of wealth . . . that have little or no correlation to the public's support for the corporation's political ideas." This ruling was overturned by *Citizens United v. Federal Election Commission* (2010).

(A) Identify the constitutional clause that is common to both *Austin v. Michigan Chamber of Commerce* (1990) and *Citizens United v. Federal Election Commission* (2010).

(B) Based on the constitutional clause identified in Part A, explain why the facts in *Citizens United* led to a different holding than the holding in *Austin*.

(C) Describe one long-term effect of *Citizens United* and its impact on modern politics.

GO ON TO THE NEXT PAGE.

4. Develop an argument that explains whether or not a strong executive is best to ensure the long-term survival of a republican form of government.

In your essay, you must:

- Articulate a defensible claim or thesis that responds to the prompt and establishes a line of reasoning.

- Support your claim with at least TWO pieces of accurate and relevant information:
  - At least ONE piece of evidence must be from one of the following foundational documents:
    - Federalist No. 70
    - The Declaration of Independence
    - The Constitution
  - Use a second piece of evidence from another foundational document from the list or your study of civil rights:
    - Federalist No. 10
    - Federalist No. 51
    - The Articles of Confederation
- Use reasoning to explain why your evidence supports your claim/thesis.

- Respond to an opposing or alternative perspective using refutation, concession, or rebuttal.

END OF EXAMINATION

Practice Test 4:
Answers and
Explanations

PRACTICE TEST 4 ANSWER KEY

1.	B		29.	D
2.	C		30.	C
3.	B		31.	C
4.	A		32.	A
5.	D		33.	B
6.	C		34.	D
7.	C		35.	C
8.	B		36.	C
9.	D		37.	A
10.	A		38.	B
11.	B		39.	D
12.	D		40.	A
13.	A		41.	C
14.	D		42.	B
15.	C		43.	A
16.	B		44.	B
17.	A		45.	B
18.	D		46.	C
19.	B		47.	D
20.	D		48.	B
21.	C		49.	D
22.	D		50.	B
23.	C		51.	A
24.	D		52.	C
25.	B		53.	C
26.	A		54.	C
27.	D		55.	D
28.	C			

Once you have checked your answers, return to page 4 and respond to the Reflect questions.

PRACTICE TEST 4 ANSWERS AND EXPLANATIONS

Section I: Multiple Choice

1. **B**   When answering a quantitative analysis question, your first job is to look for trends in the data. In this bar chart, you can see that the number of filibusters rose significantly from the early 1970s to 2014. You can eliminate answers that conflict with this data, like (A), given that between 2012 and 2014, there were a large number of filibusters despite the Democratic Party controlling the White House and Senate. This also rules out (D), as despite small downward trends, the number of filibusters grew consistently no matter the balance of power between the Senate and White House. Also eliminate choices that cite real data but make up the rationales behind them, like (C): there was no such rule against filibustering. This leaves (B) as the correct answer; in the mid-2000s, the number of filibusters started to rise at a much faster rate than it had since the trend began in the 1960s.

2. **C**   The second question in a quantitative analysis pair will often ask you to connect the data with your prior knowledge. Choice (A) can be eliminated as the legislation being filibustered by senators does not originate with the president. Choice (B) can be eliminated as the opposite is true: the parties have become more polarized since the 1970s. Choice (D) can be eliminated as this statement was also true between 1953 and 1963, when there was no discernible increase in the number of filibusters. Therefore, (C) is correct. As senators have become more partisan, they have become more willing to use the filibuster to block legislation proposed by the other party or even by less partisan members of their own party.

3. **B**   In this question, a correlation refers to the relationship between income and voter turnout. Choice (A) is incorrect as there is a clear correlation between voter turnout and income. As income rises, so does voter participation. Choice (C) is incorrect as a reverse correlation would exist if voter turnout fell as incomes rose. Choice (D) is incorrect; although 79.8% of eligible voters who make $100,000 per year or more vote, the table does not provide information on how many voters actually participate. As a result, (B) is correct as the data represents a direct correlation: as incomes rise, so does voter turnout.

4. **A**   Many factors influence whether an eligible voter votes in a presidential election. Choice (B) is incorrect given that a "small" tax deduction may not incentivize low-income working families who largely do not pay much in federal income tax. Choice (C) is incorrect as voter ID laws sometimes decrease voting participation rates as it takes time and often money to register for them. Choice (D) is incorrect as working voters may not have the time to see the presidential candidates during candidates' visits. This leaves (A) as the correct answer. Many lower-income Americans cannot afford to take time away from work to vote. If election day were a national holiday, more Americans could go to the polls.

5. **D** When answering a question like this, Process of Elimination can quickly show you the correct answer. Choice (A) can be eliminated as Republicans were slightly more popular than Democrats in 2003. Choice (B) can be eliminated as the number of Republicans and Democrats fell between 1988 and 2012. Choice (C) can be eliminated as the number of Republicans was lower in the 1990s compared to the late 1980s and early 2000s. This leaves (D) as the correct answer: the number of Independents rose from approximately 33% in 1988 to 42% in 2012.

6. **C** Pay close attention to the wording of the question. You are being asked for the answer that would have skewed the result, creating a negative outcome. Eliminate any choice that would yield a more accurate result, like (A), which would help to collect data. Eliminate (B) because rural and urban residents often have different political views, which means that collecting from both of them would have a more representative, not skewed, result. Choice (D) can also be eliminated because 10,000 people is a large enough sample size to provide accurate polling results. By contrast, (C) is correct because calling only landlines would exclude the millions of Americans who exclusively use cell phones.

7. **C** Use the data in the map—the number of federal dollars each state receives—to answer the question. Choice (A) is incorrect as the Midwest receives fewer dollars than other states receive. The statement in (B) may be true, but as the map does not show the locations of military bases, you cannot make this determination based on the information presented. Choice (D) is incorrect as spending varies among states. The remaining answer, (C), is correct, given that the majority of the states receiving the most money (California, Texas, Florida, and New York) touch the coast. (You might have noticed that Pennsylvania is landlocked. That's why answers with extreme language are often wrong, and why (C) uses softer words like "tends to be.")

8. **B** The information shown has to do with federal spending, so begin by identifying the branch of government responsible for that and then eliminate the individuals who are from other branches. The legislative branch is what you're looking for, so eliminate (A), as the executive branch can only veto spending bills, and (C), as the judicial branch can only rule on a bill's constitutionality. The two remaining choices are both parts of the legislative branch, but you can eliminate (D); while the Senate votes on spending bills, those bills do not originate in the Senate. The individual who can most directly influence spending is one who is a member of the House Appropriations Committee, which makes (B) the correct answer.

9. **D** Political cartoons expect you to use what is happening in the picture to piece together its deeper meaning, not just the literal one. In the cartoon, a justice labeled "Supreme Court" is standing on President Obama's cape, which the justice has nailed down. The dialogue makes clear that this is about how the judicial branch limits the executive branch's power. You can eliminate (A) because it's too extreme—the justice is preventing Obama from using a specific power, not from doing his job. (It is implied that Obama is trying to do something outside the Constitution.) Choice (B) may be tempting, but be careful not to make assumptions; if the cartoon wished to depict the two as enemies, the Supreme Court would be dressed as a villain to match President Obama's superhero.

Also, (B) is another example of an extreme answer, and extreme answers are usually incorrect. Likewise, be careful about (C), which is too literal. Obama is annoyed, but that's only a small part of the cartoon's message. As a result, (D) is correct as the Supreme Court checks the president when the president performs actions that are unconstitutional.

10. **A** Given the theme, you can eliminate any choice that does not have to do with the Supreme Court's ability to declare a president's actions unconstitutional. Choices (B), (C), and (D) can be ruled out because they're about whether banks can be operated by the federal government, First Amendment rights, and gerrymandering, respectively. *Marbury* ensured that the Supreme Court had the ability to strike down federal laws and actions by the president it deemed unconstitutional, which makes (A) the correct answer.

11. **B** After World War I, America debated whether to ratify the Treaty of Versailles and join the League of Nations. If you're not sure of Wilson's stance, there's a big hint in the fact that this speech was given "in support of the League of Nations." Choice (A) is incorrect as the enemies that Wilson speaks of are American. You can rule out (C) because Wilson never mentions future wars and (D) because *must ratify* is too strong a stance to support with this text. As a result, (B) is correct: Wilson wants to protect the treaty from those who oppose its ratification.

12. **D** The purpose of a speech is often to change someone's mind, so think about whom President Wilson is trying to reach, and why. You can eliminate (A) because the president can sign a treaty without the approval of foreign nations, and he says "my fellow citizens," so he must be speaking to Americans. Choices (B) and (C) can be eliminated because the passage doesn't mention World War I or veterans. Therefore, (D) is the correct answer. The Senate must ratify treaties the president signs with foreign nations, which made Wilson give speeches such as this to pressure the Senate into supporting it.

13. **A** If a question tells you to base your answer on the text, use that to eliminate any choice that doesn't directly match what you've read. Wilson clearly supports the treaty in its current form, so eliminate (B). The League of Nations was a collective security treaty, so eliminate (C). Although Wilson says "If I can catch any man with a hyphen in this great contest I will know that I have got an enemy of the Republic," he is referring only to prominent individuals that opposed the treaty, many of whom had hyphenated names, so eliminate the overly literal (D). As a result, (A) is correct as the League of Nations treaty was intended to promote future peace. Anyone "obstructing" this could be putting peace in jeopardy, in Wilson's view.

14. **D** In this speech, Murrow ponders how television will impact the nation in the coming years. Although Murrow might agree that television serves as a refuge against the truth, his use of words like "distract" and "delude" suggests Americans don't need it, which is the opposite of (A), so eliminate it. Murrow states that Americans must "recognize" what companies are doing, which suggests that they do have some idea, so eliminate (B). Likewise, Murrow announces that television "can teach, it can illuminate; yes, and it can even inspire," which means that he thinks it can be used as a tool to inform the public, thereby ruling out (C). Murrow believes that companies are using television as a form of entertainment, but it could become a tool to enlighten the public, which means that (D) is correct.

15. **C** Although the question is asking you to make an assumption, it has to be a reasonable one—that is, supported by the passage. Eliminate any choice that isn't, like (A); while Murrow is concerned, it's not about the gullibility of Americans. You can also rule out (B) and (D), which are too extreme: Murrow doesn't "solely" want to do anything, and he doesn't feel that "nothing" fictitious should be on television, but rather it should offer other things as well (like educational programming). This leaves (C) as the correct answer: Murrow is concerned about how television will affect the nation: will television be a distraction, "merely wires and lights in a box," or will it be a weapon against "ignorance, intolerance and indifference"?

16. **B** In recent years, politics has become a form of entertainment. Choices (A), (C), and (D) can be eliminated. Although networks may use eye-catching graphics or bombastic pundits to make their points, these examples all provide useful information to Americans despite how much certain examples in recent memory may align with Murrow's quote. As a result, (B) is correct as the term "horse races" refers to the media sensationalizing elections for increased viewership. Horse races, by themselves, do not educate the public or serve a useful purpose.

17. **A** The passage provides many clues concerning Murrow's opinions about the role of media in a democratic society. Choice (B) is incorrect. Although *Citizens United* led to increased political advertising on television, the ruling concerned political donations. Choices (C) and (D) are incorrect as a 24-hour news network and social media, in theory, could give Americans access to pertinent news at any time of day. On the other hand, the repeal of the Fairness Doctrine in the late 1980s led to the creation of news networks that were no longer compelled by law to present both sides of political issues. It is likely that Murrow would see these networks as mere propaganda mouthpieces, so (A) is the correct answer.

18. **D** The question asks you which Amendment to the Constitution could be used to defend either pro-life (against abortion rights) or pro-choice (supports abortion rights) positions. Choice (A) is incorrect since the First Amendment protects free speech and freedom of religion, neither of which is relevant to the abortion debate. Choice (B) is incorrect since the Fourth Amendment protects accused criminals from unwarranted search or seizure of property. Choice (C) is incorrect since it relates to states' rights. This could potentially support a pro-life view, but not the views of the pro-choice supporters described in the Harvard Journal quote. As a result, (D) is correct since the Due Process and Equal Protection Clauses of the Fourteenth Amendment could justify Hagelin's and the opposing views, respectively.

19. **B** Remember that opponents of abortion would prefer that abortion become illegal nationwide or that states have the right to make abortion illegal within their borders. Hagelin believes in the former view. This question is specifically asking how those opponents might respond to the types of arguments described in the Harvard Journal quote. Choice (A) can be eliminated since most antiabortion arguments are not economic ones. Choice (C) can be eliminated since an appeal to public opinion does not directly address the arguments in the Harvard Journal quote. Choice (D) is incorrect since most antiabortionists would likely take the same view of abortion regardless of its prevalence. As a result, (B) is correct since those who take a stance against abortion usually focus on the rights of the unborn rather than those of birthing people.

20. **D** This question asks you to choose an answer that is not only true, but also supported by the graphic. Choice (A) is true, but an incorrect choice since the number of executions in the United States is not indicated by the graphic. Similarly, choice (B) is unsupported and incorrect since executions are mostly on a downward trend. Choice (C) is incorrect. The map would indicate that the opposite is true. As a result, (D) is correct since, with a few exceptions, "blue" or Democratic states on the map tend to have bans or moratoriums on execution (California, New York, etc.), while the "red" or Republican-leaning states (Texas, Deep South, etc.) mostly allow for capital punishment.

21. **C** The number of executions in the United States fell dramatically during the mid-20th century, though the Supreme Court did impose an effective ban on the death penalty between 1972 and 1976, the time period between two landmark cases which decided upon the constitutionality of the death penalty. Choice (A) can be eliminated since there is no evidence that the Supreme Court was motivated by partisan politics. Choice (B) can be eliminated since the states that used the death penalty before 1972 tended toward political conservatism. If these states' governors reduced inmates' sentences, they would likely have lowered their chances of reelection. Choice (D) is incorrect. If there had been a federal law in place, the Supreme Court would not have ruled that the death penalty violates the Eighth Amendment's protection against cruel and unusual punishment. This leaves (C) as the correct answer; after the 1976 Supreme Court decision, some states changed their execution methods in order not to run afoul of the Eighth Amendment.

22. **D** This question asks you to correctly identify which state is paired with the correct voting restriction. Pay close attention to the iconography and eliminate choices that do not match up. Proof of citizenship is represented by the star, but Texas doesn't have that icon, so eliminate (A). Voting restrictions were introduced in California, but they weren't adopted, so eliminate (B). Alabama requires photo ID and proof of citizenship, but *not* early voting restrictions, so eliminate (C). This leaves (D), which is correct: Florida has the gavel icon that represents the passage of legislation making it harder to restore voting rights to felons.

23. **C** It is impossible to eliminate any chance of voter fraud, so eliminate (A). Choice (B) can be eliminated as many voters were not affected by the new laws: they already had a government-issued ID, did not participate in early voting, or did not change their addresses. Choice (D) can be eliminated as voting restriction laws do not lengthen or shorten the length of time voters spend in the voting booth. Therefore, (C) is correct as many people went to the polls in 2016 only to find out that they were no longer eligible to vote due to their states' recently implemented voter restriction laws.

24. **D** Despite its many flaws, the Articles of Confederation laid out the rules and regulations for how territories can become states. Choice (A) can be eliminated as the Pendleton Act was a law designed to limit the use of political patronage positions within the executive branch. Choice (B) can be eliminated as the Three-Fifths Compromise classified each enslaved person as three-fifths of a person when it came to apportioning seats in the House of Representatives. Choice (C) can be eliminated as the New Jersey Plan was a suggested framework for the legislative branch supported by smaller states during the Constitutional Convention. As a result, (D) is correct as the Northwest Ordinance was passed by the federal government under the Articles of Confederation.

25. **B** "Prior restraint" refers to the government being able to suppress news reports in the name of national security, which in itself is a limit on the First Amendment protection of free speech. Choice (A) is incorrect as *Schenck* limited Americans' right to free speech if it posed a "clear and present danger." Choice (C) is incorrect as *Engel* stuck down mandatory prayer in public schools. Choice (D) is incorrect. Although *Tinker* upheld students' First Amendment rights, prior restraint was not at issue in the case. Therefore, (B) is correct as in *New York Times Co. v. United States*, the newspaper published the Pentagon Papers, top-secret documents that chronicled 30 years of American involvement in Vietnam. The Supreme Court ruled that the government could not invoke prior restraint to suppress the Pentagon Papers' publication.

26. **A** Keynesian economics was the basis for many of President Franklin Roosevelt's economic policies during the Great Depression. Choice (B) can be eliminated as Keynesian economics promotes government intervention during a recession. Choice (C) can be eliminated as cutting taxes aligns with laissez-faire economics. Choice (D) can be eliminated as raising the discount rate leads to high interest rates, slowing down the flow of money within the economy, and suppressing economic growth. As a result, (A) is correct: by raising government spending, the government spurs job creation and increases the rate at which money flows through the economy.

27. **D** Remember that crafting government policy involves many more people than just our elected officials. Choice (A) is incorrect as these three secretaries work together as part of the president's cabinet. Choice (B) is incorrect as the army, navy, and air force are all part of the Department of Defense. Choice (C) is incorrect as the three branches of government are known as the federal government. Therefore, (D) is correct as the term *iron triangle* refers to a congressional committee, an interest group, and a bureaucratic agency that all work together in the same field to craft policy and legislation. Each part of the triangle grants political or monetary favors to the other two parts. In other words, an iron triangle is a type of symbiotic relationship.

28. **C** "You scratch my back, I scratch yours" has been a part of political life since the invention of politics. Choice (A) can be eliminated as this action is an example of pork-barrel spending. Choice (B) can be eliminated as cooperation, not conflict, is at the heart of logrolling. Choice (D) can be eliminated as logrolling must involve at least two members of Congress. As a result, (C) is correct as logrolling refers to trading favors between elected officials. Representative Smith may not agree with Representative Adams's bill, but he will vote "aye" to ensure Representative Adams's future support.

29. **D** The Bill of Rights consists of the first 10 amendments to the Constitution. These amendments were added to the Constitution to protect Americans from abuses of power by the federal government. Choices (A), (B), and (C) are incorrect. Although the Tenth Amendment concerns the states, it does not concern the states' relationship with other states, foreign nations, or private businesses. The last of these is especially incorrect, as the Constitution does not mention private business. As a result, (D) is correct as the Tenth Amendment states that whatever powers the Constitution does not grant to the federal government remain with the states. That is why states have the power to set up their own courts, systems of education, and police forces.

30. **C** The modern political landscape is split between liberal and conservative beliefs. Liberals tend to believe in a larger government with greater social services, while conservatives tend to believe in smaller government that does not intervene in Americans' daily lives. Choices (A), (B), and (D) can be eliminated as each of these policies aligns with liberal beliefs. Liberal presidents have often promoted increased funding for the social safety net (e.g., Welfare, Medicare), promoted immigration, and supported gun control laws. Therefore, (C) is correct as conservatives favor smaller government except in the area of military spending. Since WWII, conservative presidents such as Reagan have promoted expanding America's military.

31. **C** Despite having different beliefs, the Democratic and Republican parties have a near-identical structure. Choice (A) is incorrect as both parties are unified. Choice (B) is incorrect as these parties also work at the state and local levels. Choice (D) is incorrect. Although the parties have members of varying beliefs, the parties are centralized. As a result, (C) is correct as the parties are organizations that support candidates at the local, state, and national levels.

32. **A** In many ways, the Senate of the 21st century resembles that envisioned by the Constitution's framers. However, the Senate has undergone one significant change since the writing of the Constitution. Choice (B) can be eliminated as there never were any term limits for senators. Choice (C) can be eliminated as both chambers of Congress have always had the power to declare war. Choice (D) can be eliminated as the legislative branch has always been the only branch of government with the power to impeach. Therefore, (A) is correct; until the passage of the Seventeenth Amendment in 1913, state legislatures elected senators to Congress.

33. **B** Federal spending consists of two broad categories: mandatory and discretionary. Mandatory spending refers to the government's essential programs, while discretionary spending refers to spending that Congress can easily increase or decrease from year to year. Choice (A) is incorrect. Although defense spending represents a large percentage of the national budget, it is not the largest. Choice (C) is incorrect as education is a relatively small part of the national budget. Choice (D) is incorrect for two reasons: the government pays off only the interest on the national debt, and these payments represent only a small part of the national budget. As a result, (B) is correct as entitlement programs such as Medicare and Social Security make up the most significant percentage of the national budget.

34. **D** The ideological battle between the Federalists and Anti-Federalists led to the United States adopting the Constitution and a Bill of Rights. Choice (A) can be eliminated as Alexander Hamilton made this argument in Federalist No. 70. Choice (B) can be eliminated as this is an Anti-Federalist argument. Anti-Federalists pushed these protections. Choice (C) is incorrect as this describes the content of the Declaration of Independence. As a result, (D) is correct. Although Madison conceded that factions would develop, splitting the government into three independent branches would act as a safeguard against one faction taking control of the entire government.

35. **C** The founders adopted the establishment clause based on studying the history of European empires and states. Choices (A), (B), and (D) are incorrect as the establishment clause does not affect the relationship between these groups. The Tenth Amendment affects the relationship between the government and the states, and the states must follow federal law regarding racial minorities and their residents. Therefore, (C) is correct as the establishment clause bars the federal government from adopting a state religion. The federal government and religious groups operate independently of each other and do not interfere with each other's actions or beliefs. This is why religious groups do not have to pay taxes.

36. **C** Just like when someone does not budget their money, the federal government can also go into debt if it spends more money than it has. Choice (A) can be eliminated as this figure represents the approximate amount the nation spends on defense each year; the act of spending money does not on its own raise the debt. Choice (B) can be eliminated as tariffs are taxes on foreign goods. Tariffs can lower the debt. Choice (D) can be eliminated as the currency supply does not directly affect the amount the government chooses to spend each year. As a result, (C) is correct: when the government borrows money, it creates a budget deficit. Each year, the budget deficit grows while the government pays off the interest.

37. **A** It is nearly impossible for the president to prevent a bill from becoming law if the Congress has a veto-proof majority, but they might have one option. Choice (B) is incorrect as the question stated that Congress has a veto-proof majority. Congress would simply override the president's veto. Choices (C) and (D) are incorrect as the president does not have the constitutional authority to do either of these things. Therefore, (A) is correct: if fewer than 10 days remain in the legislative session, the president can choose to take no action on a bill, which leads to its defeat. This action is known as a pocket veto. The following session, Congress would have to revive the bill and pass it early in the session so that the president could not reuse the pocket veto.

38. **B** In *Wisconsin v. Yoder* (1972), the State of Wisconsin wanted to compel Amish students to attend school after the eighth grade. Choices (A), (C), and (D) are incorrect. Although the First Amendment protects these freedoms, they were not at issue in the case. As a result, (B) is correct as the Amish community argued that their religious beliefs prompted them to take their children out of school. The Supreme Court agreed with the Amish community, affecting school attendance policies in all states home to Amish communities.

39. **D** At the beginning of a presidential election year, states hold primaries or caucuses to select the Republican and Democratic candidates for president. Each election, states jostle for position to have their primaries or caucuses as soon as possible. Choice (A) can be eliminated as party conventions take place only after the final primary and caucus. Choice (B) can be eliminated as states that have their primaries near the end of the primary season usually have lower voter turnout. Choice (C) can be eliminated as news networks give more news coverage to states that have their primaries earlier in the year. As a result, (D) is correct as by the time the last state has its primary, one candidate may already have a majority of delegates. In other words, the race is over even before the final state or states have their say.

40. **A** The National Security Council (NSC) is one of many executive departments that help the president perform his constitutional duties. Choice (B) can be eliminated as NASA is the nation's space agency. Choice (C) can be eliminated as the EPA oversees the protection of the environment. Choice (D) can be eliminated as the Department of Homeland Security oversees the screening process of foreign tourists and immigrants. As a result, (A) is correct as the NSC convenes to provide the president expert advice on foreign policy situations. The president can choose anyone to serve on the NSC. Members typically include the vice president and Joint Chiefs of Staff.

41. **C** There are two ways a case can make it to the Supreme Court. Choice (A) is incorrect as this describes an *amicus* (friend of the court) brief. Organizations write these letters to potentially sway the Supreme Court's decision. Choice (B) is incorrect as no particular term applies to the Supreme Court making a ruling on a case. Choice (D) is incorrect as this describes the way a case can make it to the court without a *writ of certiorari*. Therefore, (C) is correct; when the Supreme Court issues a *writ*, it formally requests to review a case no matter where that case is in the federal court system.

42. **B** Students learning about government and civics in school is only one part of a much larger process. Choice (A) can be eliminated as "general public" refers to all Americans, not just students. Choice (C) can be eliminated as "public agenda" refers to issues that the people and government both take action to fix. Choice (D) can be eliminated as "public opinion" refers to the public's beliefs on a range of issues. As a result, (B) is correct as school, religion, media, and socioeconomic background all influence young Americans' political socialization—people forming new ideas about politics as they age.

43. **A** Remember that in a comparison question, both parts must be correct for the answer choice to be correct. *McCulloch v. Maryland* and *United States v. Lopez* were two cases that redefined the balance of power between the states and the federal government. These cases had wildly different outcomes. Choice (B) is incorrect as switching the statements would make it correct. Choice (C) is incorrect as *McCulloch* expanded Congress's implied powers, and *Lopez* was a loss for gun control activists. Choice (D) is incorrect as even though the statement for *Lopez* is correct, *McCulloch* allowed the Second Bank of the United States to remain in business. As a result, (A) is correct as *McCulloch* expanded federal power at the expense of the states, while *Lopez* expanded state power at the expense of the federal government.

44. **B** Congress's enumerated powers are those specifically granted to it by the Constitution. Implied powers are those Congress grants itself to carry out its enumerated powers. The Constitution's elastic clause allows Congress to do this. Choice (A) can be eliminated as both of these powers are enumerated powers. Choice (C) can be eliminated as both of these powers are implied powers. Choice (D) is incorrect as both of these powers are enumerated powers. Therefore, (B) is correct as raising revenue is an enumerated power and creating antipollution laws is an implied power.

45. **B** The Civil Rights Act of 1964 and the Voting Rights Act of 1965 were only two of many pieces of legislation passed by Congress in the 1960s that expanded rights for African Americans and other minority groups. Choice (A) is incorrect as Title IX barred sex discrimination in education programs receiving federal funding. Choice (C) is incorrect as *Brown v. Board of Education* barred school segregation. Choice (D) is incorrect as the statements would need to be switched to be correct. As a result, (B) is correct as the Civil Rights Act of 1964 expanded Congress's powers to end school segregation, and the Voting Rights Act of 1965 banned literacy tests for voting.

46. **C** As the similar-sounding names imply, liberals and libertarians share some political beliefs, yet there are some key differences as well. Choice (A) can be eliminated as liberals are likely to defend Medicare. Choice (B) can be eliminated as the statements would need to be switched to be correct. Choice (D) can be eliminated as liberals are unlikely to support prayer in school. Therefore, (C) is correct as liberals support a progressive tax structure and libertarians champion personal responsibility.

47. **D** The Bipartisan Campaign Reform Act of 2002, also known as McCain-Feingold, and *Citizens United v. Federal Election Commission* (2010) both centered on the question of political spending on national elections. These events had wildly different effects on political campaigns at the local, state, and national levels. Choice (A) is incorrect as *Citizens United* allowed unlimited political spending by corporations and labor groups. Choice (B) is incorrect as corporations do not have to donate to both parties, and *Citizens United* did not force candidates to reveal donors' names. Choice (C) is incorrect as it was McCain-Feingold that put restrictions on political spending by foreign-owned corporations. As a result, (D) is correct as McCain-Feingold attempted to reign in "soft money" donations, and *Citizens United* authorized unlimited political spending by corporations and labor unions.

48. **B** In Washington, D.C., lobbyists outnumber congresspersons by approximately 20:1. As a result, congresspersons meet with lobbyists on a daily basis. Lobbyists can do much to curry favor with a political ally or destroy a political opponent, but they must follow the law. Choice (A) can be eliminated as many lobbyists work for PACs that produce these ads. Choice (C) is incorrect as lobbyists and their employers can pay private citizens to perform this kind of action. However, it would look negative for the lobbying group if word of this got out. Choice (D) is incorrect as the money lobbyists spend during these kinds of meals does not go directly to the representatives. As a result, (B) is correct as giving cash gifts to a senator constitutes bribery, which is illegal not just in this scenario, but for any federal employee and person who might approach them with a bribe.

49. **D** Selective incorporation refers to a situation in which the Supreme Court mandates that one or more constitutional protections apply to laws passed by state and local governments. Choice (A) can be eliminated as not all courts make laws. Choice (B) can be eliminated as this scenario describes federalism between a state government and the federal government. Choice (C) can be eliminated: since the ruling in *Brandenburg v. Ohio* (1969), the Supreme Court kept restrictions on free speech rather than expand them. As a result, (D) is correct as, in 1965, the Supreme Court ruled in *Gideon v. Wainwright* that all criminal defendants were entitled to a lawyer even if they were being tried in a state court or were charged with a state crime.

50. **B** The Supreme Court has the final say on whether a law is constitutional. Choice (A) can be eliminated as the Supreme Court could strike down the law again. Choice (C) can be eliminated as the Supreme Court could also strike down these laws as well. Choice (D) can be eliminated as only Congress can impeach Supreme Court justices. As a result, (B) is correct: if Congress begins the process of amending the Constitution, they can effectively overturn the Supreme Court if the states ratify the amendment.

51. **A** Baron de Montesquieu wrote some of the most influential texts that the founders used to help craft the Constitution. Choice (B) is incorrect as Federalist No. 70 argued for a strong executive. Choice (C) is incorrect as no text ever set forth a recommendation on the appropriate number of Supreme Court justices. Even today there is no rule about the minimum or maximum number of justices required to serve on the Supreme Court. Choice (D) is incorrect as the Connecticut Compromise laid out the current structure of the legislative branch. Therefore, (A) is correct as Montesquieu argued for the separation of powers.

52. **C** Exit polls are a valuable tool to predict the results of an election. In this question, the term "exit poll" itself is a significant clue. Choice (A) can be eliminated as this kind of poll can be part of an opinion poll, benchmark poll, or tracking poll. Choice (B) can be eliminated as this type of poll is known as an entrance poll. Choice (D) can be eliminated as this kind of poll would have no value. As a result, (C) is correct as exit polls refer to the polling of those who have just exited a polling place, having cast their ballots. Political commentators use exit polls on election day to make predictions about the election.

53. **C** Since the 1960s, government and private organizations have used affirmative action to give minority groups greater access to educational and career opportunities. Choice (A) is incorrect as the Supreme Court ruled this practice unconstitutional in *Regents of the University of California v. Bakke* (1978). Choices (B) and (D) are incorrect as refusing to hire one or more racial groups would constitute racial discrimination. Therefore, (C) is correct as universities may take race into consideration when making admissions decisions.

54. **C** A party realignment refers to a situation in which a political party's base of support changes dramatically due to the actions of one or both of the political parties. These alignments happen only during the most extreme circumstances. Choices (A), (B), and (D) are incorrect. Although these events were important historical moments, each party's base of support did not shift or switch places as a result. Therefore, (C) is correct. When the Democratic Party passed civil rights legislation in the 1960s, many white Americans switched to the Republican Party as African Americans joined the Democratic party.

55.   **D**   After the president nominates someone to the Supreme Court, the Senate interviews that person before casting a vote. Choice (A) can be eliminated as a justice who bases their decision solely on the Constitution practices judicial restraint. Choices (B) and (C) can be eliminated as a justice who bases their decision on personal preference or the national mood practices judicial activism. Therefore, (D) is correct as *stare decisis* refers to making a ruling based on legal precedent: the results of past court cases.

Section II: Free Response

Remember that you need to answer all four free-response questions in 1 hour and 40 minutes, so you do not have time to waste, nor can you skip any questions. Nevertheless, you should take time to brainstorm some ideas and to organize what you come up with before you start to write each response. Otherwise, your responses will probably be incomplete, disorganized, or both.

You should take about 20 minutes each for Questions 1, 2, and 3 and about 40 minutes for Question 4. Make sure you read each question carefully and respond directly to each of its components in your response. The questions are about broad issues, but they ask for specific information. A general free response that fails to address specific concerns raised by the question will not earn a high score. Your replies to Questions 1–3 should be brief and to the point. The information below represents what you should consider before writing a concise answer.

Question 1

(A)   Describe a power Congress could use to address the comments outlined in the scenario.

- Congress could use its power to admit Puerto Rico as the 51st state. Congress has had this power since the Northwest Ordinance (1787). Although Congress has the power to vote on admitting new states, the president must still approve the new state just as if he were signing a bill into law.

- Instead of admitting Puerto Rico as a state, Congress could use its tax and spending powers to provide greater financial assistance to Puerto Rico to help it recover from Hurricane Maria and make sure it receives appropriate support in the future.

(B)   In the context of the scenario, explain how the use of congressional power described in Part A can be affected by Congress's interaction with interest groups.

- If Congress considers legislation to make Puerto Rico the 51st state, interest groups for and against statehood would attempt to influence Congress's decision. Conservative interest groups would likely pressure lawmakers to vote against statehood, as admitting Puerto Rico to the Union would produce two more senators who would probably align themselves with the Democratic Party.

- If Congress considers legislation to increase financial assistance to Puerto Rico, interest groups representing major industries would likely support the legislation, as these industries would win contracts to rebuild the island's infrastructure.

(C) In the context of the scenario, explain the responsibilities of the federal government as prescribed by the Constitution.

- As Puerto Rico meets the qualifications for statehood (appeal to Congress, a sizable population, and a constitution), Congress can consider its application. However, the Constitution does not force Congress to do this. Therefore, it is likely that Congress will not vote on statehood for Puerto Rico until it is politically advantageous for the party that controls Congress.

- As Puerto Ricans hold American citizenship, they are entitled to the same civil liberties and civil rights as other citizens. The federal government must ensure that Puerto Ricans' rights are not infringed on or neglected as Rep. Serrano implies in his statement.

Question 2

(A) Between 1962 and 2017, in which category did federal spending decrease the most as a percentage of the national budget?

- Between 1962 and 2017, defense spending decreased the most as a percentage of the national budget.

(B) Describe a trend in the data and draw a conclusion about how it reflects a change in federal priorities over time.

- Between 1962 and 2017, mandatory spending more than doubled. In the mid-1960s, Congress passed Medicare and Medicaid as part of President Johnson's Great Society. Since then, the United States has invested more in ensuring that older and disabled Americans have access to quality health care.

- Defense spending in 2017 made up less than half as much of federal spending as it did in 1962. When the Cold War ended in 1989, so too did the Soviet Union, which meant that the United States no longer had to invest as heavily in defense.

(C) Explain how federal spending as shown in the chart relates to the adoption of entitlement programs.

- Although the number of entitlement programs has not grown since the mid-1960s, the number of Americans on them has grown, primarily those on Social Security. This change is due to longer life expectancies. Many healthy Americans live well into their 80s, meaning they benefit from Social Security for 20+ years. As long as life expectancies increase, entitlement spending will increase unless Congress raises the age at which Americans receive Social Security benefits.

Question 3

(A)   Identify the constitutional clause that is common to both *Austin v. Michigan Chamber of Commerce* (1990) and *Citizens United v. Federal Election Commission* (2010).

- Both *Austin* and *Citizens United* center on part of the First Amendment, an American's right to free speech. In *Austin*, the Supreme Court ruled that governments could put restrictions on corporations' speech, while *Citizens United* ruled that corporations have the same free-speech rights as the people who run them.

(B)   Based on the constitutional clause identified in Part A, explain why the facts in *Citizens United* led to a different holding than the holding in *Austin*.

- Between 1990 and 2010, political spending skyrocketed in the United States. In 2002, Congress attempted to limit "soft money" donations and interest groups' influence through the McCain-Feingold Act. The Act was challenged in court throughout the 2000s, leading to *Citizens United*. In the *Citizens United* ruling, the Court ruled that the First Amendment does not allow the government to levy fines for speech, which was central to *Austin* legislation passed in its wake.

(C)   Describe one long-term effect of *Citizens United* and its impact on modern politics.

- *Negative Effect:* In the years after *Citizens United*, spending on local, state, and national elections rose more quickly than in prior decades. Political action committees, even those supporting candidates for local and state-level offices, spent millions of dollars on advertisements. The impact of this spending is that candidates without significant financial backing do not stand to gain votes or even voters' attention due to the "immense aggregations of wealth" supporting other candidates.

- *Positive Effect:* The majority opinion in *Citizens United* stated that "There is no such thing as too much speech." More money in the hands of diverse organizations, rather than solely in the control of the major political parties, allows for more diverse points of view. Although there are still restrictions on direct campaign contributions, corporations and organizations can advertise about various issues that the major parties may be ignoring. This could set the tone for future reforms or legislation. On the other hand, as corporations take on a more political role in American life, they, like any candidate for office, must court the public's support. In some cases, corporate stances on social issues have affected the decisions of lawmakers. In 2018, Delta Airlines cut ties with the National Rifle Association despite threats from Georgia Republicans that they would revoke Delta's tax credits. The state legislature dropped its threats when Delta began exploring moving its headquarters to another state.

Question 4

Articulate a defensible claim.

A strong executive is not best to ensure the long-term survival of a republican form of government.

Support your claim.

- *Declaration of Independence:* In the Declaration, Thomas Jefferson and John Adams created a laundry list of abuses perpetrated by King George III, who was a strong executive.

- *The Constitution:* The Constitution includes a detailed system of checks and balances to prevent the president from abusing his power.

- *The Articles of Confederation:* In the early United States, the founders gave all power to the legislative branch. They did not view an executive as necessary to ensure the long-term survival of a republican form of government.

Use reasoning.

- *Declaration of Independence:* The founders were wary of strong executives, and knew from first-hand experience how a strong executive could infringe on individuals' liberty.

- *The Constitution:* When the Constitution was written, the president's powers were extremely limited compared to the power wielded by modern presidents.

- *The Articles of Confederation:* As all government power rested with the legislature, the Articles of Confederation more closely mirrored a republican form of government than the government created by the Constitution.

Respond to an opposing perspective.

Claim: The Articles of Confederation nearly led to the breakup of the new nation (e.g., Shays' Rebellion).

- *Refutation*: Shays' Rebellion was caused by a post–Revolutionary War economic downturn that was exacerbated by the fact that the federal government did not have the power to tax. The lack of an executive branch did not play a role in the rebellion.

Claim: The Constitution's system of checks and balances has largely worked to control presidential abuses of power.

- *Concession*: Corrupt presidents, such as Richard Nixon and Andrew Johnson, were checked by the Supreme Court and Congress, respectively.

- *Rebuttal:* Despite some victories against presidential corruption, the power of the presidency has grown tremendously over the previous 200 years.

Claim: The nation needs a strong unitary executive to act as commander in chief during wartime.

- *Rebuttal*: Although many presidents served in the military before taking office, all presidents rely on the advice provided by the Joint Chiefs of Staff and other highly trained/knowledgeable professionals before making military decisions.

HOW TO SCORE PRACTICE TEST 4

Section I: Multiple Choice

_____ × 1.0000 = _____
Number of Correct   Weighted
(out of 55)   Section I Score
                                  (Do not round)

Section II: Free Response

Question 1   _____   × 4.5833   = _____
             (out of 3)   (Do not round)

Question 2   _____   × 3.4375   = _____
             (out of 4)   (Do not round)

Question 3   _____   × 3.4375   = _____
             (out of 4)   (Do not round)

Question 4   _____   × 2.2917   = _____
             (out of 6)   (Do not round)

Sum   = _____
        Weighted Section II
        Score (Do not round)

The following conversion chart provides only a rough estimate, as scoring ranges may vary from administration to administration. Check your online Student Tools for possible updates.

**AP Score
Conversion Chart
U.S. Government and
Politics**

Composite Score Range	AP Score
83–110	5
72–82	4
56–71	3
38–55	2
0–37	1

Composite Score

_____ + _____ = _____
Weighted   Weighted   Composite Score
Section I Score   Section II Score   (Round to nearest
                                         whole number)

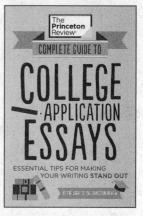